# behaviour

An Introduction to Psychology as a Biological Science

ONE WEEK LOAN

au

# behaviour

## An Introduction to Psychology as a Biological Science

## Geoffrey Hall

*Department of Psychology,*
*University of York, U.K.*

## ACADEMIC PRESS

Harcourt Brace & Company, Publishers

London   San Diego   New York
Boston   Sydney   Tokyo   Toronto

ACADEMIC PRESS INC. (LONDON) LTD.
24/28 Oval Road
London NW1

*United States Edition published by*
ACADEMIC PRESS INC.
San Diego CA92101

*British Library Cataloguing in Publication Data*

Hall, G.
  Behaviour.
  1. Behaviorism (Psychology)
  I. Title
  150.19′43   BF199

ISBN 0–12–319580–2 (paperback)
     0–12–319582–9 (hardback)
LCCCN 83–70299

Filmset by Deltatype, Ellesmere Port
Printed in Great Britain by
Antony Rowe Ltd, Chippenham, Wiltshire

# Preface

I wrote this book with a particular group of readers in mind: those undergraduate students who come to psychology either for the very first time or after experiencing a wide-ranging but superficial introductory course. Such students usually have views on what the subject is, or should be, about, and these views may turn out to be at variance with what they are then taught. They find that much of the psychology they are required to learn comes from experimental studies using contrived and artificial circumstances, often with animals rather than humans as the subjects. They find (even in those aspects of the subject concerned with human cognition) a concentration on overt behaviour as opposed to mental processes. They find explanations of behaviour couched not in everyday language but in a set of novel and abstract concepts, or in terms of the anatomy and physiology of the organism.

Some students take to this sort of psychology readily enough; others struggle with it dutifully, discovering for themselves, only after a good deal of difficulty, why it is that their teachers do the sort of psychology they do. My aim in this book has been to make this process of discovery easier by setting forth explicitly the nature of the questions that experimental psychology is asking and the reasons why it tries to answer them in the way it does. With an understanding of this (and of the basic psychological facts and concepts that such an understanding requires and implies), the student should be better able to profit from more advanced courses in, for example, learning, physiological psychology, animal behaviour, and experimental psychology generally. Even if the student goes no further with the subject, I hope that the selective survey offered here will nonetheless allow him to understand the essence of what academic psychology is about. I also hope that the book will serve the same function for the more advanced student of biology, zoology, or neurobiology who, approaching the study of behaviour from his own discipline, requires some guidance in the ways of psychologists.

Given its introductory nature, I have chosen not to load the text with detailed references for all the statements I make. (I have given the detailed reference only when the observation or experiment under discussion is of special importance or is little known, and thus not likely to be cited in an easily available general textbook.) Instead, at the end of each chapter I have given a list of the more important sources of information on the topic being considered so that the interested reader will be able to follow it up. These references should serve to put the reader in touch with what is going on in modern psychology. I am conscious, however, that, for a variety of reasons, two important areas of experimental psychology get fairly short shrift in the body of the book: they are the study of perception and of human information processing more generally. One of these reasons is that excellent introductory textbooks are already available in these areas, such as in Gregory's *Eye and Brain* (1966), Moore's *Introduction to the Psychology of Hearing* (1982) and *Human Information Processing* by Lindsay and Norman (1977).

I am also conscious that even within the areas of psychology that I have concentrated upon, I have omitted a good many of the topics that are routinely covered in books intended to introduce the reader to psychology. The explanation (and I hope justification) for these omissions can be found in my desire to present each chapter as an *argument*. I have tried to lay out in a systematic way the fundamental questions that need to be asked about a particular topic, and I have tried to answer them by citing the relevant empirical evidence. This strategy has meant the omission of some thoroughly researched psychological phenomena (and, sometimes, the inclusion of others on which experimental work is sparse and firm conclusions are difficult to reach). I plead, however, that the real importance of a psychological phenomenon is to be judged in terms of its theoretical relevance and not by the volume of work carried out on it.

Finally, I have for the most part carried my arguments through to the conclusions that seem to me the most satisfactory given the evidence available. Where these conclusions are tentative I have said so. No doubt there are places where I have reached some firm conclusion that the reader might think unjustified, perhaps because my argument has gone astray, or because of a failure to interpret the evidence correctly. I hope such cases are few. There would certainly be more but for the efforts of the following: P. J. Bailey, R. A. Boakes, C. L. M. Hall, C. Hulme, N. J. Mackintosh, E. M. Macphail and N. S. Sutherland. It is a pleasure to acknowledge the help they have given by reading earlier versions of these chapters and making suggestions toward improving them.

August 1983                                                 Geoffrey Hall

# Contents

# 1 Psychology as a Biological Science

## INTRODUCTION

The subtitle of this book needs some explanation. Clearly, if psychology is to be treated as a science at all then, since its subject matter concerns the activities of living things, it ought to be regarded as a biological one. From this point of view, to speak of the "biological science of psychology" is only to make explicit what is implied when we refer simply to the science of psychology.

But it is possible to mean more than this when the phrase "biological psychology" is used. For instance, a distinction is sometimes made between psychology as a biological science and psychology as a social science. This distinction is, however, difficult to maintain to the extent that social psychology is taken to be the objective study of social interaction. Social interactions are, after all, events of major biological significance (zoologists studying the behaviour of non-human animals have devoted a great deal of effort to investigating aggressive and sexual interactions) and we shall discuss them at some length in this book (especially in Chapters 2 and 8). Again, a distinction is sometimes made between behaviour that is culturally determined and behaviour that is determined by biological factors; and again, this is a distinction that we shall not subscribe to. Chapter 3 will discuss the extent to which some aspects of behaviour and some psychological traits can be said to be inherited but in later chapters (Chapters 4, 6, and 7, in particular) we shall also consider the way in which behaviour is modified by interaction with physical and cultural environments. Chapter 5 will discuss the structure of the nervous system and the way in which it works to determine behaviour, but nothing will be said to suggest that behaviour which has neurophysiological determinants may not have environmental determinants also. Cultural events influence an individual by producing changes in its nervous system.

The general point that has perhaps emerged is that I am using the phrase "psychology as a biological science" to refer not to some area of subject matter or to some subset of topics within psychology. Rather it is being used to mean a perspective or a way of going about the subject that is applicable to the whole of psychology. The characteristics of this perspective are what might be expected in a branch of biological science: it concentrates on observable and measurable events (i.e. on behaviour); it looks for explanations of behaviour that are rigorously formulated and can be tested by experiment and observation; it tries to relate its findings to advances in other branches of biology, especially genetics, neurophysiology, and the study of evolution; it tries to establish explanatory principles that have wide generality, applying not just to the human species but to non-human animals as well. This final point requires further comment.

## Psychology—General and Applied

In the chapters that follow we shall consider a wide range of empirical work. In some of the experiments cited the subjects under study have been men and women, or children—members of the human species. But in many others the subjects are non-human animals. To some this may seem an odd way of proceeding, especially to those whose starting point is the assertion that "psychology is about people". They, not unnaturally, view experiments with non-human animals as being sorry substitutes for the real thing, made necessary by the fact that some experimental procedures cannot be carried out ethically with human subjects. But there are other reasons for studying non-human animals. Rather than saying that psychology is about people let us start with the wider view that psychology is the scientific study of behaviour. Given this view it becomes absurd for us to restrict ourselves to human behaviour: it becomes the job of the psychologist to study behavioural processes wherever they manifest themselves.

I do not want to be taken as saying, however, that the second view of psychology is right, and the alternative necessarily wrong. There is a place for both of them, as the following analogy with another branch of biology may help to make clear. Nobody is to be heard asserting that "physiology is about people", but it is possible to distinguish a special branch of this subject known as *medical physiology*. In any textbook of medical physiology many (perhaps most) of the experiments described will have been done with non-human subjects, but the discussion and interpretation of these experiments will be directed at answering questions about the physiology of men and women. Given that medical students are going to be spending much of their time treating people with physiological disorders, this is as it should be. To the extent that psychologists are required to spend their time in analogous ways (not only in dealing with the mentally ill but in trying to cope with human behaviour more generally) they will want a psychology that treats in detail the workings of the *human* mind.

In addition to medical physiology, however, there is also a branch of physiology known as *general physiology*, the chief concern of which is the study of the general principles that underlie the functioning of all living things. Although the findings of the general physiologist may be taken up and used by the medical doctor, the general physiologist does not set out to make a contribution to medical technology: his aim is to extend the scope of his own, quite central, branch of biological science. Just as general and medical physiology can coexist so there is room for a "general psychology"; that is, for a psychology that constitutes a branch of biological science, alongside the more applied science of "human psychology".

Origins

The aims and methods of this "general psychology" can best be understood in the light of their origins. Accordingly this chapter provides a brief and selective outline of the development of experimental psychology. A chronology of the major figures and events to be discussed is given in Table 1.1. We will concentrate on the biological tradition in psychology that originates with Darwin's work of 1859; but before discussing this tradition directly it is necessary to say something about the development in Germany some twenty years later of a rather different approach to experimental psychology.

*Table 1.1.* Chronology of major events discussed in this chapter.

| | |
|---|---|
| 1859 | Darwin's *Origin of Species* published |
| 1860 | Fechner's *Psychophysics* attempts to relate quantitively psychical and physical phenomena. |
| 1871 | Darwin's *Expression of the Emotions* |
| 1872 | Darwin's *Descent of Man* helps to establish "man's place in nature" |
| 1879 | Wundt's institute established |
| 1882 | Romanes' *Animal Intelligence* |
| 1890 | James' *Principles of Psychology* and the beginnings of "functionalism" |
| 1894 | Morgan's *Introduction to Comparative Psychology* with its insistence on parsimony |
| 1906 | Pavlov's work first published in English |
| 1909 | Freud lectures in the USA on psychoanalysis and the unconscious |
| 1913 | Watson begins publicly to advocate behaviourism |

In 1879, Wilhelm Wundt (1832–1920) established at Leipzig the first academic psychological laboratory—the first institution formally devoted to the experimental study of the human mind. It is customary to cite this date as marking the beginnings of experimental (as opposed to purely philosophical) psychology. The science that Wundt and his followers developed was very influential. At the start of the present century, laboratories similar to the one in Leipzig were being set up in many universities in the English-speaking world, often staffed by workers who had served an apprenticeship with Wundt. In 1900, "psychology" meant the science that had come into being in Germany in the preceding thirty years. These laboratories still exist today but the activities that go on in them under the name of psychological research would probably surprise Wundt. The nature of psychology has been profoundly changed by the influence of a biological approach which had its origins before 1879 and was only temporarily eclipsed during the Wundtian period. It is this biological tradition which springs, like much of modern biology, from the work of Darwin, that forms the subject matter of this book. But we shall begin by looking in some detail at the nature of the science pioneered by Wundt; by comparing his approach with that of biological psychology we shall be better able to distinguish the special features of the latter.

## CLASSICAL INTROSPECTION

According to one view, the world consists of two kinds of stuff: matter and mind. The scientific study of mind has been a late developer but the scientific study of matter has proceeded apace since the Renaissance; the study of inanimate matter under the names of physics and chemistry, the study of animate matter under the name (since the early nineteenth century) of biology. Progress in various areas may have been patchy but, by the end of the last century, it seemed to many that the major problems of the most fundamental of these sciences, physics, had been solved. The success of Newton's physics had been overwhelming (and even now in the age after Einstein, Newton's view of the world is the only one that most of us can comprehend). Newton had established "the laws" of physics and these laws were held to be basic in the sense that the laws governing the behaviour of other systems could in principle be derived from them. Even those who assumed that man consists of a material body and an immaterial mind were prepared to accept, by and large, that the principles of physical and chemical science were those that governed the operation of the body. In short, the problems of the physical world seemed to be solved; it only remained for diligent workers to fill in the details left unspecified by Newton.

This must have seemed a most satisfactory state of affairs; what remained unsatisfactory was the gap in our knowledge of the world left by our ignorance of mind. But by the middle of the nineteenth century, science was working to fill the gap. Since the laws of the physical world had been established it was clear that what was needed was a parallel and basically similar set of laws which would describe the workings of the psychical world. These laws would presumably describe the constituents of the mental world—emotions, cognitions, perceptions and so on—and the way in which the parts interact with one another. They would also describe the way in which the physical and psychical worlds might interact; Gustav Fechner (1801–1887) is best known for his aptly named *Psychophysics* of 1860 which tried to relate quantitatively the world of perception to physical events. Physics which had, by default, supplied psychology with its subject matter, also supplied the elements of a methodology. Physics had been able to make headway by carefully observing its phenomena and by carrying out experiments in controlled conditions to test hypotheses and to refine the observations. These methods had proved fruitful in physiology, the science in which many of the early psychologists were trained.

Something similar could surely be done in psychology even though modifications might have to be made because of the special nature of the observations required. We can look out into the world to make observations about material objects, but to observe the mind at work we must look inwards and examine the contents of consciousness. Psychology can follow physics and physiology just so far but, so the argument ran, it must be to some extent unique in that its data are gained by introspection.

## The Experimental Method in Introspection

One of the achievements of Wundt's laboratory was that the workers there developed and refined introspection to produce a psychological method as remote from everyday soul-searching as is modern astronomy from casual stargazing. In Wundt's hands, introspection developed at least some of the qualities of a precise scientific technique. To pursue the comparison: just as the best astronomy is done by trained observers so the best psychological data could come only from trained introspectionists. These were required to be sane, intelligent adults, experienced in psychology and capable of accurately expressing their experience. And just as the best astronomy is done when the conditions are right, when the sky is clear and the background illumination low, so, good psychological observations can only be obtained in good conditions: the psychologist must have, at the very least, a quiet place free from disturbance to pursue the examination of his consciousness. And finally, just as the astronomer concentrates his efforts on one or a few aspects of his field of study so must the psychologist simplify and reduce his own field to manageable proportions.

## A Specimen Experiment

An example from one of Wundt's own experiments may help to make clear what the classical introspectionists were trying to do. The experiment is very simple. A trained observer is seated in an otherwise quiet room and asked to concentrate on the beat of a metronome. He is then asked to report on his experiences while performing the task. He will probably report that the beats of the metronome tend to fall into temporal groupings which shift from time to time; sometimes the beats will fall into groups of two, sometimes into groups of three and sometimes into more complex arrangements. We have all experienced something of the sort when listening to the tick of a clock in an otherwise quiet room.

The trained observer may also report more subtle phenomena: he may experience a feeling of tension when waiting for the final beat of a particular group of beats and a feeling of relief when it arrives; certain groupings may be accompanied by a feeling of (mild) pleasure and others less so. From an analysis of reports of this sort a psychologist might be able to work out something of the structure of the mind. Thus Wundt argued on the basis of such experiments that immediate experience consists of sensations coloured by feelings; that our feelings differ from one another only in three possible ways (they could be pleasant or not, tense or relaxed, and excited or calm) so that a particular feeling could be uniquely identified in terms of its position on these three dimensions. (see Fig. 1.1).

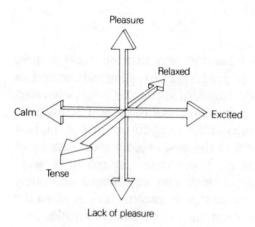

Fig. 1.1. *Wundt's three-dimensional theory of feeling. Every feeling is supposed to be capable of being located at some point in this space (i.e. to be uniquely defined in terms of its position along three dimensions).*

## Problems for Introspectionism

It would be wrong to leave the impression that Wundt's three-dimensional theory of feeling (much-cited though it is) was his major contribution to the development of psychology. Wundt's interests ranged far beyond issues of this sort. He was keen to develop what may be translated as a "social psychology" concerned with higher mental processes, with language, thinking, cultural differences, and so on. Although he did not believe that these issues could be usefully studied by laboratory experiments (he reserved these for the study of immediate experience), he began the study of topics that are now firmly included within experimental psychology. Nonetheless, the three-dimensional theory of feeling is a fair example of the sort of conclusion that experimental introspective psychology led to and it is an example that leaves one with a feeling of unease. Given the lofty intentions of introspective psychology (psychical laws to parallel the laws of physics) the actual results may seem to be a little disappointing.

But worse than disappointment is the doubt that the technique of intro-spection is at all capable of revealing how the mind works, a doubt that is provoked by considering the disagreements that flourished among the various "schools" of introspective psychology in the early years of this century. No sooner had Wundt's version of experimental psychology been introduced into America than criticisms began to be voiced by a group of native psychologists and philosophers known as the "functionalists". For these people the central question of psychology concerned not so much the structure of the mind as what the mind was *for*, and their introspections revealed a set of dynamic processes engaged in making adaptive reactions to external events. Some of them drew a very sharp distinction between their own notions of the mind and the "structuralism" of Wundt (and of Titchener, his prophet in the New World) concerned, as it was, chiefly with listing the elements of mind. A new student of psychology in 1900 could be forgiven for showing some indecision about which school he should adhere to. If the introspections of one eminent professor reveal only structures whereas another discovers dynamic processes, how is one to decide which has got it right? Or, perhaps, are these merely two different ways of describing the same thing? How is one to tell?

## Imageless Thought

Similar problems arose in Germany itself. Wundt had denied the usefulness of experimental introspection in the study of higher mental processes but one of his students, Külpe, was prepared to use the method to determine the basic elements of thinking. One possibility was that thought consisted of a compound of the elements already noted by Wundt; that it consisted of "images" constructed from sensations coloured by feeling. Külpe and his students discovered, however, that it was possible to have imageless thought. Consider, for example, the state of mind induced by the instruction: "And the following numbers". It is certain that in the interval between this instruction and the arrival of the first number some sort of thought goes on. It is much more doubtful, however, that in all people on all occasions this thought consists of images. Examples of this sort led Külpe to assert the existence of imageless thought, a conclusion that evoked a good deal of criticism from Wundt's followers. They dismissed Külpe's findings and argued that images were indeed present in thought and could be detected by a sufficiently sensitive and well-trained observer.

The debate over imageless thought was prolonged and fervent but it ended only in deadlock. Of course, there is not necessarily anything unseemly in a well-argued discussion between academics, but there is cause for alarm when the outcome is totally inconclusive. Introspective psychology was supposed to be an empirical science and in such sciences it is hoped that theoretical conflicts can be resolved by consulting empirical evidence. Here, however, was a conflict that could not be resolved in any straightforward way: when two honest and clear-sighted observers come away from studying the same event with quite different accounts of what has happened there is obviously something fundamentally wrong. When the basic empirical observations of the science are themselves a major topic for dispute one cannot be optimistic about the future development of the science. Clearly the time was ripe for a reaction against introspectionism. In America matters came to a head in 1913 when John B. Watson (1878–1958), the newly elected president of the American Psychological Association, began to propound his behaviourist view of psychology.

## BEHAVIOURISM AND THE UNCONSCIOUS

Watson asserted that psychology was, or should be, the science of behaviour. He made his assertion in a most strident and provocative manner and made many academic enemies as well as converts. "Behaviourism" still has its enemies today but, on the whole, it is fair to say that Watson succeeded in transforming psychology into his science of behaviour. An eminent British experimental psychologist has described the result of asking, in the 1960s, a group of his colleagues about behaviourism. About half replied that we are all behaviourists nowadays, whereas the remainder assured him that no one is a behaviourist these days. And indeed it is true that no psychologist at work today would be willing to accept Watsonian behaviourism in all its details (of contemporary psychologists perhaps Skinner is the man whose views are closest to those of Watson, but even Skinner has developed and refined the initial behaviourist position) and in this sense no one is a behaviourist nowadays. But it is also true that most psychologists have rejected classical introspectionism and now concentrate their efforts on studying what people do and say rather than what they say they think; in this sense we are all behaviourists nowadays.

### Features of Behaviourism*
Watson's behaviourism had many facets but its central tenet is fairly expressed by the name chosen for this approach to psychology: it is that introspection is not the unique and defining feature of the science but that the study of behaviour is. Quite what goes on during introspection is still a matter for debate and Watson was surely right in urging that no science could be securely founded on an experimental method that gives such variable results. Leaving aside disputes about imageless thought and the like, it is so often the case that we quite literally do not know our own minds: we sit down to dinner and discover that we were hungrier than we thought or we come to terms with our state of mind only when someone else remarks on our bad (or good) temper. Similarly,

* A brief definition of this and other technical terms used in the text will be found in the Glossary. For a more detailed account, read on.

introspection does not necessarily give us accurate information about the causes of our own behaviour. To take a very simple case, introspection tells us that by flexing and extending our fingers it is possible to cause movement in the tendons of the wrist (try it); but, of course we know from anatomy that the reverse is the case, that movement of the fingers is produced by movement of the tendons.

These examples may be fairly trivial but they illustrate how misleading it can be to assume that introspection gives a special and privileged insight into the workings of the mind. This is perhaps the central point. After all, when a person supplies a description of the current state of his mind he is engaging in a form of behaviour and it might be argued that such descriptions are a legitimate part of even a behaviourist psychology. But, if they are, we must remember that the behaviour that constitutes such introspective reports is itself as much in need of explanation as any other sort of behaviour. The observations yielded by introspection do not themselves explain anything and may very well be in error when they seem to reveal the mechanisms responsible for overt behaviour. Behaviourism freed psychologists from the possibility of this sort of error and gave them access to a basic subject matter that could be investigated by methods closely similar to those used in other sciences. At the very least it made it possible for two or more investigators to observe a phenomenon simultaneously and to come away having reached the same conclusion about what had happened. What people do can be recorded, scored, and measured, just as can the behaviour of inanimate material.

## The Influence of Pavlov

The rejection of introspectionism received support from a variety of sources. Pavlov's influence was at first only slight. Ivan Pavlov (1849–1936), the great Russian physiologist, turned his attention to the study of the brain at the beginning of this century, a few years before Watson started to develop his behaviourism. Pavlov's intellectual development at this time presents an interesting parallel to that of Watson. It has been reported that, on becoming interested in the workings of the brain, he turned initially to the writings of psychologists assuming that this new science must have something to say relevant to his concerns. He soon turned away showing signs of strong distaste. Here was not a science, he said, only at best (quoting William James) the hope of a science. What was needed was not introspectionism but a study of the brain using "objective" methods (or "physiological" methods—Pavlov used the two terms more or less interchangeably) and he set about devising his conditioning technique (see Chapter 7) as a way of achieving this. At this time Pavlov was unaware of the ideas of the behaviourists (although later in his life he was to write of them in approving terms) and they developed their ideas largely in ignorance of his work. (The first account of the conditioned reflex in English appeared in 1906 but it took several years for the concept to become widely known.) Watson first began to express an interest in Pavlov's work in 1916 when he realized that it provided a method by which inarticulate creatures could be trained to respond differentially to different external events, thus revealing, without any need for introspective reports, their ability to make sensory discriminations. (It can be added that Watson's mistrust of verbal reports was such that he even wanted to use conditioning techniques in equivalent experiments with adult human subjects—a most cumbersome procedure for subjects quite capable of telling the experimenter whether or not they could see a light, hear a tone, or whatever.) Within a few years, however, conditioning began to assume a central role in the behaviourist view of things with the growth of increasingly sophisticated attempts to explain all behaviour in terms of the process of conditioning.

## The Influence of Freud

That Pavlov's work should help to nurture behaviourism is readily understandable. But the rejection of introspectionism also received support from what appears at first sight to be an unlikely source. Sigmund Freud (1856–1939) is best known as the creator of psychoanalysis which as a body of doctrine (it is also the name given to a therapeutic method) incorporates many of the features that Watson wanted to exclude from psychology. For example, psychoanalysis was based at least in part on reports of the results of introspection and it postulated a complex mental structure (of id, ego, super-ego, and so on) which could be related only indirectly, if at all, to observations of behaviour. However, Freud did develop the concept of "the unconscious mind" in an interesting and important way, and it is this aspect of his work that is relevant to our present considerations. It has long been accepted that we are not conscious of many of the events and processes that are important in determining our behaviour; thus everything we say and do involves activity in nerves and in muscles of which we are almost totally unconscious. But these processes, of course, might be dismissed as being "merely physiological" and it was a much more startling suggestion that *mental* events and processes could be similarly unconscious. That we are nowadays all of us prepared to talk quite readily about unconscious motives, unconscious knowledge, and even of unconscious feelings can be put down to the influence of Freud.

The existence of mental processes which are inaccessible to introspection first became really apparent with the investigation of the phenomena associated with hypnosis when it became clear that a person in a hypnotic state could carry out quite complex mental operations without being aware of doing so. Freud, after starting to use hypnosis as a therapeutic technique soon abandoned it in favour of psychoanalysis, but he did not abandon the idea of the unconscious mind and by his method of analysis was able to reveal even more of its intricacies. His conclusion, in bald summary, was that only the smallest fraction of the contents of the mind is, under normal circumstances, open to introspection. Watson may have rejected introspection totally while Freud did not, but the suggestion implicit in the work of the latter, that introspection gives us only a very partial insight into the workings of the mind, may well have been the more important influence in turning psychologists towards more objective methods of study.

## Gains and Losses

Returning to Watson's own ideas, it should be pointed out that his behaviourism contained much more than the rejection of introspection: in particular, he argued not just that the human mind could not be adequately studied by means of introspection but that the mind was not in fact available for study at all. That is, he denied the existence of mental processes, insisting that psychologists should study behaviour in its own right. There are plenty of psychologists who are willing to become behaviourists in the sense that they are prepared to study behaviour in the hope of deducing something about underlying mental processes but there are far fewer prepared to be as radical as Watson. There are also quite a few who are prepared to denounce "radical behaviourism" in terms every bit as strong as those used by Watson in putting his case forward originally: if it accepts Watson's extreme views, it has been argued, psychology will relinquish its proper subject matter, man will be "dehumanized", human dignity and the freedom of man's will would be denied. Thus Koestler (1967) has written of the "pseudo-science of Behaviourism" which has led psychology into a "modern version of the dark ages"; he asserts that "its doctrines have invaded psychology like a virus which first causes convulsions, then slowly paralyses the victim". These are hard words and Koestler is able to find professional psychologists who agree with them. In a well-known passage Burt (1962) wrote:

> Nearly half a century has passed since Watson (1913) . . . proclaimed his manifesto. Today . . . the vast majority of psychologists . . . still follow his lead. The result, as a cynical onlooker might be tempted to say, is that psychology, having first bargained away its soul and then gone out of its mind, seems now, as it faces an untimely end, to have lost all consciousness.
>
> (Burt, 1962, p. 229)

Without attempting to resolve the dispute and to come down either for or against Watsonian behaviourism, it is only fair to add that these extreme criticisms, if they can be justified at all, are appropriate only to the more radical forms of behaviourism. Psychology has not "gone out of its mind" in that most behaviourist psychologists nowadays are quite willing to theorize about the mechanisms and processes that seem likely to be responsible for the behaviour that they observe. They may not call these "mental" mechanisms (although some do) and perhaps the name does not matter. What matters is that the theoretical notions put forward by these psychologists differ from those postulated by the introspectionists in that they are founded on verifiable observation and open to further empirical investigation.

Behaviourism has had such a consistently bad press in recent years that it is worthwhile being less apologetic and stating clearly some of the things that can be said in its favour. The first point is one that has been made already but is worth re-emphasizing: it is that the behaviourist approach has, quite simply, made a science of psychology possible by giving us a subject matter that can be objectively studied. But more than this, behaviourism has immensely widened the scope of psychology. Worthwhile introspective reports could only be obtained from "sane, intelligent adults, experienced in psychology and capable of expressing their experience". In contrast, the study of behaviour knows no such limitations; by concentrating on behaviour we are able to study equally readily non-verbal creatures, including both infants and animals, as well as the merely inarticulate; we can study the unintelligent, the mentally retarded and those with brain damage; and we can study the insane. None of these is capable of serving as a subject in an experiment which adheres to the methods of classical introspectionism, but all can and do *behave*. Seen from this point of view behaviourism can be regarded as having had not a restricting but a great liberating influence on psychology.

## BIOLOGICAL EVOLUTION AND COMPARATIVE PSYCHOLOGY*

Watson's views on psychology did not arise in a vacuum but developed in the intellectual climate of the early twentieth century in America, and although he found the introspectionist aspects of this climate unsympathetic other aspects were more congenial to him. Thus Watson was perfectly able as a psychologist to carry out experimental work with animals (he has written, "I never wanted to use human subjects. . . . With animals I was at home"), to study maze-learning in rats, the natural behaviour of terns, vision in monkeys, and to write a doctoral thesis on *Animal Education*. That research of this sort should be thought of as sensible work for a psychologist to engage in, even before the advent of an explicit behaviourism, can be traced directly to the influence of Darwin and his theory of biological evolution. Watson's behaviourism was indeed a reaction to classical introspectionism but it grew out of an older tradition of psychological thinking which was concerned to set the study of mind into a biological context.

*An outline of the principles of evolution by natural selection is given at the beginning of Chapter 2.

## The Influence of Darwin

When Charles Darwin (1809–1882) published his *Origin of Species* in 1859 the implications of his theory of evolution for psychological issues became apparent, not least to Darwin himself who remarks in a famous passage towards the end of his book:

> In the distant future I see open fields for far more important researches. Psychology will be based on a new foundation, that of the necessary acquirement of each mental power and capacity by gradation. Light will be thrown on the origin of man and his history.                    (Darwin, 1859, p. 458)

And Darwin was not prepared to leave these important researches to psychologists of the distant future but set to work himself publishing in 1871 his book *The Descent of Man* and in the following year his work on *The Expression of the Emotions in Man and Animals*. The latter work, as we can see from the title, is almost "behaviourist" in its approach (although Darwin is quite willing to comment from time to time on the thoughts that pass through the minds of animals) and is directed toward a specifically psychological issue; but both books, in fact, discuss points of interest to psychologists. For example, they introduce us to a totally new way of explaining some aspects of behaviour. To take a relatively trivial example, the erection of body hair ("goose-flesh") that sometimes occurs when we are in a state of fear seems inexplicable until we think of it in evolutionary terms as the vestige of a behaviour pattern that was once serviceable. If our remote ancestors had more body hair than we now possess it is possible to imagine that the erection of this hair might be sufficient to create the image of a creature large enough to scare away any potential predator. We are ready enough nowadays to accept this sort of explanation for odd features of behaviour but we have perhaps not accepted fully even now, over a century after the publication of Darwin's theory, the basic principle of which this explanation is just one corollary. This principle is most easily summed up in a single phrase: man is an animal.

## Man's Place in Nature

The critical feature of the theory of evolution is that it led to a radical rethinking of "man's place in nature" (the title used by Darwin's apologist, T. H. Huxley, for a work which espoused Darwin's ideas). Since man is an animal his place in nature (or at least in schemes of zoological classification) is close to the apes and monkeys, along with them and the other mammals a descendant of some long-extinct, unknown form of life. He possesses some unique features, it is true, but so does every other mammalian species; man walks on his hind-limbs and uses his fore-limbs for manipulating tools, but the dog is equipped with a superior sense of smell, the cat with agility, the race-horse is built for speed, and so on.

Each species is specially adapted to its own mode of life but each has evolved by graded steps from the common ancestor and the standard theme that underlies the variations is not difficult to detect.

A contemporary historian of psychology writes as follows about *The Origin of Species*:

> The book was indeed epoch-making, for it brought the whole kingdom of life, and by implication, Man himself, within the province of natural science . . . the explanatory concepts employed and point of view are as pertinent to psychology as to biology; necessarily so for from now on psychology becomes basically a biological science. Mind has evolved like every other piece of organic equipment . . . it is one means whereby organisms adapt themselves in the struggle for existence and reveal their fitness to survive.
>
> (Hearnshaw, 1964, p. 36)

Thus, accepting the Darwinian view of man's place in nature has implications for the way we think about his mental qualities just as it has for our understanding of his anatomy and physiology. "Mind has evolved like every other piece of organic equipment"; it may have evolved in a specialized way in the human species but it should be possible to discern the basic features of mental functioning in animals of other species. It is this suggestion more than any other that works to undermine our belief in the uniqueness of man. Before Darwin, many were willing to accept that "man is an animal" but they would also add that he is a very special one: according to Aristotle man is "the rational animal"; man is the one animal who possesses reason, who has a mind, whose behaviour is governed by intelligence in contrast to all other animals who are held to be governed by habit and blind instinct. Darwin's theory denied the reality of this distinction between man and other animals insisting instead that the rudiments of reasoning capacity should be detectable in most species. And in *The Descent of Man* Darwin himself set to work at making an explicit comparison between the mental capacities of man and other mammals. He concluded that "the difference in mind between man and the higher animals, great as it is, certainly is one of degree and not of kind" (Darwin, 1871, p. 193).

Early Comparative Psychology

It was Darwin, therefore, who laid the foundations of what we nowadays call comparative psychology—the science concerned with the origins and implications of behavioural differences between different animal species. If only for this, modern psychology is able to claim him as one of its father figures. Biologists may perhaps feel a little disgruntled that psychology should lay claim to their most famous name but there can be no doubt about the importance that Darwin himself attached to the psychological implications of his work. If Darwin adopted an intellectual heir during his lifetime that man was G. J.

Romanes (1848–1894), a man whose major work was carried out in the field of comparative psychology and whose best known book, *Animal Intelligence* (1882), was explicitly concerned with mental evolution. Romanes as an ardent supporter of Darwin saw as his major task that of bridging "the psychological distance which separates the gorilla from the gentleman" and to do this he carried out a series of experiments of his own not only with apes but with other mammals and also with invertebrates. In writing his book on animal intelligence he drew both on his own research and on the reports of a wide range of correspondents who were only too willing to present him with examples of behaviour shown by their favourite animals which seemed to them "almost human". Although he was no more credulous than his contemporaries (Darwin included), the rather uncritical way in which Romanes included in his book what seem to us now to be no more than unauthenticated anecdotes did comparative psychology (and his own subsequent reputation) something of a disservice. We cannot now read his story of the cat spreading out crumbs in order to attract birds or his comments on the emotional life of the spider without feeling that Romanes' enthusiasm for evolutionary theory on occasions got the better of his discretion.

## Parsimony in Explanation

It was Romanes' own intellectual heir, C. Lloyd Morgan (1852–1936), who supplied the necessary corrective. Morgan was the man chosen to edit and publish Romanes' uncompleted work on the latter's death. He did so faithfully, but although loyal to his predecessor as a friend he could not accept all aspects of Romanes' work. In particular, Morgan was unhappy about the low standards by which evidence was being assessed in comparative psychology. While never doubting that mental capacities akin to those shown by man could be seen in animals, Morgan thought that his case would only be damaged if he accepted as evidence for intelligence in animals observations of behaviour that could easily be explained away in other terms. He insisted on proper experiments carried out in controlled conditions and propounded his own law of parsimony which has become known as Lloyd Morgan's canon:

> In no case may we interpret an action as the outcome of the exercise of a higher psychical faculty, if it can be interpreted as the outcome of the exercise of one which stands lower in the psychological scale.
>
> (Morgan, 1894, p. 53)

Morgan's own dog was able to unlatch the front gate of his master's house but Morgan did not conclude from this that the canine mind was capable of comprehending the principle of the lever. He adopted instead the simpler explanation that the habit had been acquired as the result of a process of trial and error.

## Implications

Morgan was more of a scholar than an investigator but his views were rapidly adopted by those doing experimental work in comparative psychology. Watson, in America, was one of these and he was to carry Morgan's canon perhaps much further than its originator intended or would have wanted. He applied it, of course, in his studies of animal behaviour: he explained the way in which rats can learn their way through mazes not in terms of reason or of insight but in terms of the acquisition of new habitual patterns of movement. But he also applied it in his approach to the study of human behaviour. And why not? Darwin's theory tells us that man is an animal; why therefore should we use one standard when assessing the behaviour of non-human animals and a different one when we come to the behaviour of human animals? Why should we try to explain what a man does in terms of reason, a moral sense, intelligence, or some other mental capacity when, if the same behaviour were shown by a cat or a rat, we would try to explain it in simpler terms? The behaviourist approach can be seen essentially as one which applies Morgan's canon to the doings of man. To the extent that behaviourism created modern psychology, Darwinian comparative psychology did so too because it is in the comparative psychology of the late nineteenth century that behaviourism has its origins.

## CONCLUSIONS

To return to the more general picture, the chief importance of Darwin's theory was that it gave us a new understanding of man's place in nature. This was no doubt rather disconcerting at the time but important because it put "man himself within the province of natural science" and made psychology a branch of biological science. There are some who remain disconcerted even today, and attacks on modern psychology for its failure to deal with the uniqueness of man are not infrequent. Some of these issues will be discussed in the final chapter after we have considered the contribution made by the biological approach to the science of psychology. For the time being, therefore, we shall adopt the assumption that man is best regarded as just one species among many and that his doings are open to study on the same terms and by the same general methods as those of any other animal species.

What are these methods? The furore over the inception of behaviourism and the vigour with which Pavlov urged the use of his objective, physiological method have perhaps obscured the fact that nothing very special is being suggested. The essence of the biological approach to psychology is that the psychologist should try to deal with his subject matter in much the same way as any other specialist within the general area of biological science. That is, for example, he should proceed by making careful observations, taking exact measurements when possible; he should devise experiments in which the suspected determinants of behaviour can be manipulated and extraneous factors excluded; he should develop clearly stated hypotheses closely related to the empirical facts and these should be capable of making predictions open to test so that they can be confirmed or rejected.

These proposals are now so widely accepted that one may be forgiven for wondering why many psychologists were once so resistant to them (and why some still are). It may be of some comfort to learn that psychology is not the only branch of biology that was reluctant to adopt the scientific approach. To take an example from physiology, consider this explanation of the process of digestion provided by the sixteenth century physiologist Fernel. As outlined by Sherrington (see Zangwill, 1950, p. 1), it runs as follows: "What the stomach does is explained by Fernel by calling in three sub-faculties, 'attractive', 'concoctive' and 'expulsive' . . . divisions of the great 'nutritive faculty' . . . . Hunger resides in the wall of the stomach. When food arrives, the stomach experiences pleasure . . . ."; and so on. This so-called explanation strikes us nowadays as no more than an amusing word-game. Modern physiology has supplied us with a much better if more prosaic account of the workings of the stomach as a result of careful study of its structure, the nature of its secretions, its reactions to various sorts of stimulation, and so on. Perhaps psychology has not yet fully rid itself of the tendency to offer "explanations" for the behaviour of the whole organism similar to those offered by Fernel as explanations for the behaviour of a single organ. But it seems to me that it has made most progress when it has done so and has adopted methods equivalent to those used by the modern biologist. At any rate the work to be reported in the chapters that follow is based upon the findings of a psychology that proceeds by a careful study of the structure of the organism (in particular of its nervous system), the nature of its behaviour, and the way in which its behaviour is modified by changes in the external environment.

## SOURCES AND FURTHER READING

The quotation from Sherrington given above is cited by Zangwill (1950) in *An Introduction to Modern Psychology*. This book, although now out of date in some particulars, has as its general theme the biological approach to psychology and is still well worth reading. Another excellent introductory book is that by Miller (1962) called *Psychology: The Science of Mental Life*. This book looks at the historical development of psychology and includes a fascinating section on the work of Wundt and his contemporaries. In my account of the influence of evolutionary theory I have relied on Hearnshaw's *Short History of British Psychology* (1964), and upon *From Darwin to Behaviourism* by Boakes (1983). Further historical material can be found in the *History of Psychology in Autobiography*, Volume 3 of which (edited by Murchison, 1936) includes an interesting, if brief, contribution by Watson. A fuller account is Cohen's biography *J. B. Watson: The Founder of Behaviourism* (1979). The development of Pavlov's views is described in the introduction to his *Conditioned Reflexes* (1927) and in Gray's *Pavlov* (1979).

# 2 Evolution and Psychology

## INTRODUCTION

Having shown in Chapter 1 how some aspects of modern psychology have their roots in evolutionary biology, it is an obvious next step to turn to attempts to understand behaviour from the evolutionary point of view. At the end of this introduction we identify four important issues concerning the relationship between evolution and psychology, and discussion of these forms the bulk of this chapter. But before discussing these issues directly we must be clear about exactly what is implied by the idea of biological evolution.

### Common Ancestors

Surprisingly, for such an important and, in principle, simple concept, Darwin's theory of evolution is often badly misunderstood. In outline, there are three main points to remember. The first is the central dogma of all evolutionary theories, that all animals (and indeed plants) now living shared at some time in the past a common ancestor. This idea was accepted by some before Darwin's *Origin of Species* but it still requires something of an effort of the imagination to grasp what it implies. Obviously each of us shares with his brother or sister common ancestors in his parents; cousins share common ancestors in their grandparents, and so on. It has been widely accepted for some time that all present-day members of the human race are derived from a small number of individuals who are ancestors common to all of us. What has taken rather longer to gain acceptance is the notion that members of different species may also share ancestors; that at some time in the past there was a creature who was parent to both ape and man; that further back in time there existed an ancestor common to monkeys, men, cats, and dogs; that further back still lived the common ancestor of mammals, insects, worms, and so on. (A simplified diagram showing what we suppose to be the pattern of descent of the main animal groups is given in Fig. 2.1. Figure 2.2 shows the vertebrates—the animals with which we shall have most to do in this book—in more detail.) This is not to say, of course, that men are descended from present-day apes (or apes from men, for that matter); rather, the suggestion is that at some time perhaps as long as 20 million years ago there lived an animal neither modern ape nor modern man

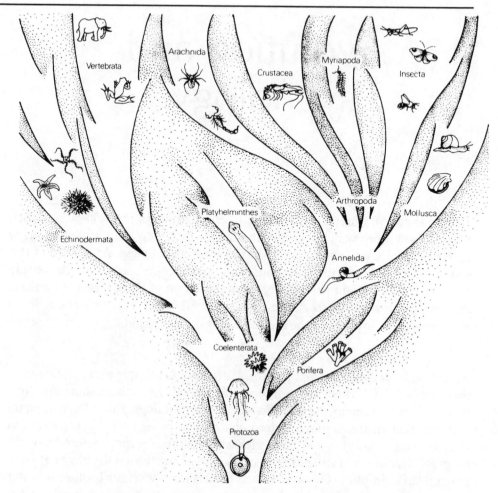

Fig. 2.1. *The evolutionary origins of the main animal groups. The fossil evidence shows that most of these groups have been in existence for at least 450 million years (after Romer and Parsons, 1977).*

some of whose offspring developed ultimately into present-day apes and others into men.

## Natural Selection

The second point to appreciate about evolution concerns the mechanism by which evolutionary change occurs. Darwin's great insight, the idea of "natural selection", concerns just this. Calling it a great insight might lead the reader to expect too much, since the process of natural selection, once it has been explained, has the appearance of a simple, self-evident truth. T. H. Huxley, Darwin's great defender in the debates that followed the publication of *The Origin of Species*, reports his reaction to the notion of natural selection as being: "How extremely stupid not to have thought of that!" (L. Huxley, 1900, p. 170).

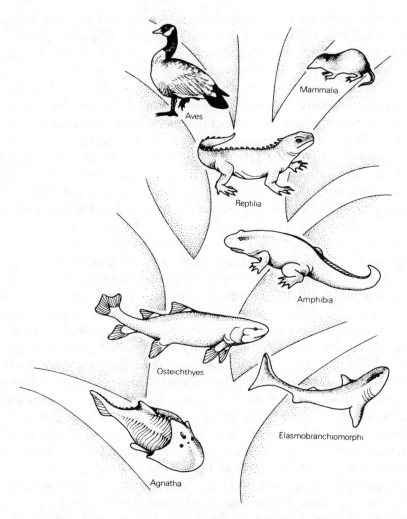

Fig. 2.2. *Relationships among the main vertebrate groups. Exact dates are difficult to give and the following figures are very approximate. The earliest vertebrates (fish called ostracoderms) were in evidence 450 million years ago (mya). The groups of fish currently extant appeared 400–300 mya, and toward the end of this time the first amphibia emerged. The first reptiles appeared some 300 mya. The mammals and birds probably originated well over 100 mya, but the first placental mammal (the group to which the human species belongs) did not emerge until about 75 mya (after Romer and Parsons, 1977).*

Central to the working of natural selection is the fact that most animal species tend to over-reproduce in the sense that each set of parents produces on average more than two children. This is certainly true of the human species at the present time and our population numbers are currently increasing in a most alarming fashion. But ours is an unusual (and perhaps temporary) situation and the numbers of most animal populations remain, within broad limits, fairly stable; it follows, therefore, that in these species many individuals must die without leaving offspring. What decides which individuals will die and which will survive to breed and to contribute to the next generation? In a way this decision is left merely to chance: an animal will die if it happens to be susceptible to disease or happens to be capable of running only slowly when confronted by a predator, and even if it survives to die of old age it may still fail to leave offspring if it is too ugly or weak to attract and keep a mate. In other words, members of a given species differ from one another in their strength, speed, intellect, their attractiveness to the opposite sex, and so on: the fortunate ones are those endowed with qualities which enable them to survive and leave offspring; the unlucky ones, not so well-endowed, die. The well-endowed are those selected by nature to be parents of the next generation.

Now, these differences between individuals which determine that one will die and another survive may just be matters of chance in the sense that the lucky ones are born that way, but the important thing to note about them is that they are often *heritable* differences, that is, they are characteristics that tend to be passed on from parent to child. Thus, healthy parents might tend, on the whole, to beget strong children whereas disease-prone parents, if they survive to breed at all, are likely to produce weakly offspring. As a consequence of the failure of many of the sickly parents to produce children it follows that the proportion of disease-resistant individuals in the next generation will be greater than in the parental generation. And as the process is repeated from one generation to the next the result will be a species that tends, on average, to grow more and more resistant to disease. The change will occur gradually but given enough time we can expect disease-resistance and, indeed, all those qualities that promote survival and reproduction in an individual, to predominate. Indeed, given very long periods of time (and, after all, life has been in existence on this planet for some 3000 million years) it would be possible for these gradual changes to accumulate and to produce a creature so very different from the original parental stock that it comes to be regarded as belonging to a totally different species. (But see below, p. 33.)

Genetic Change

The third and final point that must be made before we can move on to explicitly psychological topics concerns the question: what evolves? Clearly since evolutionary changes take place over many generations, we cannot think of an individual animal evolving. Certainly individuals change during their lifetimes: they develop and their behaviour may be modified by what they learn (we shall discuss these important topics in much more detail in subsequent chapters), but changes of this sort are of no consequence from the point of view of natural selection. Individuals do not evolve: they just live and reproduce, or die and do not. Rather, what evolves is the *gene pool*.* A population of individuals of a given species that interbreeds freely (or at least is in theory capable of doing so) can be regarded as constituting a pool of genes. Individuals die but if they reproduce sexually they leave behind in their children an exact copy of half of their own genes (the remaining half to make up a full set comes from the other parent). It is by building for themselves bodies which are efficient at surviving and mating that genes ensure their own survival from generation to generation. A genetic make-up (or *genotype*) that makes a relatively large contribution to the gene pool of the next generation is said to show superior *fitness*.

Only by appreciating that evolutionary change operates upon the gene pool can we understand the evolutionary basis of several important psychological traits. Take as an example that of altruism. At first sight we might expect natural selection to weed out those individuals who show altruistic behaviour, who put the comfort and safety of others before their own. Selfish patterns of behaviour should therefore come to predominate. But this does not always happen. Consider the behaviour of song-birds in the presence of a predator such as a hawk flying overhead. The first bird to catch sight of the predator could emit some warning signal which would serve to alert the other members of its flock but in doing so it would be likely to attract unwelcome attention. Any individual possessing a genetic make-up which promotes altruistic behaviour of this sort seems unlikely to survive for very long and its genes will perish with it. Nevertheless, this is just the behaviour that many song-birds show. To understand how this can have come about we need to make the quite reasonable assumption that song-birds which live in flocks do so along with their close relatives, that is, along with individuals having genetic make-ups similar to their own. Thus if one individual possesses the gene (or genes) responsible for the tendency to give an alarm-call it is likely that many other members of his flock will possess this gene too. And if his raising the alarm results in his own premature death this will not lead to the elimination of the gene in question from the gene pool. On the contrary, many of his relatives, each of whom possesses the gene, will escape to live on and breed producing offspring who possess the gene too. Only in recent years has it become fully appreciated that evolutionary theory must take account of *inclusive fitness*. That is, that the measure of the reproductive success of an individual must take account not only of the direct descendants it leaves but must also include the fact that other close

*A simplified account of the principles of genetics is given in the first section of Chapter 3. All we need to know for the purposes of the present discussion is that all the physical and psychological characteristics of an individual are determined in part by its *genes*. Genes are the units of hereditary transmission passed on from parents to offspring in eggs and sperm; they consist, physically, of a section of the complex molecule of deoxyribonucleic acid (DNA).

relatives will share many of that individual's genes. It is this insight that forms the basis of the "sociobiological" approach to behaviour to be discussed later in this chapter and in Chapter 8.

## The Relationship between Evolution and Psychology

Following this very brief introduction to the theory of evolution in general, we are now ready to turn to a direct consideration of the relationship between biological evolution and psychology. This is, in itself, a very wide topic and our task will be simplified by breaking it down into four main parts. First, we shall consider what role behaviour and psychological processes in general play in shaping evolution. Second, we shall consider some of the attempts that have been made to work out the evolutionary history (the *phylogeny*) of some animal groups on the basis of the behaviour that they show. Next we shall consider a related but distinguishable topic in discussing some of the attempts that have been made to work out the phylogeny of a given pattern of behaviour or a given psychological faculty. Finally, we shall discuss the extent to which the behaviour shown by animals alive today can be *explained* in terms of evolution.

## THE ROLE OF BEHAVIOUR IN SHAPING THE COURSE OF EVOLUTION

Evolutionary change occurs essentially because reproduction is non-random: if an animal does not breed or if it produces offspring which do not survive, then that animal's genes do not persist in the gene pool. They are not "selected". It is clear, therefore, that the way in which animals behave must play an important part in shaping evolution. We tend often to think of evolutionary change in terms of structural change (perhaps this is a by-product of the extensive study of fossils made by evolutionary biologists) but natural selection operates upon living, behaving organisms and it is the way in which structures function that determines whether the animal which possesses the structures will survive and breed, or die out. The behaviour that animals show (especially their behavioural interactions with other animals) helps to decide both which individuals survive and, of those that survive, which will breed successfully. We will discuss next some examples of behavioural interactions that result in selective survival and selective reproduction before turning directly to the way in which non-random reproduction can bring about the origin of new species.

### Selective Survival

*Predation.* The behavioural interaction between animals of different species that we call predation deserves first mention if only because it is this sort of interaction that comes first to mind when we think of natural selection and of "Nature red in tooth and claw".

Consider the interaction that takes place between bats and the moths on which they feed; an interaction that can be crucial in determining the chances of survival of both partners. As is well known, bats have evolved an astonishing system of echolocation which enables them to detect their prey in the dark. What is less well-known is that the ear of the moth is an excellent bat detector capable of detecting the brief, high frequency pulses emitted by bats. (These last a hundredth of a second, 10 ms, and are of about 80 kHz, i.e. 80 000 cycles per second.) Some moths, at least, react to sounds of this sort by taking appropriate evasive action, by showing an abrupt and dramatic change in their flight path, diving, climbing, or turning (Roeder and Treat, 1961; see Fig. 2.3). But not all moths show this behaviour and it is no surprise to find that those that do not do so run an increased risk of being eaten. Roeder has observed by floodlight a large number of encounters between moths and bats taking note of whether or not the moth was a reactor which showed evasive behaviour, and of the outcome of the encounter, whether the moth was eaten or whether it escaped. He found that for every 100 of the reactor moths which escaped only 60 non-reactors did so and concluded that the evasive behaviour was of great survival value. Presumably, other things being equal, this pattern of interaction will lead to a state of affairs in which the only surviving moths are reactors.

(a)

(b)

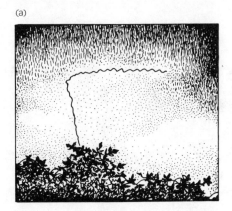

Fig. 2.3. *Flight tracks of moths before and immediately after exposure to simulated bat cries. The tracks were photographed at night as the moths flew into the beam of a floodlight. In (a) the moth simply dives at the onset of the sound; in (b) the dive is prefaced by a series of loops and turns (after Roeder and Treat, 1961).*

*Social interaction.* An individual's chances of survival may depend not only on the way in which it interacts with other species but also on the way it interacts with members of its own species. Animals of the same species living together or in close proximity are likely to be in competition for some limited resource and the individuals most effective at hunting or foraging, say, are those most likely to survive. But, in fact, the outcome of such a competition between members of a species is often determined in a more subtle manner. When animals live in a group that is fairly stable in its composition the conflict over who gains first access to food, or water, or whatever, may result not in a simple free-for-all but in the establishment of hierarchies of social *dominance*. It was noticed by scientists in the 1920s (and may have been known by farmers long before that time) that within a flock of hens there exists a highly structured social organization. Each hen either dominates or is dominated by each other hen, pecking at subordinates that get in her way and receiving pecks from her superiors (hence the term *peck order*). Not surprisingly, if the supply of grain is limited, it is the hen at the bottom of the hierarchy who goes without. Such systems of social status are not confined to birds but are found widely among mammals including, of course, man. Two features of these systems are worthy of note. First, it is of interest that clashes between members of a group are very often decided without injury to either party. Thus a fight between wolves can be a rather formal affair in which the dominant animal stands silent with raised hair and tail while the inferior animal crouches with lowered tail and flattened ears (see Fig. 2.4). Snapping of the teeth may be seen but actual biting is rare. Such patterns of behaviour are said to be *ritualized* (p. 41). In other words

Fig. 2.4. *Dominance and submission in two male wolves. The dominant animal stands with tail raised and ears up; the submissive animal points his muzzle with lips raised towards the other; his tail hangs down and his ears are flattened (after Sullivan, 1978).*

postures of threat and of appeasement or submission appear to be sufficient to maintain the social structure without the need for bloodshed. Presumably, the advantages of social living are sufficient to outweigh the disadvantages that the subordinate animals must suffer. Secondly, it is not always the biggest and strongest animals which rise to the top of a dominance hierarchy. Certainly among many species, the gorilla is an example, all adult males appear to have priority over all females but other factors may play a part. Thus among gorillas the older grey-haired animals ("silver-backs") tend to be dominant and this can be true even when the animals are to some extent enfeebled by age. But youth may not always be a disadvantage: among the howler monkeys an immature animal takes the same status as its mother.

Given the extent to which dominance hierarchies operate without actual fighting and the fact that status is often given to both the old and the young, one begins to wonder whether these systems always operate to protect the weak from the consequences of their infirmity. Such evidence as we have suggests that to be dominant in a hierarchy does have substantial survival value. Murton *et al.* (1966) have observed the behaviour of wood pigeons, scoring the rate at which they feed. They have found that even though the subordinate members of the flock may be left undisturbed by the dominant members the subordinates maintain only a relatively low feeding rate. Subordinate pigeons spent a sizeable amount of their time looking about for predators and for dominants and so on, and with less time available for feeding, lost weight and starved in times when food was short.

*Parental behaviour.* Before turning to the way in which behavioural interactions help decide which individuals breed (and here, as we shall see on p. 29, dominance again plays a part) there is one further type of interaction between members of a species which should be briefly mentioned since it has a bearing on which individuals survive and which do not. This is the interaction between parent and offspring. For many species the parent's investment in its offspring does not extend beyond the energy that is expended in producing eggs or sperm. (Many sea-living creatures simply shed their germ cells into the water and give the fertilized eggs little attention.) But for other species, including our own, that adequate parental care is essential if the young are to survive is too obvious a point to need much elaboration. One example will be considered here, taken from the large body of work carried out by Tinbergen (1963) on the behaviour of the gulls. When a baby black-headed gull has only recently hatched out it is a defenceless creature at risk from predators such as crows and herring gulls. Its survival depends upon the fact that it is rarely left without the guard of one or other of its parents. We are entitled to be surprised, then, when we discover that chicks sometimes are left unguarded for a short time because the parent bird tends to tidy the nest, flying off with the broken egg shell in its beak and dropping it some distance away. But this behaviour, too, turns out to be a part of the pattern of parental care. Tinbergen has shown that the white interior surface of a broken shell serves to attract the attention of predators to a nest which is otherwise well camouflaged.

## Selective Reproduction

We have been concerned so far with the way in which an animal's behaviour can determine its chances of survival. But selective death is only one aspect of natural selection; the fact that not all animals reproduce or do so at different rates is perhaps more important. As we have said, many marine creatures breed by simply shedding their germ cells (eggs or sperm) into the sea and hoping for the best, but for the most part sexual reproduction is a matter for social interaction. Thus, for most species the behavioural or psychological factors which control social interaction also control which animals breed and thus play a part in determining the course of evolution.

*Sexual selection.* The complex courtship displays shown by many animals (especially by birds) have long fascinated naturalists, and Darwin himself wrote about them at length in *The Descent of Man*, the book in which he developed his ideas about *sexual selection*. For our purposes sexual selection is best regarded as being one aspect of natural selection but it is of interest that Darwin regarded this form of selection as being so important that he elevated it to a special status: a novel process distinct from simple natural selection. The best known type of sexual selection is that which Darwin invoked to account for the evolution of the extreme secondary sexual characteristics of some male animals. If the female of the species has a choice as to which male she will mate with and she develops a preference for males with long beards, say, it follows that a tendency to grow long beards (at least in the males) will be passed on to the next generation. Given a consistent and persisting preference among the females of the species, beards will be prized above all other male characteristics and they may come to be selected for, even at the expense of other characteristics. In time there could evolve a species the males of which are both puny and stupid but who possess beards of great length. Resisting the temptation to draw conclusions about secondary sexual characteristics in the human species, it should quickly be added that the suggestion that males have evolved their adornments through their effects on the behaviour of females has aroused a good deal of scepticism. A fairly convincing case can be made, however, that the bizarre plumage of some birds of paradise originated in his way. The male birds station themselves at isolated points in their forest habitat and adopt characteristic postures which enable them to display their exotic plumage. A female may visit several males during the breeding season and her decision to copulate with one male rather than another must depend upon his appearance and behaviour toward her.

*Female choice.* A further case in which choice by the female may determine which males get the chance to breed is supplied by those animals which operate a system of communal mating grounds. We can take as an example the behaviour shown by an antelope, the Uganda kob, since the "arena" mating system of this animal provides part of the evidence used by Ardrey (1967) for his theories about the "territorial instinct" of man. The Uganda kob is a grazing animal which wanders in herds over the grasslands of East Africa. The female breeds all year round, and when she has weaned her latest kid she seeks a new mate. She does not, however, copulate with any male who happens to be in company with her particular herd: instead she makes her way to the arena or stamping ground that is used by, and in some sense belongs to the herd. Here there will be a dozen or so circular patches of trampled grass and in the centre of each a male antelope. Gathered around will be groups of unmated males and females watching the action but not attempting to copulate with one another. Instead, the female seeks to mate with one of the males who is in temporary possession of one of the central mating territories; her choice among the available males appears to depend not upon the personal attractiveness of any given individual but upon the territory he holds. The males themselves compete not directly for females but for possession of a territory; but since being in possession of a territory appears to give any male a strong "psychological advantage" over an intruder contests are usually decided very quickly with the intruder backing down. Territories change hands when the resident male leaves, exhausted.

*Competition between males.* The study of animals which use a system of communal mating grounds (and, in fact, the most intensive study has been carried out upon species of grouse rather than with antelopes) presents us with quite a pleasant picture of good manners in the animal world. Certainly, mating is a competitive business but the females are allowed to make a choice in a fairly decorous way, and direct and bloody confrontation between males is rare. It would be a mistake, however, to assume that this pattern is universal, for in some species the element of female choice is much reduced and that of competition between males becomes all-important.

A most extreme example is provided by the behaviour of the fur seal of the northern Pacific. In late spring, at the beginning of the year's breeding season, bull seals come ashore and establish territories at the water's edge. A month or so later the females arrive and enter the territory of a male who maintains a harem of a dozen or so. This simple description hides a number of rather grim details. The males establish their territories by fighting. Territories near the water's edge are clearly likely to attract more females and it has been found that the dominant bulls who occupy these positions perform a very high proportion of the matings. In one study of seals (elephant seals in this case) it was found that the most dominant 6% of the males inseminated nearly 90% of the females. Accordingly, the contests for these territories may be long and hard and not infrequently they result in the death of one of the contestants. Having established a territory a male will defend it night and day for a period of several weeks, not even leaving it to get food. His defence consists not only of engaging in boundary disputes with neighbouring males but includes a careful policing of the harem. Females who try to leave will be driven back (the male is roughly twice as big as the female) and a guard must be maintained against the possibility that some other male will engage in poaching. An intruder may pick up a female in his teeth and try to drag her off; the attempt of the owner to keep his property can result in a tug-of-war with the unfortunate female injured or killed. It will come as no surprise to learn that it is the female who cares for the pups and that the males treat them with total disregard so that quite a number of pups die from being crushed.

*Implications for human behaviour.* A question that inevitably arises after considering territorial and mating systems in animals concerns the way in which the human species should be described. And, in fact, it is a simple matter to give the appropriate description. Some species have a mixture of mating systems and man is such a species. In man (as in some birds such as swans) monogamy is common, but promiscuity is also found and so is polygamy. Female choice plays a part in determining mating in humans as does competition between males. And, of course, what an individual possesses (his "territory") can help to make him an attractive proposition as a mate. But having given this description it is a more difficult matter to decide what conclusions, if any, should be based on it. It is tempting to conclude, for instance, that, since man appears to be a territorial animal of sorts, his territorial nature can be elucidated by the study of territorial behaviour in other animals. While this is in part true (the study of non-human animals certainly gives us a sense of perspective by making clear what a variety of territorial systems exist in the animal world) we must be cautious about making extrapolations. All species are different and we can no more reach conclusions about the "basic animal nature" of man's territoriality by looking at the behaviour of antelopes or apes, or whatever, than we can determine the "basic nature" of territoriality in the dog, say, by looking at the behaviour of cats. We can use the same methods of study for man as we use for other animals; we can use the same concepts and terminology (of course, the term "territory" was applied to man originally and then was later extended to other animals). We cannot, however, reach conclusions about the detailed behaviour of one species from the study of another.

## The Origin of Species

We can now consider the part played by behavioural mechanisms in bringing about the origin of new species. A group of animals is regarded as being a species if its members interbreed freely producing fertile offspring or at least would be capable of doing so if brought together. It follows that there exist between species biological barriers which prevent successful interbreeding. One barrier is created by the fact that hybrids produced by crosses between species are (by definition) infertile: the mule is a useful animal but it cannot be bred to produce more, being a hybrid produced by crossing a horse and an ass. But, from an evolutionary point of view, the barrier to successful interbreeding produced by hybrid infertility comes too late—that is, the parents will have expended part of their scarce reproductive resources (see p. 52) without ensuring the propagation of their own genes. What is needed is a barrier that works to prevent mating from even getting started. Such barriers exist and are built upon differences in behaviour between the species in question. They are most evident in the elaborate *courtship displays* that are an essential preliminary to mating in many animal species.

*Courtship displays.* Consider as an example the courtship display of the guppy *Poecilia* (see Fig. 2.5). Two species of this fish live in the waters off Trinidad (*P. reticulata* and *P. picta*), but in spite of their similiarity in form and habitat they coexist without interbreeding. The reason lies in the different markings possessed by the males of the two species and the way in which they are displayed in the courtship dance. The male of *P. picta* has markings on his dorsal and tail fins and he displays these to the female by repeatedly swimming in a circle around her head. The male of *P. reticulata* has markings mainly on his

Fig. 2.5. *The courtship dance of the guppy* Poecilia. *In the upper part of the figure a male of the species* P. picta *circles the head of the female displaying his dorsal fin. The lower part of the figure shows a male of the species* P. reticulata *holding the sigmoid position in front of the female (adapted from McFarland, 1981).*

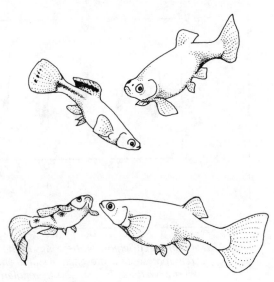

body which he shows by positioning himself in front of the female, twisting his body into an S-shape, and quivering for several seconds. An inexperienced male will perform his display to a female of either species but interbreeding will not occur since the appropriate display is necessary to persuade the female to cooperate—she will ignore or evade advances from a male of the wrong species.

Courtship displays that function in this way are said to constitute behavioural *isolating mechanisms*. They have been much studied by ornithologists and we should consider some examples from among birds. The greenfinch and the goldfinch are separate species but if kept together in confinement they will breed and produce (infertile) offspring. However, even though these two species may share the same habitat in the wild, they do not interbreed. The normal mechanisms of pair formation that are overridden in caged birds ensure that each bird mates only with its own species. In many species of birds there is an auditory component to the display. That is, male birds often sing long and frequently when they first occupy a territory, but singing declines when a female arrives and mating has been successful. The nature of the song can be an important cue in pair formation. Thus, two of the species of leaf warbler found

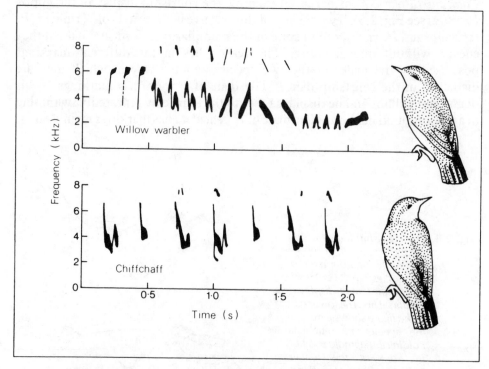

Fig. 2.6. *Sound spectrograms of the songs of the willow warbler and the chiffchaff. The dark areas represent the presence of sound energy of a given frequency at a given time. The willow warbler has a short, regularly repeated song; the chiffchaff rambles, improvising on two basic notes (after Marler and Hamilton, 1966).*

in Britain (the willow warbler and the chiffchaff) are so physically similar that naturalists can hardly tell them apart except by differences in the song produced by the males in spring. But provided that other warblers are sensitive to this difference so that females of the appropriate species are attracted by the appropriate song, this is all that matters. In spite of their external physical similarities the integrity of each species will be maintained (see Fig. 2.6).

*Isolating mechanisms and speciation.* Behavioural isolating mechanisms maintain differences between existing species; but how do these differences become established in the first place? In the introduction to this chapter (p. 22) it was suggested that a new species could originate through the gradual accumulation of genetic changes over geological time (presumably in response to a changing environment). In some cases the fossil record provides evidence for such changes. Thus the fossilized remains of early man, going back for some 500 000 years, indicate that he possessed a structure somewhat different from that of modern man but are nonetheless sufficiently similar for him to be categorized as belonging to the species *Homo sapiens*. Going back beyond that time the fossils are sufficiently different (the teeth are bigger and the braincase rather smaller—1000 cm$^3$ as opposed to 1400 cm$^3$) for palaeontologists to classify these remains as belonging to a different species, *Homo erectus* (see Fig. 2.7). It is perhaps the case that *H. erectus* and *H. sapiens* are truly distinct species in the sense that they would not be able to interbreed and produce fully fertile offspring. But such a proposal is not, of course, open to test. And in a way this does not matter. The distinction between two parts of a lineage is necessarily an arbitrary one—there can be no doubt that the very latest *H. erectus* and the very earliest *H. sapiens* would have been closely similar and interfertile. But equally there can be little doubt that the latest *H. sapiens* and the earliest *H. erectus* (or perhaps the australopithecine ancestors of this creature) would be very different and would be worth categorizing as different species.

But evolutionary change does not consist simply in the gradual change of a single lineage. Phylogenetic diagrams are tree-like (Fig. 2.2) with many branches and each fork represents a point where some ancestral species split into two. Such splits (and thus the origin of most new species) depend upon the development of behavioural isolating mechanisms of the sort described above. According to the most widely accepted account, the first step in speciation occurs when the members of an original species become divided into two geographically separated groups, as may happen when some migrate to a new habitat while others stay behind. The separate adaptation of the two groups to their differing environments will lead to the development of structural and functional differences between them that will have implications for the consequences of interbreeding should the two groups meet up again. In some cases the hybrids may be superior creatures (a phenomenon called *hybrid vigour*

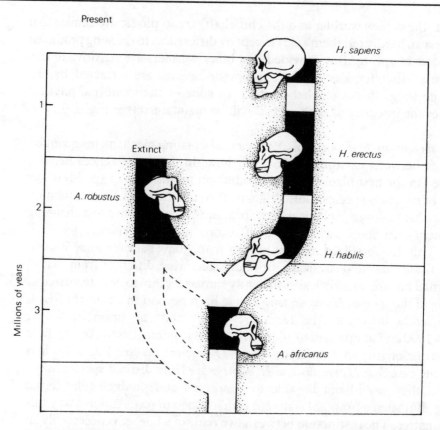

Fig. 2.7. *A possible evolutionary history for the hominids. Shaded sections represent known fossils. In addition to the doubts expressed in the figure there are many other debatable points. In particular: for a given line of descent the distinction between species is arbitrary; the remains of* Australopithecus *are very varied and some argue that there were more species of this genus than the two shown; some argue that* H. habilis *constitutes a separate line from that of the australopithecines and coexisted with them (including* A. africanus) *from some 3 mya; others suggest that* A. africanus *is not ancestral to* Homo *but that both are derived from some earlier common ancestor (based on Johanson and Edey, 1981; see also Johanson and White, 1979).*

seen when the parental stocks have declined as a result of excessive inbreeding). But in many other cases the hybrid offspring may be inferior creatures incorporating the worst aspects of each group. Within each group, therefore, those individuals least likely to breed with members of the other group will be the individuals most likely to leave offspring in the next generation. That is, each group will develop isolating mechanisms, interbreeding will cease, and there will be two species where before there was just one.

## Acquired Characteristics

It is appropriate to conclude this section with a few comments about the inheritance of acquired characteristics. I have described some examples of behavioural processes shaping the course of evolution by natural selection. In doing so I have tried to make it clear that behavioural interactions are in fact of central importance in determining evolutionary change. What I have *not* suggested, however, is that characteristics acquired during an animal's lifetime may become inherited and in this way influence the course of evolutionary change. Animals do, of course, learn new habits and acquire new skills as they interact with their environment (and we shall discuss the mechanisms involved in Chapter 7) but no mechanisms is known by which these habits and skills can become incorporated in the genes of the egg or sperm and thus be passed on directly to the next generation. Instead, habits and skills are passed on, at least in the human species, by a process in which the child imitates the behaviour of the parent or in which the parent explicitly teaches the child. Acquired characteristics may not become inherited but they can be transmitted culturally from one generation to the next. According to some, "cultural evolution", particularly when it is aided by the presence of a well-developed language as in man, can far outweigh the "biological evolution" in its importance. Discussion of the implications of this view will be postponed to the final chapter when we shall have considered in some detail the processes involved in development and learning in the individual.

## PHYLOGENY DERIVED FROM THE STUDY OF BEHAVIOUR

As well as playing its part in shaping the course of evolution, behaviour is a product of evolution every bit as much as any anatomical feature. Just like the latter, the behavioural characteristics that animals show can be used in working out phylogeny, in working out the evolutionary history of a given animal or animal group. What this means in practice is deciding which current species is closely related to another (in the sense that they diverged from their common ancestral species a relatively short time ago on the evolutionary time scale) and determining, if possible, from fossil evidence, the exact nature of the common ancestor. The branching tree diagram of Fig. 2.1 is the product of research of this sort.

The usual technique of the biologist engaged in this sort of enterprise is to look for "basic" similarities (*homologies*) and differences among living species and the fossil remains of extinct species. As well as studying the adult form of each individual he may also make extensive use of its embryological development. (A small part of the evidence favouring the idea that apes and men are closely related is that embryonic apes are hairless, have a relatively large head and look in these respects not unlike men.) Thus, for example, the biologist will decide that birds are more closely related to cats than to bees (even though the latter are unable to fly) because the cat has the same "basic" bone structure; confirmation comes from embryology which shows that young birds have proper tails (like cats) but that these disappear as the bones fuse to form the structure found in adult birds.

## Limitations

Before going any further, it should now be admitted that behavioural characteristics are not in fact very useful in tracing phylogeny, although the reasons why they are not turn out to be quite instructive. The first reason is simply that by concentrating on behaviour we restrict the range of evidence available to us. No fossils behave and there is not very much known about the embryology of behaviour. Thus we can look only for basic similarities and differences in the behaviour shown by living species. Having said this, a small qualification should be added. Fossils may not behave but features of them or associated with them may sometimes tell us a lot about the behaviour that the owner of the fossilized skeleton once showed. One of the earliest hominid forms (*Australopithecus*, see Fig. 2.7) who lived in Africa from at least two million years ago has had his near-human status confirmed by fossil evidence about his behaviour. At Olduvai in East Africa there have been found "pebble tools" made of lava and of quartz, chipped along one edge to make cutting or chopping implements and dated at about 1·7 million years old (see Fig. 2.8). (The existence of such artifacts is one of the reasons why some archaeologists want to place their makers in the genus *Homo* as *H. habilis*—"handy man".) Our knowledge of the behaviour of *Australopithecus* remains scanty but by the time we come to *Homo erectus* (see Fig. 2.7), about half a million years ago, fossil evidence supplies much more information. This creature possessed quite sophisticated flint tools that are clearly specially designed as axes and picks, and for chopping and scraping. And finding hearths with charred remains dating from about 450 000 years before the present tells us that he knew how to use fire and that, presumably, he was able to cook his food.

The second, and more important reason why behavioural evidence is of limited usefulness in tracing phylogeny can be summed up in the following truism: behaviour is very easily modified by environmental influences. To

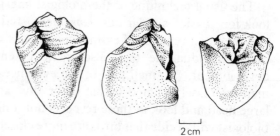

Fig. 2.8. *Pebble tools made from lava and found at Olduvai in East Africa. They are dated to about 1·7 million years (after Young, 1971).*

2 cm

amplify this point; what animals do is often a response to the immediate environment in which they find themselves. Thus a creature which is unable to maintain its body temperature at a sufficiently high level because it is not equipped with fur or blubber, or whatever, may simply get up and go to a warmer place. What is more, the sort of behaviour that an animal shows may change as a result of experience during its lifetime. That is, the animal may learn to go to a particular place when adverse conditions seem likely. The fact that behaviour is responsive to and can be modified by an animal's environment is perhaps its most important feature and this feature will be discussed at length in later chapters of this book. In tracing phylogenies, however, characteristics that are easily modified are just what is not wanted. To take a fanciful example, imagine yourself an early biologist working toward the conclusion that all the animals that we now call vertebrates are closely related because they all have four limbs. But imagine now how difficult it would be to reach this sensible conclusion if the number of limbs any individual possessed was easily influenced by environmental factors. The gross structural characteristics of an animal are not often modified by the environment in such a radical way as this but with behavioural characteristics we can be much less sure and must proceed with caution.

### Fixed Action Patterns

A case has been made, however (by Lorenz among others), that some patterns of behaviour (*fixed action patterns*) are sufficiently stable that they can be used in tracing phylogeny as readily as anatomical structures. By fixed action pattern is meant a series of movements which is more or less uniform and found in all members of a species. These patterns of movement may be elicited or "released" by stimulation from the animal's environment but once underway they are, by and large, independent of external events. A classic example is the action pattern by which a ground-nesting bird retrieves an egg which has rolled out of the nest. The bird stands up and, craning its neck, positions its beak on the far side of the egg; then it draws the egg in, moving the beak from side to side to prevent the egg from slipping away (see Fig. 2.9). In spite of the great inefficiency of this pattern (eggs often do slip away) it is consistently found among birds which nest on the ground, that is, the behaviour does not seem to

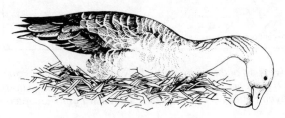

Fig. 2.9. *Greylag goose retrieving an egg (after Tinbergen, 1951).*

be susceptible to modification by environmental influence. When an egg is lost in the middle of the movement it is possible to observe just how independent of environmental events the behaviour pattern is: very often the bird will carry on with the movement bringing the now-absent egg all the way back to the nest before it can bring itself to begin the whole sequence again.

An example of the use of fixed action patterns in determining, or at least confirming relationships among living species is found in work done by Lorenz some 40 years ago in which he studied the action patterns shown by a wide range

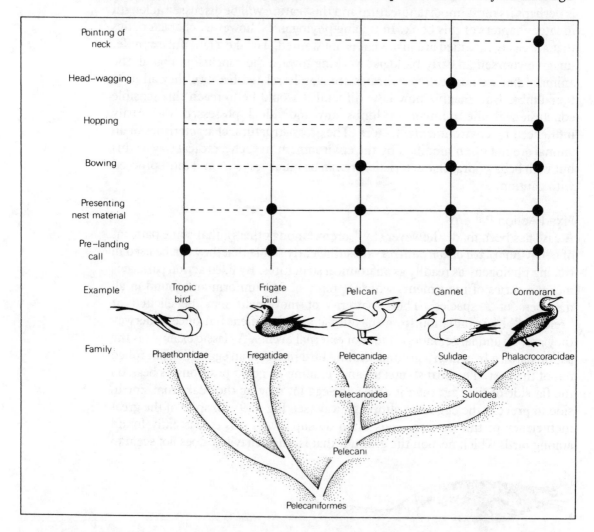

Fig. 2.10. *Relationships among pelican-like birds. The lower part of the figure shows how the various families are thought to be related on the basis of anatomical evidence. The upper part lists a series of fixed action patterns with a filled circle indicating that a given pattern is observed in a particular family (adapted from Van Tets, 1965).*

of ducks and geese. He found just one pattern that all these share (but which other birds do not) in the characteristic repetitive piping call of the lost chick. Other patterns are held in common by all the species that we call ducks but are not found among the geese and vice versa. In this way, behavioural characteristics have been found to support the phylogenetic relationships that had already been established on the basis of morphological criteria. A more modern example of this same procedure is shown in Fig. 2.10 which is based on the work of Van Tets (1965). The lower part of the figure shows a phylogenetic tree for the order of pelican-like birds (Pelecaniformes), worked out largely on the basis of morphology. The anatomy prompts us to make a major division between the Pelecani themselves and related groups that include the tropic and frigate birds. This division has been found to be reflected at a behavioural level (the top part of the figure lists some of the action patterns that have been studied with a symbol indicating when they are shown by a particular group of birds). Thus the Pelecani show a characteristic "bowing" that the other groups do not. Of the Pelecani shown in the figure it has been customary to group together gannets and cormorants as being rather different from pelicans and this distinction too appears in behaviour, "hopping" being shown only by the Suloidea and not by the Pelicanoidea.

Perhaps more dramatic are those cases in which behavioural characteristics have prompted a reinterpretation of established phylogeny derived from morphology. Mayr (1958) cites an example from those birds that it has been usual to group together as forming the family of tits. Although the various species of tit look quite similar their nest-building habits differ markedly. The long-tailed tit, for example, builds an oval-shaped nest in a tree or bush whereas "true" tits always nest in cavities such as hollow trees. Other tits show yet other forms of nest-building behaviour and Mayr concludes that the so-called family is in fact a rather artificial grouping of not very closely related groups of birds. A further example comes from studies carried out on the reproductive behaviour of the wasp genus *Ammophila*. It was noted that some individuals showed aberrant behaviour, collecting caterpillars rather than sawflies as food for the larva and collecting this food before the egg was laid rather than vice versa. It subsequently became clear that these wasps were not simply aberrant individuals of the species *Ammophila campestris* but constituted a different species which is now known, after its discoverer (Adriaanse), as *Ammophila adriaansei*.

## PHYLOGENY OF BEHAVIOURAL AND PSYCHOLOGICAL CHARACTERISTICS

In the preceding section we discussed attempts to decide which species are closely (or distantly) related to which others on the basis of the behaviour they show. In this section we turn to a related issue, considering attempts that have been made to discover the evolutionary history of a given pattern of behaviour or of a given psychological faculty. Since it is one of the few topics that have been subjected to thorough investigation we shall concentrate our discussion on the ability that some animals show to behave intelligently and ask: what is the evolutionary history of this ability?

If it were available, a full answer to this question would allow us to say that intelligence first appeared so many million years ago in a certain animal (belonging, perhaps, to a species now extinct). We could then say that since this animal is the ancestor of species A and of species B, this is why both A and B now show intelligence of some sort. In addition, our answer would also include information about what selection pressures caused intelligence to emerge in the first place and what pressures caused it to take different forms in different living species.

Unfortunately, it is not possible to give an answer as complete as this. Since fossils do not behave, the only method available to us is, again, that of comparing the behaviour shown by living species. This allows us to do no more than make plausible guesses about the origins of the behaviour in question.

### The Comparative Method: An Example

Before starting a discussion of intelligence it will be best to begin with a fairly simple example of the way in which the comparative method has been applied to a specific piece of behaviour. We can take an example again from the work of Lorenz on fixed action patterns in ducks.

When two pairs of mallard meet, the female may encourage her mate to attack using a curious action pattern known as "incitement". She lowers her

Fig. 2.11. *"Inciting" in the shelduck: the two females stand with heads lowered and pointing at the enemy (after Lorenz, 1958).*

head and points it over her shoulder at the opposing pair. Or at least the display is usually directed at the opposing pair but it may not be; if the female happens to be facing them directly she still points her head over her shoulder and hence, in this case, points *away* from the opposition. Some insight as to the origins of this bizarre behaviour is provided by looking at the behaviour of the shelduck in similar circumstances (see Fig. 2.11). In this species the female is rather more excitable than in the mallard and her reaction is to rush up to the opposing pair. As she gets closer, she becomes afraid (if we may be permitted to describe her behaviour in terms of human motives) and she turns and runs back to her mate, stopping to look back over her shoulder as aggression takes over again. Given these observations it seems sensible to conclude that the *ritualized* pattern that we see in the mallard had its origins in a behaviour pattern shown by some ancestral mallard that was like that still shown in the shelduck today.

A behaviour pattern that has become modified over the course of evolution, perhaps by becoming stereotyped or exaggerated, so as better to serve a signalling function, is said to show *ritualization*. The example just cited is simply one of many that have been discerned in observations of the threat and courtship displays of birds. Most of these displays seem to have their origin in the fact that an animal that courts or fights another subjects itself to conflict: the other animal may be a potential mate but it may also potentially be an aggressor; it may be easily beaten in a fight but it could turn out to be more powerful than it looks. The by-products of such conflict (which include not only responses whereby the animal tries both to approach and to run or fly away at the same time, but "emotional" responses such as vocalization, changes in skin colour, defaecation, and so on) will be obvious for all to see. They thus form excellent raw material for selection to work upon in producing more efficient systems for communication. To some extent, the suggestion that evolutionary change proceeds in this way remains a speculation, but comparative studies of the sort just described add weight to the argument.

### Comparative Studies of Intelligence

It is possible to apply this comparative method on a much larger scale. Instead of comparing specific patterns of behaviour in closely related species we may investigate, in a range of very different species, a range of different behaviour patterns (these being selected as reflecting some more general ability). Thus, most vertebrates seem to show at least a little "intelligence" (using the word for the time being in a casual and ill-defined way—a generally acceptable definition is hard to come by); other animals, most invertebrates, do not.

The phylogeny of intelligence has been studied by Bitterman (1965) and others by a method which involves comparing some measure of the learning ability of distantly related vertebrates. The main features of this sort of work are as follows. It takes for study a convenient example of each major vertebrate group, convenient in the sense that it is easily available and can be maintained in a laboratory. Thus Bitterman has often worked with the goldfish, with turtles (a semi-aquatic form known in Europe as terrapins) as convenient reptiles; the bird used has been the pigeon; the mammal, the laboratory rat. The next step is to devise some method for testing the intelligence of each of these species. Without a generally accepted definition of intelligence this may seem far from easy, but work of this sort has proceeded on the assumption that an animal's ability to learn gives some measure of its intellectual standing. This is not a very contentious assumption; most of us would accept that an ability to change what we do in the light of experience is an important part of what we mean by intelligence. (It is the fool who persists in his folly.)

An example of the sort of learning task used by comparative psychologists is that called *serial reversal* learning. When used with the pigeon, it works like this (see Fig. 2.12). The bird is presented with two small discs (or response-keys), one coloured red and one green, both of which it has a tendency to peck at. Pecks to the red have no consequence but pecks to the green are rewarded, the pigeon being given a small amount of food. Not surprisingly the bird learns to peck almost exclusively at the green disc. At this stage the experimenter reverses the arrangement so that food is made available only after pecks to red. The result is a pigeon which continues to peck for quite some time to what is now the inappropriate key. Given time, however (and usually this takes the bird rather longer than it took to learn the original task), a new preference is established for pecking at red. And now the experimenter reverses the arrangements again and continues to do so on each occasion that the bird develops a preference for the key associated with reward. The experimental arrangement may seem a little unkind to the pigeon but it does provide a nice technique for assessing the animal's behavioural flexibility. An intelligent animal would be one that adapted its behaviour readily to the changing demands imposed by the environment. By this measure the pigeon proves to be fairly intelligent. Given sufficient training it can come to reverse its preference quite readily, to switch to the alternative key after just a few pecks to the key that originally was preferred but which now yields no reward (Fig. 2.13). Mammals are even better at this task: the rat can learn to change its preference (in the equivalent situation) after making just a single response to the inappropriate object. Turtles and fish, in contrast, do rather badly. For some time there was no evidence that fish showed any improvement at all with protracted training on the serial reversal task; instead, they seemed to find each reversal just as difficult as the first.

Serial reversal training is just one of several "intelligence tests" that have been employed by comparative psychologists but all give roughly the same result: the species tested show a range of ability with the fish showing up worst and mammals the best. What can we conclude from this pattern of results?

Fig. 2.12. *Apparatus for training the pigeon on a discrimination learning task. A peck at the central key causes the side keys to be illuminated with, for instance, lights differing in colour. A peck to one colour yields reward, to the other colour does not. The central rectangular opening is used to present grain as the reward.*

Bitterman's conclusion was that the mechanisms employed by fish in these learning tasks were quite different from those used by other vertebrates. He went on to suggest that intelligence develops as we move up the "phyletic scale" by the addition of new modes of adjustment to environmental demands. There are a number of reasons why this notion must be treated with caution and I will outline three of them.

## Problems for Comparative Psychology

First, but probably least important, it might be argued that a simple learning task of the sort I have just described is not a good measure of intelligence. Certainly it seems to have little in common with those attributes that a person

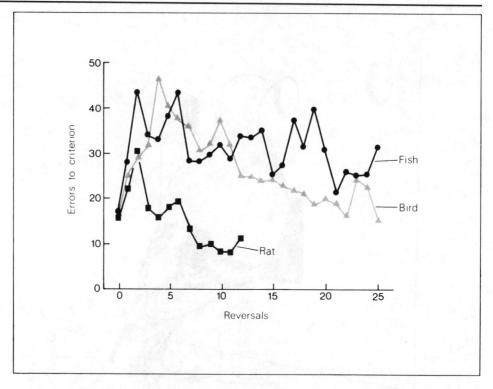

Fig. 2.13. *Performance of rats, pigeons, and fish on a series of reversals of a visual discrimination. For all species, reversals early in the series prove more difficult (there are more errors) than initial acquisition of the discrimination. There is, however, clear improvement over the series in the bird and the rat, whereas the improvement shown by the fish is marginal (adapted from Mackintosh, 1969).*

has to show before we are willing to call him intelligent. In this case, however, appearances may be deceptive. If we try to analyse and to specify precisely what qualities a person must have to be intelligent we end up with something very like my rough and ready definition of intelligence as the ability to learn and profit by experience. Intelligence is more than just the ability to do the sometimes curious tests devised by psychologists. Heim, one of the leading designers of such tests, has concluded that a person shows intelligent activity in "grasping the essentials in a situation and responding appropriately to them" (Heim, 1954). Given this definition, serial reversal learning looks like rather a good test of intelligence.

*Are the comparisons fair?* A second and more serious problem arises from the fact that it is necessary to modify the task given to one species in order to set it for some other species. At the grossest level, the fish must be tested in a tank filled with water, an environment quite inappropriate for birds and mammals. Again, the coloured stimuli used for fish and for birds cannot be used for the colour-blind rat and stimuli must be used which differ in brightness and shape. The different species require different sorts of reward to maintain their performance: the pigeon receives access to grain, the rat may be rewarded by a small pellet of sugar, the fish by being offered a small worm. All of these and other incidental details, which are forced on the experimenter who wants to study the behaviour of different species, could possibly play a role in determining the results of the experiment. That is, the difference in performance on a serial reversal task shown by the rat and the fish might arise not from any intrinsic difference in intelligence but because the different animals are necessarily being set rather different sorts of task. This problem arises in its most acute form when we consider the question of motivation. The rat is rewarded with a pellet of sugar, the fish with a worm, but are these rewards equally rewarding to the two species? If they are not then herein may lie the explanation for the difference in performance: essentially, if the fish regards a single worm as rather a paltry reward it may simply not try to solve the task, thus failing to reveal its ability to do so.

The problem I have just described is familiar to those who attempt to devise intelligence tests for people. When two individuals produced different scores on a particular intelligence test there is often some doubt that the scores reflect a true difference in intellect. If the test is one which includes tasks like "Pick the odd one" and "Complete this series", successful performance will clearly depend upon having sufficient knowledge of the English language to understand the instructions. If one of the individuals tested has a poor grasp of English, perhaps because he learned it as a second language, we would not want to say that his poor performance on the test was unequivocal evidence of a low level of intelligence. It has been suggested that a similar problem can arise even when both the individuals tested are native speakers of English. Put bluntly, the suggestion has been made that the rich and the poor (the "disadvantaged") speak slightly different versions of the language and that because the test is likely to be phrased in the language of the rich, the poor may have some difficulty in understanding the tasks they are being set.

To overcome these difficulties much effort has been expended in attempts to devise tests that are "culture-fair"—tests which require background knowledge so elementary that all the individuals being tested are sure to possess it. This strategy is not open to those who want to test the intelligence of different species. The "cultural" differences between the pigeon and the rat are so big that it is impossible to imagine a single test that could fairly be set for both animals. Instead, a different strategy has been adopted by which the conditions under which each species is tested are varied widely. It might then become possible to say, for example, that no matter how big a reward the fish is given for a correct choice and no matter how small a reward the pigeon is given, the performance of the former is always worse than that of the latter.

An alarming result of studies of this kind (alarming, at least, for those who want to argue that fish are less intelligent than birds and mammals) has come from experiments in which the techniques used for training fish have been slightly modified. The initial work with fish was done in an apparatus in which the fish pushed against an illuminated disc at one end of the tank and, if its response was correct, received a reward delivered at the other end of the tank (see Fig. 2.14). After consuming its reward the fish waited for an interval of several seconds before the start of the next choice trial. In more recent studies there have been trivial changes to this procedure. In some, the interval between successive trials has been reduced to just a second or so; in others, the site of reward presentation has been changed so that it is delivered immediately next to the disc to which the animal has responded. These differences in procedure may seem trivial but the consequences are dramatic. A fish trained by either of the modified procedures will show a fair degree of serial reversal improvement. Admittedly, no fish has yet shown performance as good as that shown by the pigeon or the rat but it must be allowed that there is now no reason (on the basis of these reversal experiments) for supposing there to be a qualitative difference

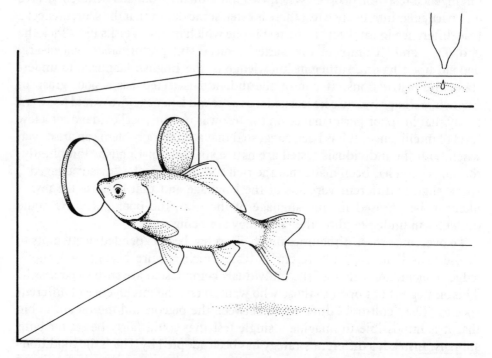

Fig. 2.14. *Schematic representation of an early version of the apparatus for training fish on a visual discrimination. The two discs are illuminated with lights differing in colour. By nosing the disc designated as correct, the fish causes food to be delivered to the back of the tank.*

in intellect between the fish and these other creatures. Furthermore, the possibility that some other small change in the training procedure might remove even the remaining quantitative difference must be acknowledged as real.

It appears, therefore, that for a number of years we have been misjudging the intellectual capabilities of fish. More worrying, however, is the possibility raised by this finding that many of our other judgements may be similarly inaccurate. Might it not be possible by a seemingly trivial change in experimental procedure to evoke behaviour from a bird as flexible as that shown by any mammal or to produce performance in a rat as accurate as that shown by the monkey? In short, any judgement that one species is more intelligent than some other must be a very tentative one and can form only a very insecure basis for wide-ranging theories of the evolution of intelligence.

*The myth of the phylogenetic scale.* The third issue raised by this sort of attempt to investigate the phylogeny of intelligence in an experimental manner concerns the evolutionary relationships between the various species that have been studied. It remains the case that, although no qualitative differences in intellect between the main vertebrate groups have been firmly established, the quantitative differences that do remain generally show mammals to be superior to birds, birds to be superior to fish, and so on. These results fit in nicely with our intuitions about the way various animals might be ordered on a "phyletic scale" (or sometimes "phylogenetic scale"). Most of us, from time to time, find ourselves referring to "lower" and "higher" forms of life, thinking perhaps of fish as an example of a lower form, of monkeys as higher forms, and even of man as the highest form of all.

Quite apart from the gratuitous insult to the fish implied by the description lower and the unjustified self-congratulation implied by regarding ourselves as among the higher animals there are good reasons for avoiding this sort of terminology. The species that are alive today must be regarded as the tips of an evolutionary tree (Fig. 2.1 and 2.2) related to each other only by way of common ancestors that are often exceedingly remote in time. Not only are they not descended directly from one another but they cannot be arranged in an orderly way along some simple continuum in the way that the higher–lower terminology seems to imply. The point may be made by reconsidering the relationships depicted in Figs 2.1 and 2.2. The fish most commonly used in behavioural experiments are bony fish (the *teleosts*, a major branch of the Osteichthyes of Fig. 2.2). As far as we can tell, on the basis of fossil evidence, the teleosts became differentiated from other vertebrates as much as 300 million years ago. The teleosts and the stock from which they emerged continued to evolve along different lines for at least 100 million years before the first mammalian forms began to diverge from the basic stock. Modern mammals and modern teleosts have their origins in quite different types of ancestral fish. The rat and the goldfish are very remotely related indeed. What is more, all the major groups of mammals (rodents, carnivores, primates, and so on) seem to have appeared more or less at the same time about 100 million years ago as the result of the almost explosive radiation of some common stock. This means that all these groups have been evolving separately for the same period of time and each is as remote from the original proto-mammal as any other. It is apparent that, however suggestive the results of experiments testing and learning abilities of these various species, we would be quite mistaken if we regarded them as allowing us to sample stages in the progress of intelligence at points along some single evolutionary scale. There is no such scale.

*Conclusions.* All these considerations force us to accept that no simple conclusion about the evolution of intelligence can be derived from the comparative study of animal behaviour. This outcome presents something of a disappointment to those of us who hoped to be able to discern the evolutionary origins of human intelligence from the study of animals. But the usefulness of comparative studies lies not in that they tell us about the "animal basis" of human intelligence. The position is essentially the same as that described earlier in our discussion of territoriality. Given what we know of vertebrate phylogeny such an enterprise would be as misguided as trying to elucidate the nature of intelligence in the dog, say, by searching for its "non-canine basis" in the behaviour of fish, or birds, and of man. If we want to investigate the so-called "biological origins" of man's intelligence by far the best way would be to study directly man himself. The same basic methods can be used. By comparing the intellectual abilities of various groups of men (the various "races" of mankind) it might be possible to work out what features they hold in common and which might therefore owe their origin to a common ancestor. Use too could be made of fossil evidence, not only fossilized skulls and the like, but also of artifacts associated with them. The tools that early man used can tell us quite a lot about how he behaved and thus something about how he thought. It is a great pity that the most informative "fossil" that a man can leave behind him, a written account of his doings, made its appearance so relatively recently. There have been only about 200 generations of history (as opposed to at least 10 000 generations of prehistory) and it seems unlikely that Darwinian evolution could produce any dramatic change in man's mental functioning over so short a time span.

## A Role for Comparative Psychology

Finally in this section, having said that comparative studies of learning in animals have supplied relatively little information about the phylogeny of intelligence, it is appropriate to redress the balance by outlining a way in which they have been and continue to be useful. Comparative studies seem to me to be best fitted to serve as tests which allow us to refine our theoretical explanations of behaviour. The variety of animal forms supplies us with scope for what might be called natural experiments. It was once proposed, for instance, that some forms of learning, notably classical conditioning (Chapter 7), would only be shown by animals with a forebrain possessing a cerebral cortex (see Chapter 5). In principle one could test this notion by taking a dog or monkey or whatever, removing its cortex, and demonstrating that conditioning is or is not possible. A number of such experiments have now been done on the rabbit and it is clear that classical conditioning can still occur. But these experiments are most difficult to perform (if only because it is difficult to keep a decorticate animal alive). It is much easier to experiment on a subject supplied by nature that already lacks a cortex. The observation that the earthworm is capable of classical conditioning is enough to demonstrate that such conditioning is not a unique property of the mammalian cerebral cortex.

Comparative studies have also been useful in testing purely psychological theories. For example, it has been suggested that man's ability to respond to the relative properties of objects (as shown by his ability to choose consistently the larger of a pair of objects, say, irrespective of their absolute size) critically depended on his possessing language. His ability to code the objects as " the larger" and "the smaller" was thought to mediate his performance on this task. But comparative studies require us to think again about this. The demonstration that non-verbal animals (rats and pigeons) are quite capable of learning a discrimination task which can be solved only in terms of the relative properties of the stimuli makes it clear that linguistic mediation is not a necessary condition for such performance. Further examples will occur in later chapters. For the time being these two cases are sufficient to illustrate a use of the comparative method that has proved increasingly fruitful in recent years (see Macphail, 1982).

## EVOLUTIONARY EXPLANATIONS OF BEHAVIOUR

In Chapter 1 we concluded that the central question asked by modern psychology takes the form: why does this behaviour occur? It is time now to summarize to what extent, if at all, the study of evolution can help to answer this question. Our conclusions will ultimately be of particular interest with respect to the behaviour of man. One does not have to look very far to discover examples of what purport to be evolutionary explanations of human behaviour; for example, the suggestion has often been made that human aggression is in some way a result of man's evolutionary history or, again, that the psychological differences between the sexes are ultimately caused by evolutionary processes.

Common though these suggestions are, it is difficult to understand at first sight just what they are meant to imply. When faced with the suggestion that man's aggressiveness has its origins in his evolutionary history one's initial reaction might be to say: but, of course; and so do all his other qualities, for all that he is and does has its origins in his evolutionary history. Furthermore, if all man's attributes have an evolutionary basis then no real explanation is being offered in the case of aggression. To understand how this suggestion might constitute an explanation we must dig a little deeper; in doing so we discover more than one interpretation of the idea that some behaviour might be explicable in terms of the evolutionary history of the species. The first of these will merely be outlined here: it is the idea that some patterns of behaviour (aggression may be an example) are a direct product of the genetic make-up that evolution has given to the species and do not arise from the experiences that individuals undergo during their lifetimes. Further discussion of this idea will be postponed until Chapter 3 which is explicitly devoted to the part played by genetic factors in determining behaviour. The other interpretations require a little more comment.

## Behavioural Vestiges

It was mentioned in passing in Chapter 1 that a knowledge of evolution can sometimes give us an understanding of "quirks" in behaviour: of why, for example, a state of fear should produce erection of the body hair in man. It may be that other, more complex, patterns of human behaviour (such as aggression) have evolutionary origins of this sort. They may be best regarded as psychological equivalents of the appendix, best regarded as features that were once useful but are so no longer. In the case of aggression it might be argued that the behaviour patterns that remain today are quite the reverse of useful, threatening as they do, not only the survival of individuals, but that of the entire species. What is being said then by this sort of evolutionary explanation is that some aspects of man's nature evolved long ago when the selection pressures acting upon him were quite different from those working today. In cases like these, any attempt to answer the question of why a certain pattern of behaviour occurs in terms of what useful function the behaviour might serve will be thwarted unless we are prepared to look back into the past.

## Adaptive Behaviour and the Experimental Method

Although evolutionary explanations can be put forward for odd features of behaviour it has been more usual to use the concept of natural selection in explaining why behaviour is adapted so as to fit each animal to the environment in which it lives, promoting its survival or at least the survival of its genes. We can develop this point by looking again at some striking examples of adaptedness in the behaviour shown by birds.

It has already been pointed out that the signals used by different song-birds in pair formation are often very different. As a consequence, mating between closely related but distinct species is made less likely, and the individuals involved are therefore less likely to waste their reproductive potential in producing inferior hybrids that are unlikely to survive. This behaviour stands in marked contrast to that shown by song-birds confronted by a predator like a hawk. In this case the alarm call is much the same in all species so that all are able to benefit from the call produced by one. Further, the alarm call has those features (it is fairly high in pitch, short in duration) which make a sound difficult to localize. It will be difficult, therefore, for the predator to detect exactly where the sound came from. Although an individual may in a sense be willing to put itself at risk in order to foster the survival of others carrying the same genes there is no point in unnecessary risks. Natural selection appears to have equipped song-birds with a tendency to raise the alarm but to have reduced the risk involved by making the call itself as safe as possible.

In this example, we already know from the results of a great many studies of auditory perception that short high-pitched sounds are difficult to localize. But in some cases fresh experiments are required to demonstrate the adaptive significance of behaviour. We have already mentioned Tinbergen's suggestion that gulls remove broken eggshells from the area around their nest so that the white interior of the egg will not be available to attract the attention of predators. This suggestion was no more than a possibility until Tinbergen and his collaborators carried out the necessary experimental test. What they did was to lay out a number of eggs in the colony, some with a broken eggshell nearby and some without. It soon became apparent that the former were taken by predators much more readily.

### The Comparative Method and Adaptation

It has often been possible to establish the adaptive significance of some behaviour patterns without resort to experimentation, simply by comparing the behaviour shown by different animals. Thus Cullen (1957) has carried out an extensive study of the behaviour of the kittiwake which, unlike other gulls, nests on ledges in steep cliffs rather than on the ground. These birds show many patterns of behaviour that the ground-nesting birds do not: for instance, young kittiwakes are less mobile than other gull chicks, they do not run when attacked, and so on. If these behaviour patterns are adaptations to cliff-nesting then it may be predicted that other species of birds that nest on cliffs should show them too. And indeed this turns out to be so—even species only distantly related to the kittiwake (such as those gannets that live on cliffs) tend to show them. It can be added that cliff-nesting birds do not show the same patterns of cleaning the neighbourhood of the nest as those shown by ground-nesting gulls. Droppings and broken eggshells are left all around, presumably because a ledge high on a cliff is relatively free from the risk of predation. This observation lends support to Tinbergen's analysis of the nest-tidying behaviour of black-headed gulls. That is, the experimental and comparative methods work together and point to the same conclusion.

In recent years this comparative method has been used increasingly in an attempt to answer more far-reaching questions about the adaptedness of behaviour (see Williams, 1966). Consider as an example the patterns of mating that were discussed earlier (p. 29). It is legitimate to ask: why is it usual for there to be competition among males with females making some sort of choice, rather than vice versa? An answer has come from the theory of *parental investment* developed by Trivers (1972), this term being used to mean anything that a parent contributes (from the germ cell itself to nourishment, protection, and education) that increases the chance of survival for an offspring. Such investments in any one offspring will necessarily be at the cost of the parent's ability to invest in other offspring. But for many species the investment made by one sex (usually the male) is relatively trivial—that is, it costs the male relatively little in time and energy to inseminate a female and having done so he can rapidly move on to the next available female. The female, on the other hand, makes a much greater contribution. For one thing she contributes eggs, cells which in comparison with sperm are very large and in rather short supply. And if she is a mammal, she grows the fertilized egg within her own body and feeds it with her own milk after it is born. Females therefore constitute a "limiting resource" within the reproductive process. They will be choosy about whom they mate with and males will have to compete among themselves in order to gain access to the resource a female represents. They might do so by becoming larger (so as to fight other males more effectively) and by developing striking coloration and patterns of display (so as to attract females).

Although this analysis is satisfying, it would be nice to take it further and to find some empirical tests of its correctness, and it is here that the comparative method again proves useful. Compare the pattern of reproductive behaviour we have just considered with that shown by that curious fish, the seahorse. In these creatures it is the female who shows aggressive courtship whereas the male shows cautious discrimination in choosing a partner. We might expect to find, therefore, that in the seahorse the male makes a greater investment in reproduction than does the female and this turns out to be so. In fact, instead of inseminating the female, the male seahorse takes her eggs into his own brood pouch and there the fertilized eggs develop to an advanced stage, taking their nourishment from his bloodstream by a placental system not unlike that used by female mammals.

## The Special Nature of Evolutionary Explanations

We have now considered several examples of animals producing patterns of behaviour that are beautifully adapted to meet their requirements. The evolutionary explanation of how this adaptation has come about is, in principle, quite straightforward. It is that behaviour *must* fit the environment since it is in a sense created by the environment: genes which produce an animal that is not fitted to his environment will perish along with the maladapted animal. Natural selection is a process that necessarily works to fit an animal to its environment. But having said this, we ought to go on and point out some curious features of this evolutionary account. These can be summed up by saying that the account in terms of natural selection provides a rather special sort of explanation since it is one that can never be proved wrong.

This may seem at first sight to be a valuable property in any explanation but it is in fact an unusual feature in a scientific explanation; most scientific explanations have implicit in them information about observations that could potentially prove them wrong. For example, if it is suggested that the amount of exploratory activity that a given animal shows is determined by how hungry the animal is then this explanation implies that exploration would increase if the animal were deprived of food for a long time. The explanation would be disconfirmed if it were found that activity was reduced by increasing the severity of food deprivation.

Now it is difficult to think of any set of observations that could be used in the same sort of way to disconfirm the suggestion that behaviour is the product of natural selection. Certainly some patterns of behaviour give the initial impression that they might present problems for the evolutionary theory, but, as so often, first impressions are misleading. To reconsider three examples that we have discussed already: it looks at first sight as though Tinbergen's gulls which abandon their chicks in order to tidy up broken egg shells are showing a behaviour pattern that would not be selected for. But when we recall that debris scattered around the nest may serve to attract predators we can see that the advantages of removing this debris might well outweigh the disadvantages of leaving the chicks unguarded for a few seconds and that natural selection could well favour the former pattern of behaviour. The second example is supplied by the alarm call of song-birds. It has already been pointed out that this call, even though it puts a single individual in some danger, could still have evolved by natural selection if it fosters the survival of other, genetically related, individuals. And thirdly, there is the possibility that some patterns of behaviour which are not now particularly advantageous to their owner are survivals from the evolutionary past when they were in fact selected for.

## Optimality in Behaviour

The view that behaviour must on the whole be adaptive since it is the product of natural selection is not a novel one, and indeed it is one of the cornerstones of the modern science of *ecology* (the study of the relationships among animals and their relationship with the physical environment). The behavioural ecologist is likely to start from the assumption that an animal will tend to behave in such ways as maximize its inclusive fitness. From this starting point he will go on to produce formal theories (often expressed in mathematical terms) that describe how a given animal behaves in a given situation and he will try to use his theories to predict how the animal will behave if circumstances change.

Thus, *optimal foraging theory* concerns itself with the strategies that animals show in finding and consuming food. It starts with the assumption that the animal in question will acquire its food as efficiently as possible since such behaviour is conducive to survival and hence to reproductive success. An item of food can be characterized by the energy it supplies when eaten ($E$) and by what it costs the animal in terms of time and energy to catch and eat (usually expressed as $h$, *handling time*). An efficient predator should therefore behave so as to maximize the ratio $E/h$. This simple idea allows us to predict how a predator will behave when two types of prey are available. Suppose that type 1 is common and easy to find ($h_1$ is low) but is not very nutritious ($E_1$ is also low) whereas type 2 is nutritious but rather rare ($E_2$ and $h_2$ will be high). Provided that the ratio $E_1/h_1$ exceeds $E_2/h_2$ then we may predict that the predator will concentrate exclusively on the more common prey and this is usually what happens. We can also predict the consequences of prolonged predation. As prey of type 1 continue to be eaten so it will become increasingly difficult to find them, that is, $h_1$ will increase. Eventually the point will be reached where $E_1/h_1$ is smaller than $E_2/h_2$ and the efficient predator will switch to feeding exclusively on type 2.

A convenient byproduct of this sort of analysis is that it supplies one possible answer to an old question about the workings of natural selection. It is clear that there is usually considerable genetic variability among the animals that make up any given population (there must be if natural selection is to work). But if, as seems likely, one animal is better fitted to the environment than all others, why do not all come eventually to possess identical genotypes correlated with this best-adapted form? There are several mechanisms all of which might function to maintain genetic diversity, and the system of predation we have just considered is an example of one of them. Some birds are said to form *searching-images* when hunting prey, that is, they fix upon a particular colour of insect, say, and search for that to the exclusion of similar insects of a different colour. This presumably is an efficient way for the bird to reduce the handling time for prey of colour-type 1. The advantage for prey of type 2 is obvious and they would be selected for survival and reproduction. Predators usually form searching-images for the more common of the alternative forms of prey and thus the less common form would have the advantage, until, of course, predation of the alternative reduced *it* to being the less common form. Thus, the less frequent of the alternatives would always be favoured with the result that both forms would survive and the frequencies of the alternative genotypes would stabilize at some intermediate level.

Although simple optimality models have had a surprising number of successes they eventually break down. Behaviour is not determined solely by the values of $E$ and $h$ and in most cases there are a host of other factors to be taken into account: an animal's hunting behaviour might well be influenced by the need to avoid its own predators for instance; its choice of food-type is likely to vary as a need for some specific nutrient develops, and so on. As a consequence, the models have grown more complicated with new parameters being added to accommodate these and other factors. But the failure of a specific model is not taken as evidence against the basic assumption upon which all such models are founded. The failure of a specific model is evidence only for the inadequacy of that model; the assumption that animals tend to behave so as to maximize inclusive fitness is itself invulnerable to disproof from evidence of this sort.

## Maladaptive Behaviour

We have argued that the evolutionary explanation of behaviour in terms of natural selection is a special sort of explanation that is not open to many of the usual forms of proof by empirical observation. In a number of the examples described above we have found the theory of natural selection to run into difficulties but we have been able to preserve it by finding hidden advantages in behaviour that seems on first investigation to be maladaptive. But it is even possible for the theory to explain behaviour that is without doubt maladaptive. Consider as an example the last act that any of us performs: that of dying. This surely must be regarded as a maladaptive pattern of behaviour; one wonders why natural selection has not produced animals equipped with efficient self-repairing biochemical mechanisms which do not therefore become senile and which live forever. Senility and death could have evolved by natural selection, however, in the following manner. Supposed a genetic mutation occurred which gave an animal outstanding reproductive ability early in its life. It would therefore be able to produce many more offspring than its competitors, the chances of their surviving would be higher, and the mutation in question would rapidly spread throughout the gene pool. But suppose also that this same genetic mutation had lethal side-effects: suppose, for example, it caused the release of some poisonous substance into the blood. Such a gene would obviously be eliminated from the gene pool except in one set of circumstances. If it happened that the lethal effects of the gene became apparent only late in the life of the animal the gene might still be selected for. Provided that animals possessing the gene could out-reproduce other members of the species early in their lives, their subsequent death from the lethal side-effects would be of no importance (at least to natural selection). The population would soon come to consist solely of mortal but rapidly reproducing animals. I should add that this account of the origins of senescence is quite hypothetical. But it raises the interesting possibility that some and perhaps many patterns of behaviour are not adaptive at all but should be regarded as the maladaptive by-products of genes which produce their beneficial effects in other ways. Given that the theory of evolution by natural selection was specifically designed to account for the way in which organisms become well adapted to their environments it may be something of a surprise to find that the theory can supply insights of this kind which further our understanding of maladaptive behaviour.

## Conclusions

To sum up, biologists are now convinced (for the reasons outlined in the introduction to this chapter) that evolution by natural selection must have occurred. Examples of behaviour which look as though they could not possibly have been selected for do not shake their conviction. Instead, they are spurred on to investigate in detail the more subtle implications of the hypothesis of natural selection; to work out how it is that the genes responsible for seemingly maladaptive behaviour manage to remain in the gene pool. When we look at it from this point of view we realize that a very special sort of explanation is being offered when it is said that the adaptedness of behaviour is to be explained in terms of evolutionary processes. Perhaps it would be better to conclude that, although there is much to be said about detailed mechanisms, once the hypothesis of natural selection has been accepted there is nothing at the general level left to explain.

Nothing, that is, from the evolutionary point of view. But the evolutionary approach is only one of several ways of trying to answer the question: why does this behaviour occur? We may accept that one reason why a particular pattern of behaviour occurs is that natural selection has favoured the survival of the genes that tend to produce it. It remains to explain how the genes have their effect; to elucidate the way in which they interact with the environment to produce a living, behaving organism; to describe and account for the ways in which the organism interacts with its environment. These are the topics discussed in the chapters that follow.

## SOURCES AND FURTHER READING

*The Theory of Evolution* by Maynard Smith (1975) provides an excellent general introduction for the non-biologist. It deals with all aspects of evolution but is particularly good on the sort of evolutionary explanation described in the last section of this chapter. These topics are also discussed in a most readable way in *The Selfish Gene* by Dawkins (1976) and in *Adaptation and Natural Selection* by Williams (1966). According to Wilson these evolutionary explanations constitute a new and important branch of biology; for advocacy of this view see his

*Sociobiology* (1975). Comparative studies of intelligence in vertebrates are discussed in detail by Macphail (1982), *Brain and Intelligence in Vertebrates*. The other topics dealt with in this chapter are well covered in the comprehensive textbook by Brown (1975) called *The Evolution of Behaviour*. Masterton and his collaborators (1976a, b) have edited two volumes devoted to the evolution of brain and behaviour which contain much useful material as does the book *Behaviour and Evolution* (edited by Roe and Simpson, 1958), but be warned that some contributions to the latter book are now rather out of date.

# 3    Genetics and
# Psychology

## INTRODUCTION

In Chapter 2 we discussed the fact that the evolutionary history of a species will influence the behaviour shown by individuals alive today. It does this by means of the genes that it "gives" to each individual, and to pursue the issue further we must now turn our attention to the way in which, and the extent to which the genetic make-up of an organism can influence its psychological make-up.

Accordingly, the introductory section of this chapter gives, in outline, those aspects of the basic principles of the science of genetics that the psychologist needs to know. We then move on to a discussion of the relative importance of the contributions of genetic and environmental factors in determining behaviour. After considering a number of alternative positions, we will reach the conclusion that all behaviour is the product of an interaction between genetic and environmental determinants. The remaining sections of the chapter discuss four different ways in which psychologists have tried to deal with the implications of this conclusion.

### Family Resemblances

The basic observation with which we must begin is simply that offspring tend, on the whole, to be like their parents. Thus, white parents almost invariably produce white children; tall parents are quite likely to have tall children; clever parents may very well have clever children. Clearly the qualification "on the whole" deserves emphasis. We can all of us think of cases in which, for example, a pair of tall parents have produced children of no more than average height. Again, the basic rule that like tends to give rise to like does not tell us what will happen when the parents differ in the characteristic in which we are interested. In some cases—skin colour is one—the child may have a value midway between that of each parent. In other cases—sex is an obvious example—the child is always like one parent rather than the other.

To some extent, the resemblances that we can observe between parents and children may derive simply from the way in which parents treat their children. If tall parents were to feed their children well while short parents starved them, the result might be a resemblance in height between parents and children. We can be thankful that parents do not behave in this way but it is quite possible that something analogous may happen in the case of psychological traits such as intelligence. It has often been argued that clever parents produce clever children only, or at least chiefly, because they provide them with a good education. The extent to which psychological traits are determined by processes of this sort will be discussed in much more detail shortly. What we need to note for the time being is that the fact that a trait tends to run in families does not necessarily mean that it is "inherited" in any simple fashion. In order to demonstrate the operation of genetic influences it is usually necessary to do experimental studies; to remove the offspring from parental influence and to concentrate upon the resemblances between parent and child that still appear. Indeed, not only should we remove the children from their parents but we should rear them in environments that are, in general, as near identical as possible. Only in these circumstances can we be sure that the likeness of each child to its own parents is not a result of the conditions in which it has been raised.

## Mendelian Genetics

Experiments of this sort, which are of course done with plants or with experimental animals, have revealed that for some characteristics the likeness between parent and offspring can be explained by making the following assumptions. (These assumptions were first formulated to explain the results of plant breeding experiments carried out in the nineteenth century by Mendel— hence the heading of this paragraph.) The offspring is assumed to receive from each parent a single factor or *gene* (one from the egg and one from the sperm in animals) which influences the characteristic in question. For some plants there is a gene (which we may symbolize as $T$) which tends to produce a tall plant while a related but different form of this gene ($S$) produces a small plant. (Alternative forms of a gene are called *alleles*.) If a plant is the product of a cross between two tall parents it may receive a $T$ allele from each and thus, with the gene complement $TT$, will itself grow into a tall plant. If, however, it receives an $S$ allele from each parent it will grow into a small plant. It is possible, of course, to receive a $T$ allele from one parent and an $S$ allele from the other. Offspring with the $TS$ gene complement may nonetheless grow into tall plants since the $T$ allele may *dominate* the $S$ allele. Genetic mixtures of this sort supply one of the reasons why like does not always give rise to like. A cross between two tall parents both of which have the genetic constitution $TS$ may well give rise to small offspring since some of these will be likely to receive the $S$ gene from each parent and thus end up with $SS$. It should be added that the genetic basis of size in most creatures (including height in man) is much more complex than this. Many different genes are involved (height is said to be *polygenically* inherited). There is no reason to assume, however, that the basic principles are different from those just described. (But is should be stated that such complexities can add very considerably to the problem of establishing experimentally the mode of inheritance of a character.)

## The Physical Basis of Heredity

The physical nature of genes is now known in some detail. Every cell in the body of the more complex animals and plants contains several pairs of *chromosomes* which are made, in part, of the substance *deoxyribonucleic acid* (DNA). A gene (of the sort we have symbolized by $T$, above) consists of a small section (*locus*) of one of these chromosomes and, hence, a small amount of DNA. For an organism with the genetic complement $TT$, the equivalent section of the other member of the pair of chromosomes will consist of an identical form of DNA. For an organism with the genetic make-up $TS$, the equivalent part of the second chromosome will contain DNA which is slightly different in its composition. An exception to the rule that every cell contains pairs of chromosomes is found, of course, in the *germ* cells: the eggs and sperm. These are formed by a special process which ensures that each contains only a single set of chromosomes and thus just one example of each gene. The union of egg and sperm can therefore produce a fertilized egg (a *zygote*) that has the full set of chromosomes. When the zygote begins to develop by dividing to produce new cells the chromosomes replicate themselves to ensure that each new cell has a full set identical to those found in the zygote itself (see Fig. 3.1).

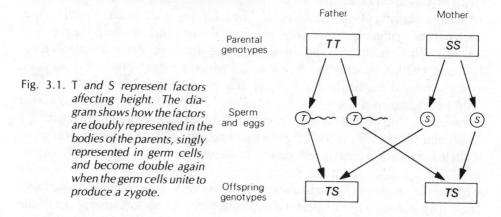

Fig. 3.1. T *and* S *represent factors affecting height. The diagram shows how the factors are doubly represented in the bodies of the parents, singly represented in germ cells, and become double again when the germ cells unite to produce a zygote.*

## The Mechanism of Gene Action

Mendel's genetic laws were derived solely from breeding experiments that allowed him to deduce that certain factors or elements (now known as genes) must be present in the germ cells, given the patterns of family resemblance that he observed. He was not able to specify the mechanism by which a given factor had its effect. But since the identification of DNA as the genetic material in the early 1950s, molecular biologists have made remarkable progress in their investigation of the mechanism of gene action. The central notion of molecular genetics is that genes can be identified with relatively short segments of the long DNA molecules of the cell. Each of these segments consists of several hundred sub-units linearly arranged, and each of the sub-units (or codons) is said to "code for" a particular *amino acid*. That is, the segment of DNA can, by a series of intermediate steps, arrange for a chain of amino acids to be built up, the nature of these and their sequence being determined by nature and sequence of the codons that constitute the DNA segment in question. A long string of amino acids makes a *protein*, a fact of significance when it is appreciated that many proteins are *enzymes*—biochemical catalysts that promote biochemical reactions that would not otherwise occur in the conditions found inside cells. The development and functioning of a cell, and thus of the organ that comprises these cells and of the body made up of organs, is determined by biochemical reactions controlled by enzymes. There is thus no mystery about the notion that genes can influence behaviour—what an organism does depends upon the development and functioning of certain structures which are in turn controlled, in part, by genetically determined mechanisms.

Take as an example the mental retardation produced by the disorder *phenylketonuria* (PKU) since this is one of the best-understood cases in which a single gene exerts a dramatic influence on behaviour. In its classic form, children suffering from PKU show severe mental retardation with IQs around 30. They differ from other mentally retarded children in that their urine contains a high level of phenylpyruvic acid. The link between these two observations is provided by a genetic defect that prevents them from synthesizing the enzyme phenylalanine hydroxylase, the enzyme that converts one amino acid (phenylalanine) to another (tyrosine). The resulting high level of phenylalanine in the blood has two consequences: it is excreted as phenylpyruvic acid but also, apparently, it interferes with the metabolism of other amino acids, depriving the developing brain of the nutrients it needs. In the cases we shall discuss below the pathway from genetic material to behaviour will be much more complex than this (indeed, in most the details are simply not known), but the principle whereby the nature of a segment of DNA can influence the biochemical make-up of cells and hence the behaviour of the whole organism is well illustrated by PKU.

Genotype and Phenotype
A final point of terminology before turning to issues of direct psychological interest, concerns the distinction between *genotype* and *phenotype*. The word genotype is used to describe the total genetic make-up of any individual; the full set of genes present in each of the cells of his body. His actual bodily make-up,

all that he is and does, is referred to as his phenotype; thus blue eyes, tall stature, IQ, and so on, are phenotypic characteristics. We can all agree that the genotype may be very important in determining a number of anatomical characteristics; eye colour and skin colour are good examples. PKU supplies an instance of how a genetic defect can influence mental development. There has been much more dispute, however, about the role of the genotype in determining behavioural phenotypic characteristics and psychological traits in normal individuals. It is this dispute that we shall consider next.

## THE RELATIVE CONTRIBUTIONS OF GENOTYPE AND ENVIRONMENT

### Two Extreme Views and a Compromise

Some authorities state or seem to imply that the genotype plays a relatively trivial role in determining psychological characteristics. Eysenck (1971) cites an official pronouncement by UNESCO on human racial differences which asserts that "the peoples of the world today appear to possess equal biological potentialities for attaining any civilizational level". Psychologists too, have held this view. It is difficult to find an example better than that expressed in the following, often quoted, statement by J. B. Watson. He wrote:

> Give me a dozen healthy infants, well-formed, and my own specified world to bring them up in and I'll guarantee to take any one at random and train him to become any type of specialist I might select—doctor, lawyer, artist, merchant-chief, and yes, even beggarman and thief, regardless of his talents, penchants, tendencies, abilities, vocations, and race of his ancestors.
>
> (Watson, 1924, p. 104)

The literary style is a good deal better but the central idea is exactly that expressed in the UNESCO statement.

In contrast, some authorities state or seem to imply that the genotype plays a critical role in determining psychological characteristics. Again, we can begin by quoting a quasi-political agency, this time the Supreme Court of the United States which gave a ruling in 1912 that "modern scientific investigation shows that idiocy, insanity, imbecility, and criminality are congenital and hereditary . . ." Scientists who have held views of this sort include Galton who began his book *Hereditary Genius* (1869) with the following statement:

> I propose to show in this book that a man's natural abilities are derived by inheritance, under exactly the same limitations as are the form and physical features of the whole organic world. Consequently, as it is easy . . . to obtain by careful selection a permanent breed of dogs or horses gifted with peculiar powers of running, or of doing anything else, so it would be quite practicable to produce a highly-gifted race of men . . . .
>
> (Galton, 1869, p. 1)

More recently, Eysenck (1971) has put forward ideas closely similar to those of the Supreme Court in suggesting that "mental illness, criminality and personality generally have strong roots in genetic constitution".

In discussing these matters we are moving onto politically dangerous ground. Those who accept either of the two extreme views outlined above are likely to find themselves subjected to abuse by their political opponents. Skinner, whose views are quite close to those of Watson, sadly relates in an autobiographical sketch (Skinner, 1967) his being called a "fascist" because of his belief that man's behaviour can be controlled by appropriate manipulation of the environment. A leaflet I received at the time of a public lecture by Eysenck which referred to "H. J. Eysenck—Hitler's 'race science' in a new guise" is enough to make it clear that a charge of "fascism" is equally likely to be brought against those who hold the second viewpoint. The only way to avoid abuse seems to be to take up a position midway between the two extremes, and perhaps for this reason, if no other, the third view I will describe had been widely adopted. It takes more than one form, but the central suggestion is that behavioural characteristics can be arranged on a continuum running from those (such as simple reflexes) that are critically determined by inherited factors to others (complex psychological traits such as intelligence) that are extremely susceptible to environmental influence. It may be allowed that all behaviour has some basis in the genotype, but it is implied that, as we move along the continuum away from the reflex, the environment adds more and more to the genetic "given".

Different as these three viewpoints are, I want to argue that all three are unsatisfactory and for essentially the same reason in each case. Although they differ in where they want to draw the line (perhaps in the case of the compromise position the division is too fuzzy to be called a "line"), all three views are willing to make a distinction between two sorts of behaviour, according to their origins. All three viewpoints accept that some aspects of behaviour can be said to be inherited, inborn, innate, unlearned, to be biologically determined, or to result from the evolutionary history of the species. These aspects of behaviour are contrasted with others that are said to be learned or acquired, or to be culturally or environmentally determined. I will argue that no such distinction can validly be made.

Difficulties in Distinguishing "Inherited" from "Acquired"
The difficulty of distinguishing two classes of behaviour, inherited and acquired, can best be seen when we try to answer the following basic question: by what criteria can we distinguish the two classes of behaviour?

*Species-specific behaviour.* On what basis do we assert that a given pattern of behaviour (or a given psychological trait) is inherited? One criterion that is commonly used asks whether or not the behaviour is species-specific, meaning by this that the characteristic is found in all members of the species under consideration. Thus, all members of the human species show the response of blinking the eye when some foreign body gets into it; all respond by jerking the leg to a tap on the tendon below the knee: in fact, all show a wide range of simple reflexes. In contrast, only some members of the species speak English or play the piano: each individual has his own accomplishments that he shares with no other individual. The argument that identifies species-specific behaviour with inherited behaviour is that since all members of the species show the behaviour it cannot therefore be a product of the idiosyncratic experience or training that different individuals undergo. It must therefore be a product of something that all members of the species have in common, that is, of the genetic make-up that all of them share.

Although superficially attractive, this argument soon disintegrates on closer inspection. Consider the fact that all members of the human species wear clothes. Thus the wearing of clothes is a species-specific behaviour, but do we want to conclude that it is genetically inherited? We do not, because wearing clothes is clearly something that we learn to do, something that parents teach their children. What this example tries to show is that not only differences between but also similarities among individuals can be produced by the environment in which they are brought up. A group of people, indeed the whole human species, may all show the same behaviour pattern simply because all have received the same sort of training. Given this fact it becomes clear that we must not make the automatic assumption that species-specific patterns are genetically based. Indeed, it is not difficult to argue that differences between individuals are as likely to be genetically based as to result from differences in training or experience. A simple example (taken from structure rather than from behaviour) is supplied by the fact that people differ in the colour of their eyes. Having brown eyes is not a species-specific characteristic (many people have blue or grey), but do we want to conclude from this that eye colour is not inherited?

*Behaviour that depends upon experience.* The criterion of species-specificity has been tried because of the assumption that species-specific behaviour could not be a product of special training given to or experience undergone by a particular individual. It turns out that this assumption is unjustified and thus that the criterion does not distinguish accurately between the two classes of behaviour we are considering. Perhaps a more direct approach might be effective. Might it not be possible to determine what behaviour *is* the product of individual training and experience? This behaviour we could then regard as being learned or acquired and the remainder of the animal's activities would be defined, by exclusion, as inherited. For example, complex behaviour like reading, writing, car-driving, or playing the piano, is clearly learned after a good deal of laborious practice. In contrast, simple reflexes like the knee-jerk and so on do not seem to be acquired in this way and perhaps should be regarded as being inherited.

The distinction being made here may seem a straightforward one but again difficulties begin to arise when we consider its implications in more detail. The first problem we come across is that in many cases we simply do not have enough information about the extent to which a particular pattern of behaviour is the result of training to enable us to categorize it at all. A more fundamental problem is that in cases where we have plentiful information we may still find it difficult to put the behaviour into its appropriate category.

Consider the way in which children come to speak their native language. To some extent, parents teach their children to talk, encourage the first attempts of the baby, correcting mistakes in the older child, and so on. Even in the rare cases where no specific training is given, adults at least provide a model that the child can imitate and learn from. But to conclude from these facts simply that language is a learned pattern of behaviour is to ignore a large body of evidence which seems to show that many aspects of the development of speech are not influenced by the child's experience. For instance, talking by the human child has its origins in the vocalizations that the child produces in infancy: the "cooing" of the three-month-old baby, the "babbling" of the six-month-old, and so on (see Table 4.1). What is of interest here is that all children produce these sounds, that they always produce them in the same sequence, and that they do so at more or less the same age. They do not have to be taught to do so; indeed we do not know of environmental changes which can promote the development of these vocalizations. Children born to deaf parents are exposed to rather different speech sounds from those heard by children whose parents hear and speak normally; further, the deaf parents are likely to make little response to the noises their children make. Nonetheless, these children go through just the same sequence of vocalization as any other child (Lenneberg, 1967). The details of speech may be learned but the basis from which it develops seems to emerge independently of experience.

I have deliberately written that the behaviour *seems* to emerge independently of experience because we cannot assert with very much confidence that it does so. We are trying to divide up behaviour into two categories: that which depends upon experience and that which does not. We may come across examples of behaviour that seem to belong in the second category but there is always room for doubt: is the behaviour really independent of experience or is it just that we have not studied it carefully enough and have therefore failed to detect the ways in which it is influenced by the environment? A concrete example which illustrates this problem comes from a study of the visual ability of cats (by Muir and Mitchell, 1973, who used a technique developed by Blakemore and Cooper, 1970). We can show that cats can discriminate a pattern of horizontal black and white stripes by training them so that they receive food after pressing a panel bearing such a pattern but not after pressing a plain grey panel. The ability to perceive a pattern of horizontal stripes may seem to be one that is developed independently of experience but experimental work has shown that this is not so. Kittens are usually raised in a world filled with varied visual patterns and are therefore exposed to objects with edges which run horizontally. This exposure turns out to be crucial. When kittens are raised in an environment in which visual experience is restricted to the inside of a cage painted with vertical stripes only (Fig. 3.2) they show no apparent ill-effects except that their ability to discriminate horizontal stripes when tested as young adults is impaired. In contrast, kittens whose experience is restricted just to horizontal stripes discriminate perfectly well. The specific conclusion to be derived from these studies is that the perceptual abilities of the adult can depend upon early visual experience (see Chapter 4). A more general

Fig. 3.2. *An apparatus for rearing a kitten in an environment of vertical stripes (after Blakemore and Cooper, 1970). The kitten stands on a glass floor positioned halfway up a long tube. The collar prevents the animal from seeing its own body. The animal spends one hour a day in the illuminated apparatus during the first few months of life, but is otherwise kept in the dark.*

conclusion, and a more important one for our present purposes, is that the influence of experience upon behaviour may be subtle and difficult to detect except by special experimental techniques. Rather than saying that a given behaviour pattern is not influenced by experience it seems much more sensible to say that the ways in which the behaviour is influenced by experience have not yet been determined.

## Interaction between Genotype and Environment

Why is it proving so difficult to find an adequate criterion that distinguishes between the two classes of behaviour, inherited and acquired? Other criteria have been suggested apart from those we have just discussed (see, for example, Lorenz, 1965) but it seems to me that all of them run into similar difficulties and it would be tedious to discuss them in detail. Particularly so in view of the fact that these difficulties arise because of a fundamental mistake we are making.

According to geneticists, it is quite inappropriate to divide phenotypic characteristics into the categories of inherited versus acquired. The point is forcefully made by one of them (Thoday, 1965) as follows:

> Every character of an individual is acquired during the development of that individual. Likewise, every character is genetic, for to acquire a character during development in any particular environment the individual must have the necessary genetic endowment . . . .

(Thoday, 1965, p. 94)

If all behaviour is both inherited and acquired then any search for a criterion that distinguishes the two types must be a wild-goose chase.

The point that Thoday is making is that all behaviour, indeed all phenotypic characteristics, arise from an *interaction* between the genotype and the environment in which the genes exist. A fertilized egg can grow into a living, behaving organism only when it is allowed to develop in a rather special environment which supplies food, oxygen, an equable temperature, and much more. The environment, of course, can do nothing without the fertilized egg to work on. Since everything the animal is and does depends upon the interaction of genetic and environmental factors we are forced to conclude that all behaviour is both inherited and acquired.

*An illustrative analogy.* The notion of genotype–environment interaction is best illustrated by a simple geometrical analogy first put forward by Hebb (1953) and depicted in Fig. 3.3. He points out that for any given rectangle its area is in a very direct sense dependent upon the interaction of two factors: the area is given by the product of its length and breadth. The area of the rectangle depends on the value of each of these parameters (changing either the length or the breadth will produce a change in area) and both must have values for the rectangle to have any area at all. It makes no sense to ask whether the area of the rectangle is determined by its length or by its breadth, for the area depends upon the values of both parameters. Now any pattern of behaviour (any phenotypic characteristic) is taken to be analogous to the area of a rectangle, and the genetic and environmental factors producing the behaviour are equated with the length and breadth of the rectangle. The genetic and environmental factors interact to produce the behaviour which can no more be said to be determined by just one set of factors than the area of the rectangle can be said to depend upon just the length or upon just the breadth. Those who try to draw a sharp line between behaviour that is inherited and behaviour that is acquired are thus bound to run into problems. Nor can one set of factors be said to be more important than the other; both are critical in determining what the result of the interaction will be. And thus it is just as pointless to try to establish a continuum running from completely inherited to completely acquired, based as it must be on the assumption that the relative importance of genetic and environmental factors can vary from one behaviour to another.

Once the relationship between genotype and environment is seen as an interaction of this sort it becomes apparent why the attempt to distinguish between inherited and acquired behaviour has proved so unsuccessful. Perhaps the conceptual confusions that are so common in this area stem in part from a basic confusion between the legal and the genetic use of the word "inherited". A child may inherit his father's car and he may also inherit blue eyes from his father. We use the same word in the two cases but we mean rather different things. In the legal sense, a physical object (the car) is passed on directly from father to son; in the other case all we see is a resemblance in colour between two, quite separate pairs of eyes. All that is physically passed on from father to son in the case of biological inheritance is a set of genes. These genes may direct the development of a new individual with eyes like his father's but they can only do so by interaction with an appropriate environment.

*Genetically produced differences in behaviour.* We have established that any item of behaviour shown by an individual is both inherited and acquired; that it is not possible to say that a particular pattern of behaviour is the result solely or mainly of genetic rather than environmental factors or *vice versa*. What then is meant by those who refer to the "genetic basis" of schizophrenia or who argue that intelligence is largely "inherited"? One worrying possibility is that those who use phrases of this sort have not really thought out properly what they do mean by them; that they have not fully appreciated the implications of the fact that behaviour is the result of an interaction between genotype and environment. In some cases, however, these phrases are used as a shorthand way of referring to the possibility that certain *differences* between individuals may be the result of genetic differences between them. This is quite a legitimate usage, for although we may not be able to ascribe a pattern of behaviour to solely genetic causes (it is the product of an interaction) it is sometimes possible to determine that people differ in a given behaviour pattern for genetic reasons (see Fig. 3.3.).

An example may be helpful here: I speak English because of my (human) genotype which developed in interaction with an environment which supplied English-speaking parents. My ability to speak English is both genetic and acquired. It is a plausible guess, however, that the linguistic differences between me and my contemporaries born and raised on the other side of the English Channel are due not to genetic differences between us (which will certainly exist) but to the differing environments in which we grew up. The difference in our native languages (speaking English rather than French) is environmentally produced. On the other hand, it seems very likely that the difference between me and my cat in the patterns of vocalization that we utter is due not to the different environments that we have experienced but to the fact that we have different genotypes. Differences of this second sort form the basic subject matter for those who study the relationship between genetics and psychology.

The example I have just cited is an extreme one, involving, as it does, a cross-species comparison. But it is a fact that all people (except identical twins, whose special features we shall consider shortly) have distinct and different genotypes—think, for instance, of the fact that everyone has his own characteristic fingerprint pattern even leaving aside environmentally caused scars and scratches and such-like. Or again, the near infinite variety of faces we see around us gives us some indication of the near infinite range of human genotypes that can exist. These genetic differences are in principle just as likely to influence psychologically important traits as they are structural phenotypic

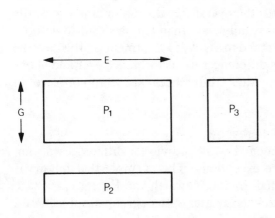

Fig. 3.3. *The areas of the three rectangles represent three different phenotypes ($P_1$, $P_2$, and $P_3$). The vertical dimension represents the genotype (G), the horizontal the environmental (E) contribution. Both G and E must have values to produce P. $P_1$ and $P_2$ differ genetically and also phenotypically although E is the same for both. $P_1$ and $P_3$ are genetically identical but differ phenotypically for environmental reasons. $P_2$ and $P_3$ differ phenotypically because of differences in both G and E.*

characteristics and the question we must consider therefore becomes: how are we, as psychologists, going to deal with the existence of genetically caused differences between individuals in their psychology and their behaviour?

We can discern among psychologists four different approaches. Some psychologists simply ignore the possibility of genetically determined individual differences; others worry about them; others set about measuring them; and yet others have tried to use the existence of these differences to further psychological knowledge. We shall deal with each of these approaches in turn.

## BY-PASSING GENETIC AND OTHER INDIVIDUAL DIFFERENCES

Most psychologists simply ignore genetic differences; many ignore all individual differences whether genetically produced or otherwise. The experimenter studying human memory is likely to begin his research report by telling us that "the subjects were 24 male undergraduates". He may add that all his subjects were roughly the same age and perhaps that they all had roughly the same level of measured intelligence but he is unlikely to tell us much more. The undergraduates are certain to vary quite widely in their nervousness, their willingness to learn, their ability to concentrate, and so on, but these differences will be ignored. Similarly, the animal psychologist working on maze-learning, say, will tell us no more than that his subjects were 24 male albino rats, 3 months old at the beginning of the experiment. And rats too can show marked individual differences particularly in their readiness to learn a given task and in the level of nervousness that they show.

In many cases this neglect of individual differences gives no cause for concern. Suppose the experimenter is investigating the effects of a certain drug on maze-learning in the rat. He will assign his 24 animals at random to two groups, one group of 12 learning the maze after injection of the drug and one group learning without the drug. The individuals within each group will differ from one another (partly for genetic reasons) but these differences should not contribute in any systematic way to the overall result: that animals with the drug tend to learn, on average, less readily, say, than animals trained without the drug. Statistical procedures designed to assess if a treatment (in this case the administration of a drug) produces differences in performance over and above these produced by inherent individual differences are commonplace in psychology.

### The Risks of Ignoring Individual Differences

Having said that in much experimental work individual differences do not matter, we must now consider the exceptions. The example that follows is imaginary but there are experimental results (Howarth and Eysenck, 1968) to suggest that it is quite plausible. An experimenter trains a group of subjects on a simple (*paired-associate*) learning task in which they must form an association between pairs of words so that when they are presented with a stimulus word from one list they can reply with the appropriate response word. After they have learned the task the subjects are divided into two groups. One group is made to recall as many of the words as possible; the second group is sent away but returns on the following day so that recall is assessed after 24 hours. It is found that the two groups achieve much the same level of performance on the recall task and it is concluded that the time interval between training and testing is of no importance. Now although such a conclusion can be fairly derived from the average results, it is possible that these may obscure effects of real psychological interest that are revealed only when individual differences are taken into account. One dimension along which people differ is said to be that of *extraversion–introversion* and questionnaires have been devised (comprising questions like "Can you easily get some life into a rather dull party?") which try to locate the position of an individual along the dimension. When a study of the effects of the training-test interval is carried out on subjects all of whom are extraverts it is found that the length of this interval makes a marked difference: extraverts perform much better when the test is given immediately. In contrast, introverts are found to do better when the test is delayed for 24 hours (Fig. 3.4). Averaging the results of a mixed group of subjects which contains both extraverts and introverts may lead us to believe that the training-test interval is unimportant when in fact it has important effects which are different for different people.

Ignoring individual differences may not only obscure important psychological phenomena, it may lead us to entirely false conclusions. Suppose that the

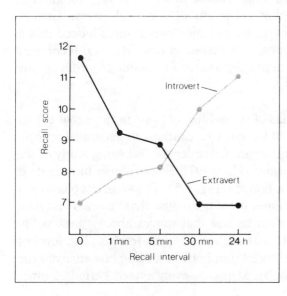

Fig. 3.4. *Number of syllables recalled (out of a maximum of 14) by extraverts and introverts tested at various times after initial learning (after Howarth and Eysenck, 1968).*

study I have just described had been carried out initially with a group of subjects that consisted only of introverts (perhaps because the experimenter found it convenient to recruit his subjects from those university students to be found in the library on a Saturday night). He might then try to apply more generally his discovery that recall is better after a day's rest and end up with nothing but confusion. The moral is that it can often be dangerous to generalize a set of findings to some population of subjects different from that used in the initial investigation. What is true of students is not necessarily true of housewives; what is true for rats need not be true for men.

## Inbred Strains

The extent to which genetic differences are responsible for the difference in personality between extraverts and introverts is still a matter for some debate. The study of animal behaviour in the laboratory, however, has yielded many examples of findings which are true for one group of subjects but which do not hold for a second group that differs only genetically from the first. Much of this work has been done with *inbred strains*. Many laboratories maintain colonies of rats or of mice in which successive generations are produced by the mating of closely related individuals (usually brother to sister matings). Thus the brown mouse (the agouti) is mated only with another brown mouse, the white (the albino) is mated only with another white animal, and the two independent strains may be maintained over many years. One result of this repeated incestuous mating is that within each strain there is a marked reduction in genetic differences between individuals; it has been computed that after 20 generations of such inbreeding all individuals will have the same alleles at 98% of chromosomal loci. Each inbred strain can be thought of, very roughly, as constituting a large and persisting collection of identical twins. Genetic differences *between* strains, however, are of major importance; indeed this is necessary so far, since all the animals are reared in near identical laboratory conditions, there is little opportunity for the environment to produce any differences.

*Open-field behaviour.* Inbred strains of mice differ not just in their coat colour but in their behaviour as well, and we must be cautious in generalizing from observations derived from just one strain. Consider the following study of the factors controlling fearfulness in mice (Hall, 1971). Fearfulness in rodents is often assessed by means of the *open-field test* (Fig. 3.5). The animal is placed in a large empty box and its activity is monitored: the mouse that "freezes" is taken to be suffering from acute fear whereas one that moves about, presumably exploring the novel environment, is thought to be less fearful. The level of activity shown by a mouse can be scored simply by recording how many of the sectors marked on the floor of the arena it crosses in a fixed period of time.

Figure 3.6 shows the average performance of 20 agouti mice of the inbred strain known as CBA, tested in an open field having a white floor. The animals tend to move about very little. Also shown are the results for a further set of 20 CBA mice tested in an open field with a black floor and it is apparent that in these conditions the animals move about much more freely.

At this stage one may be tempted to conclude that fearfulness in the mouse is determined by the intensity of the visual stimulation to which it is subjected, but the temptation should be resisted: Fig. 3.6 shows the results of a further experiment carried out with white mice of the RAP inbred strain. These animals move about readily both when the floor of the arena is black and when it is white.

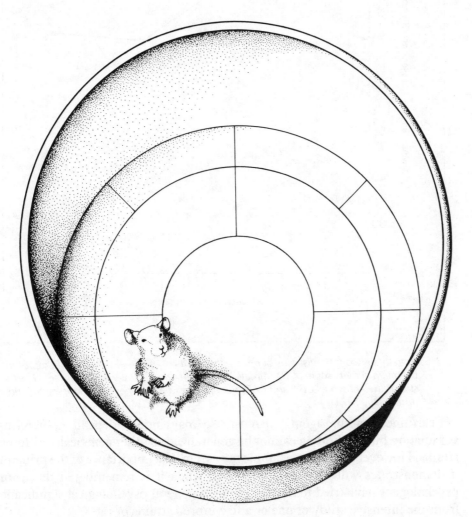

Fig. 3.5. *Rodent in an open field. The lines marked on the floor allow activity to be measured in terms of the number of lines crossed in a given time.*

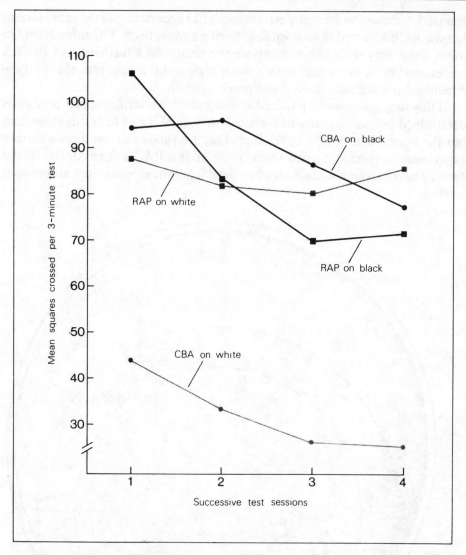

Fig. 3.6. *Activity of two inbred strains of mice in two sorts of open field. Each point represents the mean activity score of 20 animals (tested individually) over three minutes. The two strains are known as CBA and RAP; the open field had either a black or a white floor (from Hall, 1971).*

Fearfulness in the agouti CBA mouse may indeed depend upon visual stimulation but the finding cannot be generalized to other genetically different strains. However trivial this example may seem, the importance of the principle it demonstrates will soon be appreciated when it is remembered that some psychologists have tried to derive results of general psychological significance from the intensive study of one or a few inbred strains of rats.

## Implications

We have said that most experimental psychologists simply ignore genetic and other individual differences in their work on perception, memory, learning, and so on. The examples we have just considered, however, make us realize that it may not be entirely safe for them to do so. What should they do? Certainly they should continue their work: it is still worth knowing that in some rats a drug will retard maze-learning or that in some people massed training leads to better performance than does spaced training. But they must exercise extreme caution in generalizing their findings to subjects drawn from some different population. It will no doubt turn out that many experimental findings will hold good for other groups of people or for other strains of rat. But the experimenter must not assume this automatically: from time to time he must carry out his work with new and different subjects to verify that his conclusions have the generality that he hopes for.

Finally, in this section, something should be said about the problems that can arise when genetic differences are confounded with other factors that can influence behaviour. In experimental studies problems may arise when one tries to generalize from a set of results but, because subjects tend to be assigned at random to the various experimental groups, one need not worry that the outcome of the experiment derives from systematic genetic differences between the groups. With many observational studies one cannot be so sure. Suppose a psychologist wants to investigate the effects of early malnutrition on intelligence and that he does so in the following way. He tests the intelligence of a large number of children of a given age and at the same time he weighs them and measures them to determine which children have the normal weight for their height and which children are underweight. He finds that children in the latter group tend on average to score less well on the intelligence tests than those in the first group. He will be tempted to conclude that malnutrition retards the development of intelligence, but if he is a careful worker he will feel the need to check on a number of other possibilities. In particular, it may be that the difference in nutrition does not cause the difference in intelligence but that both are produced by the operation of some third factor. One very obvious possibility is that the differences between the two groups may be directly related to the social class of their parents: the well-to-do parents will be able both to feed their children well and to educate them well; poor parents may be able to do neither. The researcher will thus need to show that the association between malnutrition and low intelligence is maintained even when the children under consideration are drawn from the same social class and have the same educational background.

Most researchers doing studies of this sort are aware of the need to control for factors like social class but often they are less alert to the possible role played by genetic differences. We have assumed so far in the example we are considering that differences between children in their build reflect differences in the nutrition they have received. But suppose that all the children had been fed identically. There would still be differences in their build since some genotypes are more efficient at converting food into body tissue than others. Now if we make the assumption that genotypes which produce big children also tend to produce clever children, the observed correlation between body build and intelligence would be explained. I should add that the assumption that genes may influence more than one phenotypic characteristic is not a particularly rash one; there is plenty of evidence, some of which we shall discuss in the next section, that they may have this property.

Early malnutrition may well retard the development of intelligence but evidence of this sort cannot demonstrate the fact unequivocally. In observational studies it is often necessary to select the subjects for study on the basis of some characteristic that we *think* to reflect the environmental variable (in this case malnutrition) that we are interested in. But it is often possible that the subjects differ in this characteristic because of genetic rather than environmental factors. There is not much that the researcher who relies on observational data can do about this. He cannot, for instance, directly measure the genotypes of his various groups of subjects to show that the groups do not differ genetically in any systematic way. All he can do is exercise caution in drawing his conclusions, accepting in some cases that an alternative, genetically based explanation may be available for his results.

## THE GENETICS OF BEHAVIOUR

If some psychologists tend largely to ignore genetic differences among their subjects, others worry about them, explicitly studying the genetics of behaviour. That is, they treat some aspect of behaviour as just one more phenotypic characteristic and carry out standard genetic analysis upon it. Just as the orthodox geneticist might undertake to study the inheritance of coat colour in the mouse or of eye colour in man, so the behaviour geneticist might try to work on the inheritance of fearfulness as measured by the open field test in mice, or upon the inheritance of psychological disorder in men.

### Studies of Human Pedigrees
The human species is not ideal for investigating the genetics of behaviour: the interval between generations is long; the experimenter cannot intervene and arrange for certain kinds of matings to occur; the environment in which the population lives is not under the experimenter's control. These disadvantages are severe but not insuperable. Thus it is possible to select families for study that have been reared in fairly similar environments; often, written records have been kept for many years so that a pedigree can be constructed that

includes examples of all the sorts of mating that the geneticist might want to arrange.

Analysis of pedigrees has revealed a number of cases of phenotypic characteristics of psychological interest that show the patterns of inheritance that are to be expected on the basis of Mendel's laws. *Huntington's chorea* supplies an example. This is a rare movement disorder that appears in those affected between the ages of 30 and 50 and is characterized by the ceaseless occurrence of quick, involuntary jerking movements especially of the fingers, arms, or face. It runs in families. When an individual is found with the disorder it is always the case that at least one of his parents suffered from it too. If he marries a normal spouse the likelihood is quite high that his children will suffer from the disorder. For some marriages all the children develop chorea; for other marriages one out of every two children (on average) escapes. The outlook is even worse should he marry another individual who turns out to develop chorea (and since the disorder usually becomes manifest after the age of child-bearing such marriages do sometimes occur). Here the chances of the children developing chorea are very high: only the occasional child of such a marriage is unaffected.

Figure 3.7 shows that this pattern of inheritance is what would be expected if Huntington's chorea were produced by a single dominant gene. In the figure, $H$ represents the allele that produces the disorder and $h$ the "normal" allele. Recall (p. 59) that organisms possess two examples of a given gene (one from each parent) and that dominance occurs when just a single allele is sufficient to produce the phenotype in question. Thus individuals with the genetic constitution $Hh$ are just as likely to suffer from chorea as those having $HH$. The figure shows all possible genetic outcomes of matings between people affected by the disorder (whether they have just one $H$ allele or two) and normal individuals. Shaded rectangles indicate children who will suffer from chorea and simply by counting the affected and unaffected offspring produced by the various crosses we can see that their distribution as predicted by this analysis is much like that actually observed.

## Differences between Inbred Strains

The study of human populations has clear practical importance—it allows, for instance, of the possibility of "genetic counselling", of informing prospective parents of the extent to which psychological and other defects are likely to be passed on to their children. But the bulk of the research done on the genetics of behaviour has been carried out in laboratories, with experimental animals as the subjects. Research of this sort has one great advantage. In this, as in all experimental work in genetics, it is customary to restrict environmentally produced differences to a minimum. Since the subjects are experimental animals born in the laboratory, they can be reared under controlled conditions.

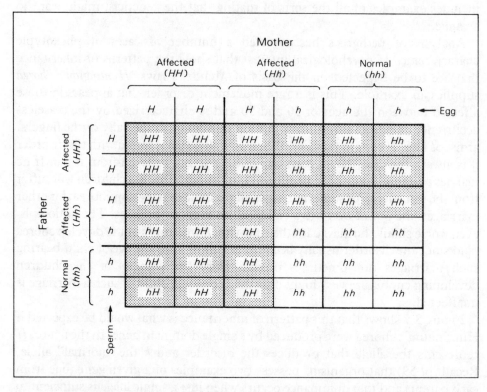

Fig. 3.7. *Huntington's chorea as the product of a single dominant gene. The unaffected parent possesses the constitution symbolized* hh; *an affected parent* Hh *or* HH. *The germ cells produced by these parents are shown along the top and side of the large rectangle. Small rectangles represent the combination of egg and sperm in a child. Shaded small rectangles represent affected offspring.*

Not only can temperature, humidity, diet, lighting, and so on, be controlled by the experimenter, he can also go out of his way to ensure that all his subjects experience the same set of conditions. He is therefore in the happy position of knowing for certain that any difference that he observes among his subjects *must* be genetically produced. This will be just as true for behavioural differences as it is for differences in coat colour, eye colour, or whatever.

The various inbred strains of rodent mentioned in the preceding section were established for the most part without regard to behavioural differences. As a first step, therefore, it is of some interest to demonstrate that there are indeed quite marked and consistent differences in behaviour between strains. Inbred strains of rats and mice have been shown to differ in their fearfulness, their exploratory tendencies, their resistance to stress, the way in which they treat their offspring, their ability to learn mazes, and in many other ways. And all these differences are genetically produced; given that the various strains are treated all in the same way, this must be so.★

Having taken this first step, where do we go from here? It is tempting to draw the conclusion that exploration, maternal behaviour, and so on, are genetically controlled, but it should quickly be pointed out that this conclusion is true only in a very restricted sense. The discovery of a strain-difference in behaviour is a demonstration only that a difference still exists when environmental causes are ruled out, and therefore that the source of the difference must be genetic. It is not a demonstration that maternal behaviour, say, in any one individual is solely genetically controlled: any phenotype is the result of an interaction between genotype and environment. Nor should we conclude that because a difference is genetic it must inevitably be present; genetically caused differences in behaviour are no more inevitable than those produced by the environment. We have already considered in the preceding section an example of the way in which the difference between the mouse strains CBA and RAP in their open field behaviour can be modified by changing the test conditions, but a further example might be useful here. Mice of most albino strains differ from pigmented strains in that they are notably sluggish and slow-moving in the open field. The difference is a genetic one but it is not inevitable. If the lighting of the open-field is changed from white to a dim red, the albino mice show increased activity and the strain-difference is thereby diminished and in some cases abolished. All that we can conclude, therefore, is that under certain carefully specified circumstances differences between animals in their behaviour can exist that are the result of genetic differences between them.

This may seem a fairly modest conclusion to reach but for some workers it appears to have been enough to motivate them to carry out more and more extensive studies of strain-differences, producing an ever-lengthening list of patterns of behaviour that can in some circumstances show genetically produced differences. Such research has provoked from one behaviour-geneticist (Hirsch, 1963) a rather irritated response. He asks:

> why so many demonstrations were necessary. Should it not have been common knowledge that within each population the variation pattern for most traits will be conditioned by the nature of the gene pool, and that this will differ among populations?
>
> (Hirsch, 1963, p. 1439)

In other words, to the extent that these experiments have set out to show that genetic differences can sometimes produce behavioural differences, then they have set out to show what should never have been in doubt.

## Breeding Experiments: Single-gene Effects

In studying the genetics of any phenotypic characteristic (including be-

★ A qualification should be noted. It is possible for there to be persisting "cultural" differences between strains. These are discussed in the final section of this chapter.

havioural characteristics) it is only a preliminary to establish populations that differ in the character in which we are interested. The next step is to carry out breeding experiments which can supply information about the genetic mechanisms involved. One might, for instance, carry out an experiment in which mice from a brown strain are mated with mice from an albino strain and observe the characteristics of the offspring (the *first filial* or $F_1$ generation). One can then go on to mate together members of the $F_1$ generation and investigate the characteristics of the grandchildren of the original strain: the $F_2$ generation. The results of such an experiment will depend upon which particular strains of brown and albino mice are used but in general they look as follows. The coat colour of all the animals in the $F_1$ generations will be brown, but in the $F_2$ generation (the *segregating* generation) a whole range of coat colours will appear from black to brown to pure white albino. The genetic basis of this pattern of inheritance is quite well understood, it depends upon just a few genes, one of which determines whether or not the coat will be coloured at all, the others determining what form the coloration will take. Animals that lack the version of the gene that produces a coloured coat on each member of the relevant pair of chromosomes turn out albinos no matter what other genes they possess.

What is of interest from our present point of view is that some behavioural characteristics of the albino show just the same pattern of inheritance as coat colour itself. The parental albino strain is inactive in the open-field but their children, the $F_1$ generation, are not. Individuals in the $F_1$ generation will have received the albino allele from one parent but from the other parent they will have received the allele for colour. One non-albino gene is sufficient to produce the coloured coat and also the higher level of activity typical of pigmented mice. Some individuals in the $F_2$ generation, however, will receive the albino gene from both parents and they develop both the white coat and the low activity level. This pattern of inheritance is a good example of *pleiotropism*—a gene is said to be pleiotropic when it can modify two or more phenotypic characteristics that are not obviously related, in this case coat colour and activity level. Although it is not immediately obvious, one possible way in which the two characters may be related is suggested by the fact that open-field activity in mice depends upon the intensity of the illumination of the apparatus. Albinos, having no pigment in the irises of their eyes, are perhaps less active because the test situation seems much brighter than it does to mice having normal pigmentation. This interpretation allows us to make sense of the observation mentioned above (p. 79) that albino mice show fairly normal levels of activity in the open-field test when the level of illumination is reduced.

Breeding Experiments in Quantitative Genetics
Although activity in the albino mouse provides a convenient example of the way in which breeding experiments can serve to elucidate the pattern of inheritance

of a behavioural character it may be rather a misleading one. Most behavioural characters depend on not just one or a few genes but are polygenically inherited; that is, when two animals differ in their behaviour for genetic reasons it is almost always the case that their genotypes differ in a large number of ways. But this does not mean that behavioural differences cannot be investigated further. The branch of genetics known as *quantitative genetics* has developed a range of sophisticated mathematical techniques which allow it to assess the extent of polygenically produced differences among members of naturally occurring populations and these will be discussed in the next section of this chapter.

*Artificial selection.* It is also possible to do breeding experiments with polygenically controlled characters and to reach some conclusions about patterns of inheritance. There has been much experimental work, for example, on strains of rats known as high-avoidance and low-avoidance strains, these being strains that differ in the readiness with which they learn to perform a response that either terminates an electric shock or prevents them from receiving a shock at all. Such strains are established by selective breeding. The animals that constitute the original stock are tested on an avoidance task, and it is observed that, although most animals perform at an average level, some show performance that is much better or much worse than the average. Such a distribution of scores on the task is what would be expected if the behaviour was determined by a large number of genes, all of which contributed in some small measure to the performance being measured. Most animals will have a mixture of genes for high-avoidance and for low-avoidance but a few will by chance have a preponderance of one type or the other. The phenotypic differences here are only quantitative: all animals can perform the required response to some extent but they differ one from another in the readiness with which they do it.

In order to establish the two strains, matings are arranged between male and female high-scorers and male and female low-scorers, and the bulk of the animals who perform at an average level are discarded. This procedure is repeated in subsequent generations with high-scorers from the high-scoring line being mated and low-scorers from the low-scoring line being mated. After a few generations the two lines begin to separate in their avoidance performance as the genes that foster high-avoidance become concentrated in the high-scoring line and those that promote low-avoidance become concentrated in the low-scoring line. Eventually the situation can be reached where even the worst of the high strain shows better performance than the best of the low strain.

*Additive and non-additive effects.* The behaviour of these two strains makes sense if we assume that the many genes that influence avoidance performance are *additive* in their effects. Each individual is likely to possess at least a few of the alleles that tend to produce the behaviour found in the other line, but the exact pattern of behaviour it shows will depend upon the relative proportions of the two types of factor. The quantitative behavioural difference is produced by differences between individuals in the quantity of certain sorts of gene that they possess. Animals with a mixture of the two types will normally show an intermediate pattern of behaviour. But this need not always be so, as an experiment by Wilcock (1972) shows. He tested young rats of the high-avoidance and low-avoidance strains on a water-escape tank. The animal was dropped into the middle of a tank of (warmish) water and the time it took to swim to the edge of the tank and climb out was noted. Figure 3.8 shows the average performance of the high-avoidance and low-avoidance strains over six trials. All animals improved a little with practice, but, not surprisingly, the high-avoidance animals were consistently more efficient. Rats from the two strains were then mated and their offspring ($F_1$) tested on water-escape. As Fig. 3.8 shows, their performance was just as good as that shown by the high-avoidance parental strain. This pattern of inheritance is an example of a form of *dominance*—in the $F_1$ animals who possess a mixture of high-avoidance and low-avoidance genes, the effects of the former dominate and obscure the latter. Non-additive effects of this sort limit the extent to which characters "breed true", something of importance to agricultural geneticists who want to produce true-breeding strains of useful domestic animals.

The attempt to quantify the extent to which phenotypic differences are due to genetic differences and the extent to which these are additive in nature has been, in part, motivated by these practical requirements. But the concept to which the attempt gave rise, that of *heritability*, has been much more widely applied, as we shall shortly see (p. 84).

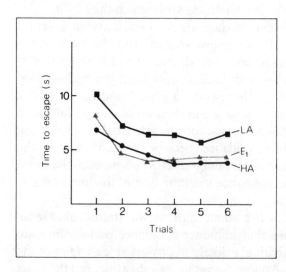

Fig. 3.8. *Average time to escape from a tank of water over six trials by three types of rat. LA and HA are low-avoidance and high-avoidance strains and are the parental stocks for the $F_1$ animals (after Wilcock, 1972).*

## Psychological Implications

It would be possible to provide now a large number of examples of breeding experiments of great complexity, directed at establishing the pattern of inheritance found in a variety of polygenically controlled behavioural characters. But at this stage it would perhaps be a good thing to pause and to ask of what interest it is to the psychologist to know that a given behavioural trait shows dominance, hybrid vigour, or whatever. The short answer must be that it is often of little interest. The geneticist, of course, will want to know all that he can about the mode of inheritance of any phenotypic character whether it be behavioural or structural, but his findings often make no contribution to answering the fundamental psychological question: why does this behaviour occur? Having said this, we should briefly consider two ways in which his findings have made a contribution.

First, knowledge of the genetics of behaviour can sometimes supply information about evolutionary selection pressures—about which behavioural traits are adaptive and put the animal at a selective advantage and which are not (a topic that is too often the subject of speculation rather than of experimental investigation). We may assume that certain traits, like the ability of rodents to produce and rear a large litter, or the ability of birds to lay a large clutch of fertile eggs, are traits that put the animals in question at a selective advantage. The inheritance of such traits often shows dominance. Other traits which we might assume to be of minimal evolutionary importance (the number of bristles shown by the fruit-fly is a good example) do not show this type of inheritance. Dominance then may be taken as an indication that the trait in question has had a history of natural selection working in its favour. One might speculate, therefore, that during the course of their evolution rats have lived sufficiently close to streams and ponds long enough for natural selection to favour those animals quick at escaping when they fall in. Such a speculation is almost impossible to prove or disprove, but the observation of Wilcock, described above, that there is dominance in the inheritance of the water-escape task can provide at least some experimental evidence that is consistent with the suggestion.

The second way in which genetic techniques can make a contribution deserves rather more discussion and receives it in the final section of this chapter. In brief outline, studies have been done which use techniques formally identical to those described in this section (that is, they look at family resemblances, at strain differences, and the behaviour shown by the offspring produced by crossing strains) but which have not been directed primarily at elucidating the genetics of behaviour. Rather, these studies have been directed at elucidating the mechanism responsible for certain aspects of behaviour and the genetic techniques have turned out to be useful tools in answering questions about these mechanisms.

## MEASURING GENETIC DIFFERENCES

We have said that individuals differ from one another (psychologically and in other ways) both because their genotypes differ and because they have been reared in different environments. In this section we discuss the work of those who have applied the techniques of quantitative genetics to psychological differences in an attempt to measure the extent to which differences between people are genetically rather than environmentally determined. This may seem to be a dry and rather academic branch of behaviour-genetics, but it has, as we shall shortly see, evoked a great deal of controversy, particularly when the psychological differences under study have included measures of intellectual ability or attainment. It will be best, therefore, to begin the current discussion with a less emotive human attribute.

### Heritability of Height

Suppose we take a sample from a defined population (say all the 18-year-old males in this country) and measure the height of each individual in the sample. Let us imagine that we find an average height of 1·8 m; there will, of course, be marked individual differences with some men being as small as 1·5 m (say) and others going on for 2 m. Thus our sample will show considerable variability in height, a variability which it is customary to express in terms of a statistic called *variance* which assesses the extent to which individual heights differ from the mean for the sample. In this example it would be obtained by subtracting 1·8 m from the height of each individual scores, squaring the resulting scores (this makes all the difference-scores positive), adding them, and then dividing by a measure of the number of scores that went into the sample.

*Heritability.* To some extent these deviations from the population mean will arise from environmental (in particular, nutritional) differences between people and to some extent they will arise from genetic differences. We want some way of measuring this latter, of finding out what proportion of the variance in the phenotypic character $(V_P)$, can be accounted for by genetic variance $(V_G)$. This proportion is known as the *heritability* of the character:

$$\text{Heritability } (h^2) = \frac{V_G}{V_P}.$$

$(V_G$ in this equation includes all sources of genetic variance and defines heritability in the "broad sense". Heritability is sometimes used in a narrower sense as the proportion of phenotypic variance due solely to additive genetic variance—see above, p. 82.) For most phenotypic characters heritability is less than one and the remaining phenotypic variance must be accounted for by environmental variance ($V_E$) and sometimes also by genotype–environment interaction ($V_{G \times E}$). This last term accommodates the possibility that there can be non-additive combinations of genetic and environmental effects: for example, two individuals with different genotypes might develop in the same way in one environment but might show phenotypic differences if brought up in some different environment.

Now we cannot, of course, completely specify the genotypes of the various individuals in our sample and see how they differ from the average. All we have got to go on is the phenotypic character itself. But we should be able to deduce something from studying the extent to which features of this character tend to run in families. A pair of brothers taken from our population will be genetically rather similar with about half the genes present in one of them also being present in the other; for first cousins about one eighth of the genes are held in common, and so on. If it should turn out that brothers tend to be much more similar in height (on average) than do cousins, and that cousins tend to be a bit more similar than do pairs of genetically unrelated individuals drawn at random from the population, then clearly we should be some way toward saying that genetic differences (and similarities) may be important in determining the observed variance in height. The problem that remains, of course, is that the similarities between close relatives may just as easily stem from the fact that they share similar environments as from the fact that they possess similar genotypes.

*Twin studies.* The principles underlying the techniques used to separate genetic and environmental influences can perhaps best be understood by considering a special case of genetic relatedness: that shown by identical twins. About one third of twin-births are *monozygotic* twins, that is, two individuals develop from a single fertilized egg cell which by some accident of development divides into two parts each of which forms a fetus. When cells divide during the course of development the genetic material in the mother cell is duplicated so that each of the daughter cells receives a complete and perfect copy. Monozygotic twins are therefore genetically identical and all the chromosomal genes present in one will be found in the other.

It will come as no surprise to discover that monozygotic twins tend to grow to much the same height. One pair of twins may differ from other pairs, of course, but differences between the members of a given pair are slight. There can be no genetically caused differences between the members of a pair, and there is usually little chance of major environmentally caused differences occurring: monozygotic twins are born at the same time, brought up in the same home, subjected to the same parental influences; they usually go to the same school, eat the same meals, and often are even dressed alike. If any of these factors is important in determining height, no effect will be apparent in normally reared monozygotic twins.

More interesting therefore are those few cases of monozygotic twins who have been separated shortly after birth with the members of the pair being brought up in different environments with different families. Separations of this sort occur for a variety of reasons. Most often they occur because the mother already has a large family and finds herself unable to cope with two more babies when she had expected only one. Tragic as they may be for the families concerned, such cases provide the psychologist or the geneticist with ideal subjects for study. If he can trace both members of the pair he will be able to assess the extent to which the different environments have produced differences in height (or whatever), secure in the knowledge that there are no genetic differences whatsoever. If he measures their heights he will find that the members of the separated twin-pair do differ rather more than do the heights of monozygotic twins brought up together, thus demonstrating that environmental differences can produce differences in height.

But he will also find that the separated twins still resemble one another quite closely. There is said to be *covariance* (i.e. shared variance) since when one twin is above average height his co-twin is also likely to be above average and when one twin is below average his co-twin is likely to be below average. A more familiar way of expressing this relationship is in terms of a *correlation*: a correlation takes the value 1·0 when each member of a pair is just the same height as his partner and the value 0 when an individual's height matches up no more closely with his co-twin's than with that of anyone else. A correlation is simply another way of expressing covariance. It is computed by obtaining a measure of covariance and dividing it by the overall variance. The correlation in height between separated identical twins is about 0·8.

Now separated identical twins have not shared a common environment but they do share all genetic variance (they are genetically identical). Their covariance in height, therefore, gives a measure of $V_G$ and dividing this by the overall variance ($V_P$) gives not only the correlation but a direct estimate of heritability in the broad sense ($V_G/V_P$). Thus the genetic variance in height as a proportion of the total variance in height has the value 0·8.

Heritability of IQ

So much for height; the point of interest to us is that it is possible to apply the same sort of analysis to any measurable phenotypic character. Given a set of monozygotic twins it would be a simple matter to compute correlations for measures of their weight, visual acuity, musical ability, of the amount of money they earn, the number of books they own, and for scores on psychological tests designed to measure personality and intelligence. This last character has provoked most interest. Since the first in the 1920s there have now been some 20 fairly large-scale studies of twins in which a point has been made of measuring IQ. All have found a high correlation between identical twins, the average value approaching 0·9. This similarity between twins is to be expected given their common genotype and their, often, near-identical environments. Perhaps more surprising have been the results produced by the few studies that have managed to get hold of identical twins reared apart. Here again the correlation between twins was sizeable: the lowest value reported was 0·62 and the highest (from work by Burt) was 0·86. On the basis of this work it was concluded that the heritability for IQ was much the same as for height, that is, about 0·8.

That the heritability for IQ should be as high as 0·8 has produced a lot of concern in some quarters and there have been attempts to show that this estimate is much too high. One line of argument has been developed by Kamin (1974) in his analysis of the work of Burt, the psychologist who has supplied us with the largest, and, so it used to be thought, the most valuable study of the IQs of twins. A careful study of Burt's work (and Kamin appears to have been one of the first to carry out such a study rather than accepting Burt's conclusion on faith) makes sorry reading. Burt's work is published only sketchily in a variety of places; important details are omitted (it is not clear, for instance, just what intelligence tests were given); many contradictory statements can be found; arithmetical mistakes and inconsistencies are common. Kamin's judgement is harsh but it is difficult to disagree with him when he concludes: "The numbers left behind by Professor Burt are simply not worthy of current scientific attention". It is worth adding that this judgement has been endorsed in a recent, sympathetic official biography of Burt (Hearnshaw, 1979). If we are to discard the results produced by Burt, as it seems we must, then we discard the study which has yielded the highest correlation between the IQs of identical twins. Our estimate of heritability is therefore reduced accordingly to a value of something rather less than 0·7.

A second reason for thinking our original heritability estimate to be too high appears when we look in detail at the way in which separated identical twins are in fact separated. In order for the correlation between such twins to be an accurate measure of the heritability of a character, their phenotypic covariance must be an accurate measure of $V_G$, that is, their genetic covariance must be the only source of their phenotypic covariance. This will be so when members of each pair are raised in "uncorrelated" environments—in environments that are, on average, just as different from each other as any pair of environments drawn at random from the population. All too often this has not been so. Identical twins are separated not according to the designs of scientists but because of special and often unfortunate circumstances in the families concerned. A mother may not be able to cope with both children but she will probably not want to banish one of them entirely. She may part with her child only to the extent of handing him on to a grandmother or an aunt or some other close relative. The "separated" twins studied by psychologists include a number of cases of this sort. One extreme example is found in a pair of twins studied by Shields (1962): the boys were indeed separated at birth but they were each brought up by one of their aunts and they lived next door to each other in the same village. Clearly, any similarity in their intellectual abilities is as likely to be mediated by their similar environments as by their identical genotypes.

It is clear, therefore that we must reduce our estimate of the heritability of IQ yet again and a value of 0·5 has been suggested as being nearer the truth. Certainly this is the sort of value that has emerged from studies comparing identical and non-identical (fraternal) twins and from studies that look at the resemblance in IQ between adopted children and their biological parents. Not everyone accepts the validity of this estimate (see Kamin, 1974) but we will not consider the evidence and arguments here. Instead, we need to move on to the wider question of what a heritability value means for psychology. Let us suppose that the heritability of IQ is agreed to be 0·5 by everyone. What does this mean for us?

## Implication of Estimates of Heritability

We should begin by spelling out two things that it does *not* mean. First, it does not mean that 50% of each individual's IQ is inherited with the remaining 50% being determined in some way by environmental influences. A moment's thought shows that this interpretation is based on a gross misunderstanding. At the risk of being unduly repetitive I should restate here that all the attributes of any one individual are both inherited and also environmentally determined since all arise from an interaction between genotype and environment. It is no more sensible to say that 50% of one's IQ is inherited than it is to say that 60% of one's hand is inherited or 70% of one's foot is inherited. When applied to phenotypic characters the word "inherited" can be sensibly applied only to *differences* between individuals: differences between individuals can be inherited or acquired or, more frequently, be produced by both genetic and environmental factors. And it is with respect to such differences that the concept of heritability is meaningful. A heritability value gives us a measure for a given population of the extent to which differences amongst its members are produced by genetic differences. Heritabilities apply to populations, not to individuals.

Secondly, a heritability is not a fixed value: if a competently conducted, well-controlled scientific study comes up with a value of 0·5 for a given population at a given time there is no reason at all why a second study carried out on a different population at some later time should not yield some radically different result. Genetic differences are not inevitable. As environmental conditions change, so the extent to which genetic differences contribute toward phenotypic differences will change also. To take a crude but revealing example, it would probably be possible to produce a dramatic reduction in the heritability of IQ simply by maltreating some of the children in the population under study. If some children are brought up in crowded homes, under-fed, and given next to no education, whereas the rest live comfortably and are well taught and fed, it seems likely that the genetic contribution to the differences among them might shrink into insignificance alongside that produced by environmental factors. Equality of treatment would have the opposite effect. As the social, nutritional, and educational differences between children have diminished in recent years so will the heritability of IQ have risen. (It is an intriguing thought that many of those most worried by the fact that estimates of IQ heritability seem rather high are also those in favour of social reforms that can only act to increase heritability.) To summarize, a heritability of 0·5 does not mean that the proportion of the variance determined by genetic factors must always be 50%.

We can turn now to what a heritability for IQ of 0·5 *does* mean for psychologists. It may indirectly have important implications for educational policy. To some extent our current educational policies embody the notion that differences between people should, so far as possible, be reduced; in particular, special efforts are made (sometimes under the heading of "compensatory education"—see Chapter 4, p. 125) to improve the performance of those who might otherwise score badly on IQ and other tests of ability and performance. Now, what a high heritability would tell us is that differences between people in the character in question are largely the result of genetic differences between them and are not much affected by the differing environments that they have experienced. It tells us, therefore, that manipulating environmental factors within their current range of variation is not likely to be very effective in reducing individual differences: different changes will be needed. It is still largely a matter of guesswork as to what sort of environment must be supplied to improve the IQ scores of potentially low-scoring individuals. But a relatively high value for the heritability of IQ does not mean that we should give up the search for important environmental influences: rather it means we should widen the scope of our search.

It is difficult to leave this topic without a few words about the concept of "equality". We are not born equal since we are all (unless we have an identical twin) endowed with different genotypes. To this initial inequality is added a wide range of environmental inequalities and the result is the wide range of individual differences in ability, temperament, personality, and achievement that we see around us every day. We most of us have a feeling that many, if not all, of the environmental inequalities are unjust and should be eliminated. Why should some starve whilst others overeat to the point of gluttony? And certainly, social policies in many countries have been directed toward removing the grossest of these injustices, the aim being to achieve "equality of opportunity". Laudable as these attempts are we must not be deceived into thinking that equality of achievement will be their consequence. When environmental sources of difference are removed, genetically produced differences will reign in their place. To many this will be acceptable, although our reasons for thinking that environmentally produced differences are unjust whereas genetically produced differences are not, have rarely been adequately specified. Perhaps it would be better to abandon the ideal of equality of treatment, to accept that people differ from one another genetically and to give, so far as possible, different treatment appropriate to each individual's genetic make-up. The programmes of compensatory education that were supplied for the children of the poor in the big cities of the USA some years ago made a start in this direction. These programmes were not very successful and came in for much criticism. One of the most notable critics was the psychologist Jensen—he criticized the studies but he did not deny the basic principle:

> Is it possible that true equality of opportunity could mean doing whatever is necessary to maximize the scholastic achievement of children, even if it might mean doing quite different things for different children in terms of their differing patterns of ability?

(Jensen, 1971)

## USING GENETIC DIFFERENCES

In a previous section we considered the way in which the examination of family pedigrees and of strain differences and the results of breeding experiments have been used to work out the genetics of behavioural characters. These same techniques can be used as "tools" in studies that try to advance our understanding of psychological processes and to test psychological theories. In this section we discuss three specific examples of the use of these tools. Family pedigrees have proved useful in the study of mental disorder in man, breeding studies in the analysis of open-field behaviour, and strain differences have helped to elucidate the mechanisms underlying mother–young interactions.

### Genetic Tools in the Study of Psychopathology

It is customary to distinguish between two sorts of mental breakdown: the milder *neuroses* and the more severe *psychoses*. Classificatory and diagnostic schemes tend to differ from one psychiatrist to another but most psychotics are usually regarded as suffering either from *schizophrenia* or from a *manic-depressive* illness. Schizophrenia, which usually first manifests itself in adolescence or early adulthood, is the condition that the layman takes as the archetype of "lunacy"—a characteristic of the sufferer is that he withdraws from reality into his own world of fantasy. The manic-depressive is said to show a disorder of "affect" (of feeling or emotion) and in its classic form the sufferer shows cyclic swings from extreme elation (mania) to profound depression. Both these disorders tend to run in families. Thus the chances of any one individual taken at random from the population suffering from schizophrenia is a little less than 1%, whereas the chances of a schizophrenic parent having a child who breaks down is more like 10%. Similar figures are found for manic-depressive illness. But more detailed analysis of these figures confirms the general view that the two types of psychosis are quite distinct. In particular, the relatives of a manic-depressive are no more likely to develop schizophrenia than are individuals sampled at random from the general population. In this way, evidence from the study of family resemblances has proved a useful way of checking upon the distinctions made in psychiatric diagnosis.

A more striking example of genetics being used as a "tool" in this sort of analysis comes from the investigation of two types of manic-depressive disorder. The true manic-depressive is said to be *bipolar*, having swings of mood from one extreme to the other. But some so-called manic-depressives show a *unipolar* form, alternating between deep depression and a fairly normal emotional state. There has been prolonged debate about whether the unipolar form is merely a reduced version of true manic-depression or whether it should be regarded as a separate disorder in its own right. Evidence to favour the latter view comes from the observation that the two forms are transmitted independently—sufferers from the unipolar form have unipolar relatives; sufferers from the bipolar form tend, on the whole, to have bipolar relatives.

Information about family resemblances has proved a simple but effective tool in "high-risk" studies of the origins of schizophrenia. Given that the onset of this disorder is usually apparent in the late teens and twenties it seems possible that some clues about its causes might be gleaned from the investigation of children, of how they behave and how they are treated, in the years before schizophrenia is diagnosed. The problem, of course, is that the investigator does not know that the children, whose development he wants to study over the course of many years, will in fact break down with the disorder. If he sampled 100 children from the general population he could expect only one of them to break down and he would gain little information from many years of hard work. The solution to the problem is to concentrate the investigation upon children who are identified as being at risk for schizophrenia on the grounds that the disorder has been seen in their close relatives (usually their parents). An investigation of 100 such children will yield evidence about the origins of schizophrenia in some 10 adults and then the enterprise becomes practical. About 20 such studies are now under way. The results are not yet in (the investigator must be prepared to wait 20 or 30 years for breakdown to occur in some of his subjects) but the tentative conclusion that has emerged so far is that the genetic predisposition toward schizophrenia is particularly likely to result in breakdown when the individual in question is subject to undue environmental stress during the course of development.

## Genetic Analysis of Open-field Behaviour

Many explanations in psychology are based on correlations. It is observed, for instance, that rodents who are poor at learning a new response in order to avoid an electric shock are also slow-moving in the open field. This correlation suggests the explanation that both these patterns of behaviour are mediated by the intrinsic fearfulness of the animal: a very fearful animal freezes in the open field and his avoidance performance is disrupted totally by the extra fear that an electric shock produces. A test of this hypothesis is provided by observations carried out on other strains of rodent that move about freely in the open field. If this behaviour really does indicate a low basal level of fearfulness and a low level is needed for learning a shock-avoidance task, then these animals should learn the latter task readily. And it has been shown that they do, thus adding support to the original hypothesis.

Equally useful can be studies which disconfirm hypotheses by showing that correlations can break down. A simple example is provided by an experiment on mice by Shire (1968). He considers two strains of mice, one very slow-moving in the open field and the other very quick, and points out that the sluggish mice are also much heavier. Perhaps then the level of open-field activity is simply a matter of how fat the animal is. Shire therefore mated the two strains to produce an $F_1$ generation and then mated these animals with members of one of the original parental strains. The product of this *backcross*

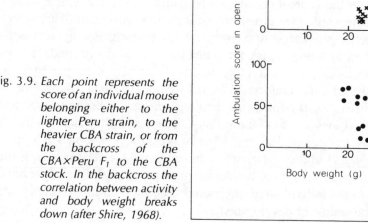

Fig. 3.9. *Each point represents the score of an individual mouse belonging either to the lighter Peru strain, to the heavier CBA strain, or from the backcross of the CBA×Peru $F_1$ to the CBA stock. In the backcross the correlation between activity and body weight breaks down (after Shire, 1968).*

comprised animals that were light and animals that were heavy; also, some animals were active in the open field and some were inactive: but the correlation between these two characteristics then broke down (Fig. 3.9). We can therefore reject the suggestion that a low activity level is a simple concomitant of having a high body weight. If this seems a rather negative conclusion it should be added that observations that disconfirm incorrect hypotheses are often thought to be of more value in science than observations which are no more than consistent with established ideas.

A positive conclusion to emerge from this sort of study concerns the physiological basis of open-field behaviour. That is, genetic differences have also been useful in exploring correlations that might exist between patterns of behaviour on the one hand, and physiological mechanisms on the other. It has been known for some time that the response to stress in mammals is mediated, in part, by the *adrenals*, a pair of hormone-producing glands that lie above the kidneys. The central core of the gland (the adrenal *medulla*) provides an immediate response to stress by releasing *adrenaline* into the blood, a substance that increases the rate of the heart beat and makes sugar available to the muscles as an energy supply. Longer-term responses depend upon hormones produced by the outer *cortex* of the adrenal. To the extent that a mouse's behaviour in the open field indicates its response to a novel, stressful situation we would expect this behaviour to correlate with measures of adrenal functioning. Shire's analysis shows that, by and large, this is so, with the more active strains of mice having larger adrenals than the less active strains.

## Mother–Young Interaction in Mice

A final example from the behaviour of mice may give some insight into the way in which genetic differences can be exploited to investigate the sort of question that is perhaps of greatest interest to most psychologists: the question of how it is that behaviour comes to be shaped and modified by the physical and social environment in which the animal lives. We feel, for example, that the way in which a mother treats her child is likely to affect the child's later behaviour. The following study (Hall, 1971) using inbred strains of mice shows this to be so. Mice of an active inbred strain were mated with mice of an inactive strain to produce offspring that were, on the whole, genetically homogeneous. The offspring could be divided into two groups, however, according to the mothering they received. It is usual practice in experiments of this sort to remove the male animal when the female becomes pregnant: the female brings up the young alone. Thus some of the mice, those whose father had belonged to the active strain, were brought up by an inactive mother; the remainder were brought up by an active mother. In this set-up, therefore, we have the perfect arrangement for investigating the effects of maternal behaviour on the young. We know that offspring of the inbred active strain are themselves active and that offspring of the inbred inactive strain are inactive, but we also know that these two groups of animals differ genetically. In the case I have described, however, the two groups of animals that we are interested in do not differ genetically in any consistent fashion. Nonetheless, the type of mothering they experience is sufficient to produce a difference between them: those brought up with a mother from the active strain prove themselves to be active when tested as adults in the open field whereas those reared by the inactive mother turn out to be rather sluggish.

This pattern of results raises two intriguing implications. The first is perhaps merely a verbal point. How are we to describe the difference between the offspring of active and inactive mothers? It cannot be a genetic difference since the two groups of animals do not differ genetically. And yet the only way in which their mothers differed was genetically and it is the difference between the mothers that produced the difference in the children. Clearly the name we apply does not matter much but it is well to be aware of the possibility that environmentally produced differences can also be the result of genetic differences working at second hand.

The second point that we should be aware of is the possibility that genetic influences may have their effects not only at second hand but also at third and fourth hand. If the mothering that a baby mouse receives can influence the open-field behaviour that the baby shows when it is grown up, might it also not affect the way in which it behaves, in turn, to its own children? If so, there is no reason why the effect should stop there. An initial genetically produced difference could be perpetuated for generation after generation by the way in which parents treat their children even in the absence of continuing genetic differences. We shall leave this phenomenon of "cultural inheritance" at this point, but there is every reason to think that it might play an important part in determining human behaviour and we must discuss it in detail in the final chapter.

## CONCLUSIONS

This chapter has been devoted chiefly to the implications of the fact that (nearly) all individuals differ genetically from one another. We have seen how these individual differences can complicate the search for general psychological principles, how it is possible to study the patterns of inheritance of behavioural differences, and how it may be possible to estimate the size of the genetic component underlying them. We have also seen how these differences may be put to use in answering purely psychological questions. But perhaps more important than any of this is the conclusion that emerged from our discussion of the contributions of genotype and environment to individual phenotypic characteristics. It was that every such characteristic is both inherited and acquired, and it means that a complete answer to the question "why does this behaviour occur?" must include information about both genotype and environment. We cannot simply answer that the behaviour is "inherited"; we must also investigate the way in which the genes interact with the environment during development.

It is not too far-fetched to divide up the science of biology into two major sections, one concerned with *phylogeny*, the other with *ontogeny*. Chapters 2 and 3 have been concerned for the most part with phylogeny, with evolution, and with those aspects that are devoted to investigating how it is that an individual comes to be equipped at conception with a certain "given". This branch of biology contains a good deal that is of interest to psychologists but most of psychology (and hence, most of the rest of this book) belongs in the section of biology that I have labelled "ontogeny". Using the word in its widest sense, the study of ontogeny is the study of the way in which the genetic "given" interacts with the environment to produce a living and behaving organism (the study of development) which continues to interact with the environment throughout its life. This branch of biology includes, of course, those subsections known as biochemistry and physiology but we shall not be much concerned with the behaviour of individual cells or of individual organs. Instead, as psychologists, we shall concentrate upon the behaviour of the whole organism, trying to describe accurately what it does and how its behaviour is determined by its past experience and the current circumstances in which it finds itself.

## SOURCES AND FURTHER READING

An admirable general textbook on genetics is that of Sinnot *et al.* (1958); for an introduction to specifically behavioural genetics a simple text is that by Plomin *et al.* (1980). A more advanced book is that edited by Hirsch (1967) entitled *Behavior—Genetic Analysis*. All these books provide general discussion of the relationship between genetic and environmental factors in determining behaviour; for more on this see Thoday and Parkes (1968) *Genetic and Environmental Influences on Behaviour*. They all also provide examples of experiments on the genetics of behaviour and of the use of genetic variables in psychological research; for further discussion of the example so frequently used in this chapter (the open-field behaviour of rodents) see Gray's (1971) *The Psychology of Fear and Stress*. There is an immense literature on the vexed topic of the heritability of psychological traits in man. It is appropriate to begin by reading the article by Jensen (1969) that provoked the recent controversy about IQ. The conclusions reached by Jensen are roundly criticized by Kamin (1974) in his *The Science and Politics of IQ* but beware that Kamin's criticisms have not themselves emerged unscathed (see Mackintosh, 1975a).

# 4 Development and the Effects of Early Experience

## INTRODUCTION

One concern of Chapter 3 was to demonstrate that any living, behaving organism is the product of the interaction between a genotype and its environment. In this chapter we turn to a closer study of the nature of this interaction, that is, to the topic of development.

In this sense, development must be regarded as a process that begins at conception and ends only with the death of the organism. For a number of reasons, however (and these will be discussed in the course of this chapter), psychologists have largely concentrated their attention on the middle part of this time span. In spite of paying lip-service to the need for a "life-span developmental psychology" they have done relatively little work on the development that occurs in the uterus or in the changes in behaviour that occur in adults. Most of their energy has been expended in studying the psychology of children, from infancy to adolescence. Things may be changing now—there has been some recent work on the psychology of senescence and an upsurge of interest in the behaviour of newborn babies—but, for the most part, the sections of this chapter that deal with human subjects will be concerned, necessarily, with the psychology of infants and children.

Developmental psychology concerns itself with two main questions. First, it asks what changes occur in the behaviour or capacities of an organism as it grows older; for example, what, if anything, is a newborn baby capable of? How well can a toddler perceive and understand the world? Second, it asks about the mechanisms responsible for developmental change: why does the two-year-old behave differently from the ten-year-old; the child differently from the adult?

The questions are not, of course, independent and most developmental psychologists are interested in both. For convenience, however, I shall treat them as if they were quite separate issues, dealing first with some studies that supply simple descriptions of the course of psychological development and then going on to consider more analytic studies that investigate the causes of development change. This analysis starts with a general discussion of the role of environmental factors in producing developmental change; then follow details of some specific cases in which the interaction of the developing organism with its environment has been studied experimentally. It concludes with a consideration of the suggestion that events occurring early in life have especially profound effects on later behaviour.

Many of these analytic studies have been done with non-human animals but descriptive studies of development in man are plentiful if only because parents like to watch their children develop and some parents are psychologists.

## THE COURSE OF PSYCHOLOGICAL DEVELOPMENT

A detailed account of the entire course of all aspects of psychological development from birth to adulthood would be well outside the scope of this book. Instead we will consider just a few aspects of behaviour and mental functioning with the intention of determining what general principles, if any, underlie the course of their development.

### The Capacities of the Newborn

The starting point for much developmental research is the behaviour of the newborn organism. Even if we restrict consideration just to mammalian species it is apparent that there is great variability in behavioural capacity from one species to another. It is customary to distinguish two main classes. The young of some animals are said to be *precocial* and are able to carry out a wide range of activities immediately after birth. Examples are to be found among the ungulates that live as herds, such as sheep and goats; presumably in these creatures when the mother is likely to be on the move, the baby must be able to follow. But ungulates are not the only precocial species: the guinea-pig supplies another, perhaps more familiar example. The second class of animals have young that are said to be *altricial*. These are more or less helpless at birth, for example, young kittens and puppies are blind and in common with the young of most primates (including man) are capable of only very limited locomotion.

A newborn altricial mammal, such as a human infant, engages, for the most part, in just two major forms of behaviour: sucking and sleeping, with two thirds or more of its time being spent in the latter activity. A few reflexes are present at birth or shortly thereafter. A human baby will show the "rooting" reflex, turning his head and pouting the lips when his cheek is softly stroked, and the Babinski reflex, stretching the foot and extending the toes when the sole of his foot is scratched. He will suck if an object like a finger (or, of course, a nipple) is placed into his mouth, will close his eyes in response to the sudden onset of a bright light, and will close his fingers around an adult's finger pressed into his palm. Given this limited behavioural repertoire it is exceedingly difficult to ascertain what mental activities an infant is capable of. We can assess the intellectual capacities of other individuals only by listening to what they say and seeing what they do. If they do not talk and do very little this may signify an absence of mental activity or it may just mean that we have no way to measure it. In order to find out about the perceptual or cognitive capacities of a newborn baby it is necessary to make full use of the little behaviour that it does show. An example is found in the following experiment reported by Lipsitt (1967).

*Learning and auditory discrimination.* The subjects were babies as young as 48 hours old. The basic procedure adopted by the experimenter was to stroke the baby's cheek gently so as to elicit, at least on some occasions, the response of turning the head toward the touch. If, when such a response occurred, the baby was allowed to suck on a teat that delivered a few drops of sugar-water, the likelihood of a head-turn being produced by a touch on the cheek was found to increase markedly. Furthermore, it proved possible to train the baby to make this response only when a specific external event occurred. Some babies received access to the teat only when a tone was sounded at the same time as they were touched on the cheek; the tactile stimulus accompanied by the sounding of a buzzer was not followed by access to the teat. Relatively quickly (after five or six presentations of each auditory stimulus) these babies learned to turn their head to the sound of the tone and not to do so to the buzzer (Fig. 4.1). These simple observations establish a number of things. First, they make it clear that the newborn baby is capable of carrying out the sensory and perceptual

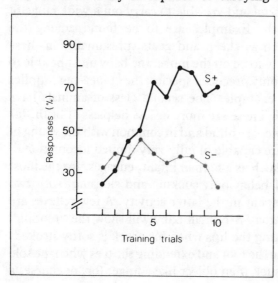

Fig. 4.1. *Auditory discrimination by human neonates. The curves show the mean performance of 16 babies over ten trials on which response to the positive stimulus (S+; e.g. a tone) was followed by reward and ten interspersed trials on which response to the negative stimulus (S−; e.g. a buzzer) was not (after Lipsitt, 1967).*

operations that are necessary for it to distinguish between a buzzer and a tone, perhaps not a very sophisticated capability but one that might surprise someone who had made no more than a casual observation of newborn babies. Second, they demonstrate that the newborn is capable of simple *associative learning*, of associating a certain pattern of behaviour with reward. Perhaps, indeed, this form of learning is not so simple as all that. Even at this early age the baby is showing a tendency for his actions to be modified by their consequences, repeating behaviour that is rewarded and eliminating that which is not. It has been argued (see Chapter 7) that learning of this sort guides much of the voluntary behaviour of adults.

The auditory stimuli used in Lipsitt's experiment were arbitrarily chosen and artificial. More recently, however, work has been done using similar techniques to show that babies younger than three days of age can discriminate the voice of their mother from other voices and indeed show a preference for it (De Casper and Fifer, 1980). The technique used exploited the babies' tendency to engage in non-nutritive sucking. It has been mentioned that a newborn baby will suck if a finger or similar object is put in its mouth. Each baby in the experiment was equipped with a non-nutritive nipple, by which sucking could be recorded, and a pair of stereo headphones. It was then arranged that if the baby sucked on the nipple in a certain way (for example, if it did so rapidly with only short pauses between bouts of sucking) it heard a recording of its mother's voice played over the headphones. Other patterns of sucking produced the voice of someone else's mother. Within a matter of minutes the babies learned to respond in the way that allowed them to hear the voice of their own mother, not only a remarkable achievement in itself but evidence that some quite rapid learning had already gone on outside the experimental situation. The babies in question had lived all three days of their life in a hospital tended and handled by a variety of women and had received, at most, only 12 hours of (postnatal) contact with their mothers before the experiment began. Nonetheless, they appear to have learned at least some of the defining characteristics of their mothers' voices.

*Vision.* Studies of the sensitivity of babies to visual stimuli have relied for the most part on the fact that infants have a natural preference for some stimuli rather than others and that they reveal their preference by their pattern of looking (Fig. 4.2). If a baby spends longer looking at one picture rather than another it is clear that he can discriminate them in some way. Thus, babies seem to have a natural preference for patterned over plain objects and will spend more time looking at a picture bearing black and white stripes than at a plain grey field of equivalent overall brightness (see Fig. 4.3). This behaviour allows us to estimate their visual acuity—if the stripes are made narrower and narrower a point will be reached where the baby shows no preference and we may assume that he is no longer able to tell the striped pattern from the plain

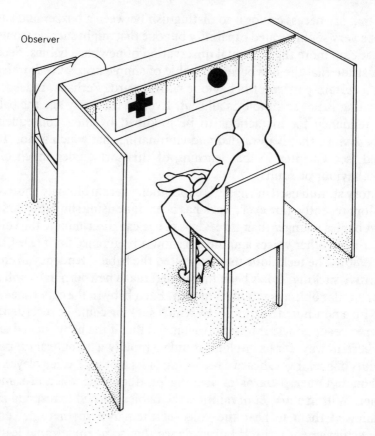

Observer

Fig. 4.2. *Procedure for studying visual preference in babies. The infant sits in a baby seat on the lap of a seated person, facing a pair of stimulus objects. The baby's direction of gaze is noted by an observer.*

grey. (At only two weeks of age a baby can detect the difference between plain grey and a pattern of stripes 3 mm wide viewed from a distance of about 25 cm.)

Preference in looking has been most widely used in studying the abilities of babies a few months old, but some of the most dramatic evidence that we have on the visual abilities of babies comes from much younger children and used a rather different technique. Meltzoff and Moore (1977) made videotape recordings of babies only two to three weeks old while the babies were watching an experimenter pull a variety of faces (such as pouting the lips, opening the mouth wide, and so on). Analysis of the videotapes suggests that these young babies are capable of imitation. They do not always do so—sometimes they pull the "wrong" face and sometimes they do not respond at all—but on average they are more likely to pull a face like that made by the experimenter than some other sort of face. If this finding can be substantiated (see Hayes and Watson, 1981) it will tell us not only about the visual discriminations that a very young

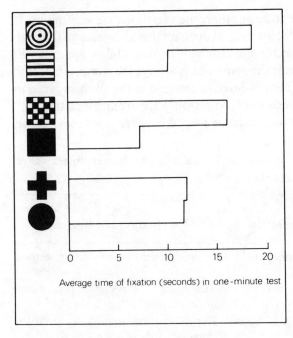

Average time of fixation (seconds) in one-minute test

Fig. 4.3. *Examples of pairs of visual patterns used to test the discrimination ability of infants. For the top two pairs the infants show a preference (more time fixating) for the more complex, but show little preference for cross over circle (after Fantz, 1961).*

baby is capable of; it will also tell us that the baby is capable of in some way equating its own unseen behaviour with that shown by others, an ability one assumes to require some quite sophisticated underlying mechanism.

*Implications.* These and similar investigations have made it clear that, whatever a baby's motor limitations, his ability to perceive events in his world is active shortly after birth. While admitting the elegance of the experiments and the important and often surprising nature of their findings, a few words of caution are appropriate here. Although it has now become fashionable to emphasize the very high level of competence that infants can show in their interaction with their environment, it nonetheless remains the case that the most salient feature of the human infant is his extreme helplessness, his total dependence upon the care supplied by others for his survival and his continued development. It is to the gradual growth of behavioural independence that we turn next.

Motor and Language Development in Man

It appears that what a baby chiefly lacks is the ability to *do* things: to walk and to talk. Certainly it is in the areas of motor and language development that the most striking behavioural changes occur during the first years of life and these changes have captured the attention of many psychologists.

Table 4.1 gives a very simplified list of the major changes that are observed as children grow older with the approximate ages at which certain features occur. Tables of this sort are very common and although those produced by different observers may differ a little, one from another, the variations are very slight. It is for this reason that the table is of interest. It appears that all babies go through this sequence of changes. The exact age at which a given ability appears will vary from one child to another but the sequence is always the same, a fact that has captured the imagination of those who have referred to the abilities given in the table as developmental "milestones". Milestones are arranged so that "2" always lies between "1" and "3" and must be passed in order as we move down the road.

*Table 4.1* Development of motor abilities and speech in the human infant (after Lenneberg, 1967).

| Age (months) | Motor development | Vocalization and language |
|---|---|---|
| 3 | Lifts head when prone; no grasp | "Coos"; produces vowel-like sounds |
| 6 | Sits; holds objects in fist | "Babbling", especially repetitions of, e.g., "ma", "mu", "da" |
| 12 | Crawls; walks when held by hand | Repetitions of sounds to produce "mama", "dada", etc. |
| 18 | Precipitate gait; grasp fully developed | Vocabulary of from 3–50 words used singly. Babbling still occurs |
| 24 | Can run but often falls | Vocabulary exceeds 50 words; two-word phrases appear |
| 30 | Can jump in air with both feet | Rapid increase in vocabulary; phrases of up to 5 words; no babbling |

It is the fixity of this developmental sequence that prompts the suggestion that at least some aspects of development are relatively free from the effects of environmental influence and are perhaps better regarded as the result of the gradual unfolding of some built-in plan. This issue is a central one in the study of development and will be discussed in detail when we come to the analysis of the causes of developmental change. For the moment we will consider the extent to which equivalent milestones can be discerned along the course of the development of thinking in children.

Stages in Cognitive Development
The work of Piaget has assumed a dominant place in the study of *cognitive* development in children (by which is meant the development of the processes underlying thinking), both attracting ardent disciples and provoking vehement criticism. Division of opinion is to be expected about the contribution of a man whose writings appear (to me at least) to present a thicket of almost

impenetrable obscurity—the reader can come away from them having extracted his own meaning rather than that intended by Piaget. Nonetheless, there appears to be a consensus that, according to Piaget, the cognitive development of the child can be divided up into four major stages or periods. The chief characteristics of each of these periods are described next. In the following section we consider some of the criticisms that have been levelled at Piaget's theory, and the problems that arise in distinguishing developmental stages more generally.

*Sensory–motor period.* During the first couple of years of its life the child is said to show only *sensory–motor intelligence* although this term must be used to cover, as any parent will know, a wide and rapidly changing range of abilities. Piaget acknowledges this fact by suggesting that the sensory–motor period should be divided up into a sequence of subsidiary stages. But if there is one thing that characterizes the very young infant during the whole of this period of his life it is his readiness to react to stimulating events in his immediate environment and with it a corresponding inability to be guided by events outside his immediate view. The young baby will look toward an object in his visual field and, when a little older, he will reach for it. But an object that moves outside the field of view (under a cushion or behind a chair) seems to cease to exist for the very young child and usually he will make no effort to retrieve it (Fig. 4.4). Only by the age

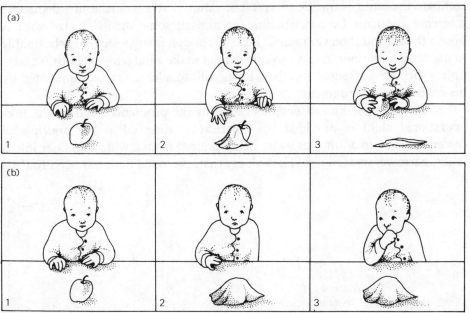

Fig. 4.4. *Observations leading to the notion that young babies lack object permanence. The six-month-old can retrieve the apple in (a) but in (b) he is unable to obtain the object completely covered by the cloth (after Bower, 1974).*

of about two years does the child show awareness of *object permanence*. This has been taken to show that the child's behaviour can now be controlled by representations of events (as opposed to immediate sensory stimulation) and the child is said to have moved into the next developmental period.

*Preoperational period.* The stage of *pre-operational* thought is said to last from about two to seven years and is the period associated with the acquisition of language. In studying the behaviour of a child of this age we have the advantage of being able to talk to him. But what emerges from our conversation is often that the child's use of words differs markedly from that of an educated adult. When the child asks: "how did we find out the name of the moon?" it becomes clear that he has yet to learn that "moon" is no more than an arbitrary, abstract symbol quite distinct from the object it signifies. (As an aside it might be added that not all adults are capable of this feat. The Russian neuropsychologist Luria has reported a case of an uneducated man who was quite prepared to believe that scientists might be able to work out how far away the stars are; he could not understand, however, how it was possible to discover their names.)

According to Piaget, a child at this stage of development is still unable to use symbols to solve problems. Piaget cites an example of a child being presented with two objects, A being bigger than B. Object A is then removed and hidden and B is shown along with a yet smaller object, C. When asked how A and C compare the child is unable to say. The adult is able to make this deductive inference, perhaps by constructing for himself some mental image with A bigger than B and B bigger than C. But the child, it is suggested, may be unable to use representations in this way and cannot make a judgement about A and C unless they are presented together. He is still, to a large extent, dominated by his immediate environment.

Perhaps the best-known demonstration of the problems faced by the pre-operational child is provided by experiments directed at the *principle of conservation*. If an adult sees water being poured from a wide container into a taller, narrower one (Fig. 4.5) he will say that, provided none has been spilled,

Fig. 4.5. *A 5-year-old child shown containers A and B will say that they contain equal amounts of water. When the contents of B are poured into C the child will say that C contains more water than A.*

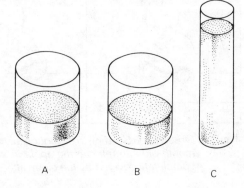

A            B            C

the second container holds the same amount as the first. The adult knows that volume is conserved in the course of such a procedure. A child of four or five years of age, on the other hand, is likely to say that the second container holds more water than the first. His judgement appears to be based on the information immediately available to his senses; on the fact that the water rises to a higher level in the narrow container than in the wide container.

*Later stages.* Mastery of the principle of conservation is one of the signs of the onset of the next developmental stage (of *concrete operations*, from about seven to about 11 years). The child now shows some ability to use symbols and to show logical thought—he is, for instance, now capable of making deductive inferences. Nonetheless, the symbols he uses tend mostly to refer to concrete objects in his immediate field of view and it is only when the child passes into the next, *formal operational* stage that he is able to deal with abstract notions, hypotheses, and so on. The example from Luria cited above might be taken to imply that not all adults manage fully to reach this stage.

## Problems with Developmental Stages

A glance at almost any textbook on developmental or child psychology will show how dominant the interest in the "stages" of development can become. Each author seems to want to divide up his own particular topic of interest be it emotional development, perception, motor skill, or whatever into ever more precisely identified stages. The artificiality of such a procedure soon becomes evident and one feels tempted to react and emphasize instead the essentially continuous nature of development. This latter view has something to be said for it but the fact that a change is gradual need not prevent us from sensibly discriminating stages. Thus, the development of motor abilities may proceed in the most gradual way but this does not stop us from distinguishing between crawling and walking and from specifying the age at which the child can do the former but not the latter.

A more serious problem arises from the fact that so often a developmental stage is defined in terms of what the child cannot do. But absence of evidence is not evidence of absence. If a given experimenter fails to find signs of a certain ability in a child this may tell us more about the incompetence of the experimenter than the incompetence of the child. Certainly, the more striking of Piaget's assertions concerning the inabilities of children at various stages of cognitive development have provoked a large number of experiments designed to show that the child may be much more competent than Piaget would have us believe.

*Object permanence reconsidered.* Consider first the notion of object permanence. Piaget's original observations are not in doubt. A child of six months will certainly lose all apparent interest if a toy is hidden under a cloth, say, in spite of the fact that he has sufficient manual dexterity to remove the cloth and retrieve his toy. An older infant (of nine months to a year) may learn to remove the cloth but he will often continue to search under this same cloth on occasions when he has watched his toy being hidden in some quite different place. What is in doubt is Piaget's suggestion that infants behave in these ways because they do not believe that hidden objects continue to exist. One obvious possibility is that, like the adult, he fully believes in the continued existence of the hidden object but that he is not as good as an adult in storing and recalling information about where it has got to.

An observation that lends support to this notion comes from studies of those older babies who have learned to retrieve hidden objects from a particular place. They will persist in searching in that place even when the object is not hidden elsewhere but is put before them in full view, that is, even in circumstances when they can be in no doubt about its continued existence. The child clearly lacks some of the skills of the adult but the ability to comprehend the continued existence of hidden objects does not appear to be one of them. We still may not fully understand the reasons why the child makes the mistakes he does but they are mistakes of the sort any adult might make (which of us has not been fooled by a conjurer at some time) and they do not require us to suppose (as the Piagetian explanation implies) that the young child possesses some form of intelligence quite different from our own.

*Inference in young children*. An example of the experimental work carried out on children supposedly in the pre-operational stage comes from the work of Bryant (1974) on deductive inference in children aged from four to six years. Bryant begins by acknowledging the accuracy of Piaget's original observation: that a child will often be unable to say that A is bigger than C after being shown that A is bigger than B (A>B) and that B>C. But, he points out, this failure may be the result of nothing more than a lapse of memory. If the child has forgotten the nature or the direction of the difference between A and B or between B and C, by the time he comes to decide about A and C then his powers of inference will be unable to show themselves. Bryant's own experiments were designed to avoid this problem.

The children were presented at various times with a range of five sticks painted different distinctive colours and varying in size from large (stick A) down to small (stick E). In the first phase of the experiment the subjects were shown pairs of sticks adjacent in size (i.e. A–B, B–C, and so on) over and over again until it was clear that their relative sizes had been fully learned. The children were shown just the ends of each pair of sticks and asked to guess which was the longer or shorter. The child was then shown whether or not his guess had been correct and training went on in this fashion until the child was reliably choosing the correct colour. Only at this stage was the critical test-combination, B–D, presented. Performance on this test provides a particularly stringent test of the child's ability to make the inference. Each of these sticks had been encountered during the first phase of the experiment equally often along with a larger stick and with a smaller stick (thus, B had been paired on some occasions with A and on others with C). This procedure excludes the possibility that the child might learn simply always to say "bigger" when shown B and "smaller" when shown C, a strategy that would enable him to come up with the correct response on the test trial. In spite of this precaution it was found that most children were able to pick out the appropriate stick when tested with B and D: six-year-old children chose correctly on 92% of B–D test trials and even four-year-olds were correct on 78% of test trials. Remember that according to Piaget children are capable of only pre-operational thought before the age of seven years.

*Conclusions.* The general point to be derived from these experiments is not that cognitive development (or any other sort of development) should not be divided into stages. Indeed the evidence just reviewed seems to suggest that early childhood constitutes a stage in which the mechanisms involved in learning and remembering function less efficiently than they do in later years. Rather it is that new evidence may appear, to reshape our understanding of what the stages might be—especially so when the stages are defined in terms of what a child of a certain age is *not* able to do.

Finally it should be said that a description of the stages of development can be only a first step toward an understanding of the topic. Many of the interesting issues in development concern the mechanisms by which one stage is transformed into the next (as Piaget himself has emphasized). It is to these issues that we turn next.

## THE CAUSES OF DEVELOPMENTAL CHANGE

### Correlation and Cause in Development

Experimental psychologists often describe behaviour in terms of *dependent* and *independent variables*. The independent variable is some event being manipulated by the experimenter: an example might be the intensity of a noise to which a child is subjected. The dependent variable is some measure of the behaviour in which the experimenter is interested: in this case he might measure the magnitude of a startle response. One aim of psychology is to work out in detail the relationship between independent and dependent variables; to put it more informally, to work out the environmental causes of behaviour.

Descriptive studies of development do not follow this pattern. There is certainly a dependent variable, such as a measure of a child's motor ability or of his speech, but there is no true independent variable that the experimenter is able to manipulate so as to demonstrate the role it plays in determining the behaviour under investigation. In these studies the part of the independent variable is filled by time, by a measure of the age of the child. In an experimental study the experimenter may plot a graph showing, to revert to the previous example, that the size of the startle response grows bigger as the intensity of the stimulus is increased. All that our studies of development allow, however, is a graph relating behaviour to the age of the child. This is depicted in Fig. 4.6a where A, B, C, etc. stand for the behaviour patterns that a child might show; for example, the motor patterns listed in Table 4.1. Such a figure would show there to be a correlation between the age of the child and the behaviour he shows: the older the child the better he is at getting about.

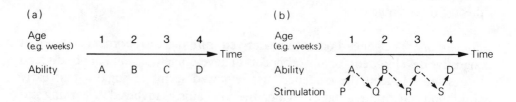

Fig. 4.6. *A, B, C, etc. represent patterns of behaviour; (a) shows how they are correlated with age; (b) shows how they could be evoked by environmental events (P, Q, etc.) that occur at these ages.*

Having got this far it is easy to jump to the conclusion that it is the passage of time that *causes* developmental change. What makes this conclusion tempting is the regularity and consistency with which each individual's development passes through its various stages. Developmental changes seem, at first sight, to be largely uninfluenced by the vagaries of the environment and to proceed at their own pace. But such a conclusion may not be justified. When we say that a loud noise causes a startle response or that an increase in the loudness of the noise causes an increase in the size of the response, it is possible to test these suggestions directly, for instance by omitting the noise and observing that the response fails to appear. No equivalent manipulations are possible when the passage of time is the "independent" variable. We cannot directly test the idea that aging in itself brings about developmental change.

What we can do is to examine the alternative hypothesis that is schematized in Fig. 4.6b. This shows the orderly succession of developmental stages A, B, C, and D, and it shows also a sequence of environmental events (P, Q, R, S) that, we are assuming, act upon the organism at various ages. The suggestion is that environmental event P causes behaviour A to appear, that Q causes B to appear, and so on. In other words, the alternative hypothesis is that developmental stages occur in their orderly sequence because they are produced by the occurrence of an orderly sequence of changes in the environment. Thus the changing pattern of vocalization shown by a baby (Table 4.1) could have its origin in the way in which the parents treat the baby, first "cooing" at it, then rewarding it for "dada" or whatever, and later encouraging it to fit words together. If this general hypothesis is at all true, the actual sequence of events is likely to be much more complex than that just outlined in that the baby's changing behaviour is certain to interact with and modify that of the parent. (This interaction is indicated by the broken arrows shown in Fig. 4.6b.) Here then is a question that can be investigated empirically: does the sequence of developmental change depend upon a parallel sequence of environmental changes? That is, can we modify the events symbolized as P, Q, etc. in the figure and show a corresponding reorganization of development?

## Modifying the Early Environment

On first inspection, such evidence as we have about the course of human development suggests that our answer to the questions posed above should be "no".

*Walking and talking.* Taking the case of motor development first, since the environmental events that might be thought to bring about such development are purely hypothetical up to this point, they cannot be manipulated in any very subtle way. But consider those children that have the misfortune to be put into a plaster cast at a very early age (a treatment sometimes used for children with congenital hip deformities). We can be fairly sure that such children are not subjected to the same sort of environmental events as normal children are. Nonetheless, when the cast is removed they appear to "know" how to walk at the stage appropriate to their age. Their muscles are weak and wasted, and so performance is initially poor, but these deficits are rapidly overcome so that their behaviour soon approximates to that of a normal child.

Much the same appears to be true of the development of speech and vocalization. Mention was made in Chapter 3 of studies of the vocalizations produced by babies born to deaf parents. These children experience an abnormal environment in that they do not hear normal speech and their own attempts are not reacted to in the same way as they would be if they had hearing parents. (It appears that deaf parents are often unable to tell from their baby's expression whether or not its mouthings are accompanied by noise.) Nevertheless, these children go through the same sequence of development (at least during the first few months of life) as children born to hearing parents. Even depriving a child of the ability to hear the sounds that he makes himself does not totally disrupt the course of development. This is not to say that hearing is not necessary for normal speech: a child who becomes deaf at the age of four of five will quickly lose the language capability that he possesses. However, a child who is born deaf develops normally up to a certain age, cooing at about three months, babbling at about six months and even producing speech sounds such as "dada" and so on (Lenneberg, 1967). Nor is practice necessary. Lenneberg reports the case history of a child who, because of a disease of the throat, needed to have a tube inserted in the wind-pipe below the larynx. The tube allowed the child to breathe but also allowed expired air to escape before it could activate the vocal cords. A day after the tube had been removed at the age of 14 months the child began to produce the babbling sounds typical of the age.

Evidence of this sort makes a point that was apparently self-evident to the ancients. Herodotus in the fifth century BC related the, no doubt apocryphal, story of a king of Egypt who arranged for children to be brought up by shepherds who were forbidden to speak to them. The intention was to see which language the children would develop; there was apparently no question of language failing to appear even in a linguistic environment as restricted as this. (We can safely ignore the conclusion of the story: that the children developed the ability to speak Greek, their first words being an appeal for bread!)

*Deprivation experiments.* In the examples given above, the children under study have, through misfortune, been deprived of some aspects of a normal environment. It is possible, using animal subjects, to do experiments (sometimes called *isolation* experiments) in which the animals are subjected to almost total deprivation receiving only food, water, and such attention as is necessary to sustain life. Experiments of this sort have produced some remarkable examples of deprived animals producing complex behaviour almost as readily as animals reared normally. Thus a chaffinch taken from the wild and reared in isolation from other birds will, when the appropriate season comes round, emit the normal chaffinch song. The elements of the song develop without apparently any special auditory experience. (But see below, p. 112.)

In an equivalent way some aspects of visually guided behaviour can in some species be shown to develop independently of what one might at first assume to be relevant visual experience. Figure 4.7 shows a piece of apparatus known as a *visual cliff*. It consists of a small central platform resting on top of a sheet of glass. On one side of the platform the glass rests directly on a solid floor but on the other side there is a sheer drop to a floor some distance away. An animal placed on the central platform will eventually move off onto the glass and, if it is capable of depth vision, it will usually move to the "shallow" side. (Birds that nest in trees present an exception here. A young mandarin duck, for example, will launch itself cheerfully toward the deep end with a little jump.) The point of interest here is that many species of animal will show appropriate behaviour on the visual cliff even when they have been deprived of visual experience. The technique is to keep the animal in the dark until it is old enough to move around

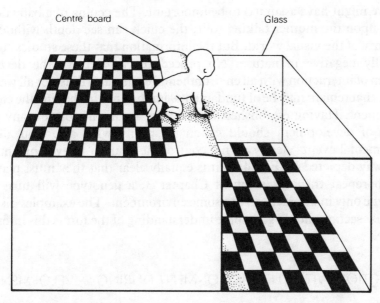

Centre board                                    Glass

Fig. 4.7. *The "visual cliff". The organism being tested is placed on the central platform, flanked by transparent sheets at different heights above the opaque floor. The side to which it steps off is noted.*

and thus be tested in the apparatus. In spite of this deprivation, rats, lambs, domestic chicks, and a variety of other animals have been found to perform well when first tested on the visual cliff.

If the primary intention of these experiments is taken to be that of removing the developing animal from the influence of external stimulation, then the most successful must surely be those carried out by Carmichael (1926) on the motor development of larval amphibians. The animals he studied show incipient swimming movements while they are still in the egg and these movements develop and strengthen both before and after hatching. It is difficult to see what environmental events could influence this behaviour but Carmichael removed any possibility of environmental effects by anaesthetizing the larvae from an early stage in their development. A more complete deprivation procedure is hard to imagine. When control (unanaesthetized) subjects had been swimming well for some time the experimental subjects were brought round. It was found that, as soon as the anaesthetic had worn off, these subjects could swim as well as the normal controls.

*Conclusions.* The question we set out to investigate was to what extent does the step by step progress of development depend upon a parallel sequence of environmental changes. Deprivation studies tell us that some patterns of behaviour are not the consequence of the environmental events that, at first sight, we might have assumed to be important. The cooing of a baby does not depend upon the mother talking to it; the chick can see depth without prior experience of the visual world. But the information that these studies supply is essentially negative in nature. No procedure can deprive the developing organism of interaction with all environmental events and thus, for all we know, the ones that remain may be of fundamental importance in shaping the course of development. Having established what events are *not* important, any proper analysis of development should go on to specify what are. And although environmental events clearly do not control the course of development in the simple way depicted by Fig. 4.6b it is equally clear that they must play some role. To repeat the conclusion of Chapter 3, a genotype will turn into a phenotype only in interaction with some environment. The examples discussed in the next section should give some understanding of the forms this interaction can take.

## INTERACTION WITH THE ENVIRONMENT DURING DEVELOPMENT

### Bird Song

We have said (p. 110) that a young male chaffinch caught in the autumn of its first year of life, long before it has started to sing, will, after being reared in isolation, produce a near-normal version of the appropriate song the following spring. A representation of the normal song of the adult male chaffinch is shown in the top panel of Fig. 4.8. In this fairly typical example the bird is emitting a string of three phrases lasting about two seconds in all, followed by a characteristic terminal flourish. That the isolated bird is capable of producing a complex utterance very like this is an intriguing observation but it is only the starting point for further analysis. It certainly does not allow us to conclude that the song of the chaffinch develops quite independently of environmental experience, as the work of Thorpe (1961) has shown.

Fig. 4.8. *Spectrograms of the song of the chaffinch. A dark patch indicates the presence of sound energy at a given frequency at a given time. (a) Normal song; (b) song produced by a bird hand-reared in isolation (after Thorpe, 1961).*

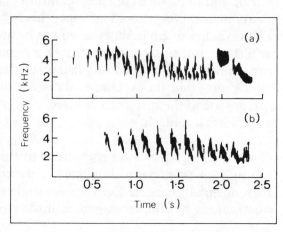

Although an isolated bird can come to develop normal song, there are circumstances in which it does not. If, rather than being taken from the wild, the young bird is bred in an aviary and hand-reared in isolation, it is observed to produce only the very inadequate version of the normal song depicted in Fig. 4.8b. The duration is about right, but only one phrase is present and there is no final flourish. Further, a young bird taken from the wild will not develop the normal song if it is surgically deafened. It may start to produce the rather rambling "sub-song" from which the proper song emerges in normal individuals, but further development and refinement does not occur. These observations suggest the following conclusions: that the isolated chaffinch will develop normal song only if it has been exposed to an example of normal song early in its life. Such exposure allows it to acquire a "template" to which it can match its own first efforts. And not only does the bird have to learn what to sing, it also needs to learn how to sing it; it needs to be able to hear its own output in order to modify it to match the template. (Note that deafening an older chaffinch that has already learned to sing does not eliminate its ability.) Thus the development of normal chaffinch song depends upon exposure to a very specific environmental event early in life and upon interaction with (self-produced) environmental events at a later stage. It cannot be interpreted as the automatic unfolding of some predetermined sequence.

## Specific and Non-specific Environmental Inputs

The example just cited is one in which a specific environmental input (the adult song experienced early in life) is necessary for normal development to occur. It might still be argued that, whatever is the case for chaffinch song, there remain a large number of demonstrations in which behaviour emerges without any such input. True, the environment must supply oxygen, food, and so on, but nothing more specific is required. To take the extreme case mentioned above (p. 111), Carmichael was able to show that even the anaesthetized larval amphibian was able to develop normal swimming movements. There may be some usefulness to the distinction being suggested here (between behaviour that requires a specific environmental input for its development and that which does not) but it is still possible to analyse the nature of the interaction with the environment that goes on even when the environment seems to contribute little. We will try to carry out such an analysis for one specific example—the development shown by the domestic chick. This example is particularly informative, for it shows two things clearly. First, it makes the point that a careful analysis can sometimes reveal a role for specific environmental events that have previously gone undetected. Second, it shows that isolating a developing organism from sources of external stimulation does not mean that quite specific sorts of stimulation play no role in determining development. Carmichael's isolation experiment was itself designed to make just this point.

He concluded about his larval amphibians that "the intricate development of such interrelated structures as receptors, nerve trunks, central apparatus and motor end-organs appears to be determined by functional stimulation within the organism itself" (Carmichael, 1926, p. 56). We shall see to what extent this is true of the development of the chick.

Development of the Domestic Chick

The domestic chick is precocial. Shortly after hatching it can stand and walk, and, as we have already observed, it will peck with rapidly improving accuracy at small specks of grit or of grain. It interacts with its mother from the start. When the mother hen finds food she emits a special food-call which attracts the chicks. She then pecks at, picks up, and drops small pieces of food which the chicks then tend to pick up and swallow (Hogan, 1973). The chicks also show an attachment to the mother, uttering a characteristic distress call when she is absent, moving towards her when she reappears, and following her quite closely when she moves about.

*Developmental stages.* Given the complexity of this behaviour it may seem that the chick is a poor subject in which to study the interaction of the developing animal with its environment. Most of the chick's most striking developmental

*Table 4.2.* Developmental stages in domestic chick (adapted from Kuo, 1967, with additions from Freeman and Vince, 1974).

| Stage | Approx age (days) | Posture and activities of embryo |
|---|---|---|
| I–IV | up to 4 | Lies on left side across yolk; first heartbeat; flexing of neck |
| V | 5–6 | Takes up characteristic crescent shape; head turning; regular flexing of trunk |
| VI | 6–9 | Movements of eyeballs, eyelids, and beak; movements now quick, jerking, and localized |
| VII | 10–14 | Wriggling and jerking movements continue. Chick begins to turn lengthwise and to sink into yolk which wraps around it |
| VIII | 15–18 | Respiratory movements begin; yolk sac shrinks |
| IX | 18–19 | Responses to sound and light; remains of yolk move to ventral surface between the legs |
| X | 19–20 | Coordinated movement; head becomes tucked under wing. Respiration begins |
| XI | 20–21 | Shell is cracked by upward pressure of beak; chick wriggles free |
| XII |  | Post-hatching behaviour |

changes appear to happen before hatching, making them difficult to observe. It might be argued further that environmental events can play little part in development since the chick develops inside a protective shell—development inside a shell can be seen as nature's own deprivation experiment. This second point will be taken up shortly. For the time being we will concentrate on describing the development that has been observed in chicks by the simple expedient of inserting a small window in the shell. Observations of this sort were pioneered by Kuo and a very condensed summary of his results (based on information provided by Kuo, 1967) is given as Table 4.2.

Once again the familiar system of division into stages is used. It will be seen that the chick embryo shows a surprisingly large amount of behaviour. Movements of the head are seen soon after it is formed, and throughout the first four or five days of life there is a regular sinusoidal flexing of the entire trunk. During the middle part of embryonic development, jerky localized movements of limbs, eyes, and beak predominate. As the time for hatching nears, complex coordinated movement is seen: the head moves out from under the yolk sac, the neck is twisted across the breast and the right side of the head is tucked under the wing in a complicated and characteristic double bend. From this position the chick can penetrate the air space that the egg contains and subsequently penetrate the shell. The early stages of post-hatching behaviour (Kuo's Stage XII) look like a simple continuation of the behaviour shown in the egg. During the first two or three hours after hatching the little bird continues to show wriggling movements, and when it attempts to use its legs it often takes rests with its legs in the same folded position that was required when the chick was encased in the egg. After four hours at most, the down has dried, normal locomotion is possible, and the chick starts to engage in the post-hatching activities described at the beginning of this section.

*Environmental influences on post-hatching behaviour.* The role played by environmental events in determining the behaviour patterns described above is not obvious but close inspection shows it to be important. Take, for instance, post-hatching behaviour. It might be supposed that the young chick tends to follow its mother "automatically" (in the same way as walking seems to appear "automatically" in 18-month-old children). But it has been known for about a hundred years now that the following behaviour of young birds depends upon a form of learning that has been called *imprinting*. Early in its post-hatching life, the chick learns the characteristics of the mother hen and forms an attachment which causes it to follow her and to shun other animals and moving objects. This can easily be demonstrated by removing the chick from its mother. In these circumstances the chick becomes imprinted upon any other largish, conspicuous, moving object that it experiences during the first day or so of life. The results may be incongruous: pictures of tiny chicks doggedly pursuing their "mother" in the form of a relatively enormous scientist are familiar enough and can still cause amusement.

*Environmental influences during the pre-hatching stage.* If an egg that is due to hatch shortly is held to the ear it may be possible to hear a clicking noise. Having tucked its head under its wing, the chick has penetrated the air space and begun to breathe and in doing so it produces clicks. Given that eggs are usually laid as clutches, the environment for any given chick includes the clicks emitted by the adjacent eggs. In some species (the domestic chick is probably not one) these clicks control the course of development. In the quail, for instance, eggs that have been laid over a considerable period of time often hatch at more or less the same time. It is difficult to see how such synchronization could be produced except by communication between the eggs in a clutch with one egg telling the others about its own stage of development, and urging the others to slow down or catch up. These effects can be demonstrated experimentally. If a relatively immature egg is placed in contact with other more advanced eggs it is found to hatch sooner than it normally would; an advanced egg put next to several immature eggs may hatch rather later than expected.

Vince (1969) has investigated these phenomena in detail and has shown that the clicks are the critical stimuli. She has artificially stimulated eggs presenting clicks at the rate of about three per second and has produced an acceleration of development. Artificial clicks presented at slower or much faster rates seem to be capable of retarding development.

This sophisticated system for synchronization may be convenient for the mother bird and, although the overall advantages presumably outweigh the disadvantages, in extreme circumstances it has unfortunate consequences for the young birds themselves. Some chicks when they hatch prove incapable of walking properly. Their legs may collapse under their weight so that they are forced to walk not on their toes but on their folded-up legs. Other birds suffer from having their toes curled up and bunched together and are incapable of putting their feet flat on the ground. The first problem can arise because the chick's development has been speeded up. It escapes from the shell at the same time as its more advanced siblings but its legs simply are not strong enough to take its weight. The second problem can arise when hatching has been held back. The chick has lain quiet inside the shell for some time but it does not stop growing. Its feet become curled up and twisted out of shape by the constriction of the shell and the consequences are more or less permanent.

The conclusion to draw from this example is that the seemingly automatic course of development can be modified by environmental events, although we must often look very carefully to discover what they are. Furthermore, relatively trivial environmental events can have profound and long-term effect on later behaviour. (The rate of presentation of some barely audible clicks can modify all the subsequent motor behaviour that a bird shows.)

*Factors influencing stage-by-stage development in the egg.* **Although the transition from pre-hatching to hatching (Kuo's Stages XI and XII) can be brought about by external events, there do not seem to be equivalent events controlling the earlier stages of development. The embryo of an egg isolated in the perfectly constant environment of an incubator will show all these stages. Developmental change depends not so much on changes in the external world but on changes in the environment that the chick supplies for itself by way of the constant stream of behaviour that it emits (Table 4.2).**

Convincing evidence, at a rather gross level, that this pre-hatching activity plays some role in the development of behaviour comes from experiments that attempt to eliminate it. Chick embryos infused with *curare* (a substance that produces paralysis) early in development prove unable to move even when the effects of the drug have worn off. This is not because nerves or muscles fail to develop but because the chicks become ossified—their joints become fixed and rigid with adhesions forming between adjacent surfaces. We can conclude that, at the very least, the high level of activity shown by the chick embryo serves the important function of preventing the young animal from becoming ossified in the fetal position. Something of the sort seems to hold for human development. Like the chick, the human embryo shows a good deal of spontaneous movement. Activity begins to appear in the 10-week fetus (which is no more than 5 cm long) and develops over the next two months into vigorous jerking and thrusting interspersed with slower "squirming" movements. It has been suggested that these movements are as important for normal neuromuscular development in the human fetus as are their equivalents in the chick. Pregnant mothers who have effectively anaesthetized their babies by taking large amounts of alcohol have provided us with a version of the deprivation procedure that was carried out experimentally on the chick, and the impoverished range of limb movements that their newborn babies show points to essentially the same conclusion (Hofer, 1981).

A more detailed analysis of the role played by embryonic activity in the development of the chick has been supplied by Kuo (1967) largely on the basis of observational data. Consider, for instance, the movements of the eyes and beak that are characteristic of Stage VI. Kuo points out that the transition to this stage can be seen as a direct result of the changes that have gone on in previous stages. As the chick grows, its legs curl over and make contact with the face. The eye and beak movements are a response to the stimulation that the chick thus provides itself, and they arise in a straightforward way as a result of growth occurring in a restricted space. Similarly, the proper development of the legs themselves (and consequently of many subsequent motor patterns) depends upon relatively simple mechanical factors. When the yolk sac moves during the course of development to the ventral side of the embryo, it moves to a position where it can press on the limbs and mould them into a shape that will be suitable for sitting, standing, and walking. Kuo has examined many cases of chicks crippled with leg and foot deformities and in the large majority of these he has found that the trouble arises because the yolk sac has stuck to the shell and failed to move into the appropriate position.

## Conclusions

These and other examples provided by Kuo show that the changes occurring in one stage of development can bring about as a necessary consequence (often for simple mechanical reasons) the behaviour seen in later stages. They imply that development should not be viewed as the automatic unfolding of some predetermined scheme. Rather, in Kuo's own words:

> the ontogenesis of behavior is a continuous stream of activities whose patterns . . . are modified in response to changes in the effective stimulation by the environment . . . both patterns of behaviour and patterns of the environment affect each other . . . changes in the environmental patterns produce changes in behavior patterns which in turn modify the patterns of environment.
>
> (Kuo, 1976, pp. 11–12)

This analysis may help to dispel some of the mystery that often seems to surround the process of behavioural development. The seemingly mysterious thing about developmental change is the way in which the organism seems to "know" what behaviour is appropriate to each stage and to move from one stage to the next without information being supplied from the environment. Closer inspection reveals that previously unsuspected environmental events may play a role. It also shows that the developing organism may create its own environment—that stage-by-stage change occurs because the things that happen in one stage provide the conditions that bring about the next stage. Analysing development in this way makes it apparent how futile must be any attempt to distinguish rigidly between the contributions made by heredity and by the environment to the behaviour of any single individual creature. It may thus give some reality to the statement so often repeated in Chapter 3 that an organism must be viewed as the outcome of an interaction between genotype and environment.

## EARLY EXPERIENCE AND LATER BEHAVIOUR

### The Possible "Special" Effects of Early Experience

Although the way in which the environment guides the course of development is still a matter for investigation and debate, it has long been accepted that events occurring early in life may have a profound effect on the behaviour shown in adulthood even when they seem to be of little consequence at the time of their occurrence. This idea, popularized by Freud, was given scientific respectability by the influential work of Hebb (1949) and it has become common to hear phrases like "the formative years of infancy" or the "critical years between birth and five". Before considering the theoretical background to views like these it will be as well to sample some of the empirical evidence from which they derive. We will consider just three areas: the effects of early experience on perceptual abilities, on personality, and on intelligence. It should be emphasized at this stage that the examples given below are just that: they are examples of the sort of work that has been done to show that early experience may have effects on these aspects of adult behaviour. The topic of early experience has provoked such a vast body of research that it would be impossible to review thoroughly in this chapter even these three areas. Nonetheless, it may still be possible to derive some general conclusions about the mechanisms by which early experience has its effects.

### Effects on Perceptual Abilities

We may begin with an intriguing and deceptively simple question: if a child blind from birth were to have his sight bestowed in adulthood would he be able to see? And if he could not see normally would he come to be able to do so as a result of experience? If the answer to these questions turns out to be "no", this would be a first indication that early (visual) experience has effects that cannot be replicated by later experience.

*Deprivation studies.* There are a few cases of individuals who, having been blind from early life, have had their sight bestowed in adulthood after a surgical operation for the removal of cataracts. One of these has been studied in detail by the psychologists Gregory and Wallace (1963). Their report, although theoretically interesting, makes sad reading. The patient who they describe as an "active and intelligent" man underwent a corneal graft at the age of 52. The initial results of the operation were satisfactory. The patient could certainly "see" in some sense: he could recognize upper-case letters of the alphabet, letters that he had learned by touch when a child, and he expressed surprise at the crescent shape of a quarter moon having expected it to look like a slice of pie. But it proved difficult to assess with any certainty just how well he could see. One technique was to ask him to supply drawings of objects that he could not have experienced by touch. The drawings that he produced of a double-decker bus (Fig. 4.9) were not good, but as Gregory and Wallace point out, it is difficult to know to what extent his poor performance was a result of a visual deficit as opposed to lack of a motor skill. More important was the fact that the seemingly successful operation produced profound emotional problems. Essentially, the patient seemed to be disappointed with his new-found visual world. After an initial period of elation and experimentation he reverted to his old ways, tending to deal with his environment using the sense of touch and choosing, for instance, to sit in the dark rather than turn on the light. These problems may represent nothing other than an understandable reaction for a middle-aged man who has undergone a major change that has upset the established habits of decades. Alternatively they may be taken to mean that visual capacities must be present early in life if they are to be developed and used normally. It is impossible to tell.

Fig. 4.9. *The first attempt at drawing a bus made by an adult patient 48 days after he had had his sight restored by means of a corneal graft operation (from Gregory, 1966).*

Similar difficulties plague the interpretation of analogous experiments carried out with animal subjects. Riesen (1947) reports an early study of the effects of total visual deprivation on a chimpanzee. The unfortunate animal was raised in darkness for the first 16 months of its life. When first brought into the light the animal showed the response of constricting its pupil but that was all. In other respects it appeared to be insensitive to visual stimulation: it showed, for instance, no tendency to blink when an object was moved quickly towards its face. One wonders, however, to what extent the animal's unresponsiveness was a product of a state of fear that the barrage of new stimulation must have induced.

*Partial deprivation and enrichment.* Perhaps more satisfactory are those experimental studies in which the early deprivation has been only partial. The experiment by Muir and Mitchell (1973) has already been described in Chapter 3. To recapitulate, it showed that kittens given early visual experience only of stripes of a given orientation showed better acuity for this orientation than for others. This procedure has two advantages. First, the animals were allowed some visual experience and this is enough to prevent the degeneration of parts of the visual system that is known to occur in some species when animals are raised in total darkness. It should also attenuate the emotional upheaval that must occur when animals are transferred from darkness to a lit testing environment. Second, any deficit in visual acuity could not, with these procedures, easily be ascribed to an emotional upset since such an effect would probably be general and not specific to one set of orientations rather than another.

Studies of partial deprivation can be seen as lying midway on a continuum running between total deprivation and experiments in which the deprivation is so slight as hardly to deserve the name. In these last, one set of experimental subjects can be regarded as "deprived" only in that they are not given some special experience bestowed upon others; the experimental treatment is best thought of as one supplying enriched experience for some of the subjects. An example is found in the work of Gibson and Walk (1956; see also Hall, 1980) who raised laboratory rats from birth in an environment which was enriched to the extent that geometrical figures were present: black, cut-out triangles and circles were suspended against the walls of their cages. Rats in a control condition were raised in standard laboratory cages. When they had grown up, all the subjects were required to learn a discrimination task in which they received food reward for choosing correctly between alternatives distinguished by the triangle and the circle. The rats raised in the normal way found this task very difficult and few of them learned it. Those raised in the presence of the stimuli, on the other hand, learned the discrimination readily. This result has been interpreted as showing that exposure to geometrical patterns early in life is necessary if they are to be perceived properly in adulthood.

## Effects on Personality

Perhaps because of the influence of Freud's ideas about infant sexuality, the notion that early experience may determine adult personality has been widely considered.

*Attachment.* Particularly influential has been the work of Bowlby (e.g. 1965, 1971), a man with a background in psychoanalysis who has also been influenced by studies of animal behaviour. The phenomenon of imprinting, whereby a young animal forms an attachment to its mother, is seen most dramatically in precocial birds, but, Bowlby urges, effects of the same general sort can also be seen in the human species. He has described the way in which infants form an attachment to an adult (usually their mothers) and the tragic consequences that ensue when a child of two to three years is separated from its mother: the initial phase of "protest" followed by "despair" and finally by "detachment" in which the child shows less obvious distress but seems no longer to care for anyone or anything. A child separated from its mother and raised in an institution may move out of its state of detachment to form attachments to substitute mother-figures, but if these are lost (the staff in the institution changes or the child is moved from one place to another) the child will become increasingly less likely to commit himself to anyone. Instead he becomes increasingly self-centred and preoccupied by material things such as sweets and toys. It is perhaps no surprise to learn that when such children grow up they are often only poorly integrated into society and suffer better than average chances of undergoing some sort of mental breakdown or of turning to a life of crime.

A famous set of experimental studies on rhesus monkeys by Harlow (e.g. 1958, 1962) helps to establish the generality of Bowlby's findings. Newborn rhesus monkeys were separated from their mothers and reared in laboratory cages (in some cases by surrogate mothers—constructions of wire or wire and cloth, see Fig. 4.10—equipped with bottles supplying milk). The infants formed an attachment to the surrogates when these were supplied, but this was not sufficient to protect them from the effects of social isolation. Monkeys raised in this way for six months turned out to be entirely passive when introduced to other animals and continued to be unable to adjust. They showed no tendency to play with their peers, a tendency toward self-aggression, and no sexual behaviour. In spite of this last point, it proved possible by the use of some ingenuity (and some sexually experienced males) to impregnate socially deprived females. As mothers these females treated their own offspring as their "mothers" had treated them, that is, they were totally unresponsive and

Fig. 4.10. *An infant rhesus monkey with two of the surrogate mothers used by Harlow (e.g. 1962; after Hinde, 1974).*

refused to feed the babies or to allow them to cling to their bellies in normal monkey-fashion. It proved necessary to remove the babies from their mothers in order to ensure their survival. In spite of the far-reaching differences between this work and that of Bowlby it is clear that maltreating a monkey in infancy will produce a severely disturbed adult just as will similar maltreatment of a human infant.

The severity of the deprivation suffered by the infant monkeys in these experiments makes direct comparison with the effects of "institutionalization" on human children a perilous business. There is, however, some evidence that milder treatment is not without effect. In one study, directly inspired by Bowlby's ideas, rhesus infants were reared by several mothers being moved from one to another every two weeks. These animals did not show the gross behavioural disturbances seen in those suffering total isolation. They were not, however, completely normal. Interestingly, they tended to be more aggressive than monkeys reared by a single mother and in adulthood they tended to rank higher in the order of social dominance than did normal animals. Another series of experiments (by Hinde and his collaborators; Hinde, 1974) has shown that there are long-term effects even of removing a rhesus mother from her six-month-old baby for just a few days (the mother-goes-to-the-hospital experiment). The baby's distress, shown chiefly by its low level of activity (it tends simply to sit in a hunched-up and very human posture), soon disappears when the mother returns. But, even if the rest of development proceeds normally, infants given this treatment still show its signs when they are more than two years of age, being much more disturbed by novel events and strange environments than their fellows who were reared normally.

*Stimulation.* The effects of early experience on personality are not limited to cases in which there is "maternal deprivation". Remaining with experimental work carried out on non-human animals we may consider as an example the effects of stimulation early in infancy on the "emotionality" of rats and mice. Individuals of these species show few differences in their behaviour that we would want to describe as being due to differences in "personality"; however, the different levels of emotionality (or nervousness) as measured by the open-field test (Chapter 3) shown by various individuals might well be regarded in this way. We have already discussed the fact that the emotionality of a given mouse will depend upon the strain from which it is derived. But this does not mean that its level of emotionality is fixed. A mouse pup that is stimulated in infancy (for instance, by being handled for a minute or so each day over the first few days of life) is usually transformed into a more stolid and placid creature even when its original tendency to be emotional is high. The origins of this effect are rather more obscure than those just described. It comes as no surprise to find that a child brought up in unusual social circumstances should have difficulty in adapting to the requirements of normal social life when it grows up. But it is difficult to see any direct connection between the handling experienced by a bald, blind, and helpless mouse pup and the mouse's behaviour as an adult in the open field. The conclusion that has been drawn by some workers in this area is that the detailed nature of the events that the young animal experiences may be of little importance and that activity of almost any sort in the sensory systems of the animal will modify its nervous and hormonal development and thus its emotional make-up. Having said this, it must be admitted that there are some observations showing that stimulation in infancy may affect the behaviour of the mouse mother (she tends to fuss over the handled pup when it is returned to her). To the extent that this change in her maternal behaviour is responsible for the altered later behaviour of the pup, we will have to allow that the effects of stimulation may themselves be simply a further example of the importance of mother–young interaction in determining adult personality.

## Effects on Intelligence

The role that early experience plays in the development of adult intelligence has been the subject of prolonged and vigorous debate. There is no doubt that people brought up in "deprived" circumstances tend on the whole to do less well on IQ tests than their better-off peers, but it is difficult to pin down the source of this difference. It could, in theory, arise from genetic differences between the two sets of people. Alternatively (or additionally) it could be produced by fairly straightforward environmental differences between the two groups—such differences would be implicated if it were found, for instance, that those who do well on the test had received special coaching on how to do IQ tests when their less well-off colleagues had not. But in spite of these confounding factors, the belief that intellectual differences have their origins, at least in part, in differing very early experience, is firmly established.

*Deprivation.* Studies of the intellectual attainments of institutionalized children provide grounds for this belief. Dennis (e.g. 1973) has carried out extensive investigation of infants and children raised in orphanages in Iran and in the Lebanon, investigations that are of special interest in part because of the severity of the deprivation the orphans suffered—even in the best cases the institutions were understaffed, the children received little or no personal attention, had no access to toys, and no opportunities for play. Testing children who had lived in the Lebanese orphanage from shortly after birth to the age of six years revealed a mean IQ not much higher than 50, a tragically low score given that we might expect a normal population to yield a mean of around 100. A problem of interpretation, of course, arises from the possibility that the children of the orphanage do not represent a sample of the normal population; that for some reason children who would be mentally retarded even if raised by their families are more likely than other children to find their way into orphanages. A second reason why the Lebanese study is of special interest is that it allows investigation of this possibility. Adoption was legalized in the Lebanon only in 1956, having been forbidden before then. It thus became possible to study the intellectual development of children who were taken away from the orphanage early in life into adoptive homes. These children quickly overcame their initial retardation and reached a mean IQ of about 100. Dennis suggests that if these children had remained in the orphanage as their predecessors had done they too would have ended up with very low as opposed to normal IQs.

*Enrichment and compensatory education.* Turning now from studies of the effects of deprivation to the effects of enrichment, a wealth of information becomes available. The belief that early experience determines later intellectual ability received its most widely publicized expression in the form of the many programmes of compensatory education (such as the federally funded Head Start programme) set up in the USA during the 1960s. One aim of these programmes was to enable the disadvantaged child to take part in and benefit from normal schooling and their method therefore was to get to the child very early in life, well before the normal school age. But there were also theoretical as well as practical reasons for using the technique of pre-school intervention, as it came to be called: many of the instigators of these programmes were explicit in their assertion that there was some critical period in infancy during which appropriate experience must be supplied if it was to be of benefit to intellectual development. Thus Bloom (1964), whose work was very influential in initiating programmes of compensatory education, argued that all later learning will be influenced by the very basic learning that goes on before the age of five years and "compensation" provided after this age will come too late.

These programmes have now largely been abandoned. There were financial and political reasons for their being run down but it is also true that their results were very disappointing. Least successful were those programmes in which the child from the poor home was simply enrolled in a nursery school, allowed to play with new toys and other children, taken on trips to the zoo and so on and generally given access to the "rich diet of experience" that their better-off contemporaries receive almost as a right. Somewhat more successful were those that explicitly set about teaching the children some of the skills (particularly linguistic skills) that would be useful to them later in life. Children exposed to this treatment have been found to show sizeable increases in measured IQ when compared with equivalent children who received no special compensatory education. But even here the gains have proved to be only temporary. After a year or so a decline begins to set in and by the time the special programme has ended and the children have experienced a year of normal schooling they have been found to differ not at all in IQ from their contemporaries.

It is difficult to reach a firm theoretical conclusion on the basis of these observations. One possibility (to be discussed in more detail at the end of this chapter) is that we were mistaken in assuming that early experience is particularly important in determining intellectual development. But a second, that cannot be dismissed, is that these programmes might have failed not because early experience is not important but because the programmes did not hit upon that aspect of early experience that is particularly important. It is even possible that some of the programmes did provide the right sort of experience but for practical reasons were not able to supply enought of it. One of the more successful schemes (the Early Training Project of Gray and Klaus, 1970) produced no very marked long-term beneficial effects. But, as the organizers of the scheme point out, the children spent no more than 2% of their waking hours during their pre-school years actively engaged in the project.

*Enrichment for non-human animals.* Experimental studies using non-human animals have been able to investigate the effects of prolonged exposure to special environments early in life (although, as we shall see, here too difficulties in interpretation arise). The most widely used procedure has compared the

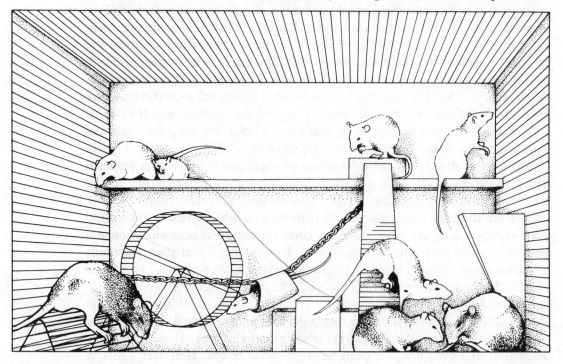

Fig. 4.11. *An example of an "enriched" environment for rats. (Based on that described by Rosenzweig et al., 1972.)*

effects on rats of rearing them in "restricted" or "enriched" early environments. The restricted environment is easy to arrange: it has usually consisted
simply of a standard laboratory cage containing nothing more than a food
container, a water bottle, and (unless the experimenter is also interested in the
effects of social isolation) some other rats of like age. Different experimenters
have devised various sorts of enriched environments but in general the
procedure adopted has been that of giving the young rats toys to play with:
blocks of wood to chew at or stand on, ladders to climb up, tunnels to go under,
and so on (Fig. 4.11).

One dramatic consequence of the sort of environment in which a young rat is
raised is that small but reliable differences in brain development are found. Rats
raised in enriched environments tend to have bigger brains than do their
restricted counterparts; in particular, the part of the brain thought to be
concerned with processing visual information (the occipital cortex—see
Chapter 5) is enlarged and there is some evidence to suggest that this represents
not just a gross increase in size but the development of more complex
connections between nerve cells (Rosenzweig *et al.*, 1972). Such a finding is
certainly compatible with the suggestion that an enriched early environment
helps to produce a clever animal but it is by no means conclusive: the
opportunity for exercise in a complex environment could well produce changes
in the brain that are quite unconnected with the general intelligence of the
animal. If it is to be shown that these changes in the brain are something to do
with intelligence than there is no substitute for a direct (that is, a behavioural)
test of intelligence.

The problems involved in assessing the intelligence of non-human animals
have been touched on in Chapter 2 where it was argued that an appropriate test
might be one in which the animal is made to learn some task that requires it to
show flexibility in its behaviour according to changing circumstances. A task of
this sort devised by Hebb (it was again the influence of Hebb that provoked
experimental work into the effects of an enriched early environment) has been
widely used. In this task (the Hebb–Williams maze, see Fig. 4.12) the hungry
rat learns to run from a startbox to a goalbox where food is available, twisting
and turning through a series of alleys some of which constitute the most direct
path and some of which involve detours. From time to time the layout of the
alleys is changed, although the general direction in which the animal must move
remains the same. Using this maze, therefore, it is possible to assess not only
how quickly it is learned initially but also the extent to which subjects can adapt
their learned pattern of behaviour to changes in the task. It has been found that
rats raised in an enriched environment tend to score more highly in the Hebb–
Williams maze than do their restricted counterparts. The interpretation of this
finding is also open to dispute—it could be argued, for instance that the good
performance of the enriched subjects reflects not their enhanced intelligence

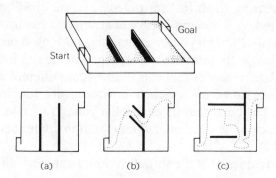

Fig. 4.12. *The intelligence test devised by Hebb and Williams (1946). The top figure gives a general view of the maze, and (a) a plan view. (b) and (c) show how the barriers can be rearranged so that the rat is required to modify its route from start to goal. The route shown at (b) would receive a high score, that at (c) a low score since it includes a number of unnecessary deviations from the appropriate general direction.*

but simply the fact that they are less disturbed by complex and novel environments than are restricted subjects. It can serve, nonetheless, as a convenient example of the sort of experimental study that has been used to implicate early experience in the development of intelligence.

### The Nature of Early-experience Effects

The effects we have been considering can be regarded as examples of the process of learning when this process is defined in the widest possible way: subjects undergo some experience and as a result their behaviour is changed when it is subsequently tested. But we should say at once that it seems to be learning of a very special sort, or at least of a type rather different from that process by which we learn to ride a bicycle or recite a poem. Many workers have tried to isolate what they take to be the characteristic features of early-experience effects, the features that distinguish them from more orthodox examples of learning. We can distinguish four such features.

First there is often a striking delay between the animal's early experience and the resulting modification of behaviour. This point has often been made with reference to the phenomenon of imprinting where it has been found that a young bird imprinted upon by an unusual object (such as an adult of some other species) shows no ill-effects until it reaches maturity at which time it begins to show inappropriate sexual behaviour, directing its courtship display toward individuals of the wrong species. Imprinting has also been said to illustrate a second distinctive feature of early experience in that it sometimes appears to be irreversible—a young bird exposed to an inappropriate object early in life appears to be stuck with the consequences of the imprinting that then occurs, and subsequent exposure to its own mother will not reverse these effects. Such irreversibility may be the product of a third feature that is said to be characteristic of early learning. This is the suggestion that there may be *critical periods* (or sometimes *sensitive periods*) during which the organism is open to environmental influence and outside which the same environmental change will be ineffective. And finally it has been argued that early experience tends to be much more general in its effects than later experience. Thus an adult animal may learn something about the other creatures it comes into contact with but such learning will not have the wide-ranging effects that exposure to another animal early in life has been shown to produce.

That early experience possesses these special characteristics has been most vigorously argued for the case of imprinting in birds (in particular by Lorenz, 1937) but they may not be restricted to this example. Thus, handling effects are not evident at the time the handling is given. They show up only in adulthood and do so not by their effects on any one simple behaviour pattern but more generally as a change in the animal's level of emotionality. Harlow's early work suggested that his monkeys had suffered permanent psychological damage as a result of their social isolation in infancy; and recent work on the visual development of kittens has implicated the first few weeks of life as being a sensitive period in which perceptual learning occurs.

One interpretation of this syndrome of special characteristics attributes them all to a single basic source. It suggests that early experience has the effects it does because it happens at a stage in life when development and maturation (particularly of the nervous system) are occurring. It is therefore able to influence the course of development, producing permanent and widespread changes, in a way that later experience cannot. It may be useful to draw an analogy with a computer. It is possible to modify the behaviour of a computer throughout its "adult life" by making changes to the way it is programmed or by altering the sort of information that is fed into it. "Experience" of this kind will produce fairly specific changes in what the machine does and changes that can be reversed by reprogramming. Contrast these effects with those that could be produced by intervening early in the machine's life when it is being designed and built. Such intervention during the sensitive period could result in a permanent and basic change in the actual structure of the machine having widespread effects on all aspects of its subsequent performance.

The analogy is a crude one and is no doubt inappropriate in many respects but it has a certain plausibility. And there is no doubt that the general view of early experience that it embodies has been widely influential. Nonetheless, there is a sizeable number of workers in this field who reject this interpretation of the mechanism by which early experience has its effects and we should consider their views next.

## An Alternative Interpretation for the Effects of Early Experience

The need for an alternative interpretation of the effects of early experience has its origins in both empirical and theoretical observations, suggesting that its special effects are not so special as all that. Thus, although early experience can have effects that are not evident until much later in life, this is scarcely a unique feature; it is not difficult for most of us to think of examples of things that we have learned as adults that have lain dormant, seemingly forgotten, until the relevant circumstances turn up many years later. Similarly, effects of great generality can be produced by adult experience just as by early experience. (Consider, for instance, the far-reaching effects that a religious conversion is capable of producing in the personality and whole way of life of an individual.)

*Irreversibility.* The notion that the effects of early experience may be irreversible has been the subject of much research in recent years since, for human infants who have suffered maltreatment, the matter is of urgent practical importance for those who want to provide some sort of therapy. This work has been reviewed by Clarke and Clarke (1976) who conclude that where evidence has been sought, recovery from the effects of early social deprivation has been found. They cite a number of case studies of children who, having suffered very greatly early in life (in one of these a little girl was kept confined in a dark room in company with her deaf-mute mother from birth until the age of about six years when she was discovered by the authorities), showed remarkable powers of recovery when given care and attention. Case-histories of this sort are always difficult to interpret since, however great the degree of recovery that the child shows, there is always room for the possibility that some deficit still remains. But support comes from controlled experimental studies of the effects of deprivation on monkeys. More recent work by Harlow and his colleagues has shown that even monkeys raised in total social isolation for the first year of life can learn to be social when they are subsequently presented with the appropriate conditions. Of these the opportunity to interact with their peers and with younger monkeys turns out to be particularly beneficial.

*Sensitive periods.* Turning to the idea that there may be some special period early in life when the organism is particularly sensitive to certain kinds of environmental influence, the first point to make is that often the observations necessary to establish the existence of such a period have simply not been made. That is, although there are often many studies showing that early experience can produce a given effect, there may be none to establish that this effect is confined to *early* experience, to show that the same experience given to an adult does not produce a similar effect. Where such studies have been done their results have not been encouraging for the traditional view. It was mentioned above that infant rats given exposure in their home cages to geometrical shapes are better able to discriminate between these shapes in adulthood. But recent research has shown that this exposure treatment can be just as beneficial when fully adult rats are the subjects. Hall (1979) gave rats that were 120 days of age (and rats are mature adults at 90 days) exposure in their home cages to triangles and circles for a period of 40 days. The subsequent discrimination performance of these animals is shown in Fig. 4.13. It clearly was much better than that shown by subjects not previously exposed to the shapes and indeed was closely similar to that shown by rats that had received exposure during infancy. Again, although experimental studies of the effects of stimulation on emotionality have usually been carried out with infant animals as the subjects, there is now evidence to suggest that similar effects can be found with adult subjects too. Inglis (1975) compared adult rats kept in standard laboratory cages with other adults given a heavy dose of extra sensory experience. These latter had cages equipped with toys and also received extra visual and auditory stimulation (noises were sounded, lights flashed, and so on). After five weeks of this treatment the rats' behaviour was observed in a novel environment. It was found that those reared in normal conditions showed less exploratory activity than the rats given the extra stimulation.

This is not to say that there may not sometimes be critical or sensitive periods for certain sorts of learning but these are perhaps just as likely to be found in the learning of adults as of infants. A female goat learns to accept her newborn kid in the period immediately after birth in the course of licking and cleaning it. If

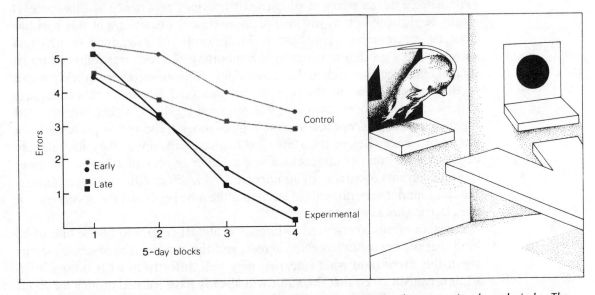

Fig. 4.13. *Performance of four groups of rats in learning a discrimination between triangle and circle. The apparatus used (inset) requires the rat to jump across a gap and push aside the door bearing the positive stimulus in order to gain access to a goal box containing food. The door bearing the negative stimulus is locked. The experimental subjects that had received prior exposure to the stimuli learned more readily than control subjects, but whether the exposure was given early in life or later made no difference (adapted from Hall, 1979).*

the kid is taken away and returned after only an hour the mother will reject it, suggesting that an important form of learning must occur during the critical one-hour period or it will not occur at all.

## Conclusions

It is very difficult, evidently, to establish clear-cut criteria by which we may distinguish the effects of early experience from those of later experience. The obvious conclusion, therefore, is that early experience is not in fact "special" and that events experienced early in life have their effects by way of the same general mechanisms as those that underlie the modification of behaviour in the adult.

What remains possible, however, (even if we accept this conclusion) is that early experience may have special effects simply by virtue of the fact that it comes first. Consider the case of an adult who in the course of his very first driving lesson loses control of the car and crashes at speed. We can imagine that this experience might produce some fairly generalized effects that would be difficult to reverse. And we might also guess that if a well-practised driver underwent a similar experience his reaction would not be so marked. The accident, when occurring as an early experience (early in this particular context), might result in a man who refuses ever to go near a car again; the later experience (later in terms of the driver's previous experience of this context) might be shrugged off as just one of those things. Something of this sort has been demonstrated experimentally. Mackintosh (1973) trained (adult) rats according to a procedure whereby the sounding of a tone was followed by an unavoidable electric shock to the animals' feet. The subjects very quickly began to show signs of fear in the presence of the tone. For these rats their first experience of the tone was that it was followed by shock. Other rats received identical training except that for them tone–shock training was presented as a later experience. Before the start of this phase of training they had already experienced a number of shocks and a number of presentations of the tone, these two events occurring in an uncorrelated fashion. After this pretraining, the rats found it very difficult to learn that the tone predicted the occurrence of the electric shock.

Now, an event experienced in infancy is almost certain to be the first of its kind that the organism has come across, and the way that the organism learns about this event (and what it learns) may well differ from what occurs in an adult organism given that the adult will already have learned quite a lot about similar events. But the special effects produced by such early learning will appear not because of some special mechanism that operates only early in life but simply because the normal mechanisms of learning that endow novel experiences with special importance will operate in infancy just as they do in adulthood.

It is thus possible to allow that early experience may have profound effects on adult behaviour without having to assume that it does so by diverting the normal course of development. Indeed such a view was only ever tenable so long as it was thought that "development" was something that went on only early in life. But it was argued in the introduction to this chapter that the process of development is a continuous complex interaction between the developing organism and its environment, a process that goes on from conception to death. If we wish to speak of environmental events influencing the course of development then we may do so but we should apply this characterization just as readily to the processes by which an adult learns as to those that operate in the young.

## SOURCES AND FURTHER READING

*Biological Foundations of Language* by Lenneberg (1967) provides a comprehensive account of motor and linguistic development and although rather advanced can be read along with any of the many introductory texts that outline human behavioural development. For an account of experimental studies of the behaviour of babies and young children see Bower's (1974) *Development in Infancy*. Perhaps the best way to approach Piaget's work is by way of one of his interpreters: the book by Flavell (1963) may be suitable. The most accessible of Piaget's own works is probably *The Psychology of the Child* (Piaget and Inhelder, 1969). It is also important to consider the views of Piaget's critics: Bryant's (1974) book *Perception and Understanding in Young Children* gives a very clear account of the way in which the issues raised by Piaget can be investigated by means of rigorous and well-controlled experiments. The account of the development of the domestic chick given above is based largely on the work of Kuo whose book *The Dynamics of Behavior Development* (1967) outlines his own very personal but fascinating approach to the whole topic of development. For a description of the intra-uterine development of the human fetus see Hofer (1981). The topic of early experience has been much written about. *Maternal Deprivation Reassessed* (Rutter, 1972) and *Early Experience: Myth and Evidence* (edited by Clarke and Clarke, 1976) discuss studies of human infants. A wider-ranging approach is provided by Sluckin's (1970) *Early Learning in Man and Animal*.

# 5    Structure and Function

## INTRODUCTION

The investigation of phylogeny and of individual development helps us to understand how the individual organism comes to be what it is. But it would be possible to undertake the study of psychology without any such background knowledge: we could simply take the adult individual as our subject-matter and try to find out why it behaves in the way that it does. The psychologist would then have a task something like that faced by an engineer presented with a quite novel and exceedingly complex machine and required to find out how it works. Without an instruction manual (and indeed without any very good idea of what was in the mind of the original designer) the engineer would no doubt start simply by turning the knobs and pressing the buttons while carefully observing the way in which the machine responded. He would probably also soon want to take the machine apart, or at least to take off the lid and look inside in the hope of identifying familiar components and of deducing something about its functioning from the way in which the various parts were put together.

In this chapter and in succeeding chapters we will be treating the behaving organism as being the equivalent of an unknown, complex machine. Our methods too will be roughly analogous to those used by the engineer. This chapter will outline the information that has been gained from "looking inside", from studying the general structure of the system and the way in which its components work and are put together. It should be admitted at the outset that an investigation of this sort will not be able to give us all the information we want about how the system works. Imagine an engineer faced for the first time with a modern electronic digital computer. His investigation of its circuit-boards and wiring, no matter how diligently it is carried out, is unlikely to tell him that the machine when subjected to a certain sort of input will respond by printing out an address list, say, or by carrying out a certain sort of calculation. But whatever its shortcomings, the result of his investigations would not be totally misleading, and although incomplete it could still be valuable. We may approach our study of the structure of the "psychological machine" in the same spirit—willing to extract what clues we can, but prepared for the fact that other methods of investigation will be required if we are to see the whole picture.

These other methods, studies of the way in which the whole organism reacts to manipulations of its environment, form the subject matter for Chapters 6 and 7; but we need to preview the broad conclusions they lead to straight away. Before plunging into any detailed description of the vertebrate nervous system we need to stand back and try to enumerate the basic characteristics of the system under investigation (or such of those characteristics as have caught the attention of psychologists).

First, the vertebrate organism is a system that is constantly doing things. Even in sleep, movements are occurring, and during its waking life there is constant movement: movement of the whole organism about its world, movement of the limbs often serving to manipulate objects in the immediate environment, and, for human organisms, movements of the throat and face producing the sounds of speech. These movements are, at least to some extent, under control of, or influenced by changes in the organism's environment. The surface of the body is equipped with a variety of *receptors*, some very localized and some widespread, that make the organism sensitive to pressure, tempera-ture, the presence of certain chemicals, light, and sound. Sometimes the appropriate activation of these receptors can clearly be seen to be responsible for evoking movements of the organism (for example, an animal will run away when threatened by a predator); but activation of the receptors also guides our more mundane and seemingly spontaneous behaviour—we need our eyes open to walk across a room without bumping into the furniture.

At this very gross level then, the organism can be seen as a device that takes in information about the state of its environment and acts in accord with it. Inspection of its internal structure should reveal the mechanisms that enable it to do this. There will be specialized *effector* systems that work the limbs, and specialized *receptor* systems to deal with the energy impinging on the sensory surface. The existence of such specialized systems makes necessary the existence of a third to integrate their activity (when the eyes detect the predator it is the legs that have to do the running away). It is the working of this third, integrating, system that has been of most interest to psychologists and it is the focus of our attention in this chapter.

## INTEGRATION AND NERVOUS CONDUCTION

### Integration Without Nerves

*Simple organisms.* The need for integration arises when an organism develops specialized sub-systems. A single-celled organism that swims more quickly when the temperature of its water is increased could achieve this if the temperature increase simply led to a speeding up of all its biochemical processes. Problems arise when only one part of the organism is sensitive to the environment and only one part is capable of movement. Thus the bacterium responsible for typhoid moves about its liquid environment when its five *flagella* (chainlike filaments that beat against the surrounding medium) work together. When movements of the flagella are not coordinated the bacterium simply tumbles over and over, and stays where it is. Coordinated activity of these effectors depends upon environmental stimulation. Should the bacterium encounter a nutrient in the medium it responds by swimming smoothly. If it moves out of the pool of nutrient, tumbling begins. (The consequence is that the bacterium tends to swim up a concentration gradient of the nutrient toward the source, for if the bacterium starts to swim away from the source, concentration of the nutrient falls, tumbling starts, and movements in that direction stops.) The receptors for this system consist of specific proteins lying on the surface membrane of the bacterium. These proteins have the ability to react ("bind") with molecules of the nutrient and this receptor-binding induces activity in enzymes within the cell. Integration of activity at these receptor sites and of the flagella is achieved by means of some compound synthesized within the cell as a result of enzyme activity, a compound that induces coordinated flagella beating.

Even quite complex multi-celled organisms can manage to integrate the activities of their various parts without the need for any complex nervous system. The coelenterate *Hydra* is a small jellyfish-type creature consisting of little more than a sac (its stomach) fringed with tentacles, used to catch live prey. The prey brushes against the tentacles and is speared by stings produced by specialized effector cells; the tentacles envelop the victim and push it into the stomach-sac. This smoothly integrated sequence of activities proceeds largely without the assistance of the primitive nervous system that *Hydra* possesses. Thus, the stinging cell is an independent operator possessing its own triggering device and it will discharge when stimulated, even when it is separated from the rest of the organism. The grasping movements of the tentacles are an automatic next step in that the wounded prey releases the substance *glutathione* (a small protein molecule that is an essential part of the biochemical system of most cells) into the surrounding water and this is sufficient to stimulate their activity.

*Hormonal integration.* In *Hydra* the non-nervous integration of activity is brought about by external chemical agencies. But in more complex multi-cellular organisms integration can be achieved by internally produced chemicals (*hormones*) especially manufactured for the purpose. An animal with an efficient circulatory system such as a vertebrate, can integrate activity at two separate sites by arranging for the first site (an *endocrine* gland) to secrete a hormone into the bloodstream so that it is carried to a second site (the *target organ*) where it affects activity. Since, in vertebrate animals, the blood supply will distribute the hormone throughout the whole body it is necessary for the target site to have some special affinity for the hormone if it alone is to be influenced. Such systems are quite common. For instance, the posterior *pituitary* gland at the base of the brain is responsible for the secretion of an *antidiuretic* hormone which is carried by the blood to the kidney where it has a quite specific effect on the tubules that control the amount of water excreted in urine, causing fluid to be retained in the body.

But, because of the fact that they are distributed throughout the body, hormones are in a sense best fitted to regulating activities that require the cooperation of many different parts of the body. Consider again an animal suddenly confronted by a predator. This emergency requires a large number of changes in bodily function. There is an increase in heart rate and a deepening of respiration ensuring a good supply of oxygen; the blood vessels in the muscles (which may soon be required for running) dilate and those in the skin and viscera contract; sugar stored in the liver is released into the blood stream for use by the muscles; the blood itself develops an increased capacity for clotting. All of these changes (and more) can be brought about by the hormones *adrenaline* (also called *epinephrine*) and *noradrenaline* (*norepinephrine*) that are released by the *adrenal medulla* (see Chapter 3, p. 93). These responses wane if stress is prolonged and activity is then coordinated by a second endocrine gland, the *adrenal cortex* which is responsible for producing a range of hormones called *glucocorticoids*. These potentiate the reactions of the blood vessels to adrenaline thus making the animal better able to respond to a new and sudden stress. They also promote the synthesis of sugars and their deposition in the liver thus ensuring a good supply of easily available energy.

## Interaction of Chemical and Nervous Systems of Integration

Some chemical methods of integration could in principle constitute a system quite independent of that provided by the nerves. Thus the secretion of antidiuretic hormone from the pituitary could in principle be the direct result of the response of that gland to the chemical changes produced in the body fluids by water deprivation. But in fact the hormone is only synthesized and stored in the pituitary. The mechanisms that detect a shortage of water are in fact in the adjacent part of the brain (the *hypothalamus*, see p. 152) and the control the release of the hormone by way of nerve fibres that connect them to the posterior pituitary (see Fig. 5.1).

The intimate interrelation between neural and chemical methods of integration is even more obvious when we consider the systems controlling response to stress. First, we have pointed out that the response to stress involves changes in the activity of the viscera and internal organs. But these organs are also controlled by nerves that constitute a distinct branch of the nervous system (the *autonomic* nervous system). Some of these nerves release noradrenaline at the points where they make contact with the organs that they innervate and thus

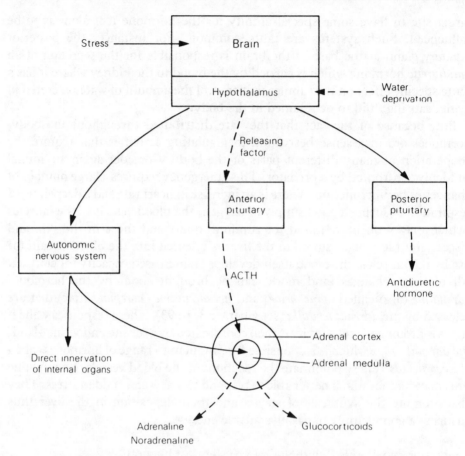

Fig. 5.1. *Interaction of chemical and nervous mechanisms in the control of some bodily functions of psychological importance. Anti-diuretic hormone controls the water output in the urine and is part of the mechanism that regulates water balance. Release of this hormone depends upon activity in the brain (the hypothalamus). The hypothalamus also plays a role, by way of the pituitary hormone ACTH (adreno-corticotropic hormone), in controlling the adrenal gland with its response to stress.*

activation of this part of the nervous system is able to produce effects like those produced by activation of the adrenal medulla. The part of the brain that plays the largest part in determining activity in the autonomic nervous system is the hypothalamus, and since we know that this structure also controls the pituitary a further link between neural and hormonal systems is established. The hypothalamus not only controls the activity of the posterior pituitary but also, by way of a chemical "releasing factor" that it secretes into blood vessels connecting them, it stimulates the anterior part of the pituitary to release a hormone into the general circulation that stimulates the activity of the adrenal cortex. It thus also plays a role in the longer-term response to stress.

This mixture of hormonal and other systems should come as no real surprise.

The response of an animal to a given set of circumstances is likely to have a number of different components. Thus when deprived of water it needs to activate mechanisms that reduce water loss (by way of antidiuretic hormone) but also it needs to get up and look for something to drink. The first part of the response is readily achieved hormonally but the latter with its requirements for relatively rapid changes in the muscles controlling the skeleton requires some other means such as is provided by nerves carrying impulses from the brain. Further, hormonal changes are not produced solely by changes in the animal's internal environment. Thus the hormonal response to stress can be triggered initially by the occurrence of some threat and this is something detected by receptors on the body surface. These receptors (in the eyes and ears, and so on) influence the rest of the body not through any chemical that they release themselves but by means of activity transmitted with great speed by nerves to the brain. It is to the mechanisms involved in nervous conduction that we turn next.

## Nervous Integration

An obvious way to integrate the activity in two parts of a system is to run a wire between them so that messages can pass between the two. Careful dissection of any vertebrate will reveal the existence of biological "wires", the nerves, emerging from muscles and sense organs. These nerves connect receptors and effectors not directly, but by virtue of the fact that they all run to a *central nervous system*. The implications of this arrangement will be taken up shortly when we consider, as an example, the integration of muscular activity with the activity of sensory systems detecting the degree of tension in a muscle. For the time being we will concentrate on the nature of the message that passes down the nerve, what its properties and what its effects are. But first we need to make clear the distinction between the terms nerve, nerve cell, and nerve fibre.

The nerve revealed by simple dissection is not a unitary structure. Microscopic examination of a nerve shows it to be a bundle of many hundreds of *nerve fibres*, the largest no more than 20 $\mu$m in diameter (a micrometre being a millionth of a metre). Further examination shows that each nerve fibre is the exceedingly long and thin extension of a nerve cell (*neurone* or *neuron*), the main body of which may be several feet away. Examples of neurones are shown schematically in Fig. 5.2.

*Conduction by nerves.* Nerves are capable of transmitting activity from one point to another. The relevant experiment has been carried out most often with the sciatic nerve removed from the leg of a frog. If one point on the nerve is stimulated electrically it is possible to observe electrical changes some distance away along the nerve. When the distance between the point of stimulation and that point at which the changes are recorded is 13 mm a burst of activity (labelled A in the Fig. 5.3) lasting about 10 ms is noted at the recording site some 4 ms after the occurrence of the stimulus. There is then a pause before further electrical changes (B) are recorded about 50 ms after the onset of stimulation; a further pause and then more activity (C) about 200 ms after stimulation (Fig. 5.3).

These times may seem short but the first point to make is that even the shortest of them means that whatever is travelling along the nerve from stimulating to recording point takes a finite time to do so: the speed of conduction works out at 40 m/s (metres per second) for the first recorded change in the frog's nerve. It is not the case, therefore, that the nerve passively conducts its electrical input in the same way (and at the same speed, i.e. the speed of light) as a copper wire would. Rather, the stimulation, which in experimental studies happens usually to be electrical (but need not be so—pinching the nerve is sometimes an effective stimulus), produces some change

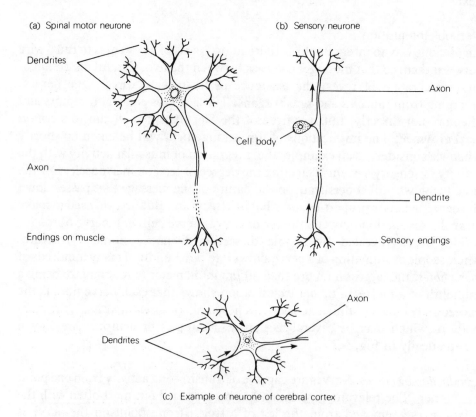

(a) Spinal motor neurone

(b) Sensory neurone

Dendrites

Axon

Cell body

Axon

Dendrite

Endings on muscle

Sensory endings

Dendrites

Axon

(c) Example of neurone of cerebral cortex

Fig. 5.2. *Some examples of neurones. The motor (a) and sensory (b) cells have myelinated nerve fibres which may be metres long and extend into the periphery. The short-axon fibre (c) is one example of the many types that are restricted to the central nervous system. In each the process that conducts impulses away from the cell body is called the axon.*

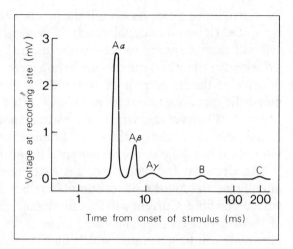

Fig. 5.3. *A schematic representation of electrical changes recorded at a point on the surface of a frog's excised sciatic nerve 13 mm away from a site of electrical stimulation. A, B, C are thought to represent the responses of different types of nerve fibre that conduct at differing velocities.*

that is conducted relatively slowly and that shows up as an electrical change some distance away. Activity at the recording site occurs in three distinct bursts because there are different types of nerve fibre in the sciatic nerve and they conduct activity at different rates. In part this occurs because some fibres are covered with a sheath of a fatty substance (*myelin*) which serves to increase conduction velocity; also, some fibres have bigger diameters than others and the bigger ones conduct more rapidly than the smaller. Thus the fibres responsible for the C response in Fig. 5.3 are both fine and not myelinated; it is thought that they conduct information from the periphery that is important in producing the feeling of pain when body tissues are damaged. Those responsible for the response labelled $\alpha$ in the figure are both large and myelinated. They include those nerve fibres that activate the muscles responsible for moving the limbs.

*Conduction in nerve fibres.* In order to find out more about the principles of nervous conduction we need to look at the properties of the single nerve fibres that go to make up the nerve. In particular, it would be useful to be able to measure the changes that occur inside a nerve fibre when it is active. Until recently, this has not been possible for the very fine nerve fibres of vertebrates. However, some of the nerve fibres of squids are much larger, having diameters of about 1 mm, and our understanding of the basics of nervous conduction comes from the study of these. It is possible to place an electrode inside the giant fibre of the squid. When this is done and a second electrode is placed in contact with the outer surface of the fibre, a small potential difference can be recorded between the two, of the order of some thousandths of a volt (millivolts, mV). The membrane of the fibre is said to be *polarized*, with the outside positive with respect to the inside.

When the fibre is stimulated there is a change in the permeability of its membrane and ions (electrically charged atoms) begin to flow into the cell from the surrounding fluid. As a result the potential difference across the membrane is reduced (it becomes depolarized). If the degree of depolarization is small the cell will use its energy to restore the normal state, but if the stimulation is sufficiently strong and the depolarization large an inrush of ions occurs and the polarity of the membrane is reversed for two or three milliseconds before metabolic processes restore normality. This change constitutes an *action potential*. Whatever the nature of the stimulation applied, the basic form of the action potential is always the same. Stimulation must pass a certain threshold but once it has done so the stereotyped impulse is generated.

The electrical and other changes that constitute the action potential are initially localized at the site of stimulation but they trigger changes in adjacent parts of the fibre. Current will flow from intact areas of membrane on either side of the depolarized part and these areas become depolarized in turn. Action potentials will be generated which then depolarize the next bit of membrane and so an impulse of electrical and chemical activity is able to progress down the fibre. Once an impulse has traversed a piece of nerve fibre, that part of the fibre is incapable of supporting further activity until a recovery period of a fraction of a second (the *refractory period*) has elapsed. The result is that nerve impulses are recorded as discrete events. Increasing the intensity of the stimulation (given that it is above threshold) does nothing to the size and shape of the impulse but increases the rate at which impulses occur until the maximum capacity of the system is reached. Thus what this "biological wire" transmits can be seen as being a sort of primitive Morse code with only two signals, "on" and "off", with only the "off" signal being variable in length (and even that unable to go below a minimum set by the refractory period).

*The generation of nerve impulses and their effects.* Nerve impulses are not normally produced by direct electrical stimulation of the fibre, nor are they usually recorded part way along its length. If the nervous system is to fulfil an integrative function, nerve impulses must be generated by energy impinging on receptors and must be conducted from there to control the activity of effectors. A simple example of such a system is shown in Fig. 5.4. The receptor shown in the figure is not one sensitive to changes in the outside world: it is a stretch receptor embedded in a muscle and sensitive to the degree of elongation or contraction of the muscle. The effector is a group of muscle fibres such as those that go to make up the muscle that extends the lower leg. It would be possible to connect receptor to effector by a single short nerve fibre. In fact, they are linked not in this way, but by the fibres of two nerve cells lying in and near the spinal cord.

The stretch receptors lie on modified muscle fibres (*muscle spindles*) attached to the main body of the muscle so that they lengthen and shorten along with the muscle. The sensory nerve fibre monitoring the state of the muscle has

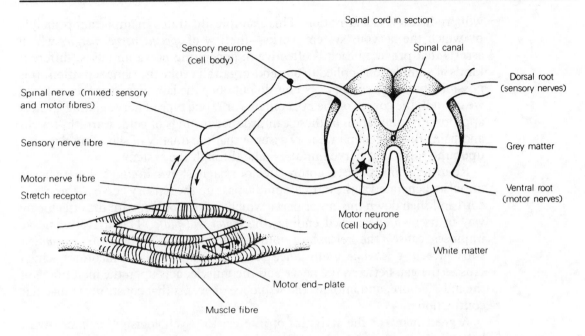

Fig. 5.4. *A schematic representation of the connection between sensory and motor nerve fibres by way of the spinal cord. The arrows represent the normal directions in which nerve impulses flow.*

branching endings that are wrapped around the central part of the spindle. Stretching this part of the spindle produces an electrical change that in turn causes nerve impulses to be evoked, the rate of discharge depending upon the degree to which the spindle has been stretched. It has already been said that nerves are sensitive to mechanical stimulation and that they respond to these events by producing nerve impulses. Specialized receptor mechanisms such as those found in the muscle spindle serve the function of making the nerve cell in question especially sensitive to certain sorts of stimulation. In part this may be achieved by the presence of accessory structures that shield them from other sorts of stimulation. In the ear, for example, the final critical event is again a mechanical distortion, but the complex system that surrounds the nerve endings ensures that the only distortion to act on them is one produced by vibrations of air molecules (i.e. by sound). Similarly the structure of the eye is such that the endings of fibres in the optic nerve lying as they do in the retina at the back of the eyeball are protected from unwanted sources of stimulation. Their special sensitivity to light, however, depends upon the presence in the retina of receptor cells (rods and cones) that are capable of responding with electrical and chemical changes when light falls upon them.

This is not to say, however, that the visual system is quite insensitive to other forms of energy. Pushing (gently) on the side of the eyeball with the finger will activate the rods that lie in the periphery of the retina and this mechanical input will produce a visual sensation. This example illustrates an important principle by which the nervous system works—the law of *specific nerve energies* which asserts that provided each is effective in generating nerve impulses, different kinds of stimulation applied to one end-organ all evoke the same sensation. It is possible that some sensory systems do not obey the law. For instance, as far as we can tell, the cornea of the eye contains only one type of nerve ending and yet appropriate stimulation of these can produce feelings of cold, warmth, touch, and pain. But in general we may assume that the quality of sensation depends upon the route that nerve impulses take through the system.

Returning now to the receptor–effector system shown in Fig. 5.4; here nerve impulses generated at the muscle spindle pass up the sensory nerve to the spinal cord and then down the motor nerve which makes contact with the effector by way of its own specialized ending, the *motor end-plate*. The arrival of nerve impulses causes the release of minute amounts of a chemical *transmitter* substance, *acetylcholine* (a substance chemically very similar to nicotine), which crosses the gap between the nerve and the muscle, acts upon the membrane of the muscle fibre, and initiates the sequence of events that constitutes muscular contraction.

A great many of the activities of interest to psychologists (i.e. most overt behaviour) are mediated by this *final common path*: motor neurone, acetyl-choline transmitter, and the contraction of a muscle. But exceptions are to be found in the autonomic nervous system (p. 137). Although some nerves within the autonomic system (those constituting the *parasympathetic* branch of the system) work by releasing acetylcholine, it has already been pointed out that those mediating the initial response to stress (the *sympathetic* branch of the system) use noradrenaline. Further, the autonomic system controls some effectors that are glands rather than groups of muscle fibres. The activities controlled by these autonomic pathways are also of psychological interest. In particular, the autonomic system is responsible for the internal changes that are associated with emotional and motivational states. It is also worth adding that our understanding of basic mechanisms of learning owes much to Pavlov's work on the control of salivary secretion (Chapter 7), work done on the activity of a gland controlled by the autonomic nervous system.

The whole system shown in Fig. 5.4, of muscle spindle, sensory nerve, motor nerve, and muscle, is arranged so that when the muscle is passively stretched it responds by contracting. Its activity can be seen in the knee-jerk reflex, the twitch of the lower leg produced by a blow just below the knee-cap. The blow hits the tendon that attaches the muscle of the front of the thigh to the lower leg and stretches the muscle. The jerk is the consequence of the reflex contraction of this muscle. In more natural circumstances this reflex serves to maintain bodily posture: when a rider leaps astride his horse, the animal does not collapse under the weight since its muscles respond by contracting slightly in response to the stretch applied to them.

*Junctions between nerve cells.* The sensory and motor neurones depicted in Fig. 5.4 come into close contact in the spinal cord but they remain discrete entities. The junction between them (a *synapse*) consists of a minute gap, about one fiftieth of a micrometre across. Small though it is, this gap is large enough to preclude the possibility, in the large majority of instances, of the nerve impulse in the sensory neurone jumping straight across to the motor neurone. Instead what happens is that the arrival of a nerve impulse at the end of the sensory neurone triggers the release of a chemical transmitter that acts upon the membrane of the motor neurone. The transmitter does not itself immediately generate a nerve impulse in the motor neurone; rather it produces a small and relatively long-lasting depolarization of its membrane. If this change lasts long enough it can summate with effects produced by the transmitter released by the arrival of later nerve impulses which may come down either the original sensory neurone or by way of other neurones that synapse with the same motor nerve cell. The summation of excitatory effects may then be enough to generate a new set of nerve impulses. Some synapses are inhibitory rather than excitatory. The arrival of nerve impulses at these junctions brings about the release of a transmitter substance that produces a hyperpolarization of the membrane of the cell on the far side of the synapse (i.e. increases the size of the potential difference that normally exists across the membrane), making it less likely that a nerve impulse will be generated.

Transmission across synapses throughout the *central nervous system* (brain and spinal cord) also depends upon transmitters. They have been the subject of much research in recent years and some thirty have now been identified. There is some evidence that molecules consisting of short chains of amino acids can act as transmitters (a suggestion that has attracted much attention because of the fact that some of the molecules in question bear a surprising similarity to the drug morphine). Better established as transmitters are rather smaller molecules, the monamines and single amino acids. Examples of the former are noradrenaline, acetylcholine (the transmitter used also at the neuromuscular synapse), and dopamine. The structural resemblance between some of the monamines and hallucinogenic drugs such as mescaline and LSD suggests that the latter may have their effects by mimicking the action of the transmitters at synapses in the brain. Gamma-aminobutyric acid (GABA), the commonest inhibitory transmitter in the brain, is an example of an amino acid. Huntington's chorea, the neurological disorder discussed in Chapter 3 (p. 77) is associated with a loss of inhibitory neurones that normally contain GABA.

The only synapse shown in Fig. 5.4 is between the sensory neurone and the motor neurone but in fact the motor neurone receives inputs at something like a hundred synapses. This allows many events other than a stretching of the muscle to influence muscular contraction. (If all that were needed was the simple stretch reflex, this could be achieved by a single nerve cell running straight from the muscle spindle to the contractile fibres.) We cannot specify what each of these synapses does but we know about some. The example we have been considering is that of a motor neurone which when stimulated activates a muscle that causes the limb to extend. Extension of the limb is also seen when an unpleasant stimulus is applied to the skin of the equivalent limb on the other side of the body and we may conclude from this that nerve impulses generated in the skin's sensory receptors make their way up the sensory nerve, across the spinal cord to an excitatory synapse on the motor neurone. This same sensory input will evoke the withdrawal of the limb to which it is applied. We may conclude from this that the input is capable of activating the motor neurones that control contraction of the muscles that flex the limb. Such flexion automatically stretches the muscles concerned with extension of the limb but the action is not opposed by the normal stretch reflex. We conclude, therefore, that the original input also activates inhibitory synapses on the motor neurone controlling the extensor muscles (Fig. 5.5).

*Conclusions.* These observations give us some idea of how the system works to generate a reflex response. Energy impinging on a receptor generates nerve impulses which are conducted up a sensory nerve fibre. The form of these impulses does not depend upon the nature or intensity of the stimulation, but their frequency can vary. Arriving in the central nervous system, these impulses bring about the release of a chemical transmitter that, if present in sufficient quantity, will generate activity in an adjacent neurone. The readiness

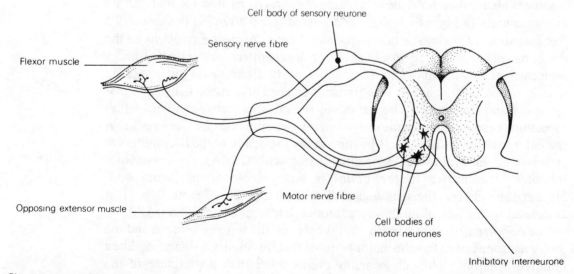

Fig. 5.5. *An inhibitory interneurone ensuring that contraction of one muscle is accompanied by relaxation of its opponent.*

of the recipient neurone to respond will also depend upon the transmitters released by other active neurones nearby, thus allowing the integration of inputs from a variety of sources. When a motor neurone is stimulated sufficiently to generate nerve impulses, these pass down its nerve fibre and activate an effector.

It should be emphasized that these conclusions are derived from the study of a very simple behaviour pattern and that consequently some important aspects of nervous functioning have been neglected. Two of these should be mentioned now. First, the stretch reflex just described is one in which there is a direct connection between a motor neurone and a sensory neurone. In most cases, however, sensory and motor neurones make contact only by way of synapses with intervening *interneurones*—nerve cells that lie solely within the central nervous system itself and that interact only with other nerve cells (see Fig. 5.5). Each of the extra synapses involved when a chain of interneurones mediates between input and output provides a site at which activity from other parts of the nervous system can interact with that from the primary sensory neurone.

Second, studies of the stretch reflex (and of many other reflexes) have been done, for the most part, on "spinal" animals, that is, animals in whom the brain has been surgically disconnected from the rest of the nervous system. We know, however, that nervous activity coming down from the brain is capable of evoking activity. How this may be achieved is something we will consider in the next chapter, after we have considered the general structure of the brain and some suggestions about how it might work.

## THE STRUCTURE OF THE CENTRAL NERVOUS SYSTEM

An engineer studying a system equipped with a variety of receptors and a range of effector-devices might not be surprised, upon looking inside, to see a tangle of wires with each receptor having its own direct link to each effector. But a more sensible arrangement would be to have some central switching station to which all wires run. The input from any given receptor could then be connected to the end of the wire leading to any of the effectors according to need. With a very extensive set of receptors and effectors a central switching system is not just sensible but is essential: it would be impossible to construct a telephone system in which every subscriber had his own personal wire connecting his telephone to that of every other person he might want to call. We shall shortly be discussing how adequate the view of the brain as a biological version of a complex telephone switchboard is, but, in terms of the gross anatomy of the system, the analogy is not inappropriate. Figure 5.6 shows the general layout of the nervous system with the peripheral nerves radiating from the central switching system, the *central nervous system* consisting of the brain and the spinal cord.

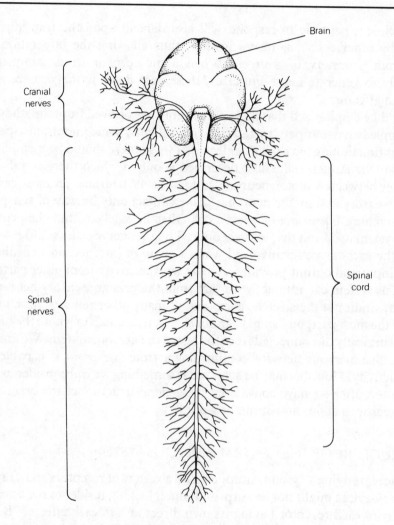

Fig. 5.6. *A disembodied human nervous system viewed from in front. The brain and spinal cord constitute the central nervous system. The origins of the cranial and spinal nerves running into the periphery are also shown.*

## The Spinal Cord

Some animals, the earthworm is an example, consist of a series of very similar segments. Vertebrates, too, can be viewed as basically segmental creatures. The structural modifications undergone by some of the segments are quite dramatic but the fundamental structure can still be seen in the layout of those peripheral nerves that arise from the spinal cord (Fig. 5.6). It will be well, therefore, to begin our description with this part of the system so as to establish the basic structural principles that underlie the complex elaboration seen in the brain.

The spinal cord consists of a long tube of nervous tissue. In man it runs from the base of the skull to the base of the spine, and is about as thick as a little finger. Wrapped around the *cerebrospinal canal* lying at the centre of the cord is a core of "grey matter", this being the colour of tissue containing many nerve cell bodies. With a few exceptions, the motor nerve fibres that innervate the muscles have their origin in cells lying in the ventral part of the grey matter (Fig. 5.4). (The part of a structure lying toward the belly is termed "ventral"; that lying toward the back, "dorsal".) The dorsal section of the grey matter contains cells that receive incoming sensory fibres. These fibres originate in cells that lie outside the central nervous system itself. As Fig. 5.4 shows, the cell body of the sensory fibre entering the dorsal part of the cord lies in a small *ganglion* (a group of neurones) positioned on the dorsal or sensory "root" of the nerve just before it enters the spinal cord. Outside the cord the dorsal and ventral roots unite to form a "mixed" nerve containing both motor and sensory fibres.

Many nerve fibres are sheathed in myelin and since this is a white fatty substance they give its characteristic colour to the "white matter" of the spinal cord that surrounds the grey central core. Some of this white tissue consists of the fibres entering from the dorsal sensory root and the fibres leaving down the ventral motor root, but in addition there are many nerve fibres that run up and down the spinal cord. Such fibre tracts are to be expected on functional grounds; without them it would be possible to integrate various activities only at the segmental level (i.e. input down a sensory fibre would be able to influence the output only of the motor fibres adjacent to it in the cord). Their existence can be demonstrated anatomically by making cuts through the cord at various levels. When a nerve fibre is disconnected from its cell body the fibre degenerates, and degenerating fibres can be identified under the microscope. A section through the spinal cord high up near the brain produces a clear pattern of "descending" degeneration indicating the existence of fibre tracts in the ventral and lateral parts of the white matter carrying information down from cell bodies in the brain. "Ascending" degeneration produced by a section lower down in the cord reveals the presence of large tracts of fibres (especially in the dorsal white matter) carrying information up to "higher centres". Although the approximation is certainly a very crude one, it is good enough for our present purposes to say that the ventral part of the spinal cord contains cell bodies and nerve fibres concerned with motor output and that the dorsal regions contain cells and fibres dealing with sensory input.

General Features of the Vertebrate Brain
The orderly structure of the spinal cord seems to be lost as it turns into the brain at the head end of the animal. No longer is there a simple tube with paired nerves emerging from it at regular intervals (Fig. 5.6); rather there is a seeming jumble of cranial nerves, running to eyes, ears, and nose, and the complex

musculature of the face, emerging from a central set of bumps and lobes of nervous tissue. Nonetheless, on closer inspection the general structure seen in the spinal cord can be found in the brain too. Thus, it is still possible to discern areas of grey and of white matter, and to distinguish parts having sensory functions (again lying dorsally for the most part) from those (lying ventrally) having motor functions. The special features of the brain become intelligible after considering the special nature of the sensory information it has to deal with.

We have said that the spinal cord consists of a tube of nervous tissue around a central canal. At its head-end this tube swells out in three places to produce a series of three major swellings. These are labelled as forebrain, midbrain, and hindbrain in the schematic diagram shown in Fig. 5.7. (You may sometimes come across them referred to as *prosencephalon*, *mesencephalon*, and *rhombencephalon*, respectively.) Each of the swellings is associated with a cranial

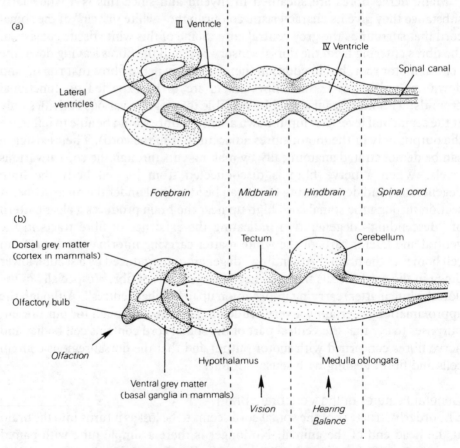

Fig. 5.7. *A schematic diagram of two sections through the brain of a "typical" vertebrate; (a) is a top view; (b) a view from the side (adapted from Romer and Parsons, 1977).*

nerve that, unlike the nerves of the spinal cord and the other nine cranial nerves, is almost totally made up of sensory nerve fibres. Counting from the head end these nerves are labelled I, II, and VIII. The forebrain accommodates the first, the olfactory nerve, and the information it carries from the nose; the midbrain takes visual information from the optic nerve (II); nerve VIII carries information from the ear (both auditory information and input from the organs of balance) to the hindbrain. We may now look in a little more detail at the constituent parts of each of these divisions.

*Hindbrain.* In the hindbrain the basic structure found in the spinal cord is still clearly discernible. The fluid-filled canal has swelled out to form a larger central cavity, the fourth *ventricle*, which somewhat distorts their appearance but there are still central masses of grey matter, the ventral tissue being motor in function and the dorsal, sensory. The arrangement may also differ from that seen in the spinal cord in that the grey matter does not always form a continuous column, becoming, in some species, fragmented into a series of *nuclei* separated by tracts of nerve fibres. This part of the hindbrain is known as the *medulla oblongata*. Arising as an outgrowth of the roof of the hindbrain is a structure that has no real parallel in the spinal cord, the *cerebellum*. (Cerebellum means "little brain". The early neuroanatomists had the happy knack of choosing simple descriptive names but the unfortunate habit of translating them into dead languages.) In this structure the usual arrangement of white matter on the outside and grey matter on the inside is reversed, the cell bodies forming a thin outer covering (or *cortex*) around a fan-shaped radiation of incoming and outgoing fibres. These fibres come from a variety of different sources but many of them originate in the eighth nerve which carries information from the organs of balance. In this way the hindbrain shows its origin as a structure developed to deal with the specialized sensory information coming down the eighth nerve.

*Midbrain.* In the midbrain the ventricle narrows to form only a small tube (the *aqueduct*) and in this respect the structure is more like that of the spinal cord. Much of the ventral part of the midbrain is filled with white matter; in particular with bundles of fibres carrying motor commands from the forebrain down to the spinal cord (where they form some of the tracts identified by descending degeneration that we have alredy discussed). There is, however, some grey matter (the *tegmentum*) which again seems to have a motor function—this area too sends tracts down the spinal cord and human patients with disorders of movement coordination are sometimes found to have suffered damage to this part of the brain. Above the aqueduct there is a mass of grey matter forming the roof (or in Latin, the *tectum*) of the midbrain, associated with the special sensory input from the second cranial nerve and for this reason often referred to, in non-mammalian vertebrates, as the optic tectum. A fish with its tectum removed surgically appears to be virtually blind. In mammals, where the visual function of the tectum is less important, the term optic tectum is not used; instead, the bumps that form the roof of the midbrain are given the descriptive name of *colliculi* (small hills).

*Forebrain.* As it moves into the forebrain the cerebral aqueduct opens out to form the third ventricle. Beyond this point the tube forks with a pair of lateral ventricles extending forward from the third ventricle. It is convenient therefore, to regard the forebrain as consisting of two main sections: the *diencephalon* (sometimes "between-brain") being the tissue surrounding the third ventricle and the *telencephalon* (or "end-brain"), the tissue surrounding the lateral ventricles (and consisting of the paired *cerebral hemispheres*). The olfactory nerves enter the brain at the tip of the telencephalon and the structures of the diencephalon have no special connection with them. These structures consist of a set of nuclei, those of the lateral walls of the ventricle being known collectively as the *thalamus*. They take their sensory input not from any nerve entering the system at the level of the forebrain, but from fibre tracts that carry information that has entered the system lower down. Similarly, the nuclei lying ventrally in the diencephalon (and constituting the *hypothalamus*) have no obvious direct efferent connections (there is a tract of fibres running to the tegmentum) but they clearly serve some motor function since electrical stimulation of them can elicit movement patterns. (As we have already seen, a good part of the importance of the hypothalamus lies in the fact that it can control glandular rather than muscular effector systems by virtue of its close association with the pituitary gland.) This lack of direct efferent and afferent connections distinguishes the diencephalon from lower parts of the brain and the spinal cord. And, leaving its olfactory input aside, the relative indirectness of inputs to and outputs from the telencephalon is even more striking. This structure deserves separate consideration.

## Comparative Perspectives on Forebrain Structure

The complex structure of the vertebrate forebrain can best be understood if we begin by making a guess as to what the telencephalon might have been like in some primitive vertebrate (now extinct) from which modern species are descended. Figure 5.8a shows a cross section of the head end of the basic neural tube with the grey matter lying around the central space divided up, for ease of reference, into five different sections on each side. In most vertebrates the central tube has pushed out laterally, by a process referred to as "evagination", to form the lateral ventricles. The development of the cerebral hemisphere around its lateral ventricle in a postulated primitive vertebrate is shown in Fig. 5.8b). According to some anatomists, a forebrain structure very like this is to be seen in some present-day amphibians.

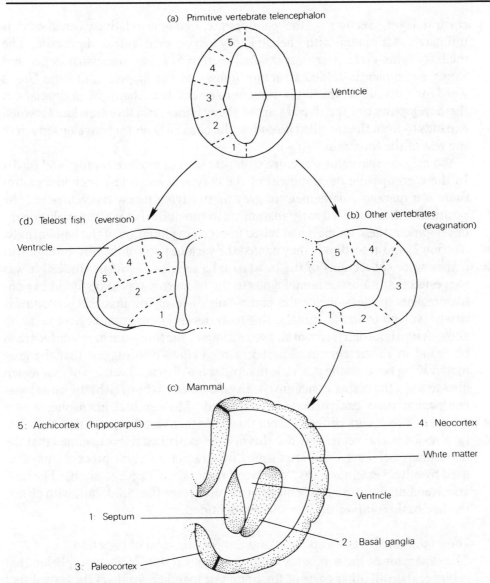

(a)  Primitive vertebrate telencephalon

Ventricle

(d) Teleost fish  (eversion)

Ventricle

(b) Other vertebrates

(evagination)

(c)  Mammal

5:  Archicortex (hippocarpus)

4:  Neocortex

White matter

Ventricle

1:  Septum

2:  Basal ganglia

3:  Paleocortex

Fig. 5.8. *Relationship of forebrain structures in the mammal to the organization assumed in "primitive" forms. Also shown is a possible interpretation of the arrangement found in bony fish (adapted from Scalia and Ebbeson, 1971).*

The development from the primitive state of affairs to that seen in a modern mammal is shown in Fig. 5.8c. The ventrally positioned blocks of tissue labelled 1 and 2 have retained their original positions next to the ventricle. That labelled 1 forms a nucleus of grey matter known as the *septum*; that labelled 2 forms a group of nuclei sometimes called the *basal ganglia*. The rest of the grey matter has migrated to the outside of the cerebral hemisphere forming a thin cortical layer. Section 3, the *palaeocortex*, remains relatively small and is intimately associated with the olfactory nerve as it enters the brain. The medially lying *archicortex* (our original section 5) grows somewhat larger and forms a complex in-folded structure known as the *hippocampus*—the Greek word for a sea-horse which it is thought to resemble in shape. Most dramatic is the development of the dorsal part of the original structure (section 4) which expands to form the so-called *neocortex*, the cortical layer that envelops much of the rest of the forebrain.

We may compare this structure with that seen in modern reptiles and birds. In these groups the development of the cortex is much less pronounced but there is a marked enlargement of grey matter lying below the ventricle. The position of this tissue led early anatomists to conclude that in their evolutionary development these animals had relied upon an exploitation of the basal ganglia (section 2) and accordingly they named the various parts of the bird forebrain as if they were subsections of the basal ganglia seen in mammals. Indeed it was suggested that no tissue homologous to the neocortex was to be found in non-mammalian species—hence the prefix "neo", implying that this structure is newly evolved in the mammals. But more recently, anatomists have come to allow that primordial forms of all five sections of the forebrain grey matter are to be found in all vertebrates. There is some evidence to suggest that the grey matter lying beneath the ventricle in reptiles is a displaced version of that which goes to form the cortex in mammals. Even in teleosts (bony fish) the same basic component parts can perhaps be identified. The cerebral hemispheres of a teleost fish look very different from those of other vertebrates in that there are no obvious lateral ventricles. But this may be explained if it is assumed that the hemispheres of such a fish are formed by a rather different process from that used by other vertebrates (by "eversion" rather than by evagination). The final arrangement of the tissue is somewhat distorted (see Fig. 5.8d) but, with effort, the five basic components can still be identified.

### The Mammalian Telencephalon and Encephalization of Function

The expansion of the neocortex in the mammals results in a telencephalon that is bigger than all other parts of the brain put together. And yet the only direct sensory input to this structure is to the palaeocortex via the olfactory nerve. However important the sense of smell may be in some mammals, it is scarcely so important as to require the full-time attention of all this nervous tissue. Direct investigation shows no sign of an olfactory function for most of the mammalian forebrain and even the palaeocortex can be shown to have functions other than the processing of olfactory input. There appears to be considerable *encephalization* of function in mammals with the head end of the neural tube having information about events occurring elsewhere and having the power to interfere in activities occurring elsewhere.

This is most clearly seen by tracing the pathways of the two main sensory cranial nerves. The eighth nerve indeed enters the brain at the level of the hindbrain and sends fibres to the cerebellum but it does not stop there. Rather it synapses with other nerve fibres which run up to the thalamus of the diencephalon (the *medial geniculate* nucleus) and from there other fibres radiate to a specialized area of the neocortex (the auditory cortex). Similarly the optic nerve having entered the brain at the level of the midbrain sends only a few fibres to the tectum. Most of the fibres are diverted, again to one of the nuclei of the thalamus (the *lateral geniculate*), from where a new set of fibres project the sensory input up to the visual cortex. Sensory information from the surface of the body also makes its way via the spinal cord to the dorsal thalamic nuclei from where it is "projected" to the somatic sensory area of the cortex. The importance of these cortical areas in processing sensory information is demonstrated by clinical cases in which they have been damaged. For instance, damage to the visual cortex of a mammal such as a monkey will produce an animal that is effectively blind, just as will damage to the optic tectum of a teleost fish.

Motor control shows similar evidence of encephalization. It has been mentioned that tracts of motor nerve fibres run through the floor of the midbrain and down to the spinal cord. The origin of most of these fibres is found in an area of cortex known as the motor strip. Damage to this part of the brain in monkeys produces an initial loss of the ability to perform voluntary movements from which recovery occurs only slowly. The ability to perform delicate and rapid finger movements may never be regained.

It used to be supposed that encephalization of function was a special feature of mammalian, and particularly of human cerebral organization. Put very crudely the argument might run: "lower" animals hear with the hindbrain, see with the midbrain, and smell with the forebrain; the mammal with its neocortex can carry out all these functions with the forebrain, with a reliance on the forebrain being most evident in the most "advanced" mammals. Support for this view was sought from observations made on the effects of forebrain damage in a variety of species. It has just been mentioned that removal of the motor cortex in a monkey renders the animal paralysed initially after the operation. A similar operation on a dog or cat, however, does not drastically disturb the animal's ability to walk or run. And a bird with the whole of the cerebral hemispheres removed, although it will show little or no spontaneous movement, is quite capable of flying, will avoid obstacles, and can land without much difficulty.

It may therefore be that the forebrain is in some sense more important in some species than in others, but from what we have already seen of the forebrain anatomy of fish, birds, and reptiles it is unlikely that their dorsal forebrain is simply olfactory in its function—they may not have the mammalian arrangement of an extensive cortical layer but their forebrains contain tissue that appears to be homologous to it. Recent anatomical work (carried out largely on sharks by Ebbeson and his colleagues) has confirmed the non-olfactory function of large parts of the forebrain in some species of fish. Thus Ebbeson (1972) has shown that the olfactory input projects to only a small part of the telencephalon and that other parts of the forebrain receive a substantial projection from the thalamus which in turn receives inputs from the spinal cord and from the visual system. And although damage to the tectum produces severe visual incapacity some visual functions remain, mediated presumably by the telencephalon. In any event, damage to the posterior part of the forebrain is also capable of producing severe visual dysfunction. In birds, where more investigations have been carried out, there is plentiful evidence that sensory input from the eyes, ears, and the skin gets to the thalamus and is projected from there to parts of the telencephalon. In these creatures it seems likely that the thalamus acts as a sensory "relay station" just as it does in mammals. Furthermore, there is evidence in birds of the existence of nerve tracts descending from the telencephalon to the spinal cord where they play some part in the control of movement. A more thorough investigation of the brains of non-mammalian species is required before any certain conclusion can be reached. Nonetheless it begins to look as though the system of involving the forebrain in motor control and in the processing of information from all sensory modalities is a general principle of the functional organization of the vertebrate brain.

## The Human Brain

*Superficial features.* Figure 5.9 shows the major features of the human brain, viewed from the left side. The dominant feature is the wrinkled (neocortical) surface of the cerebral hemisphere the growth of this structure being such as to engulf the rest of the brain. Only a part of the cerebellum is visible in this view. The brain stem (i.e. the rest of the hindbrain, the midbrain, and the diencephalon of the forebrain) is lost from sight as are the other cortical structures (such as the hippocampus) which have become folded into the middle of the hemispheres. The major fissures (*sulci*), occurring in the neocortical surface allow us to divide it up into a number of lobes. The central sulcus separates off the *frontal* lobe. Just in front of this sulcus, and lying within the frontal lobe, is the strip of cortex known as the *motor cortex*. A less clearcut series of sulci separate off the *occipital* lobe at the back of the brain: it is here that the visual cortex is found. The rest of the hemisphere is divided by the lateral sulcus into an upper part (the *parietal* lobe) and a lower part (the *temporal* lobe). The cortical projection area of the auditory nerve (the part of the cortex receiving direct input from the relay station of the thalamus) is found in the temporal lobe adjacent to the lateral sulcus; the projection area for information

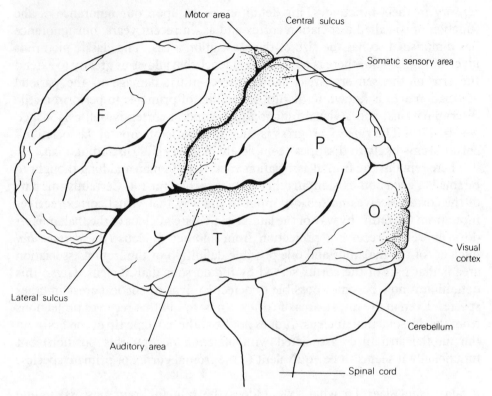

Fig. 5.9. *General view of the left side of the human brain. The four main "lobes" of the cerebrum are indicated as T: temporal; F: frontal; O: occipital; P: parietal. Only the largest folds (sulci) are shown. The shaded areas give a rough indication of the primary sensory and motor areas of the cortex. Estimates of the extent of these areas vary according to the method used to determine them.*

from receptors on the body surface is found in the parietal lobe immediately next to the central sulcus.

*Association cortex.* Figure 5.9 shows the primary sensory receiving areas in the temporal, occipital, and parietal lobes of the cerebral hemispheres and the strips of motor cortex in the frontal lobes. The rest of the cortex remains unaccounted for. The function of this "association cortex", as it has been called, will be discussed in detail below but it is appropriate to consider here the suggestion that the human brain is exceptional in having such large association areas. In particular, the large frontal lobes have often been cited as a characteristically human feature.

It proves sensible to approach this suggestion with caution. The problem arises from a difficulty we face in specifying exactly what is and is not association cortex. A standard procedure is to define the association areas by exclusion, that is, as being those areas of the cortex that are neither motor nor sensory in their function. This definition relies upon our ignorance of the function of so-called association cortex and as, in recent years, our ignorance has diminished so has the size of the association areas. The classic picture is given in Fig. 5.9 but there is now good evidence that allows us greatly to extend the size of the sensory areas shown there—thus, damage to the parietal association area is known to disrupt the ability of primates to perform tactile discriminations, and a visual function for temporal cortex is well established (see p. 170). The rate of progress is such that parietotemporal "association" cortex seems likely to disappear completely in all species, including man.

There remains the frontal association area; large in man and long thought to be small or even non-existent in other species such as the rat. Certainly this part of the cortex receives no sensory input in the way that visual cortex receives input from the retina by way of the lateral geniculate nucleus of the thalamus. It does, however, receive a projection from another nucleus (the *dorsomedial* nucleus) of the thalamus and one possible definition of the frontal association area is that part of the cortex served by the dorsomedial nucleus. Given this definition it now becomes possible to detect equivalent cortical areas in other species. Even in the rat, an area of cortex can be found that receives projections from the dorsomedial nucleus. It does not lie at the extreme tip of the brain (in the rat the structures associated with olfaction occupy this position) but functionally it seems to be equivalent to the frontal cortex of primate species.

*Relative brain size.* To what extent does the human brain possess unique anatomical features? It does not seem to possess any new components different from those that go to make up the brain in other mammalian species. Any special properties it has seem to be a function of its size. The human brain is a large structure with an average weight of about 1400 grams. Few vertebrates have brains that are bigger than this: they include those of elephants and the various species of whale. It should be emphasized, however, that our brain is not especially big in relative terms—since man is rather a big animal he might be expected to have a big brain. If we look at a range of vertebrate animals differing in body size we find that, although the brain tends to get bigger as the body does so, the relationship is not entirely simple. Figure 5.10 plots brain weight against body weight (on logarithmic scales in order to accommodate the wide range of values) for some familiar vertebrates. There is a fair amount of scatter but it is possible to see the points as lying around a sloping straight line. The slope is such that any given increase in body weight (say a doubling) is associated with a somewhat lesser increase in brain weight. Thus a lion may weigh a thousand times as much as a rat but its brain is only about a hundred times heavier. In consequence, expressing brain weight as a simple ratio of body weight can give some seemingly odd results: the relative brain size of very small animals such as shrews, when expressed in this way, exceeds that of man.

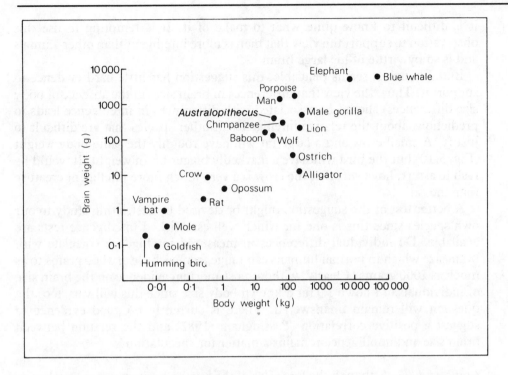

Fig. 5.10. *The relationship between brain weight and body weight for a selection of familiar vertebrate species (from data reported in Jerison, 1969, 1973).*

This simple measure of relative brain size may, however be inappropriate. The amount of brain that an animal needs just to deal with the information coming from its sense organs will depend, roughly, on the area of its body surface (since this is where most of the receptors are located). But as an animal gets bigger in volume (and in weight) its surface area increases less rapidly — doubling the length of the side of a one-metre cube, for example, will increase its volume from 1 cubic metre to 8 cubic metres but its surface area will increase from 6 square metres only to 24 square metres. The implication is that a big animal may need only a relatively small brain (in proportion to body weight) in order to deal with incoming sensory information as effectively as a small animal.

*Brain size and intelligence.* Various techniques have been adopted to avoid the difficulties inherent in comparing brain size in animals that also differ in body size. The simplest is to bypass the problem completely and to compare only animals of roughly equivalent body size. Doing this reveals that man's brain is rather larger than the brains of creatures of roughly the same body weight such as the chimpanzee, the female gorilla, or the wolf. This may seem gratifying but it is difficult to know quite what to make of it. It is tempting to use this observation to support the view that man is more intelligent than other animals and is so by virtue of his large brain.

But although it seems plausible, this suggestion has little hard evidence to support it. Thus, the view that differences in brain size (in the absence of body size differences) should be associated with differences in intelligence leads to predictions about the relative intelligence of other species that are difficult to justify. A small crow and a large rat will have roughly the same body weight (Fig. 5.10) but the bird will have a markedly bigger brain weight. It would be rash to assert, however, that the crow is a very much more intelligent creature than the rat.

A better test of the suggestion might be devised by restricting study to our own species since this is one for which well-established intelligence tests are available. Do individual differences in measured intelligence correlate with brain size which in normal humans can range from as little as 1000 grams to as much as 2000 grams? Clearly, without post-mortem evidence on the brain size of individuals of known IQ (and known body size since this will vary too) the question will remain unanswered. There is currently no good evidence to suggest a positive correlation (Passingham, 1982) and the relation between brain size and intelligence remains a matter for speculation.

*Cortical folding.* Although the large size of the human brain may not be taken as evidence for special intellectual powers it does have other implications. It has sometimes been suggested that the human brain is anatomically unique in that it has a very large cortex, deeply folded and wrinkled. In fact the human cerebral cortex is not particularly large; there is a fairly orderly relationship at least within the primates between the size of the forebrain and the amount of cortex it includes and, as Fig. 5.11 shows, the human brain has just the right amount of cortex for its size. It is, however, very deeply wrinkled in a way that the brain of the mouse or rat or cat is not. The fact that these smooth-brained animals are all relatively small (and therefore have quite small brains) is of significance. We have already mentioned the fact that an increase in the linear dimensions of a structure produces proportionately a much greater increase in volume than it does in surface area. It follows that if the brain of a cat were blown up to the volume of a human brain the relative size of its cortex would not remain the same since the cortex is a superficial layer with a fairly constant thickness across species. In order for a big brain to have the "right" amount of cortex for its size some method of increasing the surface area must be found. A pattern of folds and wrinkles does just this. In short, smooth brains are found in small animals; big animals such as man (or the horse for that matter) need to have wrinkled brains. Unless we are willing to allow that the horse is a very clever animal it becomes difficult to argue that man's intellectual powers are a consequence of his having a large and wrinkled neocortex.

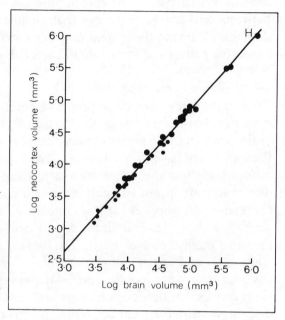

Fig. 5.11. *The relationship between the volume of the neocortex and total brain volume for primates. Large dots represent anthropoids (i.e. most apes and monkeys); small dots are prosimians (such as lemurs and bush-babies); H represents* Homo *(from Passingham, 1975).*

## HOW DOES THE BRAIN WORK?

We began this chapter by imagining an engineer taking apart a machine in order to get some idea as to how it might work from the layout of its various parts. Having surveyed the layout of the parts of the brain with an equivalent aim in view, it is apparent that no easy answers have emerged. It will be sensible, therefore, to restate what we have discovered about the workings of other parts of the nervous system. An understanding of the relatively simple might help us when we come to deal with the more complex.

### Reflex Principles
In discussing the stretch reflex we described an arrangement of receptors and effectors linked together by way of the central nervous system (the spinal cord). Energy impinging upon a receptor is converted into nerve impulses and passes to the central nervous system. There, by way of one or more synapses, it initiates activity in a motor nerve and ultimately, therefore, sets an effector into action. The connection between a given sensory input and a motor output may not be a simple one. Even in the case of the simple stretch reflex, in which the sensory neurone synapses directly with the motor neurone, many inputs other than those from the stretched muscle itself play some part in determining the likelihood of activity in the motor neurone. Nonetheless the general principles are fairly clear. They are: that input evokes output; that the input to and output

from the system consist of nerve impulses in nerve cells; that synaptic junctions between cells create pathways that channel the nerve impulses in various directions allowing the system to act as a switching device, determining what inputs (or patterns of input) should activate which effectors.

## The Structure of the Neocortex

These principles may be appropriate for the spinal cord and perhaps the brainstem but can they be applied to the neocortex of mammals, the part of the brain in which the majority of nerve cells are found? After all, each segment of the spinal cord has its own direct sensory inputs and direct connection to some effectors whereas the cortex is isolated from all but a relatively unimportant direct olfactory input, and only the motor cortex has an obvious direct link to the major effectors. A close examination of the internal structure of the neocortex shows no real signs of well defined pathways down which nerve impulses might be channelled. The cortex of the human brain consists of a continuous and fairly uniform sheet of grey matter, about 2 mm thick and covering an area of some 1000 cm$^2$. Microscopic examination of any part of this sheet reveals that the cell bodies are arranged in layers (it is usually possible to discern six) with different cell types in each. Each cell gives off very many fine fibres, some running vertically to connect the cells of the various layers, others running laterally and connecting with cells of the same and of other layers in adjacent parts of the cortex (Fig. 5.12). In itself the wiring diagram of the cortex tells us little except that all its components (neurones) appear to be connected, directly or indirectly, to all others.

A unique structure of this sort might well function according to a unique set of principles. Just as, at the behavioural level, the abilities involved in perception, learning, and memory appear to be quite different in their nature from the ability to emit a simple reflex, so, at the physiological level, the mechanism by which the neocortex works might be quite different from that used by lower parts of the nervous system. It has often been proposed that the cortex acts in some way "as a whole" in carrying out those activities that underlie perception and learning. This proposal has taken a variety of forms over the years. It is sometimes found nowadays in theories that draw an analogy between the workings of the brain and of a modern digital computer, but it was perhaps most clearly expressed many years ago by those who speculated that the cortex might be the locus of widespread "fields" of activity and we will begin by considering their ideas.

## Field Theories of Cortical Function

These theories abandon what may be taken to be a fundamental tenet of our account of the reflex—the idea that activity depends upon the spatial arrangement of the nerve cells and the way in which they are interconnected.

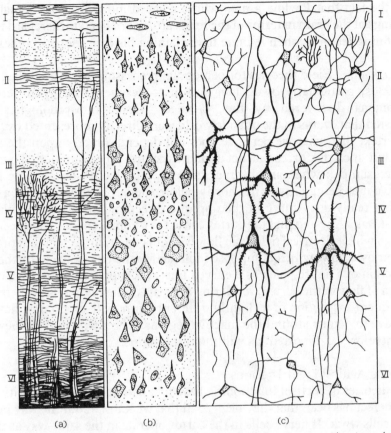

Fig. 5.12. *Three representations of six-layered cortex (layers I–VI). In (a) the tissue has been treated to reveal fibre pathways; (b) shows cell bodies; (c) shows the results of a technique that reveals a few entire cells (after Bennett, 1982).*

Instead it is suggested that fields of electrical potential can spread across the surface of the cortex as a whole.

*Pavlov.* Ironically one of the first proponents of such a theory was Pavlov, who developed his ideas in an attempt to explain the phenomena discovered during his behavioural studies of learning. According to Pavlov (see Chapter 7) the presentation of some stimulus, such as presenting food to a dog or sounding a bell, activate a specific "centre" on the surface of the cortex from which a field of "excitation" extended, like ripples spreading out when a stone is dropped into a pond. When two centres are activated simultaneously the excitation from that which is stimulated the less strongly becomes attracted to the centre that is stimulated more strongly. In this way a weakly excitatory stimulus (such as a bell) can come to evoke the response that is appropriate to the presentation of food, a response that Pavlov called a *conditioned reflex*. The irony here arises from the fact that Pavlov, a man whose avowed intention was to analyse the workings of the brain in terms of the reflex arc, felt obliged to disregard many of its defining features when it came to explaining his conditioned "reflexes".

*Gestalt theories.* Field theories for perceptual processing were developed during the 1930s, particularly by Köhler and his colleagues, to explain perceptual phenomena discovered by the so-called "Gestalt" psychologists. They suggested that events in the outside world were directly represented by fields in the cortex; that what we perceive does not depend directly upon the sensory input but upon the forces that act upon this central representation. To take one simple example: when an observer inspects a perfectly straight line he may perceive it as being curved if, shortly before, he has been looking at a similar line that really does curve in the opposite direction. In order to explain this effect it was suggested that the cortex can act as a homogeneous volume of tissue through which electrical fields can flow without constraint except that produced by their own flow, which is supposed to increase the resistance to further flow. Inspection of a figure, such as a curved line, was supposed to set up a curving pattern of flow in the cortex, rendering this part of the brain relatively inactive. Subsequent inspection of a slightly different figure will set up new fields that will have to detour around the inactive regions. The shape of these new fields will therefore be distorted, as will the resulting percept.

## Evidence Against Field Theories

Field theories of cortical functioning have met with no great popularity. Their main defect has been that they neglect all that we know about the way in which nerve cells work. If nerve cells in the cortex operate in the same way as those in the periphery, then activity in them consists of nerve impulses generated according to an all-or-none law, these impulses being transmitted via synapses from one cell to another. Such cells do not seem to provide a very good basis for fields of potential to spread in a graded way across the cortex.

*Surgical intervention.* So far we have said no more than that the field theory is rather implausible, but there is direct evidence from the experimental work of Lashley and his collaborators that seems to rule out the theory altogether. Lashley investigated the ability of rats to distinguish geometrical figures visually after undergoing surgical operations that were certain to disrupt any cerebral fields of potential. He found that fastening strips of electrical conducting material across the visual cortex did not disrupt the rats' perceptual performance, nor did cutting slits in the cortex and inserting strips of insulating material.

*Electrical recording.* It is possible, in experimental animals, to record directly (rather than just speculate about) the electrical events that go on in the cortex during visual stimulation. The results have been in accord with orthodox accounts of nerve cell activity and have given no support to those who still feel an attachment to some sort of field theory.

In a pioneering series of experiments using cats as the subjects, Hubel and Wiesel (e.g. 1979) demonstrated that cortical cells work by way of nerve impulses, just as do peripheral nerve cells; also that a geometrical figure like a straight line is represented not by any equivalent field of activity in the cortex but by the occurrence of nerve impulses in particular nerve cells. Their technique was to insert a tiny electrode into the visual cortex of an anaesthetized cat so that its tip rested close to or actually inside a single nerve cell. Various stimuli were then presented to the visual field of the cat until one was found that produced the electrical changes typical of nerve impulses at the recording site. It was found that straight lines were particularly good stimuli, eliciting in some cells a vigorous flow of nerve impulses. We have no need to suppose that seeing a straight line consists of anything other than activity in such a nerve cell.

## Reflex Principles and Cortical Functioning

The failure of these field theories of cortical functioning prompts a reconsideration of the possibility that the principles that govern the operation of simple reflexes (p. 161) might also apply to the brain. The neocortex may lack direct sensory input and motor output but it does have input and output systems of its own as we discussed in the section on encephalization of function. The motor strip of the frontal cortex (Fig. 5.9) is the origin of major fibre tracts that run down to the midbrain and the spinal cord, and artificial electrical stimulation of this area of the brain will evoke muscular responses. The various thalamic nuclei pass on "second-hand" sensory information to the projection areas concerned with hearing, vision, and the skin senses that are shown in Fig. 5.9, and nervous activity can be detected in these sites when the sense organs are stimulated appropriately.

Clearly the connections between input and output will be more complex than those found in the spinal cord but the properties of the reflex may yet serve as a "model" for all central nervous functioning. What follows is a discussion of the adequacy of this model in which we continue to concentrate (since this topic has been well researched) on the processing and use of visual information. (There is no reason to suppose that different principles will apply when behaviour is guided by other types of sensory input, and we may hope to reach conclusions of some generality.) To anticipate, we shall be forced to conclude that the brain functions according to reflex principles only when these are interpreted in the loosest of ways; but by considering the problems that the reflex model encounters we should be able to refine it and determine just what new principles are needed.

One problem arises immediately. If the neocortex does indeed work according to principles like those described above for the reflex then we ought to be able to locate pathways that transmit information such as that arriving at the visual cortex to the motor cortex where it can produce a behavioural response. But no such pathways are obvious. As Fig. 5.9 shows, the visual cortex is separated from the motor cortex by deep folds and wide expanses of other cortical tissue. There are some tracts of nerve fibre (the so-called "association" pathways, Fig. 5.13) that run through the body of the cerebral hemisphere below the level of the cortex and link various cortical areas, but the connections they make seem inappropriate from our present point of view. Thus the association fibres running from the occipital region go not to the motor cortex but to areas of association cortex in the temporal and frontal lobes.

This observation does not mean, however, that we must reject the model out of hand. It remains possible that input is linked to the output mechanisms by way of a great number of short-distance fibres running through the underlying white matter. Alternatively, the connection could be made by means of purely intra-cortical pathways: it is possible that information is handed from cortical cell to cortical cell by way of a host of synapses, and travels in this way through the intervening cortical grey matter itself.

Quite how association cortex might perform its associative function is a matter for speculation. Clearly something rather more elaborate than a direct connection is required if the owner of the cortex is to be able to discriminate between complex sensory events and to learn to perform complex patterns of behaviour according to circumstances. A direct connection can explain how a blow on the knee can lead to a jerk of the leg, but what sort of connections would be required to allow the organism to perceive the difference between friend and foe, say, and to learn to approach one and to avoid the other? We can do no more than make plausible guesses. Perhaps complex percepts are formed as the result of nervous impulses generated by much simpler sensory events coming together somewhere in the association cortex. Perhaps learning occurs because of

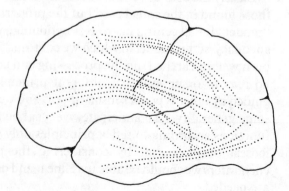

Fig. 5.13. *Some of the "association fibres" that run to and from the occipital lobe shown superimposed upon a lateral view of the left cerebral hemisphere (after Everett, 1965). These fibres lie below the cortex in the body of the hemisphere.*

synaptic changes that allow the formation of new pathways linking that part of the brain responsible for perceiving the presence of a foe and the motor cortex responsible for generating avoidance behaviour. But before speculating further along these lines we should consider some further experimental work done by Lashley since it seems, at first sight, to present some formidable problems for this sort of analysis.

### Lashley: Equipotentiality and Mass Action

Although Lashley produced experimental results contradicting the field theory of cortical function he did not turn instead to the reflex model. A series of experiments begun in the 1920s created difficulties for the reflex model just as severe as those faced by the field theories (Lashley, 1929).

*Visual discrimination.* Consider a rat that has learned to enter a lighted rather than a dark compartment in order to get food. According to the simplest reflex model of brain function, the acquisition of this pattern of behaviour depends upon some new link being forged across the association cortex allowing the input to the visual cortex to elicit an approach response. According to this view it should be possible to remove surgically the ability to learn and to perform such a visual discrimination. Cutting out the visual cortex itself should have this effect by eliminating the initial sensory input to the system; cutting out the adjacent association cortex should do so by eliminating the sensory–motor connection. But this was not the pattern of results that Lashley found. Performance on a light–dark discrimination was certainly lost when the occipital cortex was totally removed, but surprisingly it turned out that the rats could relearn the task almost as readily as before the operation. Equally surprising was the fact that damage to other parts of the cortex did not eliminate the discrimination once it had been learned–that is, the memory survived injury to those parts of the cortex in which the critical association was supposed to lie. Indeed, Lashley went on to show that a brightness discrimination learned before the operation was retained perfectly after removal of much of the cortex, provided only that some small part of the primary visual receiving area remained. He was forced to conclude that the cerebral change that underlay the learning of the discrimination was localized in the visual cortex itself. What is more, his experiments showed that it did not seem to matter which small part of the visual cortex was left intact; he referred to the visual cortex as showing *equipotentiality* for brightness discrimination learning. It is difficult to reconcile such equipotentiality with the idea that discrete new pathways between localized groups of nerve cells are formed during learning.

*Maze learning.* Equally problematic results emerged from Lashley's studies of maze learning. In some of these studies rats were trained to run a fairly complex maze in order to reach food and were then given lesions of the neocortex. Not surprisingly (for once) the brain-damaged animals tend to do rather poorly when tested again in the maze, often making the error of entering a blind alley rather than following the true path through the maze. The striking findings were, however, as follows: rats with even quite large parts of the neocortex removed were not totally incapable of running the maze; the degree of impairment suffered depended upon the size of the lesion; and no one area was critical in controlling performance in the maze (Fig. 5.14). It appears that when it comes to maze learning the neocortex shows not only equipotentiality but works according to a principle of *mass action*. All parts of the cortex work together so that the removal of any one leads to a decline in the efficiency of performance. Performance varies according to the mass of cortical tissue remaining. Again, therefore, there is no evidence for the suggestion that learning depends upon particular pathways being established between specific nerve cells; rather, the memory of how to behave in the maze seems to be present in all parts of the cortex.

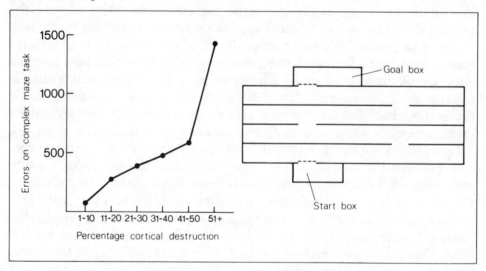

Fig. 5.14. *A summary of Lashley's results suggesting the principle of "mass action". The performance of separate groups of rats in a complex maze (inset) declines (errors increase) as the amount of cortical damage increases.*

*Implications.* Lashley's findings seem to make necessary a theory in which the cortex works "as a whole" in controlling complex behaviour. Since we have already rejected the field theories of cortical functioning, what remains? Is it possible that there is, scattered throughout the cortex, a host of general-purpose devices, each of which is capable of carrying out the processes that underlie perception, learning, and memory? This possibility, which seemed unlikely 20 years ago, has grown more plausible with the development of modern electronic computing systems based, as they are, upon the functioning of dozens of near-identical "microchips". (It is only fair to add that we are still a long way from developing a computer that could survive the equivalent of massive brain damage and still go on doing its job in a fairly adequate way.) It remains the case, however, that many workers have been unwilling to adopt some radically new model for brain function on the basis of Lashley's results. Instead they have tried hard to find some simpler explanation for them.

## Lashley's Work Reconsidered

*Critical areas.* Let us, for the moment, adopt the exact reverse of Lashley's hypothesis: let us assume that the ability to learn and remember the correct path through a maze is localized in some specific critical site in the brain. How could this notion be reconciled with Lashley's experimental results? One logical possibility is that the critical area is situated in the brain in such a way that it largely escapes small lesions of the neocortex but that larger lesions aimed at the neocortex encroach upon it more and more.

The hippocampus is a possible candidate for such a critical area. Its location is such that it is likely to suffer damage when neocortical lesions are made; further, more recent research has established that lesions restricted solely to the hippocampus severely disrupt the performance of rats in a maze, giving rise to the suggestion that the rat's ability to find its way about its environment is determined by the ability of the hippocampus to construct some sort of "map" of the external world (O'Keefe and Nadel, 1978). Perhaps, then, Lashley's lesions had their effect, not because they damaged the neocortex but because they damaged the hippocampus making less readable the map by which the rat finds its way about the maze. This interpretation frees us from the necessity of assuming that the neocortex works according to a mass action principle but it leaves us with a number of other problems. Not only does it require us to accept a theory of hippocampal function that is far from securely established but it also requires us to assume that the hippocampus itself (or whatever the critical site may be) shows both equipotentiality and mass action if we are to explain the increasingly severe effects of increasingly large brain lesions. The central problem posed by Lashley's results is not solved by this hypothesis, it is simply pushed back a stage.

*Cumulative sensory deficits.* An alternative account of Lashley's maze-learning results takes as its starting point the fact that in running a maze the rat is likely to make use of any source of information available to it. It will find its way through the maze using its sense of touch, its vision, hearing, and probably will make use of olfactory cues too. Now we have already seen that the various sensory modalities are represented in different parts of the cortex. A large cortical lesion will be capable of disrupting sensory input from all sensory systems (except perhaps the olfactory system). But smaller lesions may totally destroy the mechanisms responsible for dealing with some modalities of sensory information while leaving others intact. According to this view, Lashley's results reflect not the operation of a mass action principle but the accumulation of a series of sensory deficits produced by lesions of increasing size encroaching on more and more of the discrete sensory systems. Not only is this hypothesis quite plausible but there is experimental evidence to support it. Depriving a rat of its various senses one by one, not by damaging the brain itself but by cutting off its input peripherally, produces results very like those found by Lashley—as the number of sensory modalities available to the animal is reduced so its performance in the maze steadily declines.

*Effects of smaller brain lesions.* In response to these criticisms Lashley carried out a new series of experiments on maze learning, the general design of which was ingenious but which unfortunately gave inconclusive results. He compared the maze-learning performance of rats that had been blinded peripherally with that of rats that had suffered lesions to the occipital cortex. If the only effect of the brain damage is to eliminate the input of visual information to the brain, then the second group of rats should do no less well than the first. If, however, all parts of the cortex contribute to the animal's ability to learn and perform the maze task according to the mass action principle, then the brain-damaged rats should be at an extra disadvantage. Some experiments using this design found the results that Lashley expected, others did not, and yet others found that the outcome of the experiment depended critically on the detailed nature of the task that the animal was required to learn. Given this untidy pattern of results we may conclude only that perhaps the visual cortex does in some circumstances play a role in tasks in which visual processing is not involved, but we cannot say much about what this role is or about what the critical circumstances are.

We can say, however, that whatever role they play in maze learning, the various parts of the association cortex are not equipotential with respect to other complex learning tasks. More recent experimental work has looked at the effects of small brain lesions inflicted on particular sites in the association areas. The effects of such lesions are to produce an animal that to superficial inspection does not differ from an intact animal. Differences are found only when the animals are tested in very specific ways. Such tests, carried out largely on monkeys and apes, have shown that lesions to the temporal association cortex result in a marked deficit in visual discrimination learning. The monkeys can learn only with the very greatest difficulty to pick up one object rather than another in order to get a peanut hidden underneath. But they show no other deficits and indeed can learn a similar discrimination perfectly well when they are allowed to distinguish between the two objects by touch. A lesion in the frontal association cortex leaves visual discrimination learning unimpaired but has marked effects on a task that imposes a demand upon the animal's short-term memory. If a normal monkey is restrained and allowed to watch a peanut being placed under one of two cups he will go to the appropriate cup and retrieve the bait as soon as he is allowed to. A monkey with a temporal lesion will do this too, but the animal with the frontal lesion proves to be incapable of bridging even the briefest delay; if he is not allowed to retrieve the peanut straight away he appears to lose all knowledge of where it is, choosing between the two cups at random.

The very specificity of these effects suggests yet another explanation for Lashley's mass-action findings. The ability to run a maze is not unitary but depends upon a large number of sub-abilities: the rat must be able to discriminate between paths in the maze that are blind alleys and those that are not; it must be able to associate certain paths with reward; it must be able to remember in the short-term the turns and choices it has recently made; and so on. Lesions of increasing size may have the effect of knocking out each of these abilities one by one, thus producing a gradual worsening of performance in the maze. The argument is in principle the same as that underlying the suggestion that the mass-action effect could emerge from the summation of a variety of sensory deficits. Both these arguments can explain the results observed without any use of the notion of equipotentiality.

*Visual processing by association cortex.* There remains to consider Lashley's work on discrimination learning. The observation that damage to the temporal cortex, the part of the association cortex that is adjacent to the visual cortex, seems compatible with the reflex model. It is easy to imagine visual information from the retina going via the thalamus to the occipital cortex and being passed from cell to cell across the cortex until it reaches the temporal association cortex where it receives "higher-level processing". But this model seems to be invalidated by the fact that visual discrimination can still occur when the visual cortex is disconnected surgically from adjoining parts of the cortex. Clearly there must be other pathways by which information can get from the occipital cortex to the temporal in addition to any running through or immediately below the cortical tissue that links them directly. Mishkin (1966) has made just this argument.

Figure 5.15a is a schematic representation of a section through the cerebral hemispheres of a monkey. The occipital and temporal areas are shown on each side of the brain as are hypothetical connections between them. In each hemisphere is the link that we have already discussed: the intra-cortical connection through the intervening area of *prestriate* cortex. But the two hemispheres are linked by a broad band of fibres called the *corpus callosum*, and these fibres form a pathway whereby the occipital cortex on the left side of the brain could be connected with temporal cortex on the right side of the brain and vice versa. Figure 5.15b shows the effect of these hypothetical connections of removing the temporal cortex on one side. It leaves the remaining temporal areas still connected with the occipital cortex on both sides of brain. Visual processing should still be possible, and indeed monkeys with such a lesion can still perform complex visual discriminations; in order to see the deficit mentioned above it is necessary to carry out a bilateral temporal lesion. In Fig. 5.15c both the left temporal cortex and the right occipital cortex have been removed. An animal with this pattern of brain damage does show impairment on the visual discrimination task but its performance is still quite good compared with that shown by an animal with bilateral temporal lesions. We may guess, therefore, that some visual information does make its way across the corpus callosum by way of the connection shown in the figure. In Fig. 5.15d this final connection disappears as the corpus callosum is sectioned. There is now no route for information to get from the visual cortex to the temporal cortex.

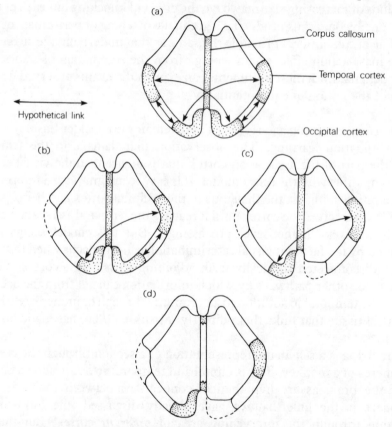

Fig. 5.15. *A representation of the stages in the study by Mishkin (1966) showing top views of sections through the cerebral hemispheres. In (a) there are four possible pathways connecting the temporal and occipital areas; in (d) all pathways have been cut.*

Mishkin found that animals with this pattern of brain damage were quite incapable of learning the visual discrimination.

It seems, then, that when all possible connections between the visual cortex and the visual association area are severed the animal is incapable of carrying out tasks requiring the analysis of complex visual information, even when (as in the case shown in Fig. 5.15d) it is equipped with one perfectly good temporal area and one perfectly good occipital area.

### "Association Cortex" Reconsidered

It will be well to restate at this point what have been taken to be the critical features of the reflex model, as applied to the neocortex: input to the brain consists of nerve impulses arriving in the sensory areas of the cortex; output consists of nerve impulses leaving the motor areas; input is connected to output by means of intracortical pathways running through or just below the association cortex. We have defended some aspects of this model, on the whole successfully against its opponents—we have rejected field theories of cortical activity and have gone some distance toward explaining away the evidence thought to require a concept of mass action. Nonetheless, we have made little progress toward explaining in detail what it is that association cortex does and we must now consider some evidence that contradicts the suggestion that its major function is that of providing a direct link between sensory and motor cortex.

*Subcortical connections.* Association cortex has been defined so far simply as being that cortex that does not have direct connection with sensory and motor nerve fibres. This indeed was one of the criteria used by early anatomists — association cortex was regarded as that part of the cortex that made only intra-cortical connections. But this view has been changed by more recent anatomical evidence. It has now become clear that just as the major sensory receiving areas receive projections from specific nuclei in the thalamus (the visual cortex from the lateral geniculate nucleus, the auditory cortex from the medial geniculate, and so on), so the association areas also receive thalamic projections. Thus the frontal cortex receives a projection from the *dorsomedial* nucleus of the thalamus and the temporal cortex (the visual association area) from the *pulvinar* nucleus. The connections of these latter thalamic nuclei are not fully known but some of those of the pulvinar, at least, have been traced. It turns out to receive a projection from that part of the midbrain that is fed directly by the optic nerve. That is, the visual association area has its own connection with the retina, independent of any going by way of the visual cortex.

The existence of this "second visual system" perhaps solves one remaining puzzle. It may explain how Lashley's rats were able to learn a light–dark discrimination even with the whole of the visual cortex removed. Even in mammals the midbrain visual system (perhaps in conjunction with mechanisms in the temporal cortex) is capable of detecting the difference between light and dark. Mammals with no visual cortex may be incapable of pattern vision but they are not totally blind. But the existence of these sub-cortical connections raises a host of new questions. No longer are we constrained to think of information winding its way from sensory to motor area by means of a long chain of intra-cortical connections. Instead the "association" areas may have their own sensory inputs and the power to integrate these with inputs passed on from adjacent primary receiving areas. What is more, they may have their own outputs since there is reason to think that some of the fibres run from the cortex to the thalamic nuclei rather than vice versa. They may even be capable of controlling the input that the cortex receives: that is, outgoing fibres from the "association" cortex may carry information that allows the thalamus to decide what information should pass up the fibres projecting to the primary sensory areas.

*Implications for the reflex model.* Given the complex "wiring" of the forebrain and in particular the existence of these connections between the cortex and sub-cortical structures, the possibilities for speculation (and for research) are endless. The general principle that emerges, however, is that although we cannot apply a simple reflex model to the activity of the whole of the cortex we need not reject it altogether. It is clearly not the case that the cortex is a system having sensory input to the receiving areas, output from the motor cortex, and pathways connecting the two. Rather it is better regarded as being a collection of a large number of interacting sub-systems. The input to many of these sub-systems will consist not of direct sensory information but will come from the output provided by other sub-systems. By the same token, some sub-systems will not influence the effectors directly but will provide inputs for others that do. The complexity of such an arrangement need not hide the fact that the principles of the reflex (as outlined above) provide an adequate model for each of the constituent parts of the whole system.

## CONCLUDING COMMENTS

We began this chapter by likening the task of the psychologist to that of an engineer trying to determine the principles by which some complex and hitherto unknown machine might work. We said that in both cases an investigation of the internal structure of the system might be a sensible first step, but it was emphasized that other information would also be needed. We are now in a position to specify what form this other information might take.

Our preliminary survey of the structure of the system has shown it to be one that is equipped to take in information about environmental circumstances and to use this information to organize its own behavioural output. Chapter 6 uses this observation as a starting point for a more detailed analysis of the interaction of the organism with its environment. And indeed, in order to say more about how the system works, what we need is a more exact specification of *what* it does. No matter how minutely a neuroanatomist studies the brain he is unlikely to discover it to be a system that, for instance, controls the response of freezing in a rat confronted with a novel environment and that transforms this response into one of exploration after a given period of time. Such facts are to be discovered only from direct study of the behaviour of the whole organism. On the basis of such a study the psychologist should be able to deduce what mechanisms must exist (mechanisms for detecting novelty, for comparing the present environment with others previously experienced, and so on) for the organism to behave as it does. Armed with this understanding at a conceptual level, the physiological psychologist will then be able to return to the study of the brain and to identify the tissues and cells, the electrical and biochemical processes in which these mechanisms are embodied.

## SOURCES AND FURTHER READING

Further information on nerves and nervous conduction can be found in any textbook of physiology, but for a detailed account of those aspects of special importance for psychology see *From Neuron to Brain* by Kuffler and Nicholls (1976). Good descriptions of the general layout of the vertebrate brain are less easy to come by. An excellent starting point is the chapter on the nervous system in *The Vertebrate Body* by Romer and Parsons (1977) although some of the suggestions they offer concerning homologies among the vertebrate classes have been overtaken by recent anatomical research. For these see Macphail's (1982) *Brain and Intelligence in Vertebrates*. Lashley's own description of his early work is to be found in his *Brain Mechanisms and Intelligence* (1929); a more up-to-date appraisal of its importance is supplied in a paper by Zangwill (1961). An extensive discussion of the implications of Lashley's work is supplied by Oatley in his *Perceptions and Representations* (1978) which gives a much less sympathetic treatment to the reflex model of brain function than that supplied by me. For a readable survey of the state of modern brain research see *The Brain*, a collection of articles by leading authorities originally published in *Scientific American* (1979).

# 6 Stimuli and Responses

## INTRODUCTION

We began our study of the structure and working of the nervous system (Chapter 5) in the hope that it might provide some clues as to why the organism behaves as it does. We have emerged with a picture of the organism as consisting of a receptor system and an effector system linked by nerves. Energy that activates the receptors can come ultimately to activate the effectors after passing, in modified form, down the pathways provided by the nerves. These observations are almost enough in themselves to provide an adequate account of the immediate causation of some very simple patterns of behaviour. That a sharp blow below the knee can cause a jerk of the lower leg is readily explained in terms of the pathway connecting a stretch receptor to the muscular effector (Chapter 5, pp. 144). This behaviour can be interpreted as being a *response* (R) to a particular *stimulus* (S).

More complex patterns of behaviour are not so readily accounted for; but it seems sensible, as we begin their analysis to work from the little that we are certain of. Accordingly we will adopt the general principle embodied in the reflex as a starting point in the analysis of the interaction of the organism with its environment. That is, we shall begin by trying to interpret complex behaviour as comprising a series of responses elicited by stimuli. For the moment these terms must remain undefined. There is no general agreement about how they should be used, and indeed one aim of this chapter is to discuss the alternatives. Faced with the problem, Watson, an early and vigorous proponent of the S–R analysis of behaviour, declared that he meant by the terms stimulus and response just what the physiologist means by them, and he left it at that. In the absence of a physiologist willing to provide exact definitions, this does not get us very far. All we can do for the time being is to cite examples: thus, a tap on the knee must be taken as an example of a stimulus, and a brief contraction of the muscles of the thigh with a consequent jerk of the lower leg can be regarded as constituting a response.

## Problems for the S–R Analysis

The attempt to analyse behaviour in S–R terms has a long history and has been widely influential. Once the distinction between sensory and motor nerves had been established by physiologists early in the nineteenth century, it was perhaps inevitable that S–R theories would develop. And indeed, the S–R analysis seems to be required by the existence of simple reflexes. But an analysis appropriate for reflex behaviour runs into many problems as soon as we try to apply it to more complex behaviour. A discussion of these problems forms the subject matter for this chapter and the next, but before embarking on this discussion it will be well to stand back and to describe in general terms what these problems are.

The first concerns the nature and organization of the response. The response element of a simple reflex consists of a discrete and easily identified contraction. Although most of the behaviour of interest to psychologists is undoubtedly the product of muscular contractions it is difficult to see it as a succession of reflex responses. Rather, behaviour seems to be emitted in a constant stream that is not easily divisible into a series of sub-units. The use of the word "emitted" in the previous sentence leads on to the next problem. A reflex is elicited by a specific stimulus. Much of our everyday behaviour, however, seems to possess a degree of spontaneity, there being no obvious eliciting stimulus. If the S–R analysis is to be applied to such behaviour it is necessary to allow that the stimulus that is actually effective in producing the behaviour may be something very different from that exemplified by a tap below the kneecap. Thirdly, even when we think we have found the effective stimulus for a given response it often turns out that the stimulus is quite ineffective when circumstances change. In some cases the organism has to be predisposed to make the response before the stimulus will elicit it. This is the problem of motivation. Finally there is the problem of learning: the fact that an animal may make a given response (or perhaps none at all) when a stimulus is first presented but, as a result of experience, may come to make a quite different response when the same stimulus is presented subsequently. The S–R analysis will clearly have to be elaborated to accommodate this phenomenon.

The topic of learning is of such importance that it is reserved for separate discussion in Chapter 7. In this chapter we consider the implications of the first three issues just mentioned for the analysis of all types of behaviour, whether these depend upon specific experience or not. Given that these three points amount to saying that much everyday behaviour does not show the properties of reflex behaviour it may seem pointless to pursue an S–R analysis. But it would be unwise to prejudge the issue in this way. Superficial appearances may be deceptive—after all, it is possible to construct a very complex building out of the simplest of bricks given enough of them. The first part of this chapter, then, will be devoted to the issue of whether the reflex can be regarded as a "behavioural building block", as the basic unit from which more complex behaviour is constructed.

## THE NATURE AND ORGANIZATION OF THE RESPONSE

The only response that has been mentioned so far is the knee jerk. This brief muscle twitch is clearly very different from the patterned sequence of muscular contractions that underlie any example of ordinary behaviour. Consider the example of a pianist picking out a tune on the piano. Each of his finger movements will require the integrated action of various muscle groups, the extensors being inhibited when the flexors are activated and so on, but such interactions are readily understood in terms of the reflexes discussed in Chapter 5. Furthermore, the whole performance can be described in S–R terms. Regarding each finger movement as a single response then we can identify for each response its eliciting stimulus. In this case the stimulus is likely to be visual: it will be the shape and position of the representation of the note in the music that the pianist is reading. By scanning from left to right across the music the pianist can be said to expose himself to a series of stimuli that evoke a pattern of responses that, in turn, produce the melody.

### The Role of Feedback

The example just discussed was chosen because it is an easy one for the S–R analysis to deal with—the behaviour can be divided up quite naturally into a series of discrete responses, each associated with an identifiable environmental event, its eliciting stimulus. But it is not difficult to think of other examples of behaviour that are not so easily dealt with. Thus, when a pianist has committed a piece to memory he may be capable of reproducing the whole of it faultlessly without any reference to a sheet of music, that is, he will emit a long chain of "responses" (of finger movements) in the absence of a parallel chain of eliciting stimuli. There may be some initial stimulus that sets the sequence of responses in motion ("play the National Anthem") but that can do no more than account for the first pattern of movements that the pianist makes.

To deal with this type of behaviour in reflex terms we must turn to the concept of the *chain reflex* for a possible account of what the pianist might be doing. The suggestion here is that the first response that the pianist makes itself produces the stimuli that evoke the second; the second response produces the stimuli that evoke the third; and so on. In this example the most obvious response-produced (*feedback*) stimulus is the note produced when the piano key is pressed, but visual events may also be important—that is, the pianist may see where he has put his finger and use this to guide his next response. Internal stimuli are also likely to be important. We have used the word stimulus so far to refer only to events in the outside world, but this usage seems too restrictive. The pianist is equipped with *proprioceptors*, with sensory receptors supplying information about the positions of his limbs and fingers. These too are a potential source of response-produced feedback, and although they lie inside the body the sort of stimuli they supply does not differ in principle from those supplied by receptors detecting response produced changes in the external world (see Fig. 6.1).

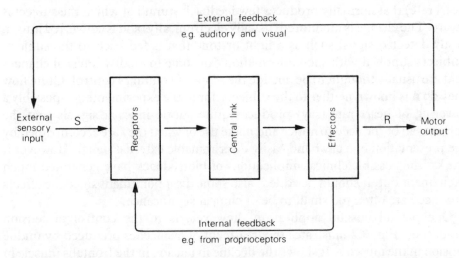

Fig. 6.1. *Schematic representation of the role of feedback in motor control. Emitting a response produces both proprioceptive changes and changes in the organism's external environment.*

*Removing normal feedback.* That feedback stimuli play an important role in human skilled performance has been established by experiments in which these stimuli are eliminated or modified in some way. In a classic demonstration of the role of auditory information the subject is required to speak into a microphone and his speech is returned to him via headphones after a slight delay. If the headphones are solid enough to exclude airborne sounds and the length of the delay is right (about one fifth of a second works best) the results can be devastating. The subject will begin to stutter, become incoherent, and perhaps find himself unable to speak at all. The role of internal feedback has been demonstrated by studies in which the subject is asked to perform some skilled movement of the fingers while a compression cuff is applied to the wrist. The effect of such a cuff is to restrict the blood flow to the nerves. The sensory nerves are more susceptible to such deprivation than are motor nerves so that (for a time) the subject is deprived of internal feedback from receptors in the joints and the skin but is still, in principle, capable of moving his fingers. Movements indeed prove to be possible in these circumstances, but the accuracy with which they are performed declines markedly—it becomes difficult to perform even a simple task in which all is required is that the subject should tap rhythmically with his finger.

*Biofeedback.* It is also possible to augment (rather than reduce or distort) feedback, and here the most dramatic results have come from studies of what has become known as *biofeedback.* In the biofeedback procedure the response used is some internal change (such as a rise in blood pressure or an increase in heart rate) that normally produces few feedback stimuli of which the subject is aware. The change is monitored (usually electronically) and is converted into an easily detected signal such as a light or tone that is fed back to the subject. Subjects supplied with such information can come to modify internal changes that are usually thought to be outside the scope of voluntary control. Quite how they do it is known neither to the subjects nor to the experimenters—possibly a lowering of heart rate (say) produces quite subtle internal signals that the subject can be induced to notice and make use of when they are accompanied by the presentation of a clear and easily discriminable external signal. However it works, the possible clinical implications of biofeedback have generated much excitement but, it should be added, also some disappointment since the effects produced are often too small to be of clinical significance.

One possibly useful application, however, is to the control of tension headaches: Fig. 6.2 illustrates the treatment of headaches produced by undue tension in the muscles. It shows the decline in tension in the frontalis muscle in subjects given 16 sessions of training with electrodes attached to the muscle to provide an external feedback signal about its state. Other subjects who were not

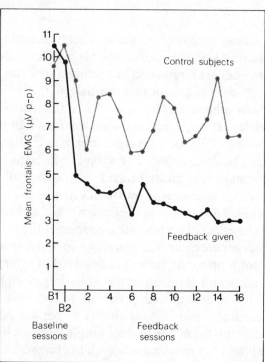

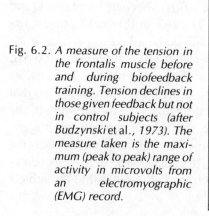

Fig. 6.2. *A measure of the tension in the frontalis muscle before and during biofeedback training. Tension declines in those given feedback but not in control subjects (after Budzynski et al., 1973). The measure taken is the maximum (peak to peak) range of activity in microvolts from an electromyographic (EMG) record.*

given explicit training (they were simply told to relax and heard irrelevant signals) show no such decline. Subjects given the biofeedback training reported a marked reduction in the frequency of their headaches.

## Chain Reflexes

By emphasizing the role of response-produced stimuli it is possible to give an S–R account for a stream of behaviour, such as that emitted by the skilled pianist, that at first sight seems to lack reflex properties. But we should be cautious about accepting this account. What is being offered is no more than a hypothesis. We have supplied evidence that response-produced stimuli exist and are important in controlling behaviour, but it has yet to be proved that they function to link a series of responses into a chain. To test the hypothesis we need an experiment in which the organism is deprived of response-produced stimuli while performing a complex activity. The chain reflex notion makes the simple prediction that an organism deprived of feedback should be able to perform no response after the first in the chain.

Studies of the mechanism controlling swimming in the dogfish yield some evidence to support this theory. Dogfish (and sharks in general—the group to which dogfish belong) swim not by waving their fins but by using their whole bodies. In the first phase of the movement the body adopts a sinusoidal posture (when viewed from above). A wave of muscular contraction passes down the body carrying the sinusoidal wave down the body, pushing the water backwards and the fish forward. This movement pattern could be a chain reflex with the stimuli produced by the response that initiates the movement eliciting the next pattern of muscular contraction and so on. The important feedback stimuli in this case are unlikely to be auditory or visual but will arise from proprioceptors. In order to test the chain reflex account it is necessary to eliminate proprioceptive information. This can be done surgically. Recall from Chapter 5 (Fig. 5.4) that sensory nerve fibres enter the spinal cord dorsally as a separate bundle distinct from the motor nerve that leaves the cord ventrally. It is possible, therefore, to cut through the dorsal roots of the spinal cord, to eliminate proprioceptive input, and yet leave the animal theoretically capable of controlling the musculature of its body.

Observations of animals subjected to this operation have yielded results compatible with the chain reflex theory. Such animals show little spontaneous movement. They do respond, however, to the stimulus provided by being put in a flow of water, by adopting the sinusoidal body posture. But no wave of undulation then passes down the body. We may conclude that the next part of the behaviour pattern needs to be elicited by the stimuli produced by the initial movement.

It would be possible now to list a number of other examples of behaviour patterns in which response-produced feedback serves to integrate the component responses. But no matter how many such cases we considered there would never be enough to prove that *all* complex behaviour is built up of S–R sub-units. It will be more instructive to look for examples in which feedback stimuli are not so important. Just a single case would require us to rethink our attempt at an S–R analysis of complex behaviour.

## Central Patterning

*Fixed action patterns.* Figure 6.3 represents the behaviour shown by a frog in catching a fly. If the fly initially appears to one side, the frog turns toward the target and then, with the fly in its sights, it shoots by flicking out its tongue. This tongue-flick is stereotyped in its form and is to be seen in all members of the species. It is elicited by the appropriate stimulus but it is not otherwise controlled by it—if the fly moves, the tongue-flick is not corrected and the fly escapes. The tongue-flick is perhaps simple enough to qualify as a reflex response but in Chapter 2 (p. 37) we considered other more complex patterns that possess some of the same properties. Thus when the greylag goose responds to an egg that has rolled away from the nest by dragging it back (Fig. 2.9) it will complete the movement once initiated, even when the egg has been removed. Perhaps motivated by a desire to discredit the chain reflex notion, early students of animal behaviour, such as Lorenz, were eager to find examples of such *fixed action patterns*, that is, of behaviour patterns consisting of a stereotyped sequence of movements that is "released" by some external starting stimulus but which appears to be free from stimulus control thereafter. It was argued that these patterns are organized centrally—that the nervous system is so arranged that it can emit the appropriate sequence of motor commands without external prompts, once it has been set into action by the starting stimulus.

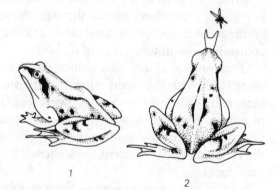

Fig. 6.3. *The stereotyped response of a frog to a fly entering its field of view. The frog turns to face the fly and then flicks out its tongue (after Tin-bergen, 1951).*

1

2

*Experimental evidence.* The existence of a nervous mechanism with these properties has been demonstrated by studies of locust flight. A locust suspended in a flow of air will respond by flapping its wings. Since the locust is held stationary, electrical recordings can be made of the rhythmic activity of the muscles that produces the rhythmic movement of the wings. The rhythm that underlies this behaviour appears to be generated by a central "pacemaker". If the wings are fixed in one position or even removed altogether the normal pattern of feedback is disrupted but the rhythm still persists. It is not the case that stimuli generated by one wingbeat reflexly elicit the next.

Central patterning is not confined to insects or birds as investigation of the coordination of swallowing in mammals has shown. The seemingly simple response of swallowing an object pushed to the back of the mouth is in fact a rather complicated matter requiring coordinated contractions in some 20 different muscles of the mouth, throat, and the diaphragm. These contractions occur in an orderly sequence that is consistent from one response to the next. It is easy to imagine that such coordination is achieved by means of a chain reflex. The initiating stimulus in this case is the ball of food at the back of the mouth. Once this stimulus has activated the first of the muscles involved, the subsequent contraction of other muscles might well be elicited by feedback stimuli from those that have contracted earlier. Indeed, the swallowing reflex looks like such a prime candidate for analysis in chain reflex terms that it comes as something of a surprise to find evidence that it is nothing of the sort.

There is no convenient surgical means in this case for removing proprioceptive feedback since swallowing is controlled by cranial nerves in which sensory and motor nerve fibres are mixed up. But the same effect as that produced by sectioning the dorsal roots of the spinal cord can be achieved by means of an anaesthetic: a substance like cocaine applied to the mouth and throat will eliminate sensation but still allow the motor nerves and muscles to work. The critical observation is that dogs injected with such an anaesthetic are still perfectly capable of performing the normal pattern of movements involved in swallowing. This behaviour pattern is not a chain reflex: rather the movement is determined by some pattern inherent in the nervous centres controlling it so that once it is initiated swallowing is independent of sensory stimulation. Swallowing, too, must therefore be regarded as a fixed action pattern. Indeed it provides a rather better example of the distinction between the chain reflex and the fixed action pattern than those more commonly cited. The most frequently cited examples are certainly free from external control once they have been initiated but there has been little experimental investigation to rule out any possible contribution from proprioceptive feedback. It remains possible, therefore, that some of them might be appropriately regarded as chain reflexes.

*Skilled performance.* For a further example of the inadequacy of the chain reflex theory we may return to the case of the pianist, with which we began discussion of the topic. It was suggested that when a pianist plays a tune from memory he is able to do so because each finger movement produces the stimuli that elicit the next. This may be true for the beginner but it cannot be true for the expert. A skilled pianist is capable of making a dozen or so finger movements in a second and the very speed of his performance is enough to rule out the chain reflex account. When movements occur as rapidly as this there is simply not enough time for proprioceptive information to travel up the sensory nerves to the central nervous system in time to initiate the next response. In some way the required pattern of movements must be centrally represented and run off as a whole. Perhaps the fact that some pianists, when they are interrupted in the middle of a piece, cannot resume where they left off but must go back to the beginning, is further evidence of this.

## Peripheral Influences on Central Patterns

The examples we have considered so far demonstrate that, although some patterns of behaviour are organized according to chain-reflex principle, this principle is not universally applicable since other patterns are controlled solely by some central pattern. Having established this latter point it should now be acknowledged that the cases we have considered so far have been extreme examples and that in many patterns of behaviour it is possible to detect the operation of some central pattern that is modulated by sensory influences. A convenient example of such interaction between peripheral and central factors is found in the mechanisms controlling respiration in mammals.

*Breathing.* The behaviour involved in breathing could be analysed into two distinct responses, breathing in and breathing out, that follow each other in a regular sequence. It is easy to imagine that a chain reflex might underlie this behaviour with breathing out producing some set of stimuli that elicits breathing in, and vice versa. One obvious source of feedback stimuli is the stretch receptors that are known to be present in the lung. Direct physiological investigation shows, however, that breathing is controlled by motor nerve cells located in the *medulla oblongata* (Chapter 5), some of which show spontaneous rhythmic activity that is independent of sensory input. It is to this respiration control centre that nerve fibres from the stretch receptors of the lung run. But sectioning the vagus nerve which carries these fibres does not abolish breathing: the depth of inspiration tends to be increased but breathing will continue as long as the respiratory centre is itself intact. The respiratory centre is best seen as being a pacemaker necessary for the basic rhythm of breathing. Its rhythmic activity is not directly controlled but is modulated by a variety of sensory influences, which include information from receptors sensitive to the chemical composition of the blood in addition to those sensitive to the degree of inflation and deflation of the lungs.

*Fixed action patterns reconsidered.* Although the example we have just considered comes from mammalian behaviour, it should be emphasized that such central–peripheral interactions seem to be the rule rather than the exception in all classes of animal. The search for centrally organized fixed action patterns revealed in a graphic way the inadequacies of chain-reflex theory but it can now be appreciated that feedback stimuli have an important role in controlling even these patterns of behaviour. Thus, although the pacemaker in the locust's nervous system will persist in its rhythmic output when deprived of normal feedback, it is not independent of it. Cutting the sensory nerves that supply information from stretch receptors at the base of the wing will produce a slowing of the rhythm. Visual feedback is important too. A locust deprived of one wing will roll to one side when deprived of vision, but if it can see, the pattern of muscular activity will be modified so as to maintain the animal at the correct orientation to its visual world. Again, the greylag goose will indeed continue with its retrieval movement should the egg roll away but the exact pattern of the behaviour becomes changed. As the goose draws the egg in, it makes small lateral movements that serve to keep the egg under its bill. When the egg slips away the inward movement persists but the lateral movements disappear. They clearly depend upon feedback information. Finally, although the tongue-flick of the frog is not under external control, the initial part of this behaviour pattern is. Should the fly move during the initial turning phase of the pattern the frog compensates so as to face it head on. The frog shows an ability to "home" on its target. We must now consider this type of behaviour in more detail.

## Orientation and "Homing"

We have seen how a stimulus can elicit a discrete response in the case of the knee-jerk reflex. We have seen also that a given starting stimulus may elicit a much more complex pattern of behaviour which in some cases consists of a chain of separate responses, each elicited by response-produced stimuli, and in other cases is co-ordinated by some central nervous pattern that may be relatively independent of peripheral influences. These examples do not exhaust the list of ways in which S and R may be related.

*Responses to light in insects.* Consider the response known as *negative phototaxis* shown by maggots of the house fly and of the bluebottle before they pupate. When exposed to a light source the maggot will crawl directly away from it. (A *taxis* is a form of orientation in which the animal moves directly toward or away from a source of stimulation.) This behaviour is not simply released or triggered by the presentation of the stimulus since, if the light is turned off once the response has started, the behaviour pattern is aborted. It is thus rather different from a reflex or fixed action pattern in which a brief presentation of the starting stimulus is enough for the pattern to go through to completion.

Close observation of the maggot will reveal what is happening. The animal's head is equipped with receptors sensitive to the intensity of light. As it crawls along it swings its head from side to side, thus effectively sampling the intensity on each side of its body (Fig. 6.4). If the intensity is greater on the right than on the left, the maggot shows a reduced tendency to turn its head to the right and thus tends to move to the left. When the light is dead astern, there is no preference for turning to one side rather than the other since both are equally illuminated. The maggot thus moves directly away from the light and "homes" on the darkest part of its environment. It is possible to "trick" this system by turning the light on every time the maggot's head swings to the right (say) and turning off when the head swings to left. The maggot will consistently circle to the left.

Animals equipped with two receptors can move toward or away from a source of stimulation directly, without swinging to and fro. Like many adult insects, the hover fly will fly or walk directly toward a light source. Suppose that when the light is first turned on the insect is standing at an angle to it. As a result, one eye will receive more intense illumination than the other. The legs on the more dimly lit side may then be seen to work more vigorously than those on the

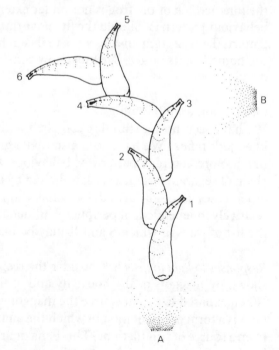

Fig. 6.4. *Phototaxis in a maggot. In response to light A the maggot moves away, by series of expansions and contractions swinging its head from side to side as it goes. At position 3, light A is turned off and light B on. The next movement to the left (4) is somewhat larger than usual. The swing to the right at 5 exposes the receptor to increased illumination and is corrected by the swing over to 6 (modified from Tinbergen, 1951).*

brightly lit side and as a consequence the insect turns toward and tends to move toward the light. When it is head on to the light there will be no difference in the intensity of light falling on the two eyes and the legs will work equally vigorously on both sides of the body. Any deviation from the true path will produce differential illumination of the eyes and the consequent difference in performance between the legs on the two sides of the body will automatically put the insect back on course. (Some insects can be made to go round in perpetual circles by painting over one of the eyes. No matter how hard the legs work on the "dimly lit" side they never manage to equalize the apparent intensity of the light falling on the two eyes.)

*Negative feedback control systems.* Here then is a behaviour pattern that, like the chain reflex, is dependent upon feedback in that the consequences of an initial movement determine the nature of the next movement that the animal makes. But it differs in the important respect that the behaviour never becomes independent of the initial starting stimulus. In the chain reflex (as described above) each response in a sequence is elicited by its own stimulus, and no new principle is introduced by the fact that some of the eliciting stimuli happen to be response-produced. In this case, however, the initial movements modify the properties of the starting stimulus, and information about these modifications is fed back into the system and influences its further behaviour. This feedback principle is widely used in man-made control systems (see Fig. 6.5). A domestic thermostat has a "set point" (the desired temperature), takes information from a receptor about the temperature of the room, and sends commands to an

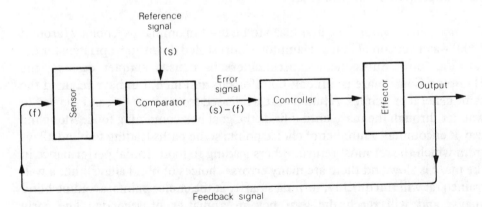

Fig. 6.5. *A feedback control system. The comparator detects the discrepancy (or error) between a reference signal (such as that provided by the setting on a thermostat) and an input signal (the temperature of the room) provided by a feedback loop. If the two signals are equal, nothing happens. If there is a discrepancy the error signal operates the controlling device (another part of the thermostat) and the controlled process (the activity of some effector) is modified. For an insect the controlled process will be locomotion and the error signal produced by the discrepancy between an optimum level of illumination and that falling on the receptors.*

effector, the boiler. When a comparison shows that the room temperature has fallen below the set point the boiler is switched on. The increasing temperature is sensed and when it exceeds the set point the boiler is turned off again. (The feedback is thus said to be *negative*.) In this way the system automatically "homes" in on the appropriate temperature. The entire system seems to show purposive behaviour, to act in ways that are directed toward a particular goal, just as the house fly maggot, whose behaviour is controlled by an analogous set of processes, seems to show purposiveness in the way it avoids light. For this reason the principles illustrated by such self-regulating systems are of great interest to psychologists. A major problem for any reflex analysis of behaviour is that it fails to account for the obvious goal-directness of much human and animal behaviour. The examples we have just considered provide some clues as to how this phenomenon might be accommodated by an elaborated version of the S–R account.

## Maze-running by the Rat

The patterns of behaviour that we have considered so far are quite remote from those usually studied by psychologists. To redress the balance we turn next to a pattern that has (according to some) been studied by psychologists to the point where it begins to look like an unhealthy obsession. A more important reason for looking at the behaviour shown by a rat when it runs through a maze is that it allows us to see how several of the principles of response organization exemplified above may interact in controlling what seems, on first inspection, to be a simple pattern of behaviour.

*Proprioceptive control.* The first maze to be used in animal psychology (around 1900) was a version of that at Hampton Court scaled down appropriately for the rat (Fig. 6.6). Subsequent experimenters have used simpler designs (the Hampton Court maze is difficult both for rats and men) but have retained the same general principles. A hungry rat is released from a start box and allowed to wander through the maze until it finds the goal box containing food. Along the way it encounters a number of choice points some paths leading to blind alleys from which the rat must return, others leading to food. Initial performance in the maze is slow and there are many errors (choices of blind alleys), but a well trained rat will run quickly, turning smartly at the choice points, avoiding blind alleys, and will reach the goal box in a matter of seconds. The early behaviourists considered this to be an example of a chain reflex, with the initiating external stimulus being the start box and with response-produced stimuli eliciting the subsequent responses that moved the animal through the maze. Watson himself laid particular emphasis on the importance of proprioceptive response-produced stimuli (as opposed to the sequence of external stimuli that the rat will subject itself to as it runs through the maze) and he provided some evidence in favour of his view. In an experiment by Carr and Watson (1908) rats were given extensive training in a complex maze (one with many choice points). Some of the alleys were then lengthened or shortened and the behaviour of the rats was found to be greatly disturbed. When the alleys were lengthened the rats tend to make their turns (or rather, try to make their turns) at the point where the junction had previously been. When the alleys

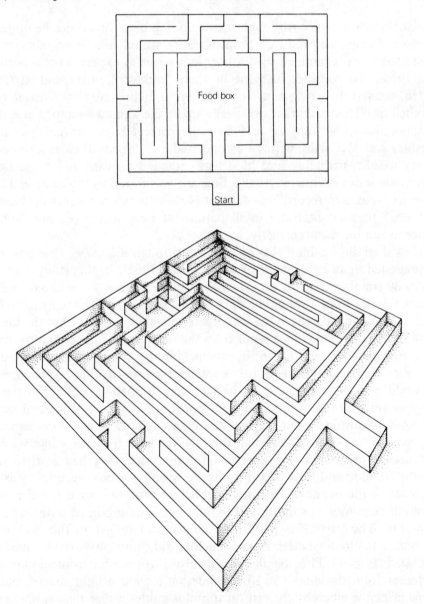

Fig. 6.6. *A complex maze, modelled on that at Hampton Court, as used in early studies of learning and performance in the rat.*

were shortened the rats ran headlong into the end wall. They were thus clearly not paying much attention to external cues, a result that goes a long way towards supporting Watson's analysis. (It remains possible, although it may seem unlikely, that the rats were running through some centrally patterned response sequence that was entirely independent of peripheral influence.)

*Control by remote cues.* Although maze running may sometimes be under the control of response-produced proprioceptive stimuli this is not always true. The matter was examined by Lashley in a series of experiments reported in the 1920s. To consider just one of these studies: Lashley and McCarthy (1926) trained the rat to run a maze before inflicting surgical damage on its cerebellum. This operation drastically upset the animal's motor pattern but did not disrupt its ability to follow the correct path through the maze. Lashley and McCarthy write of an operated rat: "She walked as if drawing a heavy weight, with fore and hind legs extended forward and dragging her along in a series of lunges. At this time she was tested in the maze and made a perfect retention record" (p. 428). It is clear therefore that this subject did not need to encounter the usual pattern of proprioceptive stimulation in order to run the maze correctly.

How then did Lashley's rat find its way through the maze? One possibility is suggested in an experiment by Mackintosh (1965). In this study, rats were given 20 training trials in a "T-maze" (a maze with just one choice point at which the rats must turn either right or left; see Fig. 6.7). After this training had been completed the maze was rotated through 180° so that the animals now approached the choice point from the north (say) rather than the south. This manipulation resulted in the rats making the wrong choice, turning into the alley that had not previously contained a reward. The explanation for this odd behaviour is found in the fact that the baited goalbox in the first stage of training was positioned next to a window. The rats learned not the response of turning right (say) at the choice point; rather they learned to approach a very obvious external stimulus, the light from the window. When the maze was rotated they carried on doing what they had learned to do during training and thus ended up in the wrong goalbox since this was now adjacent to the window. In running this maze the rats were not emitting a series of responses to stimuli; rather they were homing-in on a distant target stimulus. The particular pattern of movements to get to the goal varied according to circumstances just as much as did those employed by Lashley's operated animal. The detailed mechanisms for motor control are quite different from those seen in insects homing toward a light source, but the basic principle whereby the critical stimulus guides rather than simply elicits the response can be discerned in maze running too.

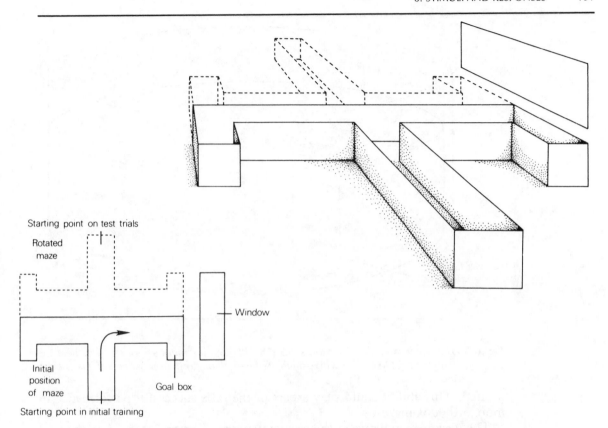

Fig. 6.7. *Investigation of the cues controlling performance in a T-maze. In the experiment by Mackintosh (1965) the position of the maze was shifted with respect to the distant cue provided by the window. The arrow shows the path that the rats were trained initially to take. The question of interest was which way will a rat turn in the rotated maze?*

In Mackintosh's experiment the rats' behaviour was guided by a distant stimulus. Recent experiments have made it clear that rats are remarkably proficient at using remote cues of this sort to find their way about the environment. Furthermore, these cues can serve to guide behaviour even when they do not themselves act as targets to be homed on, as is dramatically shown in an experiment by Morris (1981). Morris's experiment relies on the fact that rats do not like water and when put in a tank (Fig. 6.8) they will learn to swim to a small platform that allows them to climb clear of it. Since the top of the platform is arranged to be just below water level and the water itself is cloudy (achieved by adding milk), the rat cannot locate the platform directly. Nonetheless, the subjects learn to swim straight to it from whatever point they are first put into the tank. Clearly the rats are capable of learning the spatial location of the goal relative to the remote cues provided by aspects of the room in which the tank is located. This ability could well play a part in the rat's successful performance in more orthodox mazes.

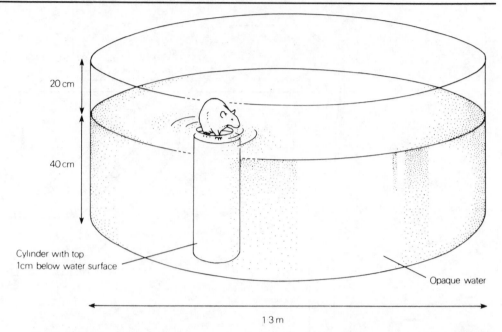

20 cm

40 cm

Cylinder with top
1cm below water surface

Opaque water

1 3 m

Fig. 6.8. *The water tank used by Morris (1981). Although it cannot see or smell or hear the target, the rat learns to swim straight to the small platform from wherever it is put into the tank.*

located. This ability could play a part in the rat's successful performance in more orthodox mazes.

The discrepancy between the results just discussed and those described by Watson makes it clear that the nature of the response underlying maze running may vary from one study to another. The experiment reported by Mackintosh casts some light on one of the factors responsible for this variation. Some rats in this experiment received not 20 but 200 training trials with the maze in its normal orientation. When these subjects were tested in the rotated maze they did not approach the window but persisted in making the same turn as that required in training. Mackintosh suggested that with extended training there may be transfer from external to proprioceptive control. Thus in the early stages of learning a maze, the animals tend to home upon a distant stimulus but with a lot of practice their behaviour becomes converted into a chain reflex. (The rats in Watson's experiments received very thorough training.) Such a transfer from external to proprioceptive control will be familiar to anyone who has worked hard at acquiring a skill such as typing, or playing the piano, or riding a bicycle, although in these cases the transfer is unlikely to be complete. *Central patterns.* It is even possible that in some circumstances, maze running might be substantially free from control by stimuli and come instead under the control of some central pattern. Taub and Berman (1968) report a series of experiments investigating motor control in monkeys. In these experiments the animals were deprived of sensory information from their arms and hands. They were then required to carry out a task involving a fair degree of manual dexterity in the absence of any useful visual cues. (They had to reach behind a screen in order to pull a lever.) Their performance was not particularly good, but that they were able to do this task at all shows that behaviour can indeed by controlled by a central pattern capable of operating independently of sensory input. Presumably in normal animals the central pattern interacts with peripheral influences. It can be envisaged as consisting of a list of instructions: reach, grasp, and pull. These instructions will be enough on their own for the movement pattern to be produced in a rough-and-ready way but really skilled performance will depend upon sensory stimuli directing the detailed execution of each of the components. Something similar may play a part in determining performance in a maze. The rat will use visual cues to identify the various choice points and proprioceptive cues will help to control the detail of individual limb movements, but the overall pattern of its behaviour might well be determined by some central plan, equivalent to a list of instructions of this sort: first on the left, second on the right, and so on. Signs of the operation of centrally organized plan have been revealed in experiments by Dabrowska (e.g. 1963). She trained rats in mazes where they had to learn a sequence of turns (such as L, R, R, L) to get from start box to goal box. When this had been learned the layout of the maze was changed so that the animals now had to learn either to reverse the direction of all their turns (i.e. they now had to follow the sequence R, L, L, R) or just some of them (e.g. R, L, R, L). She found that the complete reversal was acquired more readily than the partial reversal. The rats could learn the new problem presented by the complete reversal simply by learning to make a new turn at the first choice point but otherwise persisting with the same general scheme that worked in initial training. The partial reversal, however, requires them to adopt a new pattern.

## Conclusions

Watson's attempt to demonstrate that maze running is essentially a chain reflex stemmed from his attachment to the S–R account of behaviour. We have seen that, although complex behaviour patterns can sometimes be analysed into chain reflexes, this is by no means always true. Does this mean that we must now discard the S–R analysis?

We took as the defining example of "a response" the muscle twitch seen in the knee-jerk reflex and in doing so we were implicitly accepting Watson's view that behaviour consists of nothing but a series of muscular contractions (and sometimes glandular secretions) such as have been described by physiologists. It is interesting to note, however, that although Watson wanted to define the response in this way he often failed to abide by his own definition, referring to such "responses" as "walking", "talking", "taking food", and so on without reference to the muscle contractions that underlie them. In the terminology suggested by one of his successors in the study of maze running by rats (Tolman, 1932), he slipped from a *molecular* definition of the response to a larger scale *molar* definition.

Watson was presumably willing to do this because he believed that behaviour described at the molar level ("the rat turned left and then right") could in principle be analysed into a set of muscle contractions each evoked by its own stimulus. We have seen that this belief was mistaken, and Watson's version of S–R theory must indeed be abandoned. It still remains possible, however, to give an S–R analysis of behaviour provided we define the response at the molar level, and what is more this is surely a more appropriate level for the psychologist to work at. Playing a tune on the piano, articulating a sentence, running through a maze—these can, with care, be as well defined as the muscle twitch responsible for the knee-jerk reflex, and they are of much greater interest to the psychologist. It may be impossible to analyse these patterns into individual muscle twitches each evoked by its own stimulus but we are nonetheless entitled to regard each whole pattern as being a "response". Their origin may still be discussed in S–R terminology in that the psychologist's job remains that of specifying the events that cause the response to appear.

What we have done by adopting the molar level of analysis is to redefine the nature of R in the S–R formula so that it now refers to any identifiable bit of behaviour. We must turn next to a consideration of the way in which the concept of the stimulus must also be expanded if we are to establish a satisfactory framework for the analysis of behaviour.

## THE EFFECTIVE STIMULUS

If we adopt any version of an S–R account of behaviour, we are accepting that all behaviour consists of responses (however defined) that are elicited by stimuli. In order to explain why a particular behaviour pattern occurs it is necessary, therefore, to determine what stimulus elicits it. This may seem a simple matter in that all we need do is record what environmental events reliably precede the occurrence of the response in question. But, unfortunately, as soon as we try to do this, complications begin to arise. The most obvious problem is that animals can show behaviour that seems to be "spontaneous"—behaviour that is not immediately preceded by some environmental event. This issue is discussed at the end of this section of the chapter. First we need to consider another set of problems: those that arise from the ability that animals show to select the stimuli to which they respond, attending to some and ignoring other aspects of their environment.

### Stimulus Selection

*Examples.* During the breeding season, the male three-spined stickleback establishes a territory and will attack another male that encroaches upon it. A casual observer might suppose that this aggressive response is elicited by the sight of a small three-spined fish but his conclusion would be unjustified.

Figure 6.9 shows four not very fishlike objects that are all capable of eliciting the response. The fish shown at the top of the figure is not. In order to elicit the response the intruding fish must have a red underside (a characteristic of the male stickleback when breeding) and this feature in the three dummies of Fig. 6.9 is enough to elicit the response. Thus, organisms can exhibit a selectivity about which aspects of environmental events they attend to, and this constitutes a problem for any experimenter. If he happens to notice some aspect other than those used by his subject he will come away with a wrong conclusion about what stimulus is actually effective in eliciting the response.

Attentional effects are also evident in less natural patterns of behaviour. In an experiment reported by Reynolds (1961) two pigeons were rewarded by getting access to food for pecking at a response key (see Chapter 2, p. 42) on which was displayed a white triangle on a red background. When the key displayed a white circle on a green background pecks were not rewarded. The pigeons came to peck only at the former display. Here then is a response (pecking at the key) that is reliably elicited by a given stimulus (a key displaying a white triangle on a red background). Or so it seems until we consider the results of a second stage of Reynold's experiment. In this second stage the birds were presented on

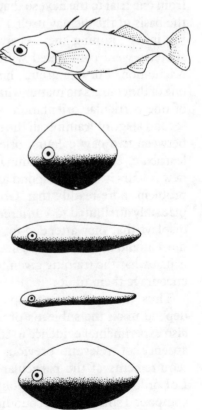

Fig. 6.9. *A male stickleback lacking a red belly and four crude models each with a red underside. The models will evoke fighting in another male but the fish will not (after Tinbergen, 1951).*

separate test trials with components of the original displays: with triangle and circle in the absence of the coloured backgrounds and with plain red and green fields. One bird responded only to the triangle and not to the red field; the other bird responded to red and not to the triangle. For neither subject was our original characterization of the stimulus (as a white triangle on a red background) a proper description of what was in fact eliciting the response. The birds proved to be capable of responding selectively to particular components of the original display.

*Experimental analysis of attention.* It is not known why the two subjects in Reynolds' experiment differed in the components that they attended to but other experiments of the same general type have provided some clues about variables that can play a part in determining the direction of attention.

A simplified version of the design of an experiment on stimulus selection by Mackintosh and Little (1969) is given in Fig. 6.10. In this experiment the pigeons were allowed to choose between two keys presented simultaneously, each of which bore a different display. Response to one of the displays gave access to reward. (The key on which each display was presented was varied from one trial to the next so that pigeons were required to make their choices on the basis of the display itself.) There were two groups of subjects, differing in the initial training they received. On each trial of this initial stage, all the subjects were confronted with displays that differed both in colour and in orientation. For one group, however, reward was delivered after response to one of the colours no matter what the orientation was; for the other group choice of one particular orientation was rewarded, regardless of the colour. In the second stage of training all the subjects were required to learn a discrimination between two new colours, orientation again being an irrelevant cue. Having learned a red–green discrimination does not tell the subject which of the two new colours it should respond to. Nonetheless, Group 1 learned the transfer test problem more readily than Group 2. This difference in performance is most plausibly attributed to a difference between the two groups in the aspects of the displays that they attended to. In order to solve the test problem the subjects must attend to colour differences and ignore differences in orientation; and this is just what the training given to the subjects in Group 1 might be expected to encourage them to do.

Thus, the aspects of a complex environmental event that are attended to may depend upon the subject's previous experience with similar events. There is also experimental evidence to show that attentional effects may be found in the absence of relevant previous experience and may be produced by the requirements of the particular experimental situation employed. Foree and LoLordo (1973) trained pigeons to press a treadle for food in the presence of a compound stimulus: the sounding of a tone combined with the presentation of a

Training stage

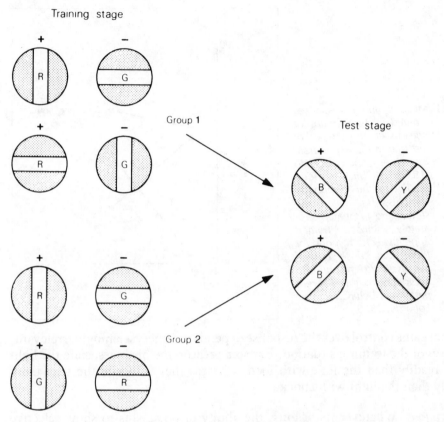

Fig. 6.10. *Schematic representation of an experiment with pigeons on attention. On each trial the pigeon chooses from two keys presented side by side; for each group two of the possible choices required are depicted. The + designates the key response to which is rewarded. Group 1 learns to respond to the red stripe regardless of its orientation; Group 2 learns to respond to the vertical stripe regardless of its colour. Both groups are then required to learn a new colour discrimination with the orientation of the stripes irrelevant.*

light. When the birds had learned to do this they were given test trials on which either just the tone or just the light was presented. The results (Fig. 6.11) suggested that the birds had attended only to the light in that they responded readily in the presence of this stimulus but scarcely at all in the presence of the tone. Other birds in the same experiment received similar initial training differing only in the nature of the event used to reward performance; these subjects learned to press the treadle in the presence of the tone–light compound because this response prevented the delivery of an electric shock. When these subjects were given test trials they showed a reverse pattern of results, responding to the tone but not to the light. We must conclude, therefore, that both the tone and the light can function perfectly well as stimuli but that which

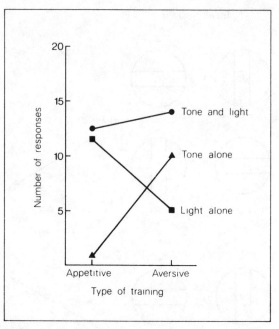

Fig. 6.11. *Mean number of responses emitted by two groups of pigeons on three types of test trial in the experiment by Foree and LoLordo (1973). All birds respond readily to the compound stimulus, but when the stimuli are presented separately those trained appetitively (to respond for food) and those trained aversively (to respond to avoid shock) show different patterns of behaviour (after LoLordo, 1979).*

of them gains control over the response depends on other, seemingly irrelevant, features of the training situation. For some reason the birds associate the light more readily than the tone with food, whereas they associate the tone more readily than the light with shock.

*Implications.* Whatever its origins, the ability of organisms to show selective responsiveness has important implications for the way in which we analyse behaviour. Our aim is to explain behaviour by pointing to the stimulus that elicits it and in order to do this we have to be able to identify the stimulus accurately. But no matter how carefully we try to do this it might easily turn out that the organism under study has ignored all the features we have identified and is responding to something that we have not noticed at all. We might find ourself confidently stating that the response is elicited by the presentation of a white equilateral triangle, apex pointing upwards, only to find that the presentation of this event on a subsequent occasion fails to elicit the response simply because we have changed the colour of the background on which it is presented. In order to provide a satisfactory explanation for behaviour (one that is capable of predicting what an organism will do) it is necessary to specify the *effective stimulus*—that feature of the environment that actually controls the response.

## Defining the Effective Stimulus Experimentally

What we have shown is that it is not possible to decide what stimulus elicits a given response by simple observation. What has perhaps emerged is that the effective stimulus needs to be determined by experiment. We may speak of an object such as a blue cube or a red square or whatever as being "a stimulus" but the effective stimulus is not itself an event or object; rather it is some property of the event that cannot be changed without changing the response. In order to determine the effective stimulus what we must do is to separate out the various properties of the original event and test them one by one. That which elicits the original response is the effective stimulus. (This is, of course, the basic technique used in the experimental studies of stimulus selection described above.) Were we simply to guess which of these properties is the stimulus that elicits the response, we could very easily get it wrong and our predictions about the organism's further behaviour would go awry.

*Perception of brightness.* The need to determine the nature of the effective stimulus experimentally is not restricted to cases in which compound stimuli are used, as the following examples drawn from studies of the perception of brightness will show.

Some stimuli when presented along with the question "what colour is it?" will elicit the response: "black". It might seem a simple matter to specify in purely physical terms those properties that an object must possess if it is to be stimulus capable of eliciting this response—to say that an object will appear black when it emits or reflects less than some certain number of units of light energy. But the matter is not so simple. Imagine yourself sitting in a darkened room waiting for a slide-show to begin. The brightest object in the room will be the white projection screen. When a black-and-white slide is then shown we see black shapes against a bright white background. The blackness of the shapes will be so convincing that it may be difficult to appreciate that no light has been subtracted from the dark areas of the screen and that they are still reflecting as much light as they did before the projector was switched on. Their blackness derives not from the amount of light they emit themselves but depends upon the contrast with adjacent bright areas. A more exotic demonstration of a similar effect is supplied by the surprise that many people showed when they were first allowed to see the moon rocks brought back by the Apollo expeditions. The surface rocks of the moon looked, even under intense illumination, much more like pieces of coal than the white marble that many of us had anticipated. They reflect only 7% of the light that falls on them, as does the moon itself. The moon looks white only because it is brightly illuminated by the sun and is viewed against a background of darkness. It seems that the perception of brightness may be determined by relative rather than absolute properties. An object can look black in one context and white in another even though it is emitting the same amount of light in both.

Phenomena of this sort are not found only in human subjects. A rat, faced with two cards differing in brightness, can be trained to push down the dark one rather than the light one if the response gives access to food. The rat's response seems not always to be governed by the absolute properties of the card associated with reward. If a trained rat is allowed to choose between the original dark card and one that is even darker, it is usually found that the original stimulus no longer elicits the same response. Rather the rat chooses the novel, even darker card—a phenomenon that has been called *transposition*. The stimulus that is effective in eliciting the approach appears to be "the darker card".

*Implications.* The implications of this conclusion are just the same as those of the findings produced by the experiments on stimulus selection. Even the simplest object or environmental event will possess many properties. (In this case the object in question will have a certain physically measured *luminance*, it may be darker than the background against which it is presented, it may be the darkest object present, and so on.) Any of these properties might constitute the effective stimulus for the response under investigation and, in order to discover which, it is necessary to distinguish them and present each separately. The studies described above can be seen as experiments that separate the physical luminance of an object from its other properties. They lead to the conclusion that physical luminance is often not the effective stimulus in the perception of brightness which depends rather upon relative properties of the stimulus object. If we are to accept this conclusion it will make necessary a radical reappraisal of what we should mean by the term "stimulus".

## What Properties of Events can be Stimuli?

Our interpretation of the transposition experiment was that the stimulus effective in eliciting an approach response was not to be defined in terms of the physically measured luminance of a particular object; rather it was "the darker card". However natural this conclusion seems it was vigorously resisted by hardline S–R theorists. Hull, their leader during the 1930s and 1940s, had urged that the stimulus should be described and defined in the language of physical science—a tactile stimulus as a force in grams, a visual stimulus in terms of the wavelength and energy of the radiation emerging from it, and so on. According to this view, the description of an object as being the darker (or the bigger, or the second from the left, or whatever) cannot be accepted as being a proper description of a stimulus. Admittedly most psychologists were content to describe objects and events in such everyday terms and were still willing to regard them as being stimuli; but it was presumably assumed that the everyday description could be translated into the language of physics when necessary.

In 1937, Hull's colleague Spence published an ingenious account of transposition that attempted such a translation. It tried to explain the phenomenon without recourse to anything other than an absolute description of the stimulus. It is worth examining Spence's theory in some detail since it presents us with a sort of test case. If it succeeds we should be encouraged to accept the Hullian definition of the stimulus. If it fails we should have to admit that properties of events other than the physically defined energy they emit can also sometimes function as stimuli.

*Spence's account of transposition.* The critical features of Spence's theory are shown schematically in Fig. 6.12. This diagram represents the strengths of the response tendencies that a subject has acquired as the result of training on a discrimination in which response to a mid-grey card (M) is rewarded whereas response to a light-grey card (H: high luminance) is not. The vertical bars represent a strong tendency to approach M and a tendency to inhibit any approach to H. Each of these tendencies is assumed to be elicited by the absolute properties of the stimuli used in training. Spence also assumes that there will be some spread of effect (or *generalization*) so that stimuli similar to those used in training will tend to evoke the response to some extent. The more similar a stimulus is to the original, the more likely it is to evoke the response. This is shown by the solid curves in Fig. 6.12. Finally, Spence assumed that the net response tendency controlled by any stimulus was to be found by subtracting any inhibition it might have associated with it from any approach tendency it elicited. The net response tendency at each point on the brightness

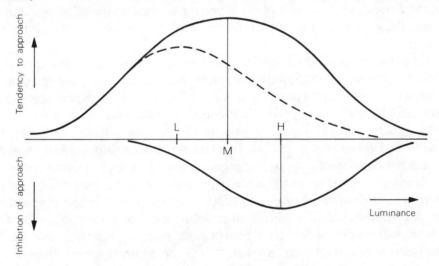

Fig. 6.12. *Generalization of response tendencies and transposition. L, M, and H represent low, medium, and high intensities of light. Reward for response to M produces a spread of effect shown in the upper curve; failure to obtain reward after response to H produces the lower curve. The resulting, dashed, curve means that there is a greater net tendency to approach L than M itself.*

dimension is shown by the dotted line in the figure which was produced by subtracting the lower solid curve from the upper.

As can be seen from the figure, the spread of effect from such trained stimulus to adjacent values means that the net response tendencies at both H and M are somewhat reduced. Nonetheless, the tendency to approach M is still greater than any tendency to approach H, and this difference is responsible for the subject's successful performance on the original discrimination task. More importantly, the spread of inhibition from H does not reach the more distant point L representing a stimulus low in luminance. As a consequence, the approach strength governed by L as a result of generalization actually exceeds that governed by the rewarded stimulus, M. A subject given a choice between M and L would thus approach L. That is, this theory can predict the occurrence of transposition on the basis of a few simple assumptions and without supposing the subject is responsive to relative properties of the events controlling its behaviour.

*Assessment of Spence's theory.* Although Spence's theory shows that a traditional S–R account can be extended to accommodate the phenomenon of transposition it still remains to establish whether or not this theory is correct. That is, the original demonstration of transposition has become ambiguous, being explicable both in terms of Spence's theory and in terms of the view that subjects may respond to relative properties of stimuli. We must therefore turn our attention to a more complicated version of the transposition task, one for which the two theories predict different outcomes, in order to choose between them.

Figure 6.13 shows the application of Spence's theory to the so-called three-stimulus problem. The dimension depicted here is that of size and the numbers represent seven objects differing in size. The subjects (in experiments of this sort these have often been pre-school children although equivalent results have been obtained with chimpanzees) are trained initially with three objects (3, 4, and 5), and are rewarded for choosing the intermediate value, object number 4. The generalization of response strength produced by such training is depicted in the figure according to the same conventions as were used in Fig. 6.12. A comparison of the two figures makes apparent the consequences of inserting a second non-rewarded stimulus. Since inhibition spreads from points that flank the original positive stimulus, the curve of net response tendency now peaks at the original positive stimulus itself. When the subjects are confronted with three stimuli from elsewhere on the dimension (such as 4, 5, and 6, or 5, 6, and 7) the theory predicts that they will choose either the original object (i.e. 4 rather than 5 or 6) or, if it is not available, the object that is closest to it in absolute size (5 rather than 6 or 7). But this is not what usually happens. Rather, the subjects show a preference for the object of intermediate size; that is, their

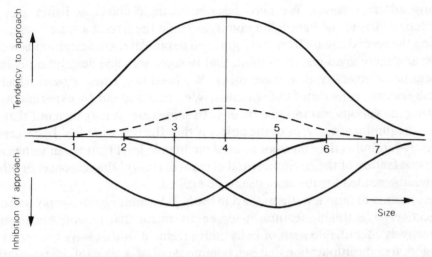

Fig. 6.13. *Generalization effects in an organism trained to choose object 4, an object intermediate in size between 3 and 5 which were not rewarded. The resulting net response tendency (the dashed curve) still peaks at 4 (compare Fig. 6.12).*

behaviour is controlled by a stimulus that is to be defined in relative terms ("approach the object intermediate in size") not by the response strengths governed by stimuli defined in absolute terms.

This is not to say that Spence's theory is wrong in all its particulars. (There is, for instance, perfectly good independent evidence that a tendency to respond to a given event will indeed generalize to similar events.) Nor does it mean that organisms are quite incapable of responding on the basis of absolute properties of objects in their environment. (Such behaviour can be induced by special training procedures.) What it does mean is that the description of the stimulus favoured by Spence and other S–R theorists is not universally applicable. In some circumstances, at least, the appropriate description of the effective stimulus appears to be closer to that suggested by everyday usage.

### "Stimulus" Redefined

At the beginning of this chapter we took as our defining example of a stimulus the blow on the knee that elicits the knee-jerk reflex. This was in line with Watson's intentions when he proclaimed that the psychologist should use the terms stimulus and response to mean just what the physiologist means by them. We have already seen that it is sensible for the psychologist to extend the term response to mean any identifiable behaviour. We are now in a position to reconsider our usage of the term "stimulus".

What we have seen is that when a given event reliably elicits a given response there may still be some ambiguity about what features of that event are effective in doing so. Any given event will possess many features (can be described in many different ways). We may describe a single object as being grey, as reflecting 50% of the light falling on it, as being the largest square present, as being the second square from the right, and so on. All these descriptions will be true and there is no reason to think that in some way one description is more scientific or objective than some other. We need not define *a priori* which of these features constitutes the stimulus. We must find out by experiment, by testing the various features one by one. In some cases it may turn out that the absolute luminance or area of the object is the effective stimulus. In others the effective stimulus may turn out to be some higher-level feature. In some cases just one feature of the environmental event will control the response; in others all will be needed for the response to be evoked.

According to this view, then, the S in the S–R formula stands simply for some objectively identifiable feature of the environment that reliably elicits some objectively identifiable item of behaviour. Defined in this way, the terms no longer carry the implication that behaviour consists of a series of reflexes; rather the S–R formula has become simply a useful shorthand way of expressing the psychologist's belief that what creatures do depends upon what happens to them.

## Spontaneous Behaviour

The belief that behaviour depends ultimately on eliciting events is clearly expressed in the attempts that have been made to deal with seemingly spontaneous behaviour—with "responses" that occur without there being an obvious eliciting stimulus.

The starling has a characteristic behaviour pattern whereby it chases and catches small flying insects. The eliciting stimulus is usually, of course, a small insect, but, according to Lorenz (1950), such behaviour may sometimes be observed when the eliciting stimulus is absent. A caged starling can show *vacuum activity*; that is, show the entire pattern of chasing, catching, and even eating a non-existent fly.

This example is particularly dramatic but we need not go to caged animals to find cases of seemingly spontaneous behaviour. The animals we see around us every day (other people) are often disconcertingly unpredictable in their behaviour in the sense that what they do does not always seem to be a product of their immediate circumstances. Even when we observe our own behaviour only rarely do we find it to be a response to some obvious stimulus; often we find ourselves doing something just because we happened "to feel like it". We often insist that our behaviour is entirely spontaneous—that we acted of our own free will. However compelling this impression may be, surely any scientific analysis of behaviour needs to start from the assumption that no behaviour is in fact spontaneous, when what we mean by spontaneous in this context is: "not attributable to some prior, causal, event". The S–R account of behaviour can be seen as being a formal way of expressing this assumption, the S being used to encompass whatever event or events cause a given R to occur. Granted this viewpoint we must say that all behaviour, however spontaneous it may seem, is in fact elicited by some stimulus. When the stimulus is not immediately obvious it is our job to dig deeper in an attempt to discover it.

*Explaining away spontaneous behaviour.* Thus the S–R account does not try to explain spontaneity in behaviour. Rather it tries to explain away, in its own terms, behaviour that seems to be spontaneous. A number of strategies have been employed.

The first, and simplest, is to argue that behaviour can appear to be spontaneous simply because we have failed to notice an eliciting stimulus that is in fact present. On many occasions I have seen my dozing cat wake for no obvious reason and walk off only to realize subsequently that this apparently spontaneous behaviour was a response to the sounds of food being prepared in the kitchen. It is an easy matter, especially when observing the behaviour of a non-human animal to miss cues to which the animal is especially sensitive and you are not.

A second strategy is to argue that some eliciting stimuli are not detected, because they are in principle unobservable, but that they exist nonetheless. A cat or a dog (or a person for that matter) may "spontaneously" start to scratch himself without there being any external irritant to evoke the response. But we can feel an itch without being tickled by a feather and so, presumably, can cats and dogs. In this case it seems legitimate to assume that an eliciting stimulus (an itch) is present even though this is the sort of stimulus that can be properly observed only by the creature suffering from it. This may seem a trivial example but it illustrates the point that stimuli arising from within an organism's body (and stimuli that are therefore unobservable) can control responses. A more important example has already been discussed when we considered the role played by response-produced internal stimuli in controlling some motor patterns.

Third, it may be argued that a response can appear spontaneous because the stimulus responsible for it lies some way back in the organism's history and for this reason has escaped detection. When an alarm-clock rings "spontaneously" early in the morning it does so because it has been set the night before. Because of its internal structure, a device as simple as a clock is able to delay its response to an environmental event. It requires no very special assumptions, therefore, for us to argue that much more complex devices (animals) should also be capable of showing delayed response to stimulation. It does mean, however, that in order to explain behaviour we need to take into account, not just the stimulation that the organism is currently subjected to, but also information about its previous experience. This issue is taken up in the final section of this chapter and in Chapter 7.

*Endogenous activity.* Finally, it has to be acknowledged that when all of these strategies have been applied there still remain examples of behaviour that appear to be spontaneous. We have already described how respiration is controlled by a central pacemaker which, although it is sensitive to peripheral influences, has its own spontaneous rhythmicity. This is not an isolated example. Many of the patterns of cyclical activity that most animals show appear to be endogenous. For instance, human volunteers who have spent long periods of time living in an unchanging environment (such as that provided by a deep cave) persisted for more than two weeks in showing a sleeping–waking cycle of about 24 hours (Aschoff, 1965). These patterns of behaviour cannot be said to be elicited by stimuli but seem rather to be instrinsic to the organism, to be directly determined by its very structure. This admission does not, however, invalidate our attempt to supply an S–R analysis for the rest of behaviour as the following example may help to make clear.

Imagine that you have never seen a motor car before and you are set the task of discovering the principles by which it works. You may come to the conclusion that it is essentially a device that responds in a predictable way to certain manipulations—that turning the wheel determines the path that it follows, that pressing one pedal makes it go faster and another makes it go more slowly, and so on. You may also discover that the engine is capable of a spontaneous rhythmic activity (the pistons move up and down in a regular fashion) that is only modulated and not controlled by the manipulations at your disposal. Such a discovery would be of interest and you might want to try to explain it by investigating the detailed structure of the engine; it would not, however, require you to abandon the S–R analysis that you had provided for other aspects of the car's behaviour.

If we wished to explain how living organisms can show endogenous rhythms it would be necessary to examine in detail the structure of the neural circuits (or whatever) that give rise to them. But our present concern is the interaction of the organism as a whole with its environment and for this a version of the S–R analysis is appropriate. It must be acknowledged, however, that the effect of a given S can sometimes vary according to the internal state of the organism (pressing the accelerator has no effect if the car's engine is not running). We consider next the implications of this fact.

## THE PROBLEM OF MOTIVATION

Consider the following simple experiment. A handful of food is put into the cage of a laboratory rat and its behaviour is observed. The outcome is that the rat walks across its cage, picks up a piece of food, and starts to eat. If the experiment is repeated day after day with appropriate variations in procedure it should be possible to demonstrate that the stimulus effective in eliciting the response of eating is the presentation of food.

Our first reaction to this "finding" might be to dismiss it as a trivial application of the S–R account and to move on to more important matters. But a closer inspection suggests that our S–R characterization of what is going on is not so much trivial as wrong (or at least, incomplete). Suppose that we did the experiment twice in the same day, presenting the rat with a second handful of food as soon as it had finished eating the first. We might well find that the rat did not eat, that the stimulus did not elicit the response. It is easy enough to understand why this should happen. The problem is clearly one of motivation: the rat refused the second helping of food because it was no longer hungry. But the fact that we can understand how the rat feels, that we can endow the rat with the feelings that we would ourselves experience in analogous circumstances, does not alter the fact that our original account of the rat's behaviour was wrong and that the presentation of the stimulus can, on occasion, fail to elicit the response. It is clearly necessary for us to modify our account of behaviour to incorporate the notion of motivation—of what value is an "explanation" of behaviour that says "R will occur when S is presented provided the organism in question wants to respond"?

### Hunger as an Intervening Variable

Chapter 4 introduced the concepts of dependent and independent variables—a dependent variable being the behaviour under investigation and an independent variable some feature of the environment that the behaviour depends upon. In our present terminology an independent variable is represented by the symbol S and a dependent variable by the symbol R. The example described above (and clearly this was just one example chosen to illustrate a more general problem) shows that it is not always possible to give an adequate account of behaviour in terms of just these variables. What is needed is a third sort of variable, an *intervening variable*. Such a variable might be used to represent some internal state of the organism and as such it would be something that "comes between" S and R. An obvious name for this state in the context of the present example would be "hunger". What is important, however, is not the name but the properties that the state must be assumed to possess.

In order to explain why the presentation of food does not always evoke consummatory behaviour we need to endow that state of hunger with the following properties. First, when it is present it must interact with the stimulus in a way that allows the stimulus to evoke the response; it has been common to think of hunger as "energizing" the response that the stimulus is trying to elicit. Next we must suppose that the state is not always present, or at least, is capable of varying in strength. Thus, when the presentation of food fails to elicit eating this is because the animal's level of hunger is very low, but the response will occur (given the stimulus) with increasing vigour as intensity of the hunger state increases.

### The Status of Intervening Variables

We have said that the name given to an intervening variable should not matter. It may, nonetheless, be misleading to choose the everyday term "hunger" for the intervening variable being introduced here. If the account of the variation in the rat's responsiveness to food that has just been put forward sounded at all convincing this was probably because the use of the term "hunger" allowed us to interpret what was going on in terms of our own experience of a state that we call by this name. In order to see the true nature of what is being said it is probably better to express our "explanation" in more neutral terminology such as the following: when an animal is in state D, food will elicit eating but it will not do so when state D is absent.

Stripped of its extraneous associations the account now sounds much less convincing. In particular it provokes the question: how can we know whether or not the animal is in state D?

Unless we know the answer to this question ahead of time we will not be able to predict whether the rat will eat on any given occasion; and a theory that is not able to predict is not offering any real explanation at all. As the theory stands at the moment, the only way by which we can tell that the rat is in state D or a hunger state or whatever is by observing that he does in fact eat food when it is presented. The only evidence for the existence of the state is the behaviour that it purports to explain.

Non-explanations of this sort have been very common in psychology: a rat may be said to wander round a maze because of its "exploratory drive"; a mother cares for her baby because of a "maternal instinct"; violent behaviour of all kinds is blamed upon "aggressive urges". The examples may sound convincing on first hearing but each of them reduces to saying nothing more than that a particular pattern of behaviour occurs because there is something that causes it to occur. In each of these cases we say no more about the observed behaviour by inventing some underlying intervening variable than we would by simply describing the behaviour itself. If an intervening variable is to be useful it must do more than redescribe the observed behaviour in fancy terminology. If it does not then we have no need to bother with it—after all, drives and instincts and the rest are not self-evident facts about behaviour that the psychologist must explain, rather they are theoretical notions that he introduces in order to help him to explain behaviour. If they are no help he can simply discard them.

### "Anchoring" an Intervening Variable

In what circumstances then is an intervening variable likely to be a useful concept? Let us try to answer this question by considering further the factors that govern a rat's responsiveness to food. We will see that the state D (for "drive") can be a useful explanatory concept when it is firmly anchored to observable events; that is, when we can specify what circumstances determine whether or not the drive will be present and when we can specify more exactly the range of effects that the drive has on behaviour.

To begin with the second of these points, we have said that it is an unsatisfactory procedure to postulate a state D to explain the occurrence of a response when the only evidence for the existence of this state is the behaviour it is supposed to explain. It might be possible, however, to use the occurrence of the response to show that the drive exists and then to demonstrate that the drive has other properties. For example, a rat that is in the drive state (as evidenced by the fact that it will eat food eagerly when it is presented) will show enhanced responsiveness not only to food itself but to other events that might be associated with food. The rat may roam around his environment as if looking for food or, if it is a laboratory rat, run quickly through a maze to get to the baited goal box. The drive state that energizes the final *consummatory act* once the goal is reached also seems to be capable of energizing a preliminary phase of *appetitive behaviour* that serves to get the animal to the goal in the first place. The concept of drive is now no longer as empty as it was: knowing that the rat is in a drive state (on the basis of his consummatory behaviour) allows us to make a prediction about the speed with which we will run through a maze. More detailed observation might reveal a whole range of behaviour patterns the likelihood or vigour of which is modified when changes occur in this drive state, and thus extend the predictive power of our account.

The circumstances that determine whether or not the drive will be present can also be determined by observation and experiment. In this case all we need do is to take note of the fact that the rat will eat food readily when previously it has been deprived of food for some hours and that it will not do so when it has previously had access to a good supply of food. Given these observations, the drive state is no longer something conjured up to explain one particular observation of behaviour. We can now specify the circumstances which produce it (deprivation) and those that remove it (eating) and we can manipulate its strength experimentally. By knowing the antecedent conditions we are now in a position to predict what a given rat will do on a particular occasion when it is presented with food.

It need hardly be said that very few of the intervening variables in common use are as well anchored as is that state we call hunger and accordingly we should be very cautious about using them. In some cases, however, there is quite good evidence that several patterns of behaviour tend to go together and this may be enough to justify our hypothesizing that a common intervening variable underlies them all. (The notion of "intelligence" may be justified in this way. There is no one thing that a person does that makes us call him intelligent. Only if he shows ability in a wide range of intellectually demanding tasks are we likely to accept that there is some general ability that underlies all of them.) But for few of the various drives, urges, and instincts that have been hypothesized has an adequate account of their antecedents been given.

The Argument from Economy

Although the concept of drive once it has been anchored in this way becomes a workable one, it may still be doubted that it is a useful one. We can say that an animal in a drive state (because it has been deprived of food for some hours) will eat food when it is presented; but we need not do so. Why not simply say: a rat that has been deprived of food will eat food when food is presented? Again, instead of saying that a drive state underlies both the readiness with which a rat eats and the vigour with which he runs through a maze we could say simply that an animal that eats readily will also tend to run vigorously. Anchoring the intervening variable to observable events appears to have made it redundant. Nonetheless there is still good reason for us to persist with such variables. The argument is that they may still serve a useful function in allowing us to economize on the number of relationships between observables that we must specify. It has been made most clearly by Miller (1959) with respect to the drive state that we commonly call "thirst".

Figure 6.14a represents some of the observations that have been made about the rat's responsiveness to water. The first is that sometimes a rat will drink when water is presented and that this may depend upon prior deprivation of water. This is represented by the central arrow in the diagram. The rat's readiness to drink may also be determined by other factors: two other arrows represent the fact that a rat will drink after it has eaten a lot of dry food or if it has been injected with a fairly strong salt solution. A willingness to drink goes along with other patterns of behaviour. Figure 6.14a represents the fact that the rat will also run quickly through a maze or will press the lever in a Skinner box if these behaviour patterns lead to water. It also shows that the likelihood of these responses is also increased by manipulations that increase the likelihood of drinking (the remaining arrows on the figure). In order to specify the effects of three environmental manipulations on three responses it has been necessary to specify nine relationships (the nine arrows in Fig. 6.14a).

Contrast this with the situation depicted in Fig. 6.14b. Here we have postulated an intervening variable (D) that underlies all three behaviour patterns, the strength of which is modified by all three of the environmental manipulations. The picture is now much simpler. Instead of having to specify the relationship between every S and every R we need only say that any event that modifies the strength of D will change the likelihood of any R that D

(a)

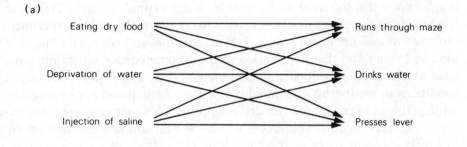

(b)

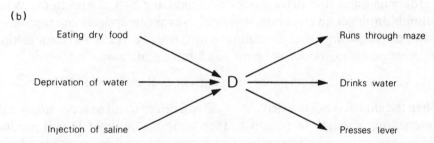

Fig. 6.14. *The arrows represent relationships between environment events and behaviour that the psychologist must specify. In (b) the introduction of an intervening variable (D) reduces the number of these relationships (after Miller, 1959).*

energizes. The advantage of economy bestowed by this system is obvious even in this case but grows dramatically as the number of Ss and Rs is increased.

Having gone to these lengths to justify the use of the drive concept as an intervening variable, it is appropriate now to examine in detail a specific theory of motivation so that we may see the concept of drive in action. The theory I have chosen to describe is that of Hull, not because it is correct in all its details (we shall shortly come across ways in which it breaks down) but because it has been so widely influential forming the basis for a host of other theories both in experimental animal psychology and in some branches of social psychology.

Hull's Theory of Motivation
Any theory of motivation has to answer three basic questions: it must specify what conditions bring about the drive state; it must specify how the drive manages to bring about the activity we suppose it does; it must specify what conditions remove or terminate the state of drive.

Hull answered the first question by suggesting that drive is a consequence of "biological need" although he was not very specific about what such a need might be. He suggested that a need existed when any of the conditions necessary for individual or species survival was lacking, but this is not very helpful given that different individuals are likely to produce very different lists if asked about the things that they just could not live without. For experimental purposes we will not go far wrong if we assume that animals have a "need" for food and water and that deprivation of these commodities will bring about a state of drive. A consequence of this view is that, although we can arrange conditions to ensure that an animal is in a drive state, it will not be possible to arrange things to ensure that no drive is present. No matter how generous we are to our experimental subjects it will always remain possible that we have overlooked one or more of their needs and that these can act as sources of drive.

Hull suggested that drive works by energizing S–R connections. When a stimulus impinges on an animal it "tries" to evoke its appropriate response but it is able to do so only when the animal is in a state of drive. This relationship can be conveniently expressed in terms of a simple equation:

$$\text{strength of response} = \text{strength of S–R connection} \times D.$$

When the animal is not in a drive state, D will be zero, and so accordingly will be the resulting strength of response. Increasing the value of D will produce a response of increasing strength. Which particular response occurs depends upon the stimulus that is presented. Thus if the subject is a rat and the stimulus is the start box of a maze, then D will energize the appetitive behaviour of running through the maze; if the stimulus is food, then D will energize the consummatory behaviour of eating. It should be noted that in this theory the drive state plays no part in determining what response occurs—that is a function of the stimulus: drive merely supplies the energy. This is not to say that an organism does not "know" that it is hungry rather than thirsty, say; the set of internal stimuli produced by food deprivation (from the empty stomach, for instance) should be quite discriminable from those produced by water deprivation. These internal *drive stimuli* can, according to the theory, function like any other stimulus and form part of the S to which the R is connected. Thus a rat can learn to turn left in a maze to reach water and right in a maze to reach food when the only cue immediately available comes from the animal's own internal state—whether it is hungry or thirsty. What the theory does imply is that all biological needs contribute to a common drive state which, in turn, determines the vigour of all aspects of behaviour.

Hull's answer to the final question about what removes the state of drive follows from what has been said already. Drive will fall to zero when the biological needs that produce it are satisfied.

## Assessment of Hull's Theory
We must now assess Hull's theory in the light of experimental and other evidence in order to detect any flaws and, it is to be hoped, build a better theory.

*Non-biological drives.* Seemingly the most obvious flaw in the theory is its assertion that all behaviour is motivated by biological need. Our feeling is that much of our own behaviour (if not that of other people) is evoked by higher motives than this. Unfortunately it is very difficult to prove the point. Anyone who has argued with a Freudian theorist determined to "reduce everything to sex" will know just how difficult it can be. Experimental studies fare no better. There have been a large number of experiments with animal subjects designed to show the existence of an "exploratory drive"; to show that a rat or a monkey that wants for nothing will still tend to explore its environment. The problem with these is that it is well-nigh impossible to prove that all the subject's biological needs have indeed been satisfied, particularly if we allow the existence of a need for safety. An animal might well explore its environment because the fear evoked by novel stimuli contributes to its drive state. Might it not be that most animals live in a perpetual state of mild anxiety engendered by novel stimuli or by stimuli that have previously been associated with unpleasant events, and that this state motivates much of what they do? It is perhaps not too far-fetched to suppose that much the same is true of people. Once this is allowed, the case for ascribing all motivation to a state produced by biological need becomes tenable, at least. Whether or not it becomes convincing is another matter. Rather than debate this issue further it seems sensible to turn to one on which hard evidence is available.

*Specific drives.* Hull's theory is more open to attack with respect to its second major suggestion, the notion that drive is a general state capable of motivating any and all behaviour. This too runs counter to our intuitions (we think of a drive *for* food as being something quite different from a drive *for* water) and it runs counter to some experimental evidence too. In particular, Hull's theory implies that different sources of drive should summate: that an animal that is both hungry and afraid should do whatever it is doing more vigorously than one that is just hungry or just afraid. This implication has been tested in many experiments that have investigated the reaction of hungry rats to stimuli associated with an unpleasant event. In these, the rat is deprived of food and allowed to obtain it in small quantities by pressing the lever in a Skinner box (Fig. 7.8). The rat is then presented with some stimulus (such as the sounding of a tone for a minute or so) that has previously been experienced along with an electric shock. Hull's theory says that the fear evoked by the tone should summate with the drive state produced by food deprivation so that the vigour with which the rat presses the lever should be enhanced. The opposite result has uniformly been obtained; in fact the presentation of the fear-evoking tone suppresses the rat's tendency to work for food.

*Termination of drive.* Hull's third major theoretical suggestion was that drive would be diminished (and that the behaviour energized by it would be terminated) when the biological need underlying the drive was satisfied. This idea, too, is in conflict with some experimental evidence. When an animal has been deprived of water and starts to drink when water is made available, its behaviour helps to remove the need that the body tissues have for water. Water deprivation raises the concentration (the *osmotic pressure*) of the body fluids and the intake of water dilutes them causing their osmotic pressure to return to normal. If the source of the drive underlying drinking is the need to restore the normal osmotic pressure of the body fluids then drinking should continue until this occurs. In fact an animal will usually stop drinking before this has had time to occur, before the water has passed through the digestive system into the blood and the tissues. Termination of the activity does not depend upon the need being satisfied. This is demonstrated most strikingly by a procedure known as "sham drinking" in which surgery on the animal's oesophagus allows the experimenter to arrange that fluids passing down the animal's throat never reach its stomach. No matter how vigorously such an animal licks at its water bottle its activity cannot rectify the abnormal osmotic pressure produced by water deprivation. Nonetheless, such an animal will sham-drink a fairly normal amount and then stop.

One possible interpretation of this observation is that drive should be thought of as constituting a limited supply of energy that is consumed in performing the consummatory behaviour. (This view has been championed by Lorenz, 1950.) If we adopt this view, it is necessary to suppose that a new supply can very quickly be generated since an animal that has been sham-drinking will usually start drinking again after only a brief pause. A more satisfactory interpretation distinguishes short-term and long-term factors influencing the termination of driven behaviour. When an animal sham-drinks it experiences a set of stimuli (from water flowing down the throat and the feedback stimuli produced by performing the response itself) that are effective, in the short term, in stopping the behaviour. The need for water still exists, however, and when the short-term effect wears off, drinking is resumed. In normal animals, of course, drinking also has the longer-term effect of restoring the body fluids to normal and so, once such an animal has stopped drinking because of the input of consummatory stimuli, it does not start again for some time.

We have concentrated on factors controlling drinking in part because the only other cases to be studied in any detail (eating and sexual behaviour) turn out to be far more complicated. Nonetheless, it is possible to sum up with a generalization that is not grossly inaccurate. Driven behaviour may indeed have its origin in a biological need but such behaviour is not terminated solely by the removal of the need; rather the drive will be reduced when the organism experiences at least some of the set of stimuli that characterize the goal object.

*Conclusions.* What then remains of Hull's theory? First, we can salvage the general structure it proposes: the suggestion that S will elicit R only in conjunction with some other, intervening variable that serves to energize behaviour. That is, we can accept the essence expressed in Hull's equation (p. 212). We must deny, however, that a single intervening variable can accommodate all the observations. The state induced by the presentation of a signal for an unpleasant event (such as electric shock) *can* energize behaviour—a rat will soon learn to run to a safe place when such a signal occurs—but, as we have seen, it does not always do so, since it will actually suppress appetitively maintained behaviour. One interpretation of this finding is that there are two major motivational systems (we might call them "hope" and "fear"), one concerned with energizing behaviour that leads to pleasant consequences, the other with energizing behaviour that allows the animal to avoid unpleasant consequences. These systems work in apposition to each other. The inhibitory interaction between them (our inability to be both hopeful and fearful at the same time) has formed the basis for techniques used in clinical psychology. A patient with a *phobia* (a strong, irrational and incapacitating fear of spiders or snakes or whatever) may be confronted with the event that causes him fear in circumstances that are otherwise pleasant and relaxing. Provided the positive motivation is strong and the fear rather weak (the snake is only a model and is at the far side of the room), the former may inhibit the latter. Such an outcome might contribute at least a starting point for successful therapy.

Next, although the importance of biological needs cannot be denied, the circumstances that induce and reduce motivational states turn out to be more complex than Hullian theory originally supposed. Deprivation and satiation are important but an adequate theory must leave room for sensory stimuli to play a role. Not only do such stimuli bring about the termination of appetitively motivated consummatory activity but they can also produce motivational states. External events (like electric shocks) can generate a motivational state and so can stimuli that were previously neutral, simply by virtue of having been associated with unpleasant events. There is some evidence to suggest that neutral stimuli may also be able to acquire the ability to generate the appetitive motivational state by a similar mechanism, that is, by virtue of having been associated with pleasant events like the consumption of food. To pursue this matter further it is necessary to consider in detail the mechanisms involved in associative learning and this we do in the next chapter.

## SUMMARY

What this chapter has tried to do is to provide a framework for the analysis of behaviour that can be used to guide our future thinking and research. The result is something that superficially resembles the theory proposed by Hull in that we allow a role for intervening variables and describe behaviour as consisting of responses elicited by stimuli. It should be made explicit, however, that what is being advocated here is really rather different from traditional S–R theory. We have liberalized our usage of the terms stimulus and response so that they now mean something very different from what the early behaviourists intended. For them, to adopt S–R theory was to adopt a particular sort of explanation about the mechanisms controlling behaviour. For us it is now simply a convenient way of speaking, but one that serves as a useful reminder that the subject matter of the psychologist is ultimately what the organism does (R) and that the psychologist's job is to find out what circumstances (S) make the organism do it.

## SOURCES AND FURTHER READING

The topics treated in this chapter are discussed in standard texts on animal behaviour such as those by Hinde (1966), by Manning (1972) and by Marler and Hamilton (1966). A more accessible rendering of Hinde's views is to be found in his *Ethology* (1982). A classic paper concerned with the nature and organization of the response is that by Lashley (1951) devoted to the problem of "serial order" in behaviour. The nature of the stimuli that control the natural behaviour of animals is discussed by Tinbergen (1951) in *The Study of Instinct*. (This book also contains a discussion of the spontaneity of behaviour.) For a detailed account of transposition see Riley's *Discrimination Learning* (1968) and for a comprehensive survey of laboratory studies of stimulus selection see Mackintosh's (1974) *The Psychology of Animal Learning*, in particular the chapter on discrimination. The book entitled *Motivation*, edited by Bindra and Stewart (1966) reprints many important, original papers on that topic and the editors themselves contribute some useful discussion of conceptual issues. Gray's (1971) *The Psychology of Fear and Stress* deals with fear and discusses its interaction with appetitive motivation. For a survey of the entire field and also a critical discussion of Hull's theory see *Theory of Motivation* by Bolles (1967).

# 7    Learning

## INTRODUCTION

Experimental psychologists have often been chastised for devoting so much of their energy to studying the topic of learning. Some critics have argued that a concentration on the mechanisms involved in learning has led to a neglect of other mental mechanisms (such as those involved in emotion) that are just as important in determining how an individual interacts with his environment. Others, particularly ethologists, have argued that experimental psychologists have been over-eager in using learning to explain the origins of behaviour, and have neglected other determinants. When asked why a given animal does a particular thing, the psychologist will almost always look for an answer in terms of the past experience of the organism, paying scant regard to the evolutionary history of the species in question.

In spite of these criticisms, the central position given by psychology to the topic of learning seems to me to be largely justified. It would not be justified if the study of learning consisted of nothing more than the study of the processes involved in acquiring a piece of information (learning a new telephone number, say) or in perfecting some new motor skill (e.g. learning to ride a bicycle). But we shall take a wider view of learning than this. We shall regard the study of learning as being the study of individual adaptation—learning is a process whereby the organism interacts with its environment, becomes modified as a result of the interaction, and is thereby (usually) better fitted to meet environmental demands. Since these interactions often involve environmental events of emotional and motivational significance, a proper theory of learning cannot confine itself to cognitive aspects of mental functioning but must deal with these other aspects too. Although the study of individual adaptation can be independent of the study of species adaptation, the student of learning does not deny the usefulness of the analysis supplied by the evolutionary biologist and the geneticist (see Chapters 2 and 3), rather he seeks to supply an analysis complementary to theirs.

## The Role of Learning in the S–R Analysis

After these grand generalizations it will be well to try to pin down learning in terms of observables. For the notion of learning, like that of motivation, requires the use of intervening variables that must be firmly anchored in observable events. The point is made most simply by considering the phenomenon of *habituation*. The sudden presentation of a brief loud noise (S) will evoke a startle response (R) consisting of changes in heart rate, respiration, and a number of other functions controlled by the autonomic nervous system, in addition to the more obvious "jump" of the whole body. When the same S is presented a second time the same R will occur but will be reduced in amplitude. With repeated presentations of the S, the R may disappear completely; that is, habituation will occur. It is not simply that the sensory system or the motor system has become fatigued, since the presentation of a changed stimulus (for example, one less intense than the S that the organism has become accustomed to) is often capable of evoking the R.

Here then is a case where, in the absence of any obvious motivational changes, the organism shows variable responsiveness to a given S. To account for this we need to introduce a new intervening variable the value of which helps to determine whether or not S will evoke R. In this particular case we need to assume that the organism is initially in a state whereby the S can be effective but that this state is changed as a result of repeated presentation of the stimulus. In other cases we must assume that the state changes from one in which the S does not evoke a given R to one in which it does, as when a rat meanders through a maze on the first trial but briskly follows the correct path after a number of trials. We may call this intervening variable a *memory* and the process by which it is established, *learning*; but, as in the case of drive, the name given to the intervening variable does not matter so much as the properties that it is supposed to have. What we are proposing is that organisms are permanently modified by experience in a way that causes them to change how they respond to given environmental events. What we need to specify is the exact nature of this change, the conditions that produce it, and how it works to modify behaviour.

## A Behavioural Analysis

Ultimately it should prove possible to do this in physiological terms: to specify what nerve cells change during learning and the way in which they do so. But detailed information of this sort is in short supply and we shall concentrate instead on trying to understand the mechanisms underlying learning at a conceptual level, paying little regard to their embodiment (see Chapter 5, p. 175). Here there is plentiful information derived from the experimental, behavioural analysis of well-defined examples of learning in non-human animals. Much of this work has concentrated on *associative learning*; that is, on the learning that results from presenting an animal with two events, one contingent upon the other. In *classical conditioning* the two events are stimuli; in *instrumental learning* the presentation of a stimulus is made contingent upon the animal's performing some response. We next discuss examples of these forms of learning in some detail so that we may go on to determine the extent to which they reveal general principles that are more widely applicable.

## LEARNING ABOUT THE ENVIRONMENT

### Pavlov's Classical Conditioning

By his discovery of classical conditioning, Pavlov (1927) provided us with an ideal experimental procedure for investigating what goes on when organisms learn about the relationship between environmental events. His basic procedure is well known. A hungry dog is isolated and restrained in a quiet experimental chamber and food is presented by remote control. A minor surgical operation bringing the duct of a salivary gland to the surface of the skin allows the response of salivation to be recorded (Fig. 7.1). Over the course of a number of trials the presentation of food is preceded by the presentation of some other stimulus such as the onset of a light. The light does not initially evoke the response of salivation (although it does evoke other responses) but after a series of light–food "pairings" it comes to do so (Fig. 7.2). This can be seen most clearly on "test trials" (the light is presented alone), but it may also

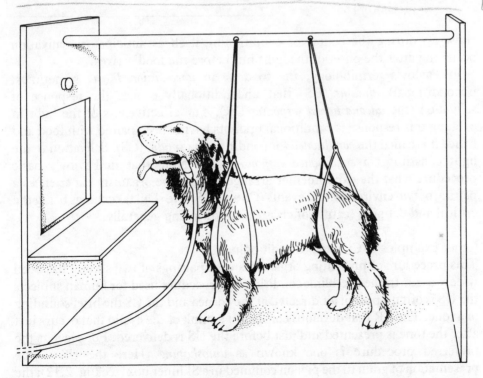

Fig. 7.1. *A version of the apparatus devised by Pavlov for the study of salivary classical conditioning in the dog.*

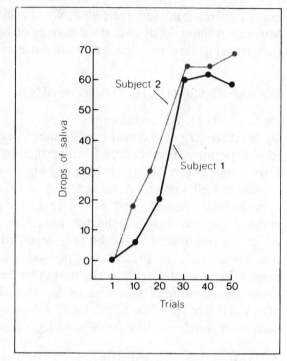

Fig. 7.2. *The development of a salivary conditioned response in two dogs given pairings of a tone and meat powder. The CRs were recorded on test trials when the CS was presented on its own (data from Anrep, 1920; after Mackintosh, 1974).*

show up during the course of conditioning itself as anticipatory salivation occurring after the onset of the light but before the food arrives.

In Pavlov's terminology, the food is an *unconditioned* (or, sometimes, unconditional) *stimulus* (US) that unconditionally evokes the response of salivation (the *unconditioned response*, UR). The effectiveness of the light in evoking this response is conditional upon its having been paired with food and hence it is called the *conditioned* (or conditional) *stimulus* (CS). Salivation to the light constitutes a *conditioned response* (CR). Note that in Pavlov's basic procedure what the experimenter arranges is that the organism experiences a pairing of two environmental events (CS and US); we shall take this as being the critical and defining feature of classical conditioning generally.

## Other Examples of Classical Conditioning

This procedure of presenting organisms with pairings of two stimuli has been widely used. In the eye-blink conditioning procedure used for human subjects the US is often a puff of air directed at the cornea and the CS the brief sounding of a tone. The CR that develops consists of a blink of the eyelid that occurs just after the tone is presented and just before the US is delivered. For pigeons the preferred procedure is one known as *autoshaping*. Here the US is the presentation of grain to the pigeon confined in a Skinner box (see Fig. 2.12); the CS is the illumination of a response key for a few seconds before the food is

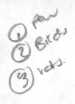

made available. Birds subjected to this procedure develop the CR of pecking at the key. As an example of a procedure used with rats we may consider flavour-aversion learning. In this procedure the CS is a novel flavour such as that produced by putting saccharine into the rats' drinking water. The US is some treatment designed to induce nausea—injection of a weak solution of a lithium salt is particularly effective. Rats given such an injection shortly after having had access to the saccharine develop the CR of shunning saccharine. (This last example provides a partial explanation of why it is difficult to exterminate wild rats. If the rat fails to eat enough of the poisoned bait to kill it on the first occasion the nausea that it experiences will be enough to stop it eating the same thing again.)

These procedures are very different from that used by Pavlov but all of them have important features in common with salivary conditioning. All are cases in which behaviour is changed in creatures that have experienced two environmental events presented in conjunction. In all a CR emerges, but note that in none is the animal actually required to make a response—it cannot earn food by salivating or avoid an air-puff by blinking: rather the US is delivered after the CS no matter what the subject does.

The Nature of the Association

Classical conditioning provides us with a clear-cut example of a case in which a stimulus (the CS), that initially does not evoke a given response (the CR), comes to do so as a result of experience. What is the nature of the change that the animal undergoes and that permits this outcome? The most obvious answer to this question (at least within the perspective of our S–R analysis of behaviour) is depicted in Fig. 7.3a. The circular symbols represent parts of the brain that are assumed to be active in certain conditions. That labelled US represents the cerebral "centre" that is activated when the subject tastes food; that labelled CS is the centre that detects the CS (in this example, a light); that labelled R is the cerebral mechanism responsible for controlling the response; and the arrow connecting US and R represents the connection that enables food to elicit salivation unconditionally. The dotted arrow represents the suggestion that what happens during conditioning is the formation of a new S–R association: that the concurrent activation of the CS centre (by presentation of the light) and of the R centre (by way of food presentation) in some way allows a link to be forged between them. This link may be presumed to have the same properties as the pre-existing link between US and R. By way of it, presentation of the buzzer is now able to activate the R centre and to elicit salivation. Salivation now becomes a CR rather than a UR.

The principal assertion of this account—that conditioning effects depend upon the formation of associations—has been universally accepted. It is

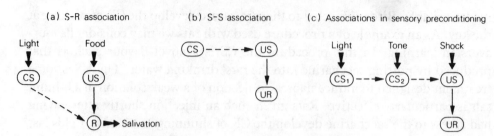

Fig. 7.3. *Possible associations (broken lines) formed between the internal representations of events as a result of classical conditioning. (a) S–R associations; (b) S–S associations; (c) S–S associations in sensory preconditioning.*

doubtful, however, that the association is in fact one between S and R, as shown in the figure. We may consider two of several relevant lines of evidence.

*Conditioning with the response prevented.* The first comes from experiments showing that it is possible to get learning as a result of classical conditioning when the animal is not capable of making the response. Thus, Zentall and Hogan (1975) carried out a conditioning experiment using the autoshaping procedure in which the pigeons received 300 trials each consisting of the brief illumination of a key-light followed by food presentation. An S–R account requires the CS to become associated with the R of pecking, a response elicited by the presentation of food. But in their experiment Zentall and Hogan prevented this response from occurring by blocking the entrance to the food tray with a plastic screen—the birds could see the food but could not peck directly at it. In spite of this the CR of pecking at the key was still acquired. Conceptually similar experiments have been done with animals paralysed by the drug curare (a drug that blocks the neuromuscular junction; see Chapter 5). Such animals can do no more than sit and take the CS and US during conditioning. But when they recover from the paralysis they start to show the CR to the CS.

*Sensory preconditioning.* The second line of evidence comes from experiments on *sensory preconditioning* (see Fig. 7.4a). As an example, Prewitt (1967) reports an experiment with rats in which the CS was a tone and the US a mild electric shock delivered to the rats' feet. The CR was assessed by observing the extent to which the CS disrupted ongoing activity (drinking water from a tube). The tone–shock pairings constituted only the second stage of Prewitt's experiment. Before they received this training the rats experienced a sequence of conditioning trials in which the paired events were a light and a tone; that is, the CS was a light and the tone stood in the place of the US. After the second stage had been completed, testing the light showed that this stimulus too, in spite of the fact that it had never been paired directly with the shock, was quite capable of

(a) Sensory preconditioning

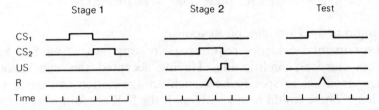

(b) Second order conditioning

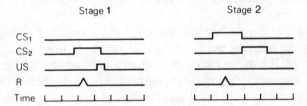

(c) Blocking

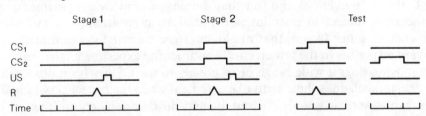

Fig. 7.4. *Sequence of events in three conditioning procedures: (a) sensory preconditioning; (b) second order conditioning); (c) blocking. In each procedure several, perhaps many, trials will be given to each stage of training. (See text for further explanation.)*

disrupting drinking. By virtue of its association with a tone which only subsequently was paired with shock, it acquired the capacity to evoke the CR.

This last finding leads to the suggestion that the association formed in classical conditioning is between S and S rather than S and R. The suggestion is depicted in Fig. 7.3b for simple conditioning. Figure 7.3c shows how the idea is applied to sensory preconditioning: in the first stage of training a link is formed between the "centres" labelled $CS_1$ and $CS_2$; in the second stage $CS_2$ and US become linked; in the test stage the light is able to evoke a response by way of this chain of associations. More generally, what is proposed, both for sensory preconditioning and for simple conditioning, is that the concurrent activation of the cerebral representations of stimuli allows a link to be formed between them so that the first presented can excite the centre for the second. The stimuli need not evoke responses for these links to be formed.

## The Origin of the Conditioned Response

The experimental evidence requires us to suppose that an S–S association underlies classical conditioning. Having accepted this conclusion it now becomes essential to specify how such an association can come to modify behaviour. There would be no problem if the S–R account were correct, since this theory of conditioning explicitly states that the CR is just the UR transferred to a new stimulus. By adopting the S–S account we run the risk of having a theory that allows the animal to "know" that food follows the buzzer but is incapable of predicting what it does as a consequence of knowing this.

*Stimulus substitution theory.* Even if we reject the account of conditioning given by S–R theory our starting point for an analysis of the origin of the CR must be the fact that the CR usually bears more than a passing resemblance to the UR. In some cases it seems to be identical with the UR and when differences occur they can sometimes be explained away. Thus it has been pointed out that the CR in Pavlov's original conditioning experiments is merely an anticipatory version of the UR—all that the dog does in response to the CS is to salivate; it shows few of the other responses that a dog emits when given food itself. But to argue this is to overlook the fact that the dogs in Pavlov's experiments were deliberately subject to restraint (see Fig. 7.1) in an attempt to exclude the influence of other factors that might interfere with the development of the salivary response. In the few classical conditioning experiments that have used free-moving dogs a wide range of responses to the CS has been observed. In particular, such dogs show signs of excitement when the buzzer is switched on: they run toward it eagerly, lick at it, and on occasion, try to bite it. Such behaviour is reminiscent of that shown by a pigeon subjected to the autoshaping procedure where the bird moves across the Skinner box toward the illuminated response key and starts to peck at it as if it were food.

The conclusion prompted by these observations is that the CS–US link formed as a result of conditioning allows the CS to take on some of the properties of the US itself. According to such a *stimulus substitution* theory the CS becomes a surrogate for the US, and the CR takes the form it does because the animal behaves toward the CS as if it were the US. Perhaps the strongest support for this view (a version of which was proposed by Pavlov himself) comes from an experimental study of autoshaping carried out by Jenkins and Moore (1973). The pigeons in this experiment were both hungry and thirsty and conditioning was carried out concurrently with both food and water USs. The presentation of food was always preceded by the illumination of one response key; the presentation of water by the illumination of a different key. Classical conditioning occurred with both USs; that is, the birds began to approach and make contact with whichever of the keys was lit on a given trial. But detailed observation of the birds' behaviour showed that the way in which the key was operated differed according to whether it preceded food or water. Responses to the "food key" consisted of sharp, discrete pecks, usually with the mandibles of the beak apart and coming together at the moment of contact. This is the pattern of pecking that a pigeon shows when eating grain. Responses to the "water key" were quite different. The birds tended to "snuggle" against the key rather than striking at it and sometimes showed the pumping movements of the throat that are characteristic of drinking in the pigeon. In short, we may say that the birds tried to eat the food key and to drink the water key.

*Limitations to the theory.* As a first approximation, the suggestion that classical conditioning causes the animal to behave toward the CS as if it were the US is satisfactory. We must, however, acknowledge two important limitations to this conclusion. The first, and fairly obvious point, is that the animal can behave toward the CS as if it were the US only to the extent that the physical properties of the CS allow this. Thus, the hungry pigeon can move toward a response key (as it would to a supply of food) and can begin to peck (as it would to food) but it cannot go on to complete the parallel by ingesting and masticating the key. To this extent at least, some CRs are bound to be "anticipatory". In some cases, indeed, the CS may prove incapable of supporting any obvious CRs at all. Autoshaping experiments have been done in which the CS is a non-localized event such as the sounding of a tone. In these circumstances there is simply nothing for the bird to approach and peck at. But the absence of a CR does not mean that no CS–US association has been formed. The existence of such an association can be revealed by means of a procedure known as *second-order conditioning* (Fig. 7.4b) in which a previously trained CS is used in the place of the US in a second stage of training. When the pigeon is trained with a keylight preceding the presentation of the previously trained tone, it is found that the bird comes to peck at the keylight. We must conclude that the tone has taken on some of the properties of the original US although this does not show directly in behaviour. But these properties can be passed on to the keylight in the second phase of the experiment and can there show up in the usual way as keypecks.

The second limitation arises from the fact that in talking of "the US" in conditioning experiments we have been guilty of a gross over-simplification. The US is always an event with a large number of properties and, as with any stimulus, we have no right to assume that all its properties will be attended to (see Chapter 6). Thus, when we say that "food" excites a central representation of the US (Fig. 7.3) there is a good deal of room for doubt about what aspects of this event are actually represented. There may be a representation of a given quantity of sucrose in the mouth, say, or it may merely be a representation of "something pleasant". When the US is a shock the animal may encode details of its position and intensity (1 milliamp (mA) to the cheek, say) or alternatively it may simply learn about it as being "something unpleasant". Which of these representations enters into an association with the CS will help determine the form that the CR takes. Thus if the animal does indeed learn about the details of the shock the appropriate CR to the CS will be an eye-blink. But if all it learns about the US is its general aversiveness the CS will be able to do no more than evoke a general state of fear. Which of these CRs is formed seems to depend upon the details of the conditioning procedure employed. Evidence on this matter is sparse but there is some to suggest that subjects will fail to encode details of the US when there is a long delay between the onset of the CS and the presentation of the US. Thus a rat trained with a CS lasting a minute or more that terminates with the presentation of an electric shock will show little by way of discrete CRs; rather its behaviour during the tone seems indicative of a general state of anxiety. The suggestion that emotional states can be conditioned has evoked a good deal of interest and will be discussed further below (p. 230).

## The Conditions Necessary for Association Formation

We have outlined the nature of the change in the animal produced by conditioning and have gone some way toward saying how this change comes to modify behaviour. We must now specify in more detail what conditions are necessary to establish the CS–US association in the first place. All we have said so far is that classical conditioning occurs as a result of CS–US pairings. It has perhaps been noticed, however, that in all the experiments discussed so far the CS had been presented in advance of the US. In some procedures, indeed, the US is not presented until the CS has acutally terminated. It has been usual to assume, therefore, that activation of the representation of the CS, once initiated by the onset of that stimulus, will persist for some time. It may still then overlap the activation of the US centre produced by presentation of the US itself and in this sense the CS and US may still be said to be paired.

An implication of this view is that conditioning should proceed less readily as the interval between onset of the CS and onset of the US is lengthened (assuming that the activation of the CS representation will tend to die away during this interval). Figure 7.5 shows the results of an experiment on classical conditioning in the rabbit in which the CS–US interval has varied. The US was an electric shock delivered next to the eye, a stimulus that elicited a twitch of the subject's eyelids. The CS was a tone 50 ms (millisecond: a thousandth of a second) long presented, for different groups of subjects, at different times before the onset of the shock. On certain test trials the tone was presented for a full second unaccompanied by shock and its ability to evoke a CR (an eyelid twitch) was noted. The figure shows that a CR was most likely to occur in

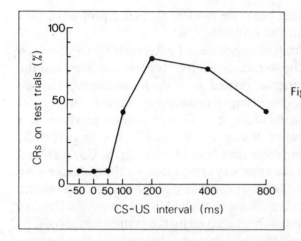

Fig. 7.5. *Classical conditioning of the rabbit's nictitating membrane ("third eyelid") response with a 50 ms tone CS and a 50 ms shock US. Different groups were conditioned at the different intervals and the results are for test trials when the CS was presented alone (after Smith et al., 1969).*

animals trained with a CS–US interval of about 200 ms but that the frequency of the CR declined as the interval was increased.

It might be expected, according to this account, that conditioning would proceed most readily if the CS and US were truly paired, both stimuli coming on and going off at exactly the same time. Figure 7.5 shows, however, that the conditioning is less likely to occur as the CS–US interval falls below 200 ms and that no CRs were recorded in subjects trained with simultaneous presentation of CS and US. It is not clear whether or not the reasons for this failure of conditioning are of any great theoretical significance. Part of the problem is that it is difficult to detect a CR in such circumstances since it may well be masked by the UR elicited by concurrent presentation of the US. Presenting the CS on its own as a test trial offers no solution: if no CR occurs it could merely be that the response has been disrupted by the surprise that the subject must experience on being confronted with the CS alone.

There are, however, several conditioning procedures in which no CR is developed in spite of the fact that the subject experiences paired presentations of a CS and US, and which cannot be explained away so easily. Consideration of these will allow us to refine our ideas about the conditions necessary for association formation.

Three Failures of Conditioning

We have said that conditioning may occur when the CS precedes the US because the activity engendered by the CS persists until the US arrives. By the same token it should be possible to produce conditioning by a procedure in which the US precedes the CS (*backward conditioning*). Figure 7.5 shows the results produced by a group of subjects trained in this way (−50, in the figure) and it is apparent that no conditioning occurs. This has been the usual outcome of experimental studies of backward conditioning—there have been a few reports of success early in training but it seems clear that after prolonged US–CS pairings the CS does not come to evoke the CR.

Our second example comes from an experiment by Rescorla (1968) in which the subjects were rats, the CS the sounding of a tone for two minutes, and the US an electric shock. Conditioning was carried out in the normal manner in that the US was preceded by the CS. One group of rats received shocks, on average, after only every tenth presentation of the CS. This procedure produces less rapid learning than does consistent pairing of CS and US, but, nonetheless, these subjects eventually began to show the CR of fear during the CS. A second group of subjects was treated in the same way except that for them shocks were also presented from time to time (with a probability of $0.1$ in each two minute period) in the intervals between conditioning trials. No CRs were observed in these animals in spite of the fact that they received just the same number of CS–US pairings as did the first group of subjects. It seems that learning fails to occur when the US is just as likely in the absence of the CS as in its presence.

A third example is provided by the phenomenon known as *blocking* (Fig. 7.4c). It is possible to carry out conditioning with a CS made up of separable elements put together as a compound. For example, a rat might be trained with a tone and a light presented simultaneously and in advance of a shock US. On test trials the elements can be separated and it will be found that both the tone and the light are each capable of evoking the CR when presented alone. In the blocking procedure the subject is given initial training with just one of the elements, say the tone, paired with the US, before the phase of training with the tone-light compound. It is found that such preliminary training prevents the light from coming to evoke the CR. The tone is said to "block" conditioning to the light. Clearly, pairing the light with the US in the compound phase of training is not a sufficient condition for learning to occur.

### The Predictive Power of the CS

One interpretation of the standard conditioning procedure is that the CS supplies information about the likely occurrence of the US; since it precedes the US it may be said to function as a signal for, or as a predictor of, the US. The implication of the three failures of conditioning just described is that it is this feature of the CS–US relationship that is important in determining whether or not learning occurs.

Consider the experiment by Rescorla (1968). Here the addition of extra shocks was arranged so as to ensure that shocks were just as likely to occur in the presence of the CS as in its absence. The procedure was thus one in which the CS did not supply any very reliable information about the likelihood of occurrence of the US, and in consequence it did not acquire the power to elicit the CR. Similarly, in the blocking experiment, the added stimulus element (the light) supplied no new information since the occurrence of the US was already fully predicted by the pretrained tone. Accordingly the light was not learned about. And, of course, no learning could be expected with the backward conditioning procedure since the CS could not possibly predict the occurrence of a US that has already happened.

This last point is worth pursuing in a little more detail in the light of recent experimental work showing that learning of a sort can be produced by prolonged experience of the backward conditioning procedure, even though the CS does not come to evoke the expected CR. What has been found is that a CS that has consistently followed the US can acquire the power to inhibit the CR evoked by another CS that has been paired with the US in the standard fashion. Thus if the US is shock and the "forward CS" evokes a fear response, the "backward CS", although it appears to do nothing when presented on its own, will prevent the subject from being fearful when presented along with the forward CS. The nature of the association underlying such "inhibitory" learning has been the focus of much discussion that is outside the scope of this book. The discovery of this phenomenon, however, is enough to add support to the general point being made here. In backward conditioning the CS cannot signal the US but it does signal the start of a fairly long period of time (the inter-trial interval) in which the US is guaranteed not to occur. That such a CS acquires inhibitory properties reinforces our suggestion that the learning produced by conditioning procedures depends upon the predictive power of the CS.

## The Significance of Classical Conditioning

Some writers on the subject of learning consider classical conditioning briefly and dismiss it quickly before moving on to other supposedly more interesting examples of learning. For them, classical conditioning is merely a way whereby simple reflexes (like salivation) can be persuaded to occur in an anticipatory form. Some reasons for rejecting this view as too restricted deserve mention.

*Movement about the environment.* The first point to emphasize is that classical conditioning effects are not restricted to simple reflexes. The eye-blink or the response of salivation can be used as convenient indices of conditioning but they are no more than that. According to our view, conditioning is a procedure that endows one stimulus (the CS) with many of the properties of another stimulus (the US). When the US is a motivationally significant event (such as food or electric shock) the CS will acquire the power to evoke a whole range of responses. In particular it will acquire the power to evoke movements of the entire animal. Just as the animal tends unconditionally to approach pleasant events and to shun unpleasant events so it will tend to approach CSs associated with pleasure and to avoid CSs associated with aversive events. The importance of this point becomes clear as soon as we realize that much of what any animal does most of the time consists of moving toward some features of its environment and avoiding others. That is, a great deal of the locomotion and (for animals equipped with hands or something similar) manipulative behaviour shown by animals can be regarded as a series of conditional responses to classically conditioned stimuli.

The power of this analysis is extended by the existence of second-order conditioning and sensory preconditioning. A stimulus may become a CS by virtue of the fact that it has been associated with some other stimulus that has been directly paired with a US at some other time. Thus a stimulus may evoke an approach response because it is the first event in a chain of associated stimuli that eventually make contact with the central representation of some pleasant event. Something of this sort may underlie maze-running by the rat (Chapter 6). When a rat has run through a maze and received food in the goalbox the stimuli arising from the goalbox will become a CS associated with the food US; stimuli that characterize the choice point will become associated with goalbox stimuli; startbox stimuli will become associated with choicepoint stimuli. Each of these sets of stimuli will then be able to elicit the approach normally elicited by food itself. The rat will therefore be able to get from the startbox to the food by approaching a series of conditioned stimuli that become available to him in sequence. There is no reason to suppose that this process is restricted to the behaviour of rats in mazes: the ability to link together a number of neutral stimuli that ultimately lead to some goal provides a plausible account of how other animals, including you and me, are able to find their way about their environment.

*Conditioning of motivational states.* Not only does classical conditioning explain how animals move about the environment it also goes some way toward explaining why they should want to. When an animal forms a tone–shock (CS–US) association it not only learns that a shock is likely to occur after the tone it also learns to be afraid in the presence of the tone. That is, the CS acquires the emotional or motivational properties of the US itself. Presentation of the tone will then evoke not only those responses that serve to move the animal away from the CS but will also elicit those behaviour patterns (such as changes in heart-rate and so on) that we regard as characteristic of the state of fear. We ended our discussion of motivation in Chapter 6 by saying that external stimuli are sometimes capable of inducing drive states. It is by way of classical conditioning that they are able to do this. It may be added that we have no need to suppose that conditioned motivational properties will be restricted to CSs associated with aversive USs. A CS associated with food should be capable of evoking an appetitive motivational state (perhaps we should call it "hope") just as an aversive CS can evoke the state of fear. This source of appetitive motivation may be every bit as important in energizing behaviour as that produced by the effects of deprivation and this is an issue that is currently the focus for much experimental work. Although this topic is investigated most easily in animal subjects and with events like food and electric shock being used to generate these states, the results should be of much greater generality. Cross-question anyone about the reasons underlying any given piece of behaviour and, if you go on long enough, you should be able to reduce his answer to one of two fundamental reasons: "to obtain pleasure" or "to avoid pain", or words to that effect. The terms "hope" and "fear" are perhaps often unduly melodramatic as descriptions of human motives but, regardless of the names we give them, the states associated with the anticipation of pleasant or unpleasant consequences are surely the fundamental motives underlying much of what we do.

*Learning about causal relationships.* Finally something should be said about the fact that conditioning occurs only when the CS is a predictive event supplying information about the likely occurrence of the US. This, in itself, is enough to dispose of the view that conditioning is a simple, trivial, and "automatic" process. It leads instead to the view, now becoming increasingly popular, that classical conditioning is a sophisticated process whereby an organism is able to build up an internal representation of what has been called the "causal structure" of its environment. In order to survive, any complex organism needs to be capable of learning what circumstances bring about pleasant events, what bring about dangerous events, and to ignore stimuli that have only a spurious correlation with these events. Classical conditioning embodies a mechanism that allows the organism to do this.

## LEARNING TO CONTROL THE ENVIRONMENT

We have described classical conditioning as a process whereby organisms learn about the relationship between events that occur in the environment. The fact that this learning often produces a change in behaviour has been treated as if it were almost an accidental by-product. But animals can also learn to *do* things. A child learns to ride his bicycle, an adult to drive a car, Morgan's dog learned to unlatch his master's gate (Chapter 1); surely these changes in behaviour cannot be attributed to classical conditioning. However obvious this conclusion may seem today, it took psychologists a long time to realize that learning of this sort involved procedures quite different from those used in classical conditioning. This was in part due to the influence of Pavlov himself who insisted that "it is obvious that the different kinds of habits based on training, education and discipline of any sort are nothing but a long chain of conditioned reflexes" (Pavlov, 1927, p. 395). It may not have been "obvious" to everyone but Pavlov's assertion proved difficult to refute—since no one knew just how it was that a complex motor response was acquired, it remained possible that a basic classical conditioning mechanism lay hidden beneath the complexity. Progress began to be made with attempts to produce response-learning in very simple experimental paradigms.

## The Instrumental Learning Procedure

The first systematic experiments on what we shall be calling *instrumental* learning or conditioning were done by Thorndike around 1900. The first clear distinction between instrumental and classical conditioning made in the West was by Grindley (1932). (The distinction had been proposed a few years earlier by the Polish psychologist and neurophysiologist, Konorski.)

Grindley carried out a learning experiment; his subject was a guinea pig which, like one of Pavlov's dogs, was restrained in a sound-proof enclosure during training. The animal was permitted to move its head from side to side, this being the response under study. Grindley also used a discrete, initially neutral stimulus of the sort used by Pavlov (in this case, a buzzer) and a device by which a small amount of food could be presented immediately in front of the animal by remote control. The training procedure was as follows. A trial was initiated by the sounding of the buzzer. This stayed on until the animal moved its head 30° in a specified direction (the right, say); the buzzer was then turned off and food was presented. The initial head-turn took about 100 seconds to occur but with continued training its latency gradually declined until after 100 trials or so the response usually occurred within a second of the onset of the buzzer (Fig. 7.6). In a second phase of training, an attempt was made to reverse the habit acquired in the first phase, the animal now being required to turn its head to the left to obtain the food. During the early trials of this phase the animal tended to turn its head to the right and latencies were long, but this habit soon disappeared and was replaced by a rapid and efficient turn to the left (Fig. 7.7).

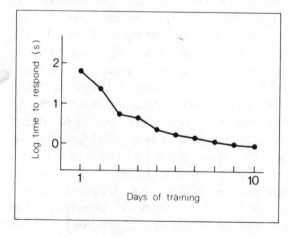

Fig. 7.6. *Averaged results for four guinea pigs given five trials each day. For each animal a turn of the head 30° in a specified direction yielded access to food presented centrally. The time to make the response from the onset of the stimulus declines with training (after Grindley, 1932).*

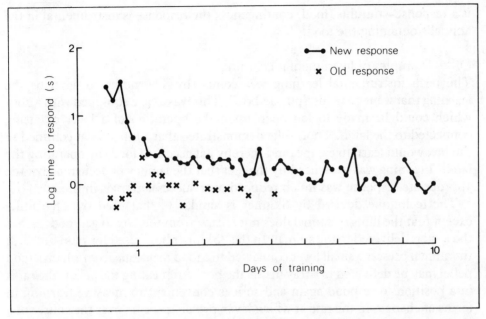

Fig. 7.7. *Results from individual trials for a guinea pig required to turn its head to the left after initial training on turning to the right. Early in training the time to make the new response is long and the old response tends to occur; times to make the first old response on any trial are given (after Grindley, 1932).*

This procedure certainly has some features in common with classical conditioning: there is the initially neutral buzzer which could be regarded as a CS; there is the presentation of food (a US); behaviour is modified as a result of experience. It is difficult to see, however, that the change in behaviour observed could be the consequence of a CS–US association being formed. We may allow that such an association will probably be formed and that the buzzer will take on some of the properties of food. But, since the food was presented centrally, it does not follow from this that the buzzer should start to elicit the response of turning the head to the right. And even if we were to allow that such a CR might somehow develop as a result of the formation of the CS–US association we would still have no explanation for how the same association comes to evoke a quite different CR in the reversal phase of training. *with the dog* 9. *p.g*

Grindley concluded that the learning he had observed was not classical conditioning. The critical feature of his experiment, he suggested, was that the food was presented only *after* the response, a feature that might be expected to produce quite different effects from those observed in Pavlov's experiments where the response under investigation is one elicited by the US. In classical conditioning the experimenter arranges for one stimulus (the US) to be contingent upon another (the CS). In instrumental learning, by contrast, there is a response–stimulus (food) contingency; the response is instrumental in the animal's obtaining the food.

### Other Examples of Instrumental Learning

The term instrumental learning was coined by Thorndike to describe the learning that went on in his "puzzle-box". This was a cage equipped with a door which could be made to fall open upon the operation of a lever or string connected to the latch. Thorndike demonstrated that a hungry cat confined in the box would learn to escape (and thereby get access to food) by operating the latch. Learning was evidenced by the fact that the latency of occurrence of the appropriate response was much reduced over successive trials in the box.

The technique devised by Skinner is similar to that used by Thorndike except that the hungry animal does not escape from the box to get food; rather the food is delivered to the animal. In the "Skinner box" used for rats (Fig. 7.8) the animal presses a small lever connected to a food magazine from which a food pellet may be delivered to a tray inside the box. After eating the pellet, the rat is in a position to respond again and so it is convenient to measure learning in terms of changes in the rate at which lever-pressing occurs over the course of a session of an hour or so. Skinner refers to this procedure as *operant conditioning* (the animal operates upon its environment to produce some effect) but the basic principle it embodies, that of making some consequence dependent upon a specified response, is identical to that seen in Thorndike's instrumental training situation. Given that the purpose of these artificial learning procedures is to

Fig. 7.8. *A version of the apparatus devised by Skinner. Pressing the lever can bring about delivery of a food pellet. The measure taken is usually the rate at which the response occurs.*

allow the study of some specified aspect of behaviour in as controlled a way as possible, Skinner's procedure is less nearly ideal than those used by Pavlov and Grindley (in which the experimental subject is restrained so as to exclude interference from other possible responses that the animal might make). Nonetheless, Skinner's procedure is much more convenient (both for the experimenter and the subject) and the Skinner box is now very widely used for the study of instrumental learning.

## The Law of Effect

Returning now to the experiment by Grindley, the critical feature of his results, that made them difficult to interpret as a form of classical conditioning, was the fact that the change in the animal's behaviour depended upon its consequences. Grindley accepted the need for an additional principle of reinforcement like that suggested by Thorndike some years earlier in his *law of effect*:

> Of several responses made to the same situation, those which are accompanied or closely followed by a state of satisfaction to the animal will, other things being equal, be more firmly connected with the situation, so that, when it recurs, they will be more likely to recur.
>
> (Thorndike, 1911, p. 244)

This statement of the law has a number of features (it asserts, for instance, that S–R associations are formed, that "satisfiers" are responsible for reinforcing these associations) that have not been widely accepted. Discussion of these features can be postponed for the time being while we concentrate on the law's central point—the assertion that the probability of occurrence of behaviour can be modified by its consequences. This assertion (sometimes called the "empirical law of effect") has been accepted as an important principle even by those (like Skinner) who reject all its other features.

Skinner's approach to the law of effect was not to theorize about it, but to use it. For him a *reinforcer* is defined as any event that can bring about a change in the likelihood of behaviour on which it is consequent. There is no talk of changes in the strength of S–R links or whatever; instead reinforcement is a technique for controlling behaviour. Again, a reinforcer may be an event, like the presentation of food, that we might want to call a "satisfier" but it need not be. An event like the presentation of a light that has previously been paired with food, will increase the rate at which rats press a lever when this behaviour produces the light. The light is therefore a reinforcer even though it seems improbable that its occurrence is satisfying in itself. The uses to which the empirical law has been put include attempts to change not only the behaviour of experimental animals but also men. To take just one example: some psychotic patients so withdraw from the world that they refuse ever to speak to anyone—some have gone for 20 years or more without speaking. A first step in the treatment of such patients is to retrain the behaviour of speaking by reinforcement techniques. At first any sound, a cough or a grunt, will be reinforced. When these increase in frequency, only approximation to words will yield reinforcement. Then phrases will be required, and so on. The reinforcer used will depend upon the patient—perhaps a cigarette for one, a piece of chocolate for another—but its nature does not matter. If it is effective in increasing the frequency of the desired behaviour, that is enough.

Skinner's empirical approach to reinforcement is both useful and logically sound. Nonetheless, other psychologists have remained interested in the more theoretical propositions embodied in Thorndike's statement of the law. They still want to try to specify what properties of events that have been shown to be effective as reinforcers allow them to be so; also, to determine what changes go on in the organism, as a result of reinforcement, that produce the change in behaviour. We shall see that experimental analysis of both issues requires us to reject the suggestions put forward by Thorndike and thus to reject his theoretical version of the law of effect.

## Varying Size of Reward

Food is an effective reinforcer for a hungry rat. If the animal is placed in the startbox of a runway and allowed to make its way to a goalbox containing food at the other end of the runway, learning will occur. On subsequent trials in the runway the rat will come to move from start to goal with increasing speed. Thorndike's law of effect explains this by saying that, of the many responses elicited by the stimuli of the runway, only that of moving to the goalbox is followed by food. Behaviour changes because one S–R connection becomes so strong that the R of running is always evoked rather than any other R to which the S is only weakly connected. The necessary conditions are that the R should occur in the presence of the S and be closely followed by the food.

The results of an experiment by Crespi (1942) quickly show that this analysis is, at best, incomplete. Figure 7.9 shows the level of performance reached by two groups of rats after 20 trials in a runway. One group received 256 food pellets in the goalbox, the other only 16 pellets. This difference in reward size produce a marked difference in behaviour with the former group running much more rapidly. Common sense might anticipate this result but it is not to be expected on the basis of Thorndike's theory—since receiving 16 food pellets is an effective reinforcer clearly capable of strengthening the hypothesized S–R connection why should it be that animals given this reward end up running more slowly than those given 256 pellets?

Yet more troublesome are the results from a second phase of Crespi's experiment. From trial 20 the subjects that had previously received the large reward had it reduced to a mere 16 pellets. Once the animals had experienced the smaller reward their speed of running declined sharply, even falling below the speed shown by rats that had experienced only the small reward (Fig. 7.9).

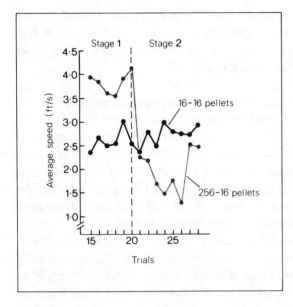

Fig. 7.9. *Average running speeds of two groups of rats over a series of trials in a runway. In stage 1 the groups received a different number of pellets in the goalbox (256 or 16); in stage 2 both groups received 16 pellets (after Crespi, 1942).*

Crespi referred to this as a "depression" effect; it is also known as *negative contrast*. Such a result is not predicted by Thorndike's law of effect. The smaller reward is a perfectly good reinforcer as is shown by the behaviour of the subjects that experienced this reward throughout. Animals pretrained with the large reward are thus receiving an effective reinforcer after performing an R in the presence of S. But the behaviour appears to be weakened rather than strengthened by this procedure. It is not the case that a "reinforcer" automatically strengthens the behaviour upon which it is contingent; rather the effectiveness of a given event depends upon the animal's previous experience of other reinforcers, that is, on the discrepancy between what the animal expects and what actually happens.

### The Nature of the Association in Instrumental Learning

Although Thorndike's account of the nature of the reinforcer is not adequate, it still remains possible that his notion of an S–R association is correct. Another possibility is suggested if we draw a parallel between classical and instrumental learning. In classical conditioning, the experimenter arranges a contingency between one stimulus (the CS) and another (the US). The result is the formation of an S–S association. In instrumental training, he arranges that a given stimulus (the reinforcer) should follow a response. Perhaps then what the subject learns consists of an R–S association. We might propose, much as we did for classical conditioning, that the near simultaneous occurrence of activity in those points of the brain that organize a response and those that are sensitive to the receipt of an unexpected amount of food allows the formation of a link between them; that this link grows stronger with repeated pairings; and that the rate or vigour of the response depends upon the strength of this link. According to this account, the "reinforcer" does not merely strengthen some other association, rather it enters into an association itself.

*Devaluing the reinforcer.* This new hypothesis was investigated in an experiment by Adams and Dickinson (1981) in which use was made of the fact discussed above, that flavour aversions can be established by means of classical conditioning. The essence of this experiment was as follows: hungry rats were trained to press the lever in a Skinner box, each response being followed by the delivery of a sucrose pellet. This stage of instrumental training was followed by classical conditioning in which the rats were injected with lithium chloride after consuming sucrose. Pairings of sucrose and illness stop the subjects from eating the sucrose pellets; but does it have any other effects? If instrumental lever-pressing depends upon the existence of an association between the response and the reinforcer then we might expect this to be affected too. The sucrose will no longer be a desired event since, by classical conditioning, it will have taken on some of the properties of the illness with which it has been associated. And indeed, when the rats returned to the Skinner box they showed a marked reluctance to press the lever in comparison with control subjects that had not received pairings of sucrose with illness.

This result may seem unsurprising (why indeed should a rat press a lever in order to obtain something that makes it ill?) but it is nonetheless important. It is a result predicted by the theory of response–reinforcer association that is not to be expected on the basis of the law of effect. According to the law of effect, responding during the test phase of the experiment should be determined simply by the number of reinforced S–R pairings experienced during training. Procedures designed to devalue the reinforcer when administered after training should be unimportant since by this stage the reinforcer has already done its job.

*Devaluing the response as a predictor.* A different experimental approach to the issue of response–reinforcer association pursues the parallel between classical and instrumental learning. All we have said so far is that a response–reinforcer association will be formed when the two events are paired. In classical conditioning we found that the formation of a CS–US association depended upon the CS providing information about the likely occurrence of the US. That the same sort of thing may be true of instrumental learning is suggested by the following experiment by Pearce and Hall (1978).

Rats were intially trained to press the lever in a Skinner box in order to receive food. Once responding had been established a schedule of *partial reinforcement* was introduced (Fig. 7.10a). No longer did every response

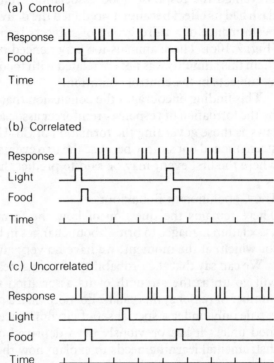

(a) Control

Response

Food

Time

(b) Correlated

Response

Light

Food

Time

Fig. 7.10. *Relationship between responses, food, and light in the various conditions of the experiment by Pearce and Hall (1978). With sufficient training, conditions (a) and (c) generate higher rates of response than does condition (b).*

(c) Uncorrelated

Response

Light

Food

Time

produce a food pellet: food was made available only once a minute on average.) (The actual interval between reinforced responses was varied over a wide range so that the rats had no way of knowing that any particular response would be successful in producing food.) The rats continued to respond, emitting, on average, about 15 responses each minute, only one of which produced a food pellet. Clearly even a limited number of response–food pairings is capable of maintaining instrumental responding. Another way of looking at this is to say that even though the response is not a perfect predictor of the reinforcer (since may responses go unreinforced) it is still the best predictor available (since food is never delivered unless a response has just been made).

The implication of this latter view is made clear by considering the performance of a second group of rats trained in the *correlated* condition (Fig. 7.10b). These animals received training just like that given to the subjects in the control condition except that a novel stimulus, a brief flash of light, was introduced. The flash was produced by and immediately followed reinforced responses; it therefore immediately preceded the delivery of food. These animals proved to be much less willing to press the lever. Thus the introduction of a stimulus that predicted the delivery of the reinforcer better than the response (the light flash occurred only and always before the delivery of food) prevented the response–food association from being strengthened. That the flash had its effect because it predicted the delivery of food was confirmed by the performance of a third group of subjects trained in an *uncorrelated* condition (Fig. 7.10c). These animals too experienced presentations of the light but for them this stimulus was not correlated with food. They responded just as readily as subjects in the control condition.

(This finding encourages the conclusion that instrumental learning proceeds by the formation of response–reinforcer associations that obey the same general laws as those governing the formation of CS–US associations. Associations are strengthened not simply because the two events are paired but in circumstances where the first event may be said to predict the second.)

## The Generation of Behaviour

There remains the question of how the formation of a response–reinforcer association manages to bring about changes in behaviour, and this is a question for which, at the moment, we have no very good answers.

We can say that the probability of a given response (such as pressing a lever) will go up as the strength of its association with food increases, but, for a number of reasons, this can be no more than a partial account. For one thing, it is true only under a special set of circumstances—a rat will not lever-press for food unless it has previously been deprived of food. An adequate theory of instrumental learning needs to explain how the state that is produced by food deprivation can energize the performing responses that are associated with food.

Second, the existence of a response–reinforcer association will not lead to the emission of responses unless the stimulus conditions are right. Obviously a rat will not be able to press the lever in a Skinner box if there is no lever present to be pressed, but the point is more subtle than this. Recall that Grindley's guinea pig, having formed an association between the response of turning its head and food, came to perform this reponse only in the presence of the buzzer. How is this phenomenon (known as *stimulus control* of responding) to be accommodated?

One obvious possibility is that the introduction of a stimulus such as the buzzer, allows classical conditioning to go on alongside instrumental learning. When the animal turns its head it receives food, and thus the response–food association will be formed. But the training set-up is such that the presentation of food is also preceded by the buzzer and thus there is scope for a buzzer–food (CS–US) association to be formed as well. The buzzer will therefore come to evoke the range of CRs that are typical of a stimulus associated with food. As we have seen (p. 230), these CRs may be construed as constituting a state of "hope", a motivational state that helps to energize responding. Responding will therefore be confined to the presence of the stimulus because the stimulus supplies the motivation to respond.

The theory just described (which has been called *two-process theory* because it depends upon the interaction of both instrumental and classical conditioning processes) is perhaps the theory of learning most widely accepted today. It is not without its problems, however, and it would be misleading to move on without mentioning one of them. The theory requires that a CS–US association be formed (a buzzer–food association in this example) during the course of instrumental learning. Now, although buzzer–food pairings do occur, there will also be occasions on which the buzzer is presented and is not followed by food, given that food is presented only after the subject has made the designated response: sometimes, especially early in training, the buzzer will sound but the animal will not turn its head. In consequence, the correlation of buzzer with food will be poor; the response itself will be a much better predictor of food. The situation is the converse of that arranged in the correlated condition of the experiment by Pearce and Hall (1978). In that experiment a stimulus, the flash of light, was better correlated with food than was the response. The outcome was that the response–food association did not become strengthened. In Grindley's experiment (and in most other studies of instrumental learning) the response is better correlated with food than is the stimulus and on these grounds we might expect that the stimulus would become only weakly associated with food, if at all. Since the instrumental training situation is less than ideal for the formation of stimulus–reinforcer associations it may seem unwise to attribute the powerful effect of the stimulus in controlling the emission of the instrumental response to the existence of such an association. It must be admitted, however, that a better theory of stimulus control still remains to be specified adequately.

## The Significance of Instrumental Learning

Although some have dismissed instrumental learning as being mere trial-and-error learning, others have had no doubt about its fundamental importance in controlling the day-to-day activities of animals and men. In particular, Skinner has often pointed out that the study of operant conditioning (as he calls it) is, in essence, the study of "voluntary" behaviour. Although they may come under stimulus control, operant responses are not directly elicited by identifiable stimuli and are not, therefore, to be equated with simple reflex responses. Rather, the operant response is controlled by its consequences, increasing in probability when it leads to a pleasant state of affairs and (although we have not discussed this explicitly) becoming less likely when it leads to aversive consequences. This sort of control, according to Skinner, is the central feature of the behaviour that we call "voluntary" in everyday usage.

Certainly, our investigation of the conditions under which instrumental learning occurs leads us to reject the description of it as "mere" trial-and-error learning. As in classical conditioning, the formation of the relevant association appears to depend upon the first event (in this case, the response) serving as a predictor of the second; mere pairing of the response and reinforcer may not be enough. Just as classical conditioning may be regarded as a process whereby animals learn about causal relationships between environmental events, so instrumental learning may be regarded as the process whereby animals can learn about the causal relationships between their behaviour and its consequences.

## LEARNING AND ADAPTIVE SIGNIFICANCE

The few experiments mentioned above are but a minute sample from the mass of work done using classical and instrumental conditioning procedures. Our discussion of the significance of these two types of conditioning has hinted at the reason for all this interest—it stems from the assumption that the study of laboratory animals in artificial and well-controlled conditions can help to lay bare mechanisms that are of general applicability and importance.

In recent years this assumption has come under attack from some ethologists and comparative psychologists who lay stress on the adaptive significance of learning. They argue that the mechanisms responsible for learning have evolved like all other attributes that an organism possesses, and that they should be viewed as specific adaptations that help a given species to survive and reproduce in the particular habitat in which it evolved. They argue that research prompted by this view shows that

> our principles of learning no longer have a claim to universality . . . that learning depends in very important ways upon the kind of animal that is being considered, the kind of behaviour that is required of it, and the kind of situation in which the behaviour occurs

> (Bolles, 1979, p. 165)

The evidence cited in favour of this conclusion is of two complementary types. First are the cases in which learning occurs with dramatic ease in spite of the fact that, according to the traditional laws of conditioning, circumstances are such that learning should be difficult. Second are the cases in which learning does not occur (or occurs only slowly) in spite of the fact that the circumstances thought to promote rapid conditioning have been specifically arranged. We will analyse in detail examples from each of these categories.

### Flavour Aversion Learning

Perhaps the most frequently cited example of inappropriately rapid learning is that of imprinting in young birds. Flavour aversion learning by rats runs it a close second and we will concentrate on this phenomenon here, partly because imprinting has already been discussed (Chapter 4, p. 128), and partly because flavour aversion learning poses a challenge to our traditional concept of classical conditioning in a most clear-cut way. In particular, the procedure used to induce a flavour aversion, that of presenting a distinctive flavour and following it by some treatment designed to induce illness, can readily be interpreted as one of classical conditioning with the flavour as the CS and the lithium injection as the US. Indeed the procedure was introduced above (p. 221) in just this context.

Whatever the formal, procedural similarities between flavour aversion learning and more orthodox conditioning procedures, it must be allowed that the former shows some unusual features that cannot be predicted from studies of the latter. Perhaps the most striking characteristic of the flavour aversion is its time course. Recall (Fig. 7.5) that conditioning of the rabbit's eye-blink response was best achieved when the CS–US interval was about half a second. On the basis of this finding it has been suggested that the optimum CS–US interval for classical conditioning in general must be about half a second and that conditioning cannot occur with intervals much longer than this. Flavour aversion learning, however, will develop fairly well with an interval of several hours between the rat's exposure to the flavour and its being subjected to the procedure designed to induce illness. Just one such training trial can be enough to produce the effect. This result has been taken to suggest that the "laws" of classical conditioning do not apply to this form of learning—that evolution has equipped the rat with special mechanisms that allow it to learn very readily about biologically, relevant relationships between events. The further implication is that each species may be equipped with its own idiosyncratic special mechanisms.

Support for this conclusion comes from a famous experiment on flavour aversion by Garcia and Koelling (1966), shown schematically in Fig. 7.11. Rats were allowed to drink from a bottle containing sweetened water and were then subjected to a treatment designed to produce a suppression of drinking. Some animals were poisoned so as to induce a flavour aversion; others received an electric shock to the feet immediately after drinking from the bottle. As the figure shows, the first treatment was successful but the second was not. This result on its own might be interpreted as showing nothing more than that these experimenters had chosen a shock intensity too weak to sustain learning; but the results from two further groups of rats show that this is not so. The remaining animals in the experiment received equivalent treatment except that, for them, the distinctive stimulus accompanying drinking was not a flavour but was auditory-visual—each lick at the bottle caused a burst of noise, and lights to flash. For these subjects the shock was effective in suppressing drinking whereas the illness induced by poisoning was not (Fig. 7.11). It seems that rats are especially "prepared" to associate external cues with the painful consequences of an electric shock and to associate illness with taste cues. The adaptive significance of such an arrangement is readily apparent.

| | | Consequence | |
|---|---|---|---|
| | | Illness | Pain |
| Cue | Taste | Drinking suppressed | No suppression |
| | Auditory-visual | No suppression | Drinking suppressed |

Fig. 7.11. *The results produced by the four main groups in the study by Garcia and Koelling (1966).*

## Analysis of Flavour Aversion Learning

To acknowledge the adaptive value of a given feature of behaviour does not free us from the obligation to try to analyse the mechanisms that underlie it; and flavour-aversion learning has been subjected to a thorough theoretical and experimental analysis.

*The special problems of flavour aversion learning.* First we should be clear about the ways in which this form of learning is and is not "special" when compared with more orthodox forms of classical conditioning. The fact that it can occur in a single trial is not particularly noteworthy. Many conditioning procedures produce one trial learning, particularly those using an aversive event, such as a strong electric shock, as the US. Nor is the fact that a CS–US interval longer than half a second can be used in itself enough to give this form of learning special status. The interval of about half a second is indeed best for conditioning the rabbit's eye-blink but studies of other preparations used in the conditioning laboratory have shown that there is no single optimum interval—it depends upon the particular preparation used and many work well at much longer intervals. Further, studies of the CS-US interval in flavour aversion learning itself have shown there to be an orderly relationship between the interval and the strength of the aversion (Fig. 7.12) that accords well enough with the account of classical conditioning developed above (p. 226).

What remains is the fact that, although learning may be incomplete, it can still occur with a very long CS–US interval; also there remains the evidence from Garcia and Koelling (1966), for a special readiness on the part of the rat to form associations between taste cues and illness. In fact these two can be reduced to a single point. The surprising feature of learning with a long CS–US interval is that the association is formed between the US and the taste CS in spite

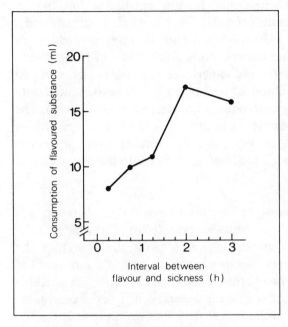

Fig. 7.12. *Consumption of flavoured water during a 10 minute test trial after training at a range of flavour-sickness intervals. Control subjects given no training consume between 15 and 20 ml (after Garcia et al., 1966).*

of the fact that there must be many other events occurring during the interval, and thus occurring in closer proximity to the illness-inducing US. In particular, the rat is handled and injected with the substance used to produce illness but the cues constituting these events do not prevent it from forming an association between the illness and a taste cue. Long-delay learning is thus a further example of preferential association between taste and illness.

Flavour aversion learning does not constitute the only case of preferential association formation. In recent years several other examples have emerged from studies using more orthodox conditioning procedures. One such case has already been discussed. The experiment by Foree and LoLordo (1973; see Chapter 6, p. 198) has been taken as showing that pigeons are predisposed to associate an aversive event with an auditory cue and an appetitive event with a visual cue. It seems to be a general principle that, for a given species, some pairings of cues are better learned about than others.

*An hypothesis.* By what mechanism is this selectivity in the formation of associations achieved? We do not yet know and all that can be offered here, as a tentative hypothesis, is an example of the sort of explanation that might be appropriate.

Mackintosh (1973) has shown that rats given uncorrelated presentations of a CS and a US (e.g. a tone and electric shock) learn that the two events are not related. They therefore show only poor conditioning when subsequently the tone and shock are paired, although they remain capable of forming an association between the CS and some other US, such as food. In other words, prior experience with the events to be used in the conditioning procedure can modify the rate at which learning occurs. Now adult rats will bring to the flavour aversion experiment a lifetime of experience with taste cues, external cues, and with internal states of illness or well-being. In this experience, taste cues will have been consistently correlated with internal states whereas the other cues will not. It seems possible, therefore, that the special features of flavour aversion learning might be generated by transfer from (informal) conditioning that the rat has experienced before it comes to the experimental situation.

*Conclusions.* It is too early to know yet whether or not this explanation will survive further experimental analysis. But whatever its fate (and whatever the mechanism underlying selective association) it remains the case that the readiness with which learning occurs does indeed depend upon the nature of the animal being conditioned, the type of stimuli used, and so on. To accept this need not necessarily undermine the search for general principles of conditioning: it means that we must add some more. And it is even possible (as the hypothesis discussed above implies) that the new principles that emerge will be able to accommodate both flavour aversion learning and the results of other, more traditional conditioning procedures.

Failures of Conditioning

According to the law of effect (p. 235), a reinforcer (such as the presentation of a pleasant event or the termination of an aversive event) will increase the probability of the behaviour that produces it. There is no implication that the "law" applies only to some patterns of behaviour, to only some reinforcers, or to only some combinations of response and reinforcer. Accordingly it should be a relatively simple matter to train a pigeon to peck a lit key that signals an impending electric shock when the keypeck prevents the shock from occurring. In fact, this turns out to be almost impossibly difficult, in spite of the fact that the pecking response is one that pigeons emit readily and one that can easily be trained using food as the reinforcer. It is not that pigeons are impervious to the effects of electric shock—pigeons will acquire with little difficulty the response of running from one end of a box to the other when this behaviour is reinforced by the omission of a shock that would otherwise have occurred.

This is not an isolated example. There is now a growing list of experiments in which instrumental conditioning has been found to be ineffective in modifying behaviour, in spite of the fact that the animal under study appears to be perfectly intelligent, the response required one well within its capabilities, and the reinforcer one that is perfectly effective in other circumstances. Many of these experiments involve the use of aversive events. Thus, rats have difficulty in learning to press a lever in order to avoid shock, but are good at learning to run in a running-wheel when this achieves the same effect. Frogs (to choose an example from a less widely studied animal group) find it difficult to learn to jump from one compartment of a box to another in order to avoid shock, but amphibia are quite capable of rapid learning about aversive events when circumstances are more propitious. Brower *et al.* (1960) demonstrated that toads would attack a bumblebee dangled before them on a string, but would do so just once. (Control subjects presented with bees from which the stings had been removed persisted in attacking.)

Unexpected failures of conditioning have also been demonstrated with food as the reinforcer. An amusing example is supplied by Breland and Breland (1961) who tried to teach a pig the trick off inserting large wooden "coins" into a slot (in a piggy bank) in order to receive food. The pig is apparently an intelligent animal and easily motivated. Nonetheless, after initial signs of success the training programme had to be abandoned when the pig began to play with the coin, tossing it in the air and rooting at it, instead of putting it in the bank. This behaviour appeared and peristed despite the fact that it cost the animal the opportunity of earning food. An experimental study using the food as the reinforcer is reported by Shettleworth (1975) who rewarded hamsters with food for performing certain, naturally occuring patterns of behaviour. A selection from the results is shown in Fig. 7.13. Here we see that when animals

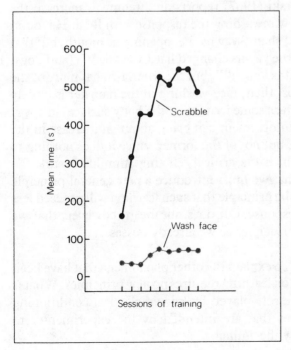

Fig. 7.13. *Mean number of seconds in 20-minute sessions spent scrabbling or face-washing by golden hamsters. Separate groups of subjects were reinforced for each behaviour pattern; a 2-second bout of the appropriate activity caused the delivery of food (after Shettleworth, 1975.*

receive food for scrabbling (that is, scraping with their forepaws on the wall of their cage), the frequency of this response increased dramatically; but they would not learn to wash their faces even though they were hungry and doing so for two seconds brought about the delivery of a food pellet.

These effects (sometimes referred to as examples of "constraints on learning") are summarized in Seligman's (1970) notion of *preparedness*. It is suggested that animals of a given species are especially prepared to associate certain responses and reinforcers; other associations will be *contraprepared*. Thus, for the hamster, scrabbling appears to have some sort of special affinity for food reinforcement that face-washing lacks. Again, the phylogeny of the pigeon makes it easy for this animal to learn to peck food, but not to peck to avoid shock, where running away is more easily learned. A possible implication of this view is that such special adaptations may render fruitless the search for general principles of learning.

### Analysis of Preparedness in Instrumental Conditioning

*The role of the eliciting stimulus.* Why will the hamster not learn to wash its face for food reward? A possible explanation is that some behaviour patterns are much more strongly tied to eliciting stimuli (i.e. are closer to the traditional notion of the reflex) than are others. Consider the behaviour of yawning. The eliciting stimulus may not be immediately apparent but, without it, to emit a "true" yawn is rather difficult. Konorski (1967) reports an attempt to increase the frequency of yawning in a dog by rewarding the response with food. He found that the dog took to performing "sham" yawns (i.e. opening its mouth) but that the frequency of occurence of true yawns changed hardly at all. We (and dogs, so it appears) can open our mouths "at will", but the true yawn has more of the properties of the reflex. Perhaps, then, face-washing in the hamster is closely tied to an eliciting stimulus (such as some irritant on the body surface) in a way that scrabbling is not. Food reinforcement can bring about an increase in the frequency of the latter response but not of the former, since it does nothing to increase the frequency with which the critical, eliciting stimulus occurs. To adopt this explanation means that we must introduce a new general principle into the instrumental learning (the principle that such learning will proceed less readily with more reflex-like responses); it does not mean, however, that we need to abandon such general principles as we already possess.

*The role of classical conditioning.* To explain the other phenomena that have been regarded as showing constraints on learning requires no new principles. What is needed is an appreciation of the role played by known classical conditioning processes in training procedures that are intended by the experimenter to require instrumental learning by the animal.

In classical conditioning pairing a CS and a US will endow the former stimulus with some of the properties of the latter (p. 224). A trained subject will therefore tend to approach and make contact with a CS that has been associated with a food US and will move away from a CS that has been associated with a shock. The form that these CRs take is closely similar to the response that the animal makes unconditionally to the US itself. Little wonder, then, that it is so easy to train a pigeon to peck a lit key to obtain food. This instrumental training procedure has embedded within it the elements of a classical conditioning procedure in that the pigeon always sees a lit key (just as it emits the response) before food is delivered, so that the key can become a CS for the food US. Autoshaping (p.220) will therefore occur and will generate a tendency to peck the key that will work along with and enhance the instrumentally reinforced tendency to do so. Learning will be poor, however, when the instrumental response required is opposed by the CR elicited by the classical conditioning that is occurring concurrently. Animals find it difficult to learn an instrumental response that requires them to approach some event in order to avoid a shock when that same event, by virtue of its association with shock, become a CS eliciting the CR of withdrawal.

These unintended effects of classical conditioning can be very powerful. For the pig trained by Breland and Breland the "coin" that had been associated with food became such an effective CS that the animal spent much of its time playing with this symbol that stood for food and thus failed to obtain the food itself. Is it too fanciful to think of the human miser as caught in the same trap, as someone so obsessed with objects associated with pleasant events that he finds himself unable to part with the former to obtain the latter?

## Conclusions

Evolution has equipped the various animal species with a variety of special adaptations that allow them to cope with the peculiar demands of their environments. That these adaptations might extend to features of the way in which animals learn, comes as no special surprise. We can readily acknowledge as a wonder of Nature the fact that (for instance) the rat is equipped with a flavour aversion learning ability that fits it admirably for its way of life as a scavenging and opportunistic feeder. But having done this, our next step must be to try to analyse the ability. We can try to discern its origins by the methods outlined in Chapters 2 and 3. We can also (and this was the intent of the analysis presented above) try to determine the nature of the mechanisms at work in the animal as it exists in the world today. The two approaches are complementary. To discover the mechanisms does not detract from the usefulness or validity of the evolutionary account.

Our analysis has allowed us to add some new general principles of learning to those that were extracted from studies of standard classical and instrumental conditioning procedures, but it has not required us to abandon those original *principles. Indeed the explanatory power of the notion of associative learning that constitutes the essence of our account of conditioning is such as to provoke the question of whether there are any* forms of learning that are not reducible to association formation. It is to this question that we turn next.

## NON-ASSOCIATIVE LEARNING

The mechanism that underlies both classical conditioning and instrumental learning has been shown to be one of association formation. In classical conditioning the association may be taken to represent the organism's knowledge about the relationship between events in its environment; the instrumental association, knowledge about the consequences of its actions. An animal capable of these two types of associative learning seems well equipped to deal with its world. Nonetheless, it has often been suggested that associative learning is just one of several types; that animals (and especially man) are also capable of adapting to environmental demands by way of "complex" learning mechanisms that are not associative in nature. In particular, it has often been argued that the mechanisms by which man learns language (and the thought processes that language allows) fall outside the scope of the analysis presented so far. Discussion of this important issue will be postponed until the final chapter. In this chapter we will confine discussion to other, less species-specific cases of supposedly non-associative learning, trying to determine which of them can be reduced to the operation of known associative mechanisms, and to determine what mechanisms are involved in those that cannot.

We begin by considering two much discussed examples of complex learning both of which have been considered to involve a process of concept formation (as opposed to association formation). We shall see, to anticipate the discussion that many features of these examples can be accommodated by associative learning theory, but that both display features that seem to require a mechanism whereby animals can learn to attend to some aspects of stimuli and to ignore others. We move on, therefore, to a direct consideration of attentional and perceptual learning. The experiments to be discussed under these headings can hardly be regarded as examples of "complex" learning since, for the most part, they utilize versions of the basic conditioning procedures. But, perhaps because of their apparent simplicity, they allow us to see more clearly the nature of non-associative learning mechanisms.

### Visual Concept Formation

*Examples.* Associations are formed between well-defined events, between stimulus and stimulus, or response and stimulus. At first sight, therefore, the learning that underlies the formation of concepts seems to lie outside the area covered by associative learning mechanisms; for the essence of concept formation is that it allows the same response to be made to a wide range of very different stimuli. To take a very simple example: when a child first learns to use the word "chair" he makes a verbal response to a particular object. (Since the child is probably praised by his parents for his behaviour, it might be appropriate to regard this as a case of rewarded instrumental learning with the response coming under stimulus control.) But given time and experience the child will come to apply the word chair to (make the same response to) many new objects quite different from the first. By the time he has acquired the adult's concept of a chair he will apply the word not only to wooden objects with a seat, four legs, and a back but also to objects made of cloth, leather, or steel with one leg or three legs or none at all, and so on.

Examples of such concept formation are not solely to be found in the human use of language. Experiments done with pigeons (subjects chosen because of their excellent visual capabilities, not because it is supposed that they are particularly clever) show that these animals are capable of similar achievements. For pigeons the response under study is not, of course, that of enunciating a word; rather it is the response of pecking at a response key onto which a picture is projected. By using a large number of slides as the stimuli it has proved possible to teach the pigeon the concept of "a person". The pigeon is shown a series of pictures of everyday scenes and is rewarded for pecking at only those that include a human figure. This the bird learns to do. It is not the case that the bird learns separately to make the response in the presence of each individual positive instance. When presented with quite new pictures that have not been used during training, the bird will still respond appropriately. By similar techniques it has been shown that pigeons can acquire the concepts of "water", "man-made object", and even of "pigeon". (This last is more remarkable than it sounds, given that the pictures presented to the experimental subjects included some of extravagant "fancy" breeds that no normal pigeon is ever likely to come across in everyday life.)

*Analysis.* There is no doubt about the reality and widespread occurrence of a form of learning that leads to concept formation, but from one point of view the challenge that it poses to associative learning theory may be more apparent than real. Recall our discussion of the nature of the stimulus in Chapter 6. There it was pointed out that an environment that reliably evokes a given response will have many different aspects, and that only by experiment can we discover what the effective stimulus might be. The necessary experiment involves presenting a whole range of potential stimuli so that the effective stimulus may be identified as that feature which is common to all events that are capable of eliciting the response. The same analysis applies to concept-learning experiments. In these, the subject makes the same response to a variety of stimuli, but the fact that this is possible indicates that all these stimuli probably contain some common element or set of elements that constitute the effective stimulus.

Stimulus set A                          Stimulus set B

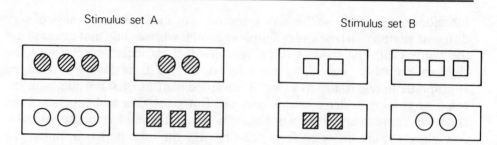

Fig. 7.14. *Eight stimuli for an experiment on concept formation. The subject's problem is to discover the rule that distinguishes set A from set B (based on an experiment by Dennis et al., 1973).*

Having made this assertion it must now be allowed that there appear to be some cases in which there is no single element or set of elements common to all stimuli that evoke a given response. An example is given in Fig. 7.14. This shows a set of eight stimuli which vary from one another according to the number of figures they contain, whether the figures are black or white, and whether the figures are circles or squares. They have been divided into two sets of four and although there is no obvious single feature that distinguishes set A from set B, subjects can learn (with difficulty) to respond consistently in one way to instances of set A and in another way to instances of set B. The reader may be entertained to try to work out for himself or herself the rule that defines which set a stimulus falls into, before reading on. The answer is that a stimulus is classified as an A if it possesses at least two out of three of these properties: black, made of circles, and containing three constituent figures. Similarly a stimulus is a B if it is at least two of: white, squares, made up of two constituent figures. The "concept of an A" is thus a statistical matter: a display need contain only two of three relevant properties in order to be classified as an A. Presumably many of the natural concepts that we use in everyday life are of this statistical sort. To revert to our previous example, there is no one set of features that defines a chair and we apply the word to objects that have next to nothing in common apart from the fact that they all possess at least some of the features of the "ideal chair". The implication of this conclusion is that it may very often be difficult to specify precisely the nature of the effective stimulus for some patterns of behaviour. It does not, however, require any radical change to the account of concept formation given above.

In experiments of this sort the experimenter needs to analyse very carefully the various objects and events that he uses as stimuli in order to discover the effective stimulus that controls the response. No new mechanism of learning need be postulated to explain the way in which that stimulus, once identified, has its effect. What still needs explaining, however, is how, with training, the subject can come to identify the properties of the effective stimulus so readily. Some form of learning is involved here; at the very least, the subject must be capable of learning to ignore irrelevant features of the stimulus display. How is this to be explained in associative terms? We turn to this issue after discussing examples of a rather different form of concept formation.

## Rule Learning

One of the earliest challenges to the view that associative mechanisms can provide an adequate account of all learning came from observations thought to show "insightful" problem solving in primates. The cat in the puzzle-box may solve the problem of how to get out by a process of trial and error, but other animals, it was suggested, could solve problems by other means. A chimpanzee may simply sit and stare at two sticks for some time; then, after a flash of insight, it gets up and fits the two sticks together to produce an implement long enough to reach food that was previously out of reach. How can such behaviour be a product of associative learning?

*Learning-set formation.* Before trying to answer this question it is necessary to specify more precisely what point is at issue. It is now accepted that learning of some sort plays a part in insightful problem solving. Primates given access to sticks will play with them and try to fit them together even when there is no food to be retrieved. It is known that the more of this sort of experience the animals have had, the more likely they will be to solve a problem involving the use of sticks. It seems, therefore, that the animals are capable of learning principles about how to use sticks and that these principles can be transferred from one situation to another. A more controlled demonstration of the same phenomenon is provided by studies of *learning-set* formation. In this procedure the ape or monkey is presented with a pair of objects and rewarded with a small amount of food for choosing one of them. The animal is given only about half a dozen trials with these objects before they are replaced with two new ones. (Every primate laboratory needs to be equipped with a large collection of small items of junk that can be used as stimuli in learning-set experiments.) After a few trials with the next set of objects they are changed again, and so on. Early in training, six trials is usually not enough for the subject to solve any given discrimination. But performance begins to improve as more and more problems are attempted until finally it reaches perfection (Fig. 7.15). That is, after extensive training with the learning-set procedure, the subject faced with two objects neither of which it has seen before will pick one of them and, if it is rewarded, will consistently choose it thereafter; if the initial choice is not rewarded the subject will switch to the other object and consistently choose that. Thus the animal appears to be able to learn some rule about how to behave in this situation that allows the near-instantaneous solution of a problem that it has never met before.

*Analysis of learning-sets.* Associative learning theory can go some way toward explaining learning-set performance in that it can supply some explanation of why the tendency to make errors declines with training. For instance, one of the

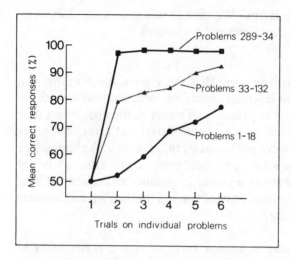

Fig. 7.15. *Performance of rhesus monkeys given 344 six-trial discrimination problems. On each problem the animal's performance begins at chance but the rate at which learning then occurs is more rapid for problems presented at the end of the series than for those presented earlier in the series (adapted from Harlow, 1949).*

factors that leads to inaccurate performance on a two-choice discrimination task is the tendency that many animals have to adopt position habits. If a monkey has a natural preference always to reach for the object on the left it will never score more than 50% correct over a series of trials given that the two objects are swapped at random from left to right between trials. The effect of a series of non-rewards for making the preferred response will be to weaken this response tendency and allow choices of the object on the right to appear. This response, too, will be rewarded on only 50% of occasions and the animal may revert to its original response for some time. The effect of such a pattern of reward and non-reward over a large number of trials will be to equalize the strength of the two response tendencies. In the absence of a position habit the animal will be much more likely to come up with the correct pattern of responding which requires it to choose a given object regardless of its position.

Although the elimination of *error factors* (such as position habits) un-doubtedly plays some part in learning-set formation, it cannot supply a complete explanation. It remains the case that a well-trained animal may be capable of solving a new discrimination problem after just a single trial and this finding has been taken to mean that the subject must have learned something positive about how to solve problems of this sort. In particular, it is said that the animals learn a *win–stay, lose–shift* strategy. To express this idea more fully: the animals seem to learn that, when faced with two objects in a discrimination task, they must choose one of them; if this choice is rewarded they should persist with it; if this choice is not rewarded they should then choose the other. The central feature of this interpretation is that the outcome of one trial (whether the animal receives a reward or not) can come to serve as a stimulus that controls responding on the next trial. Evidence to support it comes from the observation that increasing the interval between trials (and thus allowing the trace produced by one trial the chance to dissipate before the next trial occurs) produces a decline in the accuracy of performance in animals familiar with the learning-set procedure.

We have talked of the animals learning a "strategy" that guides their further learning. It is not clear, however, that the operation of this strategy, in itself, requires new mechanisms outside the scope of traditional, associative accounts of discrimination learning. That reward or non-reward can act as a stimulus requires no special assumptions; nor does the notion that these events can become associated with particular objects. The special features of the learning set is that these stimuli and associations can come to dominate the animal's behaviour to the exclusion of all others, to allow near-perfect performance on all trials (but the first) of a learning-set problem. The explanation must again be that animals can learn to attend to classes of cues that are accurate predictors of reward and learn to ignore classes of cues that are uncorrelated with reward. (Experimental evidence showing attentional learning of this sort has already been described in a different context; see Chapter 6, p. 196.) It is this aspect of learning-set formation that seems to require new mechanisms in addition to those involved in association formation and we must next consider this issue directly.

## Attentional Learning

We have so far considered rather complex experimental procedures in our search for mechanisms of non-associative learning. But attentional learning is perhaps demonstrated most clearly by considering a much simpler procedure —that of habituation, which consists of nothing more than the repeated presentation of a given stimulus. When a stimulus is presented in either of the basic conditioning procedures or in the complex learning procedures just discussed, it is presented along with some other event, such as a response or another stimulus. An interpretation in terms of association formation is thus usually possible and, in some cases, almost inevitable. With the habituation procedure, by contrast, there seems to be nothing available for the stimulus to become associated with. Nonetheless, something is learned.

The most obvious sign of learning is that the *orienting* response initially evoked by the stimulus becomes less and less likely to occur. Further, if the habituated stimulus is then used as the CS in a classical conditioning paradigm, learning will proceed only slowly. Figure 7.16 shows the results produced by two groups of rats given 10 sessions of training in each of which a 30-second light was presented 10 times preceding the delivery of food. Both groups developed the CR of approaching the cup to which food was delivered and pushing their noses into it; but subjects that had experienced 60 presentations of the light alone, prior to the start of conditioning, learned more slowly than control subjects for whom the light was novel at the start of conditioning.

One interpretation of these results holds that organisms are capable of learning to ignore an event that does not reliably signal consequences of

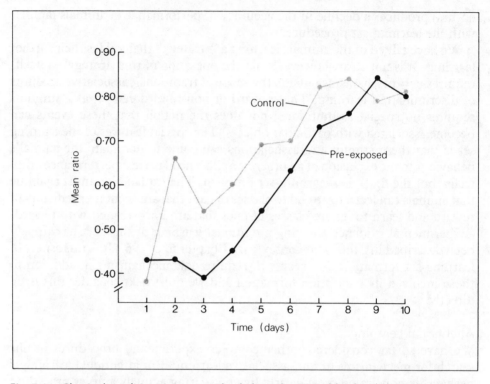

Fig. 7.16. *Classical conditioning in rats with a light as the CS and food as the US. The CR is the tendency to approach the site of food delivery when the light is turned on. Since the rats sometimes approach the food tray in the absence of the light, conditioning is assessed by means of a ratio score: approaches in the presence of the light/total approaches. Animals that have been pre-exposed to the light learn relatively slowly (after Channell and Hall, 1983).*

importance. They will stop orienting to such an event and, having learned to ignore it, they will take some time to start attending again when (as in the experiment outlined above) circumstances are changed, and it starts to signal an important consequence. This learning is unlikely to be associative in nature since it occurs precisely because the event in question is not correlated with others in the environment. Recent theories of classical conditioning (e.g. Mackintosh, 1975b; Pearce and Hall, 1980) have accordingly been extended to allow the existence of two types of learning. One, of course, is an associative process whereby CS and US become linked; the other is a non-associative process whereby the attention-getting power of the CS can be modified by experience.

It should be mentioned that some learning theorists (e.g. Wagner, 1976) have continued to seek an associative account for habituation and related phenomena. When habituation training is given, the stimulus is presented in a particular context, a special experimental room for the human subject, a

Skinner box for the rat. There is therefore a possibility that an association will be formed between the stimulus and the context in which it occurs. (In everyday language, the rat might be said to learn that loud tones tend to occur in the Skinner box.) In this way, habituation can be interpreted as being a special case of classical conditioning with the context being a CS that predicts the likely occurrence of loud tones (USs). According to this account, the only special feature of the habituation procedure is that conditioning is not measured in terms of the development of a CR but as the waning of the unconditioned response as the US becomes associated with the CS. Evidence for this view of habituation has been sought in studies of procedures that bring about *dishabituation*, the reinstatement of an habituated response. One of the most effective ways of achieving this is to introduce a novel and intense stimulus shortly before a test trial with the habituated stimulus. Since the organism has never before experienced the test stimulus in the novel context produced by the presentation of the dishabituator, there will be no association between it and this context. The response to the test stimulus should therefore reappear, and this is just what is observed.

In spite of its successes, even the most ardent supporter of the associative account of habituation would not claim it to be a complete account. The best procedure for promoting the formation of a context–stimulus association is one in which a fairly long interval is allowed between successive presentations of the stimulus. This procedure produces a long-lasting decline in the subject's responsiveness to the stimulus. But if quick results are wanted, rapid habituation can be produced by presenting a series of stimuli in very quick succession; the effect is not long-lasting (when tested the following day the subject will respond to the stimulus quite readily) but the short-term decline in responsiveness (during the course of the training session itself) will be very profound. This effect is not the result of association formation; rather, the presentation of a given stimulus has short-term consequences that reduce the effectiveness of the same stimulus when presented a second or so later. It is this feature of habituation more than any other that requires us to postulate the existence of some further, non-associative form of learning. It constitutes just one example of a more widespread phenomenon.

## Short-term Learning

Short-term learning is more familiar (and has been more extensively studied) in the context of human verbal learning. When a person hears or reads a short list of words he is usually able to repeat them accurately immediately afterwards. But, unless the list is repeated many times, no permanent impression is made. Having once heard the list of digits that constitute a new phone number, the information will persist long enough for us to dial the call but will probably be gone by the time we have finished our conversation. It seems that the mere presentation of a stimulus can produce a short-lived activation of some internal representation of that event. Why the activation so produced should be so short-lived has long been a matter for debate. One possibility is that the level of activation spontaneously decays with time; another is the occurrence of further events after the presentation of the target stimulus tends to interfere with the processes that maintain the state of activation. Given that any time interval during which decay might be occurring is also certain to contain some potentially interfering events, it is very difficult to decide between these two suggestions. But, whatever the mechanism, the evanescence of short-term memory is a fact of everyday experience.

Although short-term learning has been introduced here as a novel phenomenon, its existence was implied during much of our discussion of associative learning. We said of classical conditioning that an association would be formed between the central representations of the CS and US as a result of "pairings" in which presentation of the CS preceded that of the US. In order to explain this we suggested that the cerebral activity produced by the CS persisted until the US arrived. In other words, we assumed the existence of a form of non-associative learning in order to explain the association formation that underlies classical conditioning. Since classical conditioning is not effective when the gap between CS and US is too long, we are also required to assume that the central change produced by presentation of a stimulus is only short-term in its nature.

These varied findings have been drawn together in a theory of learning developed by Wagner (e.g. 1976) that may be summarized as follows. The mechanism involved in learning consists of a set of "centres", each sensitive to a given environmental event. Presentation of a stimulus produces activation of the appropriate centre (and if the stimulus is of the sort that we have been calling an unconditioned stimulus a response is also elicited). A centre that has just been activated has its sensitivity reduced for a short time and cannot easily be reactivated by another presentation of the stimulus—hence the short-term habituation effect. When two stimuli are presented together there will be concurrent activation of two centres, and if this occurs sufficiently often a link will be formed between the two. When the link is between a stimulus and the context in which the stimulus is presented the result will be the long-term habituation effect discussed above. When the link is between a US and a previously neutral stimulus, a classically conditioned response emerges. According to this view, short-term non-associative learning forms the basis for the development of long-lasting associations.

## Perceptual Learning

Although the details of Wagner's theory are still a matter for debate and investigation, the general principle that it embodies (with long-term learning being associative and short-term being the temporary activation of the centres between which associations are formed) provides a convenient and widely accepted framework for thinking about learning. It leads straight on to a further question, however, which may be crudely put as: how do the central representations of particular stimuli become established? It is not difficult to imagine that, simply as a result of the normal processes of developement, an animal might come to a conditioning experiment already equipped with centres that are activated by a tone or a buzzer or the presentation of electric shock. But the stimuli used in learning experiments are often more complex than these. Do we need to suppose, for instance, that all rats are automatically equipped with cerebral centres activated by the presentation of a black equilateral triangle on a white background? There has been a persistent suggestion (touched on, briefly, during our discussion of early experience in Chapter 4) that animals may actually learn to perceive such stimuli as a result of exposure to them. That simple exposure to complex events can bring about changes in behaviour was demonstrated in our discussion of song learning by birds (p. 113); and imprinting has often been regarded as a process which allows animals to learn the characteristics of the imprinting stimulus as a result of exposure to it.

Evidence in favour of this view comes from experiments like that reported by Gibson and Walk (1956) and discussed in Chapter 4. In this experiment, it may be recalled, rats were exposed in their home cages to geometrical figures (black triangles and circles) before being required to learn a discrimination between triangle and circle. Such exposure was found to facilitate the formation of the discrimination and it was suggested, in explanation, that it did so because it helped to establish the mechanisms whereby rats are able to perceive complex stimuli. A rat that has available a central representation of "black equilateral triangle" will be better able to form an association between this and food than will a rat who "sees" only "straight edge", "corner", "black area", and so on.

Perceptual learning of this sort may not be outside the scope of associative learning theory if the following argument is allowed. We know from studies of sensory preconditioning (p. 222) that organisms can form associations between paired neutral stimuli. Perhaps perceptual learning can be reduced to sensory preconditioning. When an animal is exposed to a complex object then it is necessarily exposed to concurrent presentations of the simpler constituents of the object. If these simpler elements activate central representations then associations should be formed between these representations; the perception of the event as a whole would thus be the product of associations established between its constituent elements. In the absence of any direct experimental evidence this account of perceptual learning must be regarded as nothing more than a tentative hypothesis and, for the time being it may be safe to allow that the learning produced by mere exposure to complex stimuli may be non-associative in nature.

## Conclusions

Our investigation of non-associative learning has not revealed the existence of new and subtle forms of learning. We have discovered that some cases of supposedly complex learning can be reduced to associative mechanisms. The best evidence for non-associative learning comes from rather simpler procedures that imply the existence of processes of attentional or perceptual learning, processes that are subservient to associative mechanisms. On reflection, this is perhaps not very surprising. We have viewed learning as the process whereby an organism can be influenced by its environment, becoming adapted to meet the environment's demands. A well-adapted organism would be one equipped with information about events of motivational significance (the events that we have been calling USs or reinforcers). It would know what behaviour yielded food (say) and what behaviour repelled predators. It would know how to find food and to avoid predators by using, as cues, environmental events that commonly go along with them. In short, the critical features of any animal's environment are to be found in the correlations that exist between various aspects of that environment, and between certain aspects and behaviour. The importance of associative learning mechanisms is no more than a reflection of the critical importance to the animal of correlations between events that occur in its environment.

## SOURCES AND FURTHER READING

A clear elementary introduction to the systematic analysis of the phenomena of learning is provided by Bolles (1979) in his book *Learning Theory*. Bolles deals with all the major theorists including Pavlov, but for a fuller account of his life and work the biography by Gray (1979) entitled simply *Pavlov*. For a readily accessible account of the views of Skinner see his *Science and Human Behavior* (1953) which contains not only an outline of the principles of operant conditioning but a (controversial) attempt to apply them to human affairs more generally. A comprehensive account of experimental work on associative learning is to be found in Mackintosh's (1974) *The Psychology of Animal Learning*; a more selective survey in *Animal Learning* by Bitterman *et al.* (1979); and for a thoughtful analysis of the theoretical interpretations of associative learning see Dickinson's (1980) *Contempory Animal Learning Theory*. This book is quite advanced but it repays effort. "Constraints on learning" are covered by Bolles (1979) and in the book by Bitterman *et al.* Non-associative learning is nowhere covered very well but there are many textbooks available that try to integrate the study of associative learning in animals with other aspects of learning: see, for example *Animal Learning and Conditioning* by Davey (1981), or *The Psychology of Learning* by Borger and Seaborne (1982).

# 8   Animal Behaviour and Human Psychology

## INTRODUCTION

The conclusions reached in the preceding chapters have been based on empirical work done with subjects drawn from a wide range of species. For the most part the subjects have been vertebrates but for any given experiment the creature under study is just as likely to be a pigeon, a rat, or a dog, as a human being. In choosing a particular experiment for discussion I have been guided by the desire to supply the clearest possible example of the phenomenon being considered, one that is free from the doubts raised by confounding or uncontrolled factors. For the most part I have disregarded the species of the animal being investigated.

In the introduction to Chapter 1 we briefly discussed a justification for this approach, drawing a distinction between "general" psychology and a psychology devoted specifically to human affairs. Having reviewed the first sort of psychology in the intervening chapters we are now in a position to consider the implications of the distinction in more detail. In particular we want to ask whether the general principles that have emerged during our survey are truly relevant to the behaviour of man. For all psychologists, no matter how "general" their interests, are likely to have a special interest in the behaviour of the species to which they themselves belong, and they would be disappointed, to say the least, if the general principles they discovered from the study of other species turned out not to apply to their own. Now, of course, it has often been suggested that the human species possesses a number of unique features that make its psychology distinctively different from that of other animals. Indeed, there are many who hold this truth to be so self-evident that they are unwilling even to argue the case for it. But the possibility exists that this view is no more than a reflection of our self-centredness as a species: would not every other animal, dog, or cat, or laboratory rat, perhaps regard its own species as being special and not as others are? If we are to reach a conclusion on this issue it will not be by asking unanswerable questions of this sort. We must, however, be willing to argue the case for or against the view we hold, with due regard for the relevant empirical evidence.

In this chapter we shall proceed as follows. First we shall try (what may be impossible) to look at our own species as an outsider might, in an attempt to decide what its important unique features are. We shall then consider each of these features to see if any of them allows man to transcend the basic behavioural principles that have been outlined in previous chapters of this book. Before doing this we need first to clarify what is meant by the assertion that the human species is unique.

## HUMAN UNIQUENESS

Every animal species is unique in some way; if it were not there would be no grounds for distinguishing it as a separate species distinct from its close relatives. Any given individual is defined as belonging to a particular species in terms of its reproductive capabilities (members of the same species can interbreed and produce fertile offspring) but along with these goes a range of structural and functional peculiarities. Now, many of the special features that various species possess are unimportant from the point of view of those seeking general laws. Every species of bird, or fish, or mammal has its own characteristic pattern of mating (this is one of the things that keeps species distinct—see Chapter 2) but these differences do not hinder the geneticist in his attempt to establish general principles underlying patterns of inheritance. These laws of inheritance apply as much to man as to non-human animals.

It may be hoped that something analogous is true for the study of behaviour. We must accept that every species has its own characteristic patterns of behaviour and is thus, in one sense, unique. In the preceding chapters, however, we have tried to discern general principles underlying these patterns—laws of behaviour, perhaps equivalent to their generality to the laws of inheritance developed by geneticists. The implication is that the individual patterns of behaviour that go to define each species as unique are, in principle, explicable in terms of these general laws. (See Chapter 7, pp. 242–250, for a discussion of this issue with respect to the generality of the laws of learning.)

To suggest that man is psychologically unique is to question the adequacy of the general laws in his case. When we talk of our species as being unique we do not usually mean just that it can do certain things that other species cannot. That much is accepted by everyone. Rather we are suggesting that man's behaviour shows features that are not to be explained in terms of the supposed general laws of behaviour. This suggestion can take a number of forms. Its most extreme version accepts that there are general principles that govern the behaviour of non-human animals but asserts that man possesses unique features that enable him to transcend these laws altogether. A weaker version accepts that the general principles that apply to other animals also apply to man but argues that these deal only with trivial aspects of his behaviour and do not explain those features that are of real importance. In either case the important implication is that new principles are required if psychology is to accommodate properly the behaviour shown by the human species.

What then are the unique features of human behaviour that prompt this view? In order to achieve an appropriate perspective that will allow us to provide some answers to this question it will be worth making the effort of trying to stand back in order to view our own species as an outsider might.

## The Outsider's View

As Chapter 1 showed, only since *The Origin of Species* has the fact that man is an animal been properly appreciated; but even after more than 100 years of Darwinism, most of us only half believe it. No such doubts would trouble the mind of some biologist from another planet visiting the Earth and looking for the first time at this new species. What sort of questions would such an outsider ask about our species and what special features would he (or she or it) notice?

First he might want to count them. If he could manage this he would find that there are some 3500 million: a figure that is neither specially high or low when compared with the numbers of other species. (It is difficult to give exact numbers, but some insect species are much more numerous, and we know of several species of vertebrates that are in danger of extinction with total populations numbered only in tens or hundreds.) He would then investigate their distribution and habitat. He would find their distribution to be very patchy, some land areas having a dense population (Java has about 450 people per km$^2$) others having practically none (e.g. Tibet has only about 1 person per km$^2$). The population would be found to be concentrated on low-lying land in temperate regions, especially in river valleys and sea shores. Most of the planet's surface has not been exploited by this species, especially the 70% that is covered with water.

He would want next to examine the structure of individual members of the population and would perhaps note first of all that man is rather a large animal, his body size being well above that of the average Earth species. He would note that the body plan shows bilateral symmetry and a good deal of specialization with different parts subserving different functions. He might also categorize man as a *polytypic* species, although it is difficult to be sure that the difference between various types (or "races"), so important to some of us, would be particularly striking to an outsider. He would also want to ask questions about the physiology of the species. He would note that it subsists by consuming both plants and other animals and oxidizing their tissues; that it reproduces sexually producing haploid gametes that must fuse to form a zygote in order to survive; that it enters into social relationships that are varied and long-lasting and are not solely concerned with the reproductive cycle.

Finally he would want to establish the relationship between man and the other animal species. If his classification system came out anything like ours, he would place man along with the apes and monkeys in a group of mammals that still possess what may be taken to be the primitive or basic mammalian form (in contrast to the special adaptations shown by bats, and whales, and so on). We call this order of mammals the Primates, although there is no reason to suppose that an outsider would want to endow it with primacy. Nor is it clear that an outsider would want to assign *Homo sapiens* to a special sub-group (Hominidae) distinct from that encompassing the great apes, as human taxonomists do. Recent biochemical studies of the chromosomes of man and chimpanzee reveal a high degree of genetic relatedness and if this is used as the criterion (rather than amount of body hair, say) it would be necessary to classify these two species much more closely together.

## Man as a Primate

Leaving this last point aside, Fig. 8.1 gives a simplified version of the classification scheme usually applied by (human) taxonomists to the primates. Concentrating just on the primates found in the Old World (it is almost certain that *Homo* first emerged in Africa, and emigrated to the Americas relatively recently) we see that the major division is between apes and monkeys, and that

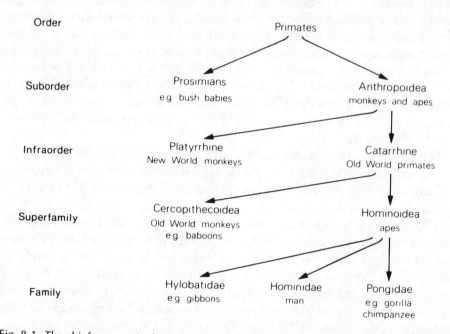

Fig. 8.1. *The chief taxonomic divisions used for primates. This scheme is much simplified; for instance, the various subdivisions of the New World monkeys have been omitted entirely.*

man is assigned to one of the three main families of the apes. His closest relatives are thought to be found among the Pongids and so, to find out what man's unique features are, we need to compare him with the chimpanzee and the gorilla.

Looking first again at numbers and distribution, we now see that man is a very numerous species as a primate and is found over a much wider geographical range, gorillas and chimpanzees being confined to the forest and forest edge in central and eastern Africa. Structurally man shows two striking sets of differences from the other hominoids: first, his body is largely hairless and liberally covered with sweat glands; second, man walks on his hind legs and has a grasping hand equipped with a powerful thumb. *Homo* shows a fair degree of sexual dimorphism (the male is bigger than the female; the female has pronounced breasts not seen in other primates) but this is perhaps no more marked than that shown by the gorilla where the male is much bigger than the female and has somewhat bigger canine teeth. There is no doubt, however, that *Homo* possesses a much larger brain than do the other primates: the human brain weighs, on average, about 1500 g; that of the chimpanzee about 500 g. Figure 8.2 plots brain weight against body weight for a variety of species of monkeys and apes. It is apparent that the human brain is much the biggest; but, as we have already discussed in some detail in Chapter 5 (pp. 158–160), it is difficult to know just what to make of this fact in the absence of an accepted scheme for relating brain size to body size, or for relating behavioural capacities to brain size.

Turning now to physiology and behaviour; it used to be thought that man was unique among the hominoids in that his diet was not wholly vegetarian. Some human groups have domesticated plants and animals, others simply

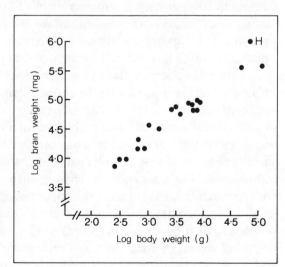

Fig. 8.2. *Brain and body weight for a range of species of monkeys and apes. H represents Homo (after Passingham and Ettlinger, 1974).*

gather wild plant food and hunt game, but all eat both plants and other animals. Most other apes are largely vegetarian but it has become apparent in recent years that many will eat meat when they can get it. Chimpanzees in particular have been observed to form into bands for the cooperative hunting of small game. They even show food-sharing to a limited degree (females and young animals will beg meat from a successful hunting male). Man's reproductive pattern does, however, seem to be something rather special among the great apes. Chimpanzees are promiscuous, with mating being a free for all among members of the troop. Gorillas are polygynous with one senior male controlling a harem of several females. Man is, on the whole, monogamous (the qualification being made necessary because of the wide variation in mating practices seen among different human groups). The human female is sexually receptive at all times (or at least there is no fixed breeding season) and, so it has been suggested, this may be an important factor in maintaining the male – female bond. These sexual arrangements are reflected in the social groupings that the various species adopt. Gorillas live as a group of about a dozen or so, consisting usually of one dominant male, his females and their young, plus a few younger males. The chimpanzee troop, by contrast, consists of about 50 individuals, the only consistent sub-units of the troop being those formed by females and their young; otherwise there is a constant shifting of relationships within the troop with small groups of animals coming together for a particular reason (such as a band of males for hunting) and then breaking up again. Human groupings may be seen as a variant of the chimpanzee system with the addition (in Western society) of an important sub-group consisting of a male, a female, and their young.

The existence of social groups implies the existence of some means of communication among group members. This is particularly well developed among chimpanzees who communicate by pulling faces, by gesturing (the open-handed begging gesture is recognizable to any human), and by making noises. Although it is difficult for anyone other than a chimpanzee to assess the flexibility and variety of their language, it seems apparent that it is extremely impoverished compared with the spoken language used by man. It cannot be doubted, however, that in his use of writing man possesses a quite novel means of communication. Until relatively recently (with the advent of the telephone and of radio and television) this was the sole means by which special-purpose social groups could be established and maintained among widely separated individuals. The existence of writing also constitutes an example of the widespread human use of tools. Chimpanzees show some tool-use (they prepare small sticks for extracting termites from holes and crevices, and large sticks for defence against potential predators) but its extent is negligible in comparison with that shown by man. Man not only possesses hammers and screwdrivers and so on but uses them to create further "tools": "tools" for sitting on, for writing at, "tools" for living in, and so on. With them man is able to create his own environment.

Conclusions

A general view of the human species reveals nothing special, but the comparison of man with other closely related primates allows certain interesting features to emerge. In spite of the fact that he is, at least on a gross level, not too dissimilar structurally from them, he is strikingly more numerous and widespread than they are. This difference rests in part upon structural adaptations. Man has been able to spread from the African homeland that he used to share with the apes and to occupy new territories (that seem quite inappropriate for an ape bred in the tropics) because of changes in his body size and shape, his skin colour, amount of superficial fat, and so on. But surely more important are the behavioural capacities that have allowed our species to shape these new environments to suit itself. This has been achieved in part because of behavioural capacities that are found in each individual—each of us can manipulate tools of various sorts in order to establish and maintain our own environmental niches. Just as important seems to be the social behaviour of the species. Our possession of a rich language allows each individual to enter into a wide range of complex social relationships. At least some of these are cooperative and mutually beneficial. Not only can a group of men working together catch a game animal (or build a house, or play a string quartet for that matter) in a way that would be outside the capacities of one man working alone, but social interaction allows also for the beneficial consequences that can follow from division of labour. If particularly skilled individuals are allowed to specialize in hunting, or tilling the land, or inventing some new tool and the outcome of their efforts is then shared among the social group, progress can be made that would not be possible if each individual had to devote all its time to feeding and clothing itself.

The social behaviour of the species may also have implications for the capacities of individual members. It has often been suggested that language serves not only to allow communication with others but also functions as a "tool of thought": that by talking to himself man is able to solve problems that would otherwise be beyond him. It is certainly the case that the communication system provided by human language allows each individual to learn new skills and acquire new information without having to go through the laborious process of learning them or acquiring it for himself. He has only to listen and he can benefit from the accumulated wisdom of the older generation, and if he can read he can benefit from the knowledge acquired by individuals he could never meet. Our ability to use artifacts to shape the environment to suit ourselves is probably secondary to these other skills. It took a rare talent to invent the first hand-axe, say, but given the instructions we could all of us now learn to make and use one; or if not we could use our communicative skills to persuade someone else to do it for us.

*Two questions.* It follows that our major concern in this chapter must be human language and its consequences. It will be useful to distinguish two separate issues. First: does human language allow the individual to interact with his environment according to principles quite different from those described earlier in this book (particularly in Chapters 6 and 7)? Second: does the communicative function of language allow man to establish social relationships that transcend the principles discussed earlier (especially in Chapter 2)? An affirmative answer to either of these questions might mean that we would have to set about constructing a distinctly human psychology importantly different from that applicable to the behaviour of most other species.

It is worth making one further point before starting our discussion of these two questions. The features of man's behaviour that I have picked out as distinguishing him from all other primates are not in fact totally unique in the animal world. If we consider the social insects we can find examples of highly developed languages (the best known case being the "dance-language" of the honey bee) and of creatures that work on their environment transforming it to meet their needs (the building work of the termites is the best example here). Since our central interest in this chapter is the human species we have no need to consider the social insects directly. But it may be a useful check on any incipient feeling of self-importance to know that our species is unlikely to be the only one for which a claim for exemption from the principles of general psychology might be justified.

## LANGUAGE AND THOUGHT

### Language and Problem Solving

Consider a rhesus monkey faced with the following task. The animal is shown a piece of food being placed under one of two identical cups. A screen is interposed between the animal and the cups so that only after a delay (i.e. when the screen is removed) can the animal reach for the cup covering the food. With a very brief delay performance is perfect, but it falls off rapidly as the delay is increased; after a delay of about 5 seconds the monkey is capable of choosing the correct cup on only 70% of occasions (Fig. 8.3). It is possible to carry out an exactly similar experiment with human subjects. The outcome of such a study will surprise no one—the human subject performs almost as accurately after delays of 5, 10, or even 20 seconds as he does when there is no delay.

The reason for our excellent performance on this task is not hard to find. Ask any human subject how he does it and he will explain that he simply memorizes the verbal label for the baited cup (perhaps repeating "left" to himself

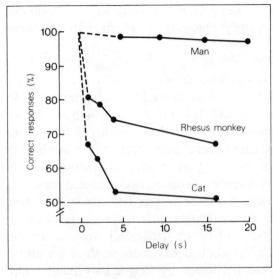

Fig. 8.3. *Per cent correct responses as a function of delay in a delayed response task for three mammalian species tested under approximately equivalent conditions (after Miles, 1971).*

throughout the delay period) and then uses this to guide his choice when the delay is over. This is a trivial example but it helps to make clear how our ability to manipulate symbols can help us to solve problems beyond the capacities of other animals. It would be possible to extend the list of such examples practically indefinitely and fortunately it would be pointless to do so; it is beyond doubt that the influence of human language is so all-pervasive that it is difficult to imagine any problem that an adult human might be set in which language would not make a contribution toward its solution.

What is less clear, however, is that in using language to solve problems, man is using a mechanism that is qualitatively different from those used by other animals. The view that he is has been most clearly expressed by those psychologists and linguists who have argued that, although he may share many mental mechanisms with other animals, man is alone in possessing a unique *language acquisition device*. Only our species has the special cerebral structures that constitute this device, the existence of which, it is argued, is most clearly demonstrated by the way in which a human infant is able to acquire an understanding of the rules that underlie language from exposure to a very limited sample of its native language. Accordingly, it is concluded, only our species can develop "true" language and the thought processes that this implies or allows.

One reason for uncertainty about the validity of this view is found in the well-publicized and partially successful attempts that have recently been made to teach a version of human language to non-human animals. If an ape can be taught such a language, then, it has been argued, the necessary mental mechanisms must be present. It has to be allowed that these mechanisms must be fairly primitive (chimpanzees do not spontaneously hold protracted conversations with their human keepers or even with each other) but it remains possible that they play some part in the problem-solving behaviour that these animals do show.

## Problems in Teaching a Spoken Language to Apes

Two attempts were made some 40 or so years ago to teach young chimpanzees to talk by bringing them up in human households and treating them essentially like human infants. The results were unimpressive: the more successful of them produced an animal that could articulate no more than three or four words, and indistinctly at that. The problem lies, in part, with the anatomy of the chimpanzee's vocal tract. Figure 8.4 shows a comparison between man and chimpanzee. In man, sounds produced by the larynx (the voice box) pass through the pharynx and the buccal cavity. Movements of the tongue can alter the shape of either of these cavities and hence the sound emitted. In the chimpanzee the larynx lies much higher in the vocal tract and there is thus no equivalent pharyngeal cavity that can be shaped by tongue movements. The range of sounds (particularly vowel sounds) that can be produced is thus rather restricted.

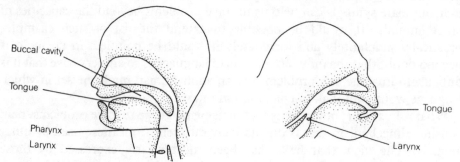

Fig. 8.4. *Sections through head and neck of man and chimpanzee to show the differing vocal tracts (simplified, after Lieberman, 1975).*

These failures constituted the only attempts to teach language to an ape for a surprisingly long time. After all, if we found that a human infant was unable to talk for some reason we would still want to teach him a language of some sort— we would teach him a sign language or we would teach him to read or write. Human language does not have to be vocal. Nor does that of the chimpanzee, and once this was realized a flood of new experimental studies was released. The best-known of these (and the first to be started) are the studies by Gardner and Gardner (e.g. 1969, 1975), and by Premack (1976). In the first of these a young female chimpanzee (Washoe) was, as in the earlier studies, brought up more or less in the family of her human keepers who took care to communicate with each other and with Washoe only American Sign Language, the language used as a

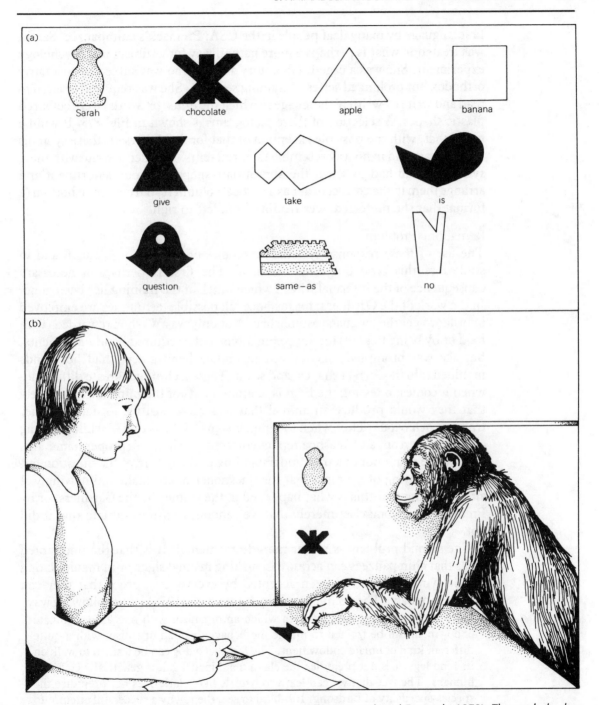

Fig. 8.5. *Some of the plastic symbols used by Premack (after Premack and Premack, 1972). The symbols also differed in colour.*

first language by many deaf people in the USA. Premack's chimpanzee, Sarah, was treated in what is perhaps a more natural way for a subject in a psychology experiment. She was a caged, laboratory animal who was subjected to a fairly orthodox but prolonged series of training sessions. She was required to learn to read and write a "written" language in which the units (or words) were coloured plastic shapes. A selection of these pictograms is shown in Fig. 8.5. It will be noted that, with the possible exception of that for Sarah herself, these symbols are arbitrary and in no way resemble their referents. In order to write with these symbols Sarah had to select the appropriate shapes from an assortment and arrange them in the correct order as a vertical column read from top to bottom (a format that she preferred over reading from left to right).

## Remaining Problems

The use of these response-systems overcomes one of the problems found in studies of this type but others remain. The first is perhaps a necessary consequence of the informal way in which much of the training has been done. In the work of the Gardners, for instance, all possible techniques are employed in order to get the language established. Not only was Washoe rewarded (with food or by being tickled) for approximations to the required hand movements, but she was prompted, encouraged to imitate her trainers, had her hands moulded into the correct shapes, and so on. These techniques create difficulties when it comes to testing the linguistic attainments of the pupil. It seem likely that they would produce an animal that was very sensitive to details of her trainers' behaviour. Thus when the trainer signs "Who is that?" while pointing at another person, and Washoe replies correctly by signing a proper name, this may be the result not of a true understanding of the nature of the question but simply a copying of prompts that the questioner might make unknowingly. I am not saying that this is what happened in the studies by the Gardners, or by Premack or anyone else; merely that we cannot be entirely certain that it did not.

The second problem is rather more fundamental. It is that the undoubted skills that chimpanzees can acquire in making manual signs or in manipulating plastic symbols have not been accepted by everyone as proof that they can acquire language. The point is made by Fodor *et al.* (1974) in the following way:

> there are very many clear cases in which an organism with one kind of innate endowment can be trained to mimic the behaviour of an organism with a quite different kind of innate endowment. The fact that a dog can be trained to walk on its hind legs does not prejudice the claim that bipedal gait is genetically coded in humans. The fact that we can learn to whistle like a lark does not prejudice the species-specificity of birdsong. It is hard to see, then, why a successful attempt to teach a chimpanzee to talk should have any bearing on the innateness of language in people

(p. 451)

Given this sort of scepticism, it is hard to see just what a chimpanzee would need to be able to do before everyone would admit that it had learned language. The difficulty is that we have no generally accepted abstract definition of what it would be to have a language. It is to this issue that we must next turn our attention.

Acquiring a Vocabulary

In order to teach Sarah the word for apple in her new language, the following technique was adopted. The appropriate plastic symbol was presented repeatedly along with a piece of apple and the animal was encouraged to pick up the symbol and to "write" the word by fixing the symbol to a specially prepared writing surface. Reward was then given, often a small piece of food. The system used with Washoe was similar in principle. When being offered a cup, for instance, the trainer would make the sign for "drink", encourage the chimpanzee to imitate, and reward good performance (often by "social reinforcement"—tickling—in this case). Given patience (on the part of the chimpanzee as well as the trainer) an animal can acquire quite a large vocabulary in this way: the Gardners report that Washoe had available more than 100 different words at the time when they stopped training her.

The sceptic might object at this point to our saying that the chimpanzee has acquired a vocabulary of various words. Why not simply say that the animal has been rewarded for making certain arbitrary responses in the presence of certain well-defined stimuli? Why not describe the results not in the terminology of language acquisition but in that of associative learning? After all, the performance shown by these chimpanzees does not seem to differ much from that shown by a pigeon that has learned to peck one response key rather than another in order to receive access to food. One possible reaction to this objection is to accept that associative learning plays an important part in the acquisition of a vocabulary and that the two seemingly different descriptions of the empirical findings are not, in fact, incompatible. However reasonable this reaction, most of us would nonetheless want to see something rather more sophisticated from the chimpanzees before we allowed the claim that they had acquired a language. In particular, we would want to see them use the words they have learned in grammatical sentences, that is, in combinations with the words appearing in the appropriate order.

Sentences

Washoe has, indeed, been observed to emit a large number of compound (usually two-word) utterances, as has Nim, another chimpanzee trained in sign language by Terrace and his collaborators (1979). Terrace has analysed these utterances in detail and has found them to be largely grammatical in the sense that the animal tends to adopt the word-ordering preferred by its trainers. Thus an animal wanting to be tickled would correctly sign "more" and then "tickle". But if it used the same word "tickle" in a sentence involving a pronoun, then "tickle" would move to the first position in the sentence, as in "tickle me". In Premack's study care was taken to inculcate the importance of word-order right from the start. For instance, Sarah was required to arrange the symbols for "Mary" (one of the trainers), "give", and "apple" in that order if she was to receive a piece of apple, and she was quite capable of learning that the sequence "apple give" had quite other implications.

Behaviour of this sort has been taken as evidence for the chimpanzees having a rudimentary understanding of syntax. But the sceptic may still be un-convinced. He might object that when they produce ordered strings of words the animals are doing nothing that they have not been explicitly trained to do. Rather than saying that Sarah understands the semantic difference between "give apple" and "apple give" all we need note is that she has been rewarded for emitting one sequence of responses and not for the other. Something similar is true of the signing chimpanzees. These animals have frequently been rewarded for aping their trainers and it would be surprising, therefore, if they did not sometimes put two signs together just as they have frequently seen their trainers do. In fact Terrace's analysis of video-tapes of the performance of his subject Nim reveals that many of the animal's signings were best interpreted as direct imitations of the movements just made or currently being made by the trainer.

What is clearly needed, if this objection is to be overcome, is for the chimpanzee spontaneously to produce some new, grammatical, multi-word sentence. (A feature of human children is that, after a couple of years of training, they start to show creativity, using words in new but grammatical combinations.) We would be more impressed if Premack's Sarah, having been trained to ask for apple, proved capable of writing "John give orange" when the appropriate circumstances arose.

Even then some would not be convinced. The sceptic could appeal to the fact that chimpanzees are capable of learning rules about how to behave in order to receive reward (see Chapter 7). In this case he could say that the animal had learned that when a symbol previously associated with some desired object is put in place after two other symbols (one of these being the symbol associated with the person who happens to be present) then the reward is provided. This may seem a complex thing to learn but it is, perhaps, rather simpler than what we usually suppose to be involved in learning a language.

Is there *any* behaviour that a chimpanzee could show that would convince a sceptic that that the animal had command of a language in the human sense of the term? This is, of course, the central problem that makes it difficult for us to interpret these studies. We have no generally accepted set of criteria by which we may decide whether or not we have succeeded in teaching language to a chimpanzee. We can all accept that the acquisition of a vocabulary is likely to depend upon associative learning mechanisms and also that the capacity to acquire a vocabulary is not, in itself, enough to justify the claim that the individual in question has acquired language. What is also needed is evidence that the pupil has knowledge of a set of rules that determine how the elements of the vocabulary may be used: what order they should occur in and (when appropriate) with what inflections. These rules constitute the *grammar* of the language. Linguists and psycholinguists have argued that such rules are in some way "built into" the structure of the human organism and are not to be acquired by way of associative learning. Thus, when it is demonstrated that the communicative skills possessed by a chimpanzee, which superficially appear to be linguistic in nature, are perhaps explicable by orthodox learning theory, the psycholinguist is constrained to deny that the animal has really learned a language. If we adopt this view we come perilously close to prejudging the whole issue; to accepting a definition of linguistic behaviour as being behaviour that cannot be produced by the mental mechanisms that non-human animals possess. The issue will only be resolved when linguists supply us with a specification of the rules of the "universal grammar" said to underlie all examples of human language. Only when this is done will we be able to judge whether or not these rules lie outside the scope of the rule-learning capacities that have been demonstrated in non-human animals.

## Reasoning

We began this section of the chapter by asking whether man had available to him, underlying his language or in the language itself, a set of mental mechanisms that other animals lack. We have so far reached no conclusion but this may be because we have so far discussed only the less important of the consequences that follow from possessing a language. Although it is true that both the human child and the chimpanzee can be trained to use symbols in order to obtain a drink or a piece of apple, the two species seem to differ in that the child grows up into an individual who is able to use language in his thinking. He is thus able to solve problems that would otherwise be impossible.

*Deduction.* A human being, asked whether Aristotle was mortal, would be able to answer correctly if he was also given the information that Aristotle was a man and that all men are mortal. The use of symbols in solving such problems is clearly demonstrated by those who resort to pencil and paper and to drawing diagrams in order to reach an answer. There have been no observations of chimpanzees manipulating plastic shapes or whatever in order to solve otherwise insoluble problems, but we may still look for other signs of the ability to reason in non-human animals.

Although he has not gone so far as to ask a chimpanzee to solve a syllogism,

Premack has made some progress in this direction by attempting to train Sarah to use appropriately a plastic symbol for the logical operator *if-then*. Sarah's favourite food was chocolate. Accordingly, she was trained with sentences of the following sort: "Sarah take apple if-then Mary give Sarah chocolate", and "Sarah take banana if-then Mary give Sarah chocolate". Sarah learned to take the appropriate fruit in order to get the chocolate. She was then tested with new sentences such as "Sarah eat apple if-then Mary give candy Sarah", and she made no errors in five such tests. It may appear that the rudiments of an ability for logical thought are present in this animal but an alternative account for this behaviour should be mentioned. In these tests Sarah was able to obtain the chocolate without paying attention to the second part of the sentence. All she needed to do was to obey the instruction contained in the first part ("Sarah take apple") and the reward was given. Premack acknowledges this difficulty of interpretation and has carried out further experiments that try to deal with it. The results have been inconclusive, and rather than describing them we may turn to a much simpler sort of study for direct evidence of a process akin to deductive reasoning in non-human animals.

*Deduction in conditioning.* Consider the following experiment reported by Holland and Straub (1979). The subjects were rats, trained initially in a procedure in which the presentation of a noise was followed by the delivery of food pellets. The animals learned something as a result of these noise-food pairings since they developed a tendency to approach the site of food delivery when the noise was turned on. In a second stage of training the rats were given free access to food pellets and were then injected with lithium chloride and thus made ill (see Chapter 7). This too produced learning in that the rats became unwilling to eat the food pellets. In a final test stage the animals again received presentations of the noise and it was found that this stimulus was no longer

Fig. 8.6. *Both groups of rats learn to approach the food tray in the presence of the stimulus (Stage 1). Pairings of food and illness for the experimental subjects (E) reduces the frequency of this behaviour in the test phase (after Dickinson, 1980; data from Holland and Straub, 1979). P: pretest.*

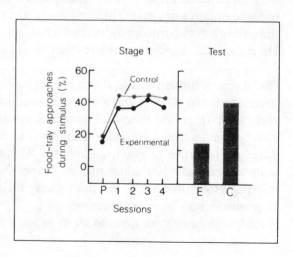

effective in eliciting the response of approaching the food tray (Fig. 8.6).

At first sight this experimental procedure must seem remote for others employed to study reasoning, but its relevance should become clear when we consider what must be going on for the rats to show the behaviour they do. Let us assume that, in the first stage of training, the rats learned something equivalent to, in human language, "the noise leads to food". In the second stage they are taught: "food causes illness". They are therefore equipped with two separate items of information. What the test phase shows is that they are capable of putting the two facts together: they behave as if they had worked out a relationship between the noise and feeling ill. That is, the rats have carried out what, surely, is an important part of any task requiring deductive reasoning — they have taken two separate facts and integrated them in order to derive a third. Holland and Straub's experiment is not the only example of this phenomenon to be found in studies of simple conditioning. We have already discussed (in Chapter 7) the procedures known as sensory preconditioning and second-order conditioning (see Fig. 7.4). These procedures are effective with a wide range of species (e.g. dogs, cats, rats, rabbits, pigeons). In both of them the subject learns initially the relationship between A and B; it is then taught a relationship between B and C; finally it is tested with A. The behaviour that the animals show to A suggests that they are in some way capable of working out the relationship between A and C.

It is difficult to interpret these findings with any confidence. Admittedly they derive from the simplest of conditioning procedures but perhaps they should be taken as showing that "simple" conditioning can be far more sophisticated than popular prejudice allows; that the basic mechanisms underlying reasoning are as widespread as those of classical conditioning and are thus to be found even in animals that do not possess (human) language. Alternatively we might want to say merely that some cases of classical conditioning can mimic some of the features of true deductive reasoning but that true reasoning involves mechanisms more sophisticated than those engaged by conditioning procedures. This second interpretation requires us to specify the nature of these "more sophisticated" mechanisms. This is not easy but they are perhaps exemplified by the ability of the human logician to use the word "some". To the logician "some" means not none (at least one, perhaps all). Given the information that some As are Bs and that some Bs are Cs, the logician knows that he can reach no conclusion about the relation between A and C. What we know of non-human animals is that they can behave appropriately when they have been taught the equivalent of: all As are Bs, all Bs are Cs. We do not yet know how they would behave if trained with other quantifiers.

*Reasoning by analogy.* Better evidence for a reasoning process that may not be reducible to more basic learning mechanisms comes from a study of Gillan *et al.*

(1981). They investigated not deductive but a form of inductive reasoning that they refer to an *analogical* reasoning. A human subject may be said to reason analogically if he replies "kitten" when asked: dog is to puppy as cat is to what? Such problems are widely used in tests designed to assess human intelligence. Gillan *et al.* asked the chimpanzee Sarah to solve equivalent problems. Figure 8.7a depicts one way in which this was done. Sarah was presented with three objects with which she was familiar. One pair, arranged horizontally in the figure, bore a particular relationship to one another (a closed lock and a key in problem I; a marked sheet of paper and a pencil in problem II). Sarah's task was to choose one of another pair of objects to make a fourth along with the closed, painted can shown in the figure. Thus, for problem I she was required to choose the can opener, and for problem II, the paint brush. Sarah did remarkably well on these and similar problems, choosing the object that correctly completed the analogy on 15 out of 18 different tests. Gillan *et al.* discuss several possible associative accounts of their results but none of these can be readily applied to a slightly different form of reasoning test that they used, and that is shown in Fig. 8.7b. Here Sarah was presented with unfamiliar objects: cardboard cutouts that could differ along a number of dimensions such as size, shape, colour, and so on. Her task was the same; that of choosing a fourth object from a pair of

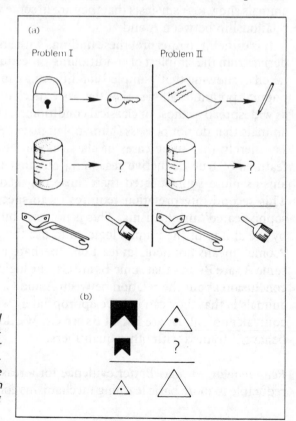

Fig. 8.7. *Examples of problems used to test for analogical reasoning in a chimpanzee (after Gillan et al., 1981). (a) represents two examples of the tests using real objects; (b) an example of a test using geometrical shapes.*

alternatives so as to complete the analogy. Thus, to solve the particular problem shown in the figure she was required to choose the small triangle bearing the spot. Given 60 of these problems, she chose correctly on 45, performance well above chance level. Gillan *et al*. conclude that Sarah is capable of reasoning by analogy.

## Conclusions

After reviewing this fascinating experimental work, it is disappointing to have to admit that we are in no position to reach any firm conclusions on the major questions of interest to us.

We have said that many psychologists are firmly of the opinion that man possesses a unique *language acquisition device* that makes him mentally, qualitatively different from non-human animals. To test this proposition by trying to teach a human language to a chimpanzee seems, at first sight, eminently reasonable. Unfortunately, the partial success shown by the subjects of such training programmes, makes the results difficult to interpret. Certainly much of what they do can be accounted for in terms of known associative learning processes. Does this mean that they have not acquired true language; or does it mean that language in general might be explicable in terms of these processes?

The picture is no clearer when we consider the ability of animals to solve problems that, it might reasonably be supposed, depend upon their having some form of language. Here we find that at least one of the important aspects of deductive reasoning can be discerned in the classical conditioning paradigm and thus in all creatures capable of associative learning. The ability to reason by analogy is difficult to explain in associative terms but this ability is clearly not unique to man having been demonstrated in the chimpanzee.

Perhaps the only safe conclusion to reach on the evidence available to us is that we cannot yet say whether or not man's language indicates or confers on him special mental mechanisms that other species lack. This is not to say that the system of symbolic representation used by man does not give him an advantage in some circumstances. To return to the example with which we began this section of the chapter; when a rhesus monkey picks the correct cup after a delay of a few seconds its does so because it has formed and retained some representation equivalent to our "food is on the left". The monkey's failure to choose the correct cup after a delay of a minute shows that its version of this statement is less effective than ours in allowing good performance on this task. What it does not prove, however, is that man's linguistic abilities allow him to solve the problem by some mechanism that is different from that used by the monkey.

## SOCIAL BEHAVIOUR AND CULTURE

We have been concerned so far with the impact of language on the thought processes of the individual. But the major importance of human language is usually supposed to lie in the fact that it allows efficient communication between individuals. From such communication spring the complex societies that are a feature of our species. In the previous section of this chapter we considered the suggestion that man's language led to an important intellectual difference between him and other species. What we must now consider is the suggestion that man's social interactions work according to principles that are quite unimaginable in other creatures.

## Ethics and Evolution

The problem posed by human society is not one for that branch of psychology concerned with the immediate causation of behaviour. We can accept that the individual perceives his fellows, learns from them, remembers what they do, and so on, by way of the mechanisms we have discussed in previous chapters. Rather, it seems to present a problem for our account of the origins of behaviour. In particular, human society seems to operate according to ethical principles that are difficult to square with the account of the evolutionary origins of behaviour given above (Chapter 2).

Darwin himself, concerned as he was to demonstrate the continuity of the species, was particularly worried about this. He wrote in *The Descent of Man* (1871): "I fully subscribe to the judgement of those writers who maintain that of all the differences between man and the lower animals, the moral sense or conscience is by far the most important" (p. 148). This is an interesting view given that most of us would (I suspect) think first of a difference in intelligence when asked to distinguish between man and other animals. It takes only a little reflection, however, to see the cause of Darwin's concern about moral differences. Man lives in societies that are, on the whole, cooperative. The smooth running of a social group, be it a family, a club, or a nation depends upon individual members of the group subordinating their own interests to those of the group as a whole. Such behaviour undoubtedly occurs: parents make sacrifices for the good of their children and soldiers run the risk of battle for the sake of their country. But if human behaviour is a product of natural selection, how could it occur? Any individual who puts himself at risk for the good of others stands a better than average chance of being killed and failing to leave any offspring. Any individual who shirks his duty stands a better than average chance of ensuring that his genes are represented in the next generation. To the extent that these patterns of behaviour have a genetic basis, antisocial behaviour should come to predominate. That it does not (or at least not totally), poses a challenge to evolutionary theory. Does it mean that human social behaviour is governed by some novel set of principles?

## Kin Selection

Evolutionary biology first faced up to this general problem when it tried to explain not human social behaviour but similar properties that are found in the behaviour of social insects. The result was the branch of evolutionary theory that some have called *sociobiology* and that we discussed in Chapter 2. This approach has had success in explaining altruistic social behaviour without departing from evolutionary orthodoxy, but by developing the full implications of hitherto neglected parts of the theory.

A good example is found in the use of the notion of *kin selection*, a term used to describe the fact that a gene may be selected for even when it produces behaviour that puts an individual at risk, provided that the behaviour in question tends to foster the survival of close relatives who also possess the gene. Consider the application of this concept to the social behaviour of honeybees. The worker bee is a sterile female who looks after the interests of others (feeding and tending the offspring of the queen bee) but who does not herself reproduce. Bee society depends upon her labour. How could such behaviour (and such a society) manage to evolve and be perpetuated since the worker bee is incapable of passing her altruistic tendencies to the next generation by genetic means? The answer is given in Fig. 8.8 which shows that male bees (drones) have an unusual genetic constitution. They develop from unfertilized eggs and are therefore *haploid* having only one example of each chromosome rather than the usual pair (the *diploid* condition). Figure 8.8 shows examples of the genotypes that are produced when two diploid individuals mate. The mixing of the genes that occurs ensures that each of the parents has 50% of genes in common with each of the offspring and that each of the offspring holds (on average) 50% in common with its siblings. Contrast this with the result of crossing a female bee and a haploid drone. As the figure shows, the products of this cross (which will be females since they are fertilized) have 75% of their genes in common. Thus if any individual worker bee "wanted" to ensure the survival of its own genes it would do so better by looking after its sisters than by mating to produce its own children which would hold in common only the usual 50% of genes.

All normal humans are diploid and so we could not expect the genetic basis of human social behaviour to be as elegant as that of the honeybee. Nonetheless, the same basic principles will apply, in that individuals might be expected to behave in ways that foster the survival of their close relatives and thus of genes that closely related individuals are likely to hold in common. Any genes that cause a mother to care for her own children are clearly likely to be perpetuated since there is a 50% chance that they will be present in the children. So, also, will those that induce her to care for her grandchildren or her sister's children since there is a 25% chance that the genes will be present in these individuals too. And, depending on the amount of effort expended, there may even be a pay-off in looking out for the interests of relatives even more remote than these.

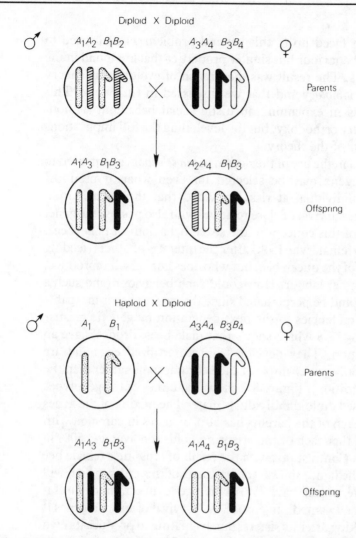

Fig. 8.8. *The diploid cell is represented as having two pairs of chromosomes (the As and the Bs) each having different alleles of a given gene (the subscript numerals). Two possible products of a cross between diploids are shown; they have half their genes in common with their mother and with each other. The haploid–diploid cross produces offspring that, since they all have their father's genes, hold three-quarters in common with each other (based on Smith, 1975).*

In short, there is nothing about the cooperative social behaviour of groups of related human beings that is, in principle, inexplicable by contemporary evolutionary theory.

## Reciprocal Altruism

It may be objected that human beings are capable of making sacrifices on behalf of others who are quite unrelated to them (although we might feel that such behaviour is not so common as one might wish). But however infrequently such behaviour occurs it will pose a problem for evolutionary theory. The solution to this problem has been sought in the concept of *reciprocal altruism*. The terminology is odd (behaviour can hardly be said to be altruistic if it is done in the hope of getting something in return) but the principle is sensible enough. One individual may put himself out to help a second provided that the second then helps the first sometime later; the chances of survival of both, and of the genes that induce them to behave in this way, will thereby be enhanced.

The problem with such a social system (it hardly need be said) is that some individuals are bound to arise who try to cheat, that is, who take help from another and then refuse to pay back what they owe. Such individuals are likely to thrive, to reproduce readily, and it might be thought that after a few generations they would come to predominate so that the system would break down. But this need not be the case. If one individual relies on another for some essential service then the cheat who takes this service without payment is dependent upon the survival of honest individuals for his own survival. If he reproduces so successfully that he squeezes out all his honest colleagues then he deprives himself of a service that he needs and effectively cuts his own throat. In such circumstances, although cheats may appear in a population they will not be able to overwhelm it. The system will be self-correcting and will settle down to some stable condition with cheats forming some small proportion of the population. The analogy with a parasite that feeds off, but does not kill its host is appropriate. The picture is not a pretty one but it does serve to show that cooperative behaviour among unrelated individuals can occur without necessarily contravening the basic principles of evolutionary biology.

## The Role of Culture

Sociobiological accounts of human social interaction have provoked strong resistance in some quarters. The objections have taken many different forms but the essential feature of most of them is well expressed in the following rhetorical question posed by one of the critics: "How can a theory that proceeds entirely in terms of genetic processes possibly take adequate account of the cultural variables in human social behaviour?" (Freeman, 1980, p. 212). We must examine, therefore, what cultural variables might be and why they should be thought to invalidate the sociobiological view.

*An illustrative example.* In part because of his linguistic skills, man is particularly adept at learning from his fellow man. This ability allows him to show a form of adaptation to environmental demands different from that produced by natural selection working on his genetic constitution, as the following example will show. Imagine a tribe of early men who, like modern men, are unable to see in the dark. Imagine now that one of their number, perhaps because of some chance genetic mutation, grows up to be exceptionally intelligent—clever enough to invent some means of kindling fire. This man might die and leave no offspring and his remarkable set of genes would die with him. But provided his fellows learned the trick of lighting a fire from him before his death, a new phenotypic characteristic (which, among other things, allows man to see at night) would be established in the population without the need for any genetic change. If parents teach this trick to their children the characteristic could persist over generations; the habit of using fire would show "cultural inheritance". Some separate tribe of men might have its own genius who invented his own means of kindling and among these people a different means of lighting fires would be established and perpetuated. In this way culturally determined differences in behaviour could be established between groups of individuals that do not differ genetically in ways relevant to the behaviour in question.

As an aside, it is worth making clear at this stage that the importance of cultural influences on human behaviour does not mean that man is no longer susceptible to the forces that produce biological evolution. If there are heritable differences between individuals that lead to differential reproduction, then evolution by natural selection must still occur. All that cultural invention does (in this context) is to help determine what factors are conducive to reproductive success. To take an obvious example: until fairly recently it was presumably the case that individuals having strong sexual urges tended to mate more often and produce more children. A strong "sex drive" would therefore be selected for. But the invention of contraceptive devices means that procreation is no longer a necessary consequence of sexual activity. It is still true, however, that some people will have more children than others; that, if the term can be allowed, the "drive to procreate" will be stronger in some people than in others. Natural selection will continue to occur but with a strong drive toward procreation rather than a strong sex drive now being selected for. Thus, cultural factors may modify the direction in which natural selection works but they do not stop it from operating.

*Culture in non-human animals.* Cultural effects are not confined to the human species. In Chapter 3 we discussed how patterns of cultural inheritance can be established in strains of laboratory mice. Their spontaneous origin has been observed in other species, especially in primates. In monkeys they have been well documented among Japanese macaques. One example will suffice here. The troop of monkeys under investigation were supplied with food by man and were faced with the laborious task of picking grains of wheat from the sand on which it had been spread. One animal (a four-year-old female) devised a new way of doing this. She took handfuls of the mixture and put them in water. The result was that the sand sank and the floating grain could be collected relatively easily. Her invention was quickly copied by some of her colleagues (particularly the younger animals) and it gradually spread throughout the troop. This pattern of behaviour (which constitutes a culturally determined difference between this and other groups of monkeys) will presumably be maintained from one generation to the next as the infants learn it from their parents.

*The importance of culture in man.* Although other examples of cultural transmission and of cultural differences could be cited, it is clear that in no other species do cultural factors have the enormous influence that they do on human behaviour. Contrast the way of life of a member of a modern Western society with that of his ancestor living before the invention of agriculture, say about 12 000 years ago. Or contrast your own way of life with that of a member of a modern hunter–gatherer society such as that of the Eskimos of the Arctic or the Bushmen of the Kalahari. (Perhaps the contrast is better made with the behaviour shown by these people a generation or so ago; there have been many recent changes.) The differences are overwhelming. Of course, these differences could have their origin, at least in part, in genetic differences between the groups being compared. We have no way of assessing the extent of these genetic differences or their importance in determining patterns of behaviour (although the recent rapid changes undergone by the hunter–gatherers provide some evidence that their behaviour can easily be modified by changes in their environment). Let us assume, however, since this would constitute the most severe test of the theory under consideration, that all these differences in behaviour are the product of cultural differences. If cultural factors can produce such profound differences in patterns of human social behaviour, how can it be possible to account for this behaviour in terms of the genetic and evolutionary principles favoured by the sociobiologists?

## A Misconception about the Role of Culture

In order to give a proper answer to this question it is important first to dispose of a misconception that commonly arises. It may be expressed as follows: much human behaviour is demonstrably determined by cultural influences; sociobiology is concerned solely with the genetic determinants of behaviour; therefore the notions of sociobiology cannot be sensibly applied to human behaviour.

To give a concrete example: Bushman women tend to space the births of their children so that they occur at roughly four-yearly intervals. This pattern of behaviour has been explained on sociobiological lines as follows. The Bushman woman supplies most of the food needs of her family by gathering nuts and other plant matter. To do so she has to walk long distances and to carry any infant she may have. Any genetic tendency to produce children more frequently than once every four years would be counterproductive since it would mean that she would have to cope with two infants on her journeys; she would not be able to care for either of them properly and their chances of survival would be reduced. It is better to produce a few children who survive than many, all of whom fail to live and reproduce; and any genetic tendency to behave in this way would be selected for (Blurton Jones and Sibly, 1978).

The (misconceived) objection to this view goes as follows. Although the sociobiological explanation seems plausible it cannot in fact be right since the reproductive pattern of Bushman women is determined not by genetic but by cultural factors. And we know that it is culturally determined by looking at the reproductive patterns shown by women in other societies. These women, we have assumed, do not differ genetically from Bushman women in any major respect but they show quite different reproductive patterns according to the culture of which they are a part. Consequently a cultural rather than a genetic explanation must be provided for this (and perhaps for most other) patterns of human social behaviour.

The central misconception that underlies this argument is the one that was discussed at length in Chapter 3. In that chapter we established that it is not sensible to say of a particular pattern of behaviour that it is genetically rather than environmentally (culturally) determined or vice versa. Any pattern of behaviour is the product of an interaction between a genotype and environmental (including cultural) factors. Thus it becomes a truism to say that the pattern of reproductive behaviour seen in the Bushman is environmentally determined —there is no behaviour pattern that is not. But to say this does not mean that it is not genetically determined too. What the genes do will be decided by their interaction with the environment in which they exist. Imagine, if you can, a baby girl taken from her home in an affluent suburb of some Western city and transported to the Kalahari. Left at home she would have produced in adulthood say three children spaced at two-yearly intervals. But brought up in the Bushman culture she would no doubt adopt the customary reproductive pattern of her adopted society. (Clearly this must be so since we have adopted the assumption that there are no major genetic differences between various sub-groups of our species.) What this imaginary experiment shows is not that genetic factors play no part in determining reproductive patterns. Rather it shows that flexible genetic mechanisms have been evolved that, in interaction with differing environments, can produce differing patterns of behaviour, each one appropriate to the special demands made by that environment.

## Limitations on the Sociobiological Account

Against this background we are better able to see the true nature of the limitations that culturals variable impose on the sociobiological account. We have said that different societies may show different behaviour patterns for cultural reasons; *ex hypothesi* these differences are not genetically produced and therefore sociobiology cannot attempt to account for them. This does not mean that sociobiology is "wrong" in some way, just that some phenomena lie outside the scope of the theory.

What it can do, however, is to try to describe the evolutionary and genetic mechanisms that are at work within a given culture; to specify the various selection pressures that are at work within that culture and to give some understanding of how that culture's behaviour patterns might have evolved. The account it provides must necessarily be incomplete. Information about a genotype can never give a full explanation of a phenotypic characteristic since what the genotype produces depends upon the environment with which it interacts. Thus the sociobiological account does not preclude other ways of explaining a given pattern of behaviour, but rather it is complementary to them. Having determined the evolutionary background to the pattern of reproduction shown by the Bushman we are fully entitled to go on and specify the cultural mechanisms, whereby this pattern is achieved. The central point here is the one that was made in a somewhat wider context at the end of Chapter 2. It is that evolutionary (sociobiological) explanations of behaviour are explanations of a special sort. They are not trying to establish that some behaviour is determined by genetic mechanisms established by evolution whereas other behaviour is not. We accept as a starting point that *all* behaviour is produced by a genotype (interacting with an environment) and that the genotype is itself a product of evolution by natural selection. The task of sociobiology is to reveal the evolutionary background (that we already know must exist) of patterns of behaviour that perhaps, at first sight, look as though they could not be the result of natural selection.

## Implications for Human Social Behaviour

A common reaction to the claims of sociobiology runs as follows: such notions may be adequate explanations for the behaviour shown by the bee, or the chimpanzee, or my cave-man ancestor, or even for the Bushman; but they cannot apply to me since my behaviour is culturally determined. We have dissected out the element of truth in this assertion by accepting that sociobiology does not deal with culturally produced differences in behaviour between individuals that do not differ genetically.

But the assertion itself is clearly untrue. Since the behaviour of any individual organism is a phenotypic characteristic determined by the genotype – environment interaction, to that extent the behaviour of any individual is determined by the environment. This is as true of the bee as it is of you and me. This fact imposes limitations (as we have already admitted) on the completeness of the explanation that sociobiology can provide but these limitations are general and apply to non-human animals every bit as much as they apply to man. There is no need to suppose that human social behaviour is governed by some novel set of principles not found elsewhere in the animal kingdom.

## CONCLUSIONS

It seems to me that many attempts to establish a "general psychology" in which man is given his proper place have been perverted from the outset because they start with the assumption that "man evolved from the animals". Given this starting point, it is accepted (and this at least is a good thing) that we can learn things of interest about human nature by studying non-human animals. But it leads on to a discussion of a range of sterile (because ill-formulated) questions about the relationship between man and the animals. Is man controlled by his genetic make-up (as the animals are supposed to be) or does his possession of culture free him from this control? Is man still a slave to his basic animal instincts or does his possession of language bestow on him a rationality that sets him apart from other animals? And so on.

The trouble with these questions is that they are based on an unjustified assumption. They assume, what is not the case, that there is a fairly uniform group of creatures, "the animals", from which man has evolved. Rather, man himself is an animal and like them has evolved from other animals, now long extinct. Any animal species has certain unique features that make it what it is and we can do for any species what we have tried to do in this chapter for the human species: that is, we can try to identify what these features are and to what extent they give exemption to psychological principles that are otherwise generally applicable. That in this chapter we have been through this exercise for man reflects nothing more than the fact that we have a very natural interest in the species to which we ourselves belong. The conclusion we have come to, that there is no necessity for us to adopt a distinctly human psychology importantly different from that applicable to other species, does not detract from the unique features that he does possess. By setting them in their proper context it may help us to understand them better.

## SOURCES AND FURTHER READING

Young's book *An Introduction to the Study of Man* (1971) is specifically concerned to introduce the beginner to the possibility of studying man in a scientific manner. It covers a much wider range of issues than those covered in this chapter but it provides an excellent background for them. For a clearly written and more extensive discussion of the critical issues debated in this chapter see Passingham's (1982) *The Human Primate*. The issue of language acquisition by animals has been covered by many authors. Linden's *Apes, Men, and Language* provides an easily accessible popular introduction. But it is important also to look at Terrace *et al.*'s (1979) work for a rather different view of sign language in apes. Premack's contribution is described in his *Intelligence in Ape and Man* (1976). For background information on human language see Miller's (1981) *Language and Speech*. On sociobiology generally see *Readings in Sociobiology*, a collection of papers edited by Clutton-Brock and Harvey (1978) that includes most of the seminal original contributions to this area. The application of sociobiological concepts to man is advocated by Wilson (1978) in his *On Human Nature*. This controversial work deserves a critical reading, something that might be helped by looking also at the collection edited by Montagu (1980): *Sociobiology Examined*.

# Glossary

*Note:* technical terms are usually defined in the text when they are first introduced. This glossary (which is intended to convey the substance of how the various terms are used in this book, and does not go in to subtleties of interpretation) should help when a technical term is encountered at some other place in the text. Words italicized in an entry are themselves to found in the glossary.

*Acetylcholine* Substance released at the end of cholinergic nerve fibres when *nerve impulses* arrive there and that stimulates activity in the adjacent nerve cell or muscle fibre.

*Action potential* A local and rapid reversal in the electrical potential that normally exists between the inside and outside of a nerve fibre (in the resting state the inside is negative with respect to the outside). It constitutes an important and readily detectable part of the *nerve impulse*.

*Adrenal glands* A pair of *endocrine* glands located above the kidneys, having a medulla that secretes *adrenaline* and noradrenaline and an outer cortex secreting a range of *hormones*.

*Adrenaline* A *hormone* secreted by the *adrenal* medulla in response to stress. Also called *epinephrine*.

*Afferent nerve* A nerve that transmits impulses from the periphery into the *central nervous system*.

*Allele* A particular form of a given *gene*.

*Altricial* Refers to young animals that are helpless for a substantial period of time following birth (or hatching); or to the species itself (see *precocial*).

*Amino acid* One of the twenty or so organic compounds that go to make up *proteins*; a protein consists of a chain of hundreds of amino acid molecules.

*Appetitive behaviour* Initial phase of activity often shown by animals seeking some goal. It may often appear to be exploratory, and rather variable in contrast to the stereotyped *consummatory behaviour* shown when the goal is reached.

*Arena* An area consistently used by a given animal group for courtship displays; often called a "lek" for birds.

*Asexual reproduction* Any form of reproduction (e.g. budding) that does not involve the fusion of *germ cells*.

*Association cortex* Those parts of the *cerebral cortex* not identified as being *sensory* or *motor cortex*.

*Associative learning* In this book, the learning that results from presenting an animal with a contingency between two events: e.g. two stimuli as in *classical conditioning*, or a response and a stimulus as in *instrumental learning* (see also *perceptual learning*).

*Australopithecus* Genus of "ape-men", possibly ancestral to modern man, that lived in Africa around two million years ago.

*Autonomic nervous system* Those parts of the nervous system in vertebrates that regulate the activities of internal organs, smooth muscle, and glands. Divided into the *sympathetic* and *parasympathetic* divisions.

*Autoshaping Classical conditioning* procedure used with pigeons in which the birds come to peck an illuminated key presented immediately before the delivery of food.

*Axon* The fibre of a *neurone* that transmits impulses away from the cell body.

*Backcross* Mating of a hybrid (produced, for example by crossing *inbred strains*) with one of the parental strains.

*Behaviourism* The approach to psychology that regards the subject as the study of behaviour; as a philosophical position, one that denies the existence of mind.

*Biofeedback* Training procedure in which bodily changes of which a subject may be unconscious (e.g. heart rate) are monitored and transformed into a more easily discriminated cue.

*Blocking* Observation that training a subject with one stimulus as a signal for a *reinforcer* prevents the subject from learning about a second when both are presented together along with the reinforcer.

*Central nervous system* In vertebrates, the brain and spinal cord.

*Cerebellum* Outgrowth of the roof of the hindbrain of vertebrates concerned with the coordination of movement.

*Cerebral cortex* The surface layer of *grey matter* of the *cerebral hemispheres*.

*Cerebral hemispheres* The paired structures of nerve cells and fibres that constitute the *telencephalon* of vertebrates.

*Chain reflex* Relatively complex pattern of behaviour that can be analysed into a sequence of *reflexes*, one response providing the stimulus that elicits the next.

*Chromosome* Structure, composed in part of *DNA*, found in the nucleus of a cell and bearing the *genes* of the cell; arranged as homologous pairs in *diploid* cells.

*Classical conditioning* Procedure for generating *associative learning* in which two stimuli are paired. Usually one (the *conditioned stimulus*) is presented shortly before the other (the *unconditioned stimulus*). A *conditioned response* to the first stimulus may appear.

*Comparative psychology* Branch of psychology that compares the behaviour shown by different animal species, usually with a view to determining their evolutionary history; sometimes used to mean the study of the behaviour of non-human animals more generally.

*Comparator* The device in a control system that compares a *feedback* stimulus against a reference signal and generates a correcting signal when there is a discrepancy.

*Concrete operational period* Phase of cognitive development in Piaget's account lasting from about age 7 to 11 years. The child of this age is said to be able to think logically about objects and events immediately present (he shows, e.g., *conservation*), but is not capable of fully logical thought.

*Conditioned response* The response evoked by a *conditioned stimulus* as a result of *classical conditioning*.

*Conditioned (conditional) stimulus* A stimulus which, as a result of *classical conditioning*, is able to evoke some new response.

*Conservation* Principle that an object (or a quantity of fluid) does not change in quantity when it changes in shape.

*Consummatory behaviour* Stereotyped response pattern shown (e.g. in feeding or mating) when an animal has reached some goal (cf. *appetitive behaviour*).

*Correlation coefficient* A statistic indicating the degree of correspondence between two sets of paired scores.

*Corpus callosum* The band of nerve fibres that links the two *cerebral hemispheres*.

*Critical (sensitive) period* A phase in development during which an organism is especially receptive to certain environmental influences.

*Curare* Drug that blocks activity at the *neuromuscular junction* and thus produces paralysis.

*Cultural inheritance* Process whereby *phenotypic* characters may run in families not for immediate genetic reasons but because parents supply the environment that ensures the appearance of the character in their offspring.

*DNA (deoxyribonucleic acid)* Large organic molecule found in the *chromosomes* and constituting the physical basis of the *genes*.

*Dependent variable* A measure of behaviour, changes in which may be attributed to changes in some *independent variable*.

*Diencephalon* Along with the *telencephalon* constitutes the forebrain of vertebrates; its chief parts are the *thalamus* and *hypothalamus*.

*Diploid* A cell with a nucleus containing *chromosomes* as homologous pairs (see *haploid*); also refers to the organism itself.

*Discrimination learning Associative learning* procedure in which a subject receives a *reinforcer* in the presence of one stimulus (the positive) but no reinforcer (or some different reinforcer) in the presence of a different stimulus.

*Display* A behaviour pattern that serves to communicate information (e.g. in courtship); often a *ritualized* form of a pattern that once served some other function.

*Dominance (genetic)* The ability of an *allele* to produce a given *phenotypic* characteristic in spite of the presence of a different allele on the homologous *chromosome* of the pair in a *diploid* organism.

*Dominance hierarchy* Pattern of social organization in which some individuals by means of aggressive acts or *displays* acquire higher status than others and use it to gain access to limited resources; relative standing in the hierarchy is usually stable over time.

*Dizygotic twins* Non-identical twins, developed from separate eggs (see *monozygotic twins*); also called fraternal twins.

*Ecology* The study of the relationship between an organism and its environment, both the physical environment and that supplied by other organisms.

*Effect, law of* Thorndike's suggestion that the consequences of a response will determine its likelihood of further occurrence (see *instrumental learning*).

*Effector* Part of an animal (muscle or gland; organ or limb) by which the animal acts, usually to effect a change in its environment.

*Efferent nerve* A nerve that transmits nerve impulses from the *central nervous system* to the periphery (e.g. the muscles).

*Electromyogram* Record of the electrical activity occurring in a muscle during contraction.

*Emotionality* Used particularly (but not exclusively) of rodents to describe a dimension along which their behaviour varies (fearfulness); tested by observing behaviour in the *open field*.

*Encephalization of function* The process whereby mammals come to have in their *cerebral cortex* areas devoted to functions carried out by areas of midbrain and hindbrain in "lower" vertebrates or in the postulated extinct ancestors of the mammals.

*Endocrine gland* A ductless gland that secretes a *hormone* into the general circulation.

*Enzyme* A protein that catalyses specific biochemical reactions.

*Epigenesis* Account of development which emphasizes the gradual, step-by-step nature of the process, with each step providing the necessary conditions for the appearance of the next.

*Equipotentiality* Lashley's suggestion that all parts of the *cerebral cortex* are equivalent in their ability to perform certain psychological functions such as learning (see *mass action*).

*Ethology* The zoological study of animal behaviour laying emphasis upon observations carried out in the animal's natural environment and upon the evolutionary background to the behaviour.

*Extraversion* A proposed dimension of personality (from introvert to extravert); can be equated, roughly, with how out-going a person is.

*Feedback* Information about the activities of an *effector* returned to the control system that governs the activities of that effector.

*Fixed action pattern* In traditional *ethology*, a stereotyped pattern of behaviour, more complex than a simple *reflex* but elicited as a whole and not controlled by a sequence of *feedback* stimuli as in a *chain reflex*.

*Flavour-aversion learning Classical conditioning* procedure in which animals are exposed to a novel flavour, this experience being followed by some procedure that induces nausea. The animals subsequently reject the flavour.

*Formal operational period* Final phase of Piaget's account of cognitive development in which the ability to deal with abstract notions and to entertain hypotheses appears.

*Frontal lobe* That part of the *cerebral hemisphere* that lies in front of the central fissure.

*Ganglion* A collection of nerve cell bodies (also, nucleus).

*Gene* The basic unit of heredity; the section of *chromosomal DNA* that codes for a *protein*.

*Gene pool* All the genes in a population.

*Generalization* The observation in conditioning that stimuli similar to the *conditioned stimulus* can also evoke the *conditioned response* to some (usually lesser) extent; the process whereby this occurs.

*Genotype* The genetic constitution of an individual (contrasted with *phenotype*).

*Germ cell* A *haploid* cell (egg or sperm) that by fusing with another produces a *zygote* that can develop into a new *diploid* individual.

*Grammar* A system of rules that specifies what sentences are permissible in a language.

*Grey and white matter* Nervous tissue: cell bodies appear grey, bundles of nerve fibres appear white.

*Habituation* The waning of a *unconditioned response* with repeated presentation of its eliciting stimulus.

*Haploid* Cell with a nucleus containing only one member of each pair of homologous chromosomes (see *diploid*).

*Heritability* The proportion of the variance in a *phenotypic* character in a population that can be ascribed to *genotypic* differences.

*Hippocampus* Part of the cortex of the mammalian forebrain having a different microscopic structure and evolutionary history from the rest of the *cerebral cortex*.

*Homology* A fundamental similarity between two structures or features of behaviour shown by different animals that is assumed to be produced by their having descended from a common ancestor.

*Hormone* The secretion of an *endocrine gland* carried by the circulation to some site where it affects activity.

*Hybrid vigour* Increased vigour (e.g. fertility) produced by a cross between two genetically different strains as contrasted with the results of a cross between individuals both drawn from one of the parental strains.

*Hypothalamus* A part of the *diencephalon* of the vertebrate brain having intimate links with the *autonomic* nervous system and the *endocrine* system; important in emotion and motivation.

*Imprinting* Originally the learning process whereby newly hatched birds (e.g. ducklings) come to show filial responses towards an object or animal experienced shortly after hatching; more generally the process whereby vertebrates form attachments early in life.

*Inbred strain* Strain of animals, essentially genetically identical, produced by repeating brother to sister matings from generation to generation.

*Inclusive fitness* The contribution of one *genotype* to the next generation (relative to that made by other genotypes) including any influence it may exert on the fitness of its close relatives (see *kin selection*).

*Independent variable* An event under the control of the investigator, changes in which produce changes in some *dependent variable*.

*Intelligence* When applied generally (i.e. to non-human animals as well as to man): the capacity of an animal to show a modification in its behaviour (as a result of learning) so as better to meet the demands of the environment.

*IQ (intelligence quotient)* The score yielded by psychological tests of human intelligence. Classically derived by dividing the subject's mental age (as determined by his performance on age-graded tests) by his chronological age and multiplying by 100.

*Instrumental learning (conditioning)* Procedure for generating *associative learning* in which a stimulus (e.g. the delivery of food) is made contingent upon the occurrence of some response; also called *operant conditioning*.

*Intervening variable* An inferred process used to link *independent* and *dependent variables* in theory construction.

*Introspection* As a method of research: that whereby trained observers attempt to describe mental content in specified and controlled conditions.

*Isolating mechanisms* Properties of an individual (often behavioural as in courtship *displays*) that prevent interbreeding between populations that occupy the same habitat.

*Kin selection* A form of *natural selection* produced by individuals influencing the survival or reproduction of relatives who possess the same genes.

*Language acquisition device* The mechanisms (hypothesized by some to be "innate") that allows children to acquire *grammar* from the sample of spoken language that they hear.

*Learning set* As a procedure: that of requiring the subject to solve (or attempt to solve) a long series of *discrimination* problems of the same general sort; also the consequences of this procedure which allows learning of later problems to occur very rapidly.

*Locus* A position as a chromosome at which there is one *gene* or *allele*.

*Lloyd Morgan's canon* The principle of parsimony in explanation as applied to behaviour; in particular the assertion that intelligent behaviour should be explained where possible in terms of known mechanisms of associative learning without recourse to concepts such as "insight".

*Luminance* Physically measured intensity of a visual stimulus; related to its perceived brightness.

*Manic-depression* A *psychosis* characterized by swings in mood from elation to despondency.

*Mass action* Proposal, due to Lashley, that, although the *cerebral cortex* may show *equipotentiality* for certain functions, its efficiency in performing these functions depends upon the mass of cortex available.

*Medulla oblongata* Hind-most part of the roof of the vertebrate brain, merging into the spinal cord; contains nerve cells important to the control of respiration, circulatory function etc.

*Molar/molecular* Used in psychology to distinguish large-scale versus detailed description of behaviour; a molar description (e.g. "walking") can often be reduced to a molecular description of individual muscle contractions.

*Mesencephalon* Midbrain: middle of the three divisions evident in the embryonic vertebrate brain; its roof is the *tectum*.

*Monozygotic twins* Twins developed from a single egg; identical twins.

*Motor cortex* Region of *cerebral cortex* in the *frontal lobe* from which nerve fibres run to the muscles and electrical stimulation of which can generate movements.

*Natural selection* The process whereby genetically different individuals make differential contributions of offspring to the next generation.

*Neocortex* Those parts of the *cerebral cortex* of mammals that show six well-defined layers of cells (cf. *hippocampus* and olfactory structures).

*Nerve impulse* Travelling wave of chemical and electrical (see *action potential*) changes that is conducted down a nerve fibre. Its characteristics, once generated, are independent of the nature of the eliciting event.

*Neuromuscular junction* Point at which the *axon* of a motor *neurone* makes contact with muscle fibres.

*Neurone* Nerve cell: the unit of which the nervous system is built; consists of a cell body from which thread-like processes project (see *axon*); also spelled neuron.

*Neurosis (psychoneurosis)* Psychological disorder, milder than *psychosis*, commonly characterized by excessive or inappropriate anxiety.

*Object permanence (understanding of)* The ability to comprehend that objects that have passed from immediate view still continue to exist.

*Occipital lobe* Part of the *cerebral hemisphere* posterior to the *temporal* and *parietal* lobes; its cortex is concerned in mammals with visual function.

*Ontogeny* The course of development through an individual's life history; contrasted with *phylogeny*.

*Open-field test* Procedure used with rodents in which the animal's reactions (particularly ambulation and defaecation) to a novel environment (a large open-topped box) are noted; thought to measure exploratory tendencies and *emotionality*.

*Operant conditioning* Skinner's term for the procedure otherwise known as *instrumental conditioning*.

*Optimal foraging theory* Theoretical analysis of the ways in which animals obtain and consume food which regards this behaviour as consisting of a set strategies that function to ensure maximum intake at minimum cost.

*Orienting response (reflex)* Complex of bodily changes mediated by the *autonomic nervous system* evoked by presentation of a novel stimulus; also the reaction in which the head and body turn toward the source of the stimulation.

*Osmotic pressure* The pressure required to stop the flow of a solvent (such as water in the body fluids) across a membrane (such as a cell wall) into a more concentrated solution (the cell contents).

*Paired-associate learning* Learning of pairs of words in which the subject is required to respond with the second member of the pair when presented with the first.

*Parasympathetic division* Part of the *autonomic nervous system* with *efferent* nerve fibres leaving the *central nervous system* via cranial nerves and at the hind-end of the spinal cord, and running to internal organs. To some extent antagonistic in function to the *sympathetic division*.

*Perceptual learning* In this book: learning brought about by mere exposure to environmental events.

*Parental investment* Behaviour shown by a parent to its offspring that increases the likelihood of survival of the offspring but reduces the opportunity of the parent to reproduce further.

*Parietal lobe* Section of the *cerebral hemisphere* bounded by the *occipital lobe* posteriorly and by marked fissures that separate it from the *temporal* and *frontal lobes*.

*Partial reinforcement schedule* Rule governing the delivery of *reinforcers* in *operant conditioning* whereby the response is reinforced on only some proportion of occurrences.

*Peripheral nervous system* That part of the nervous system in vertebrates that lies outside the skull and spinal canal (cf. *central nervous system*). Includes parts of both the *autonomic* and *somatic* nervous systems.

*Phenotype* The characteristics displayed by an individual (as contrasted with the set of genes, *genotype*, that it possesses).

*Phobia* An intense and seemingly irrational fear; form of *neurosis*.

*Phylogeny* Evolutionary history of a species or other animal group.

*Pituitary Endocrine gland* lying immediately below the *hypothalamus*; the posterior part produces anti-diuretic *hormone*, the anterior part of a range of hormones that control other endocrine glands (e.g. adrenocorticotropic hormone).

*Pleiotropy* The phenomenon of a single gene having effects on more than one *phenotypic* characteristic; also called pleiotropism.

*Polygenic inheritance* Patterns of inheritance whereby differences in a *phenotypic* character are influenced by many genes. Individually each gene exerts a very small effect and the character tends to vary quantitatively among members of the population.

*Polytypic* Of a species: having many different forms or "races".

*Precocial* Refers to young animals that are active immediately after birth (or hatching); or to the species itself (see *altricial*).

*Preoperational period* Second major phase in Piaget's account of cognitive development in which the child begins to use symbols, but fails to use them as an adult would. The child fails to show *conservation*. Extends, roughly, from age 2 to 7 years.

*Primate* A group (order) of mammals containing the monkeys and apes (including man).

*Projection area* Of the *cerebral cortex*, an area served by a tract of nerve fibres originating in a nucleus of the *thalamus*, that nucleus itself being served by nerve fibres connected to *receptors*. Thus the retina projects to the lateral geniculate nucleus, and the lateral geniculate to the cortex of the *occipital lobe*.

*Proprioceptor* A *receptor* that detects the position of and changes in the position of the body or its parts: thus the receptors found in the muscles and joints and in the organs of balance of the inner ear.

*Prosencephalon* The forebrain: the end-most of the three divisions apparent in the embryonic brain of vertebrates; consists of *telencephalon* and *diencephalon*.

*Protein* Complex organic molecule composed of a chain of *amino acids*.

*Psychoanalysis* Freud's theory of the structure and development of personality and its disorders; also a system of therapy for neurotic disorders.

*Psycholinguistics* Branch of psychology concerned with how people learn, understand, and use language.

*Psychophysics* The study of the relationship between stimulus energy impinging upon a subject and what the subject reports perceiving.

*Psychosis* Severe psychological disorder (e.g. *schizophrenia, manic-depression*).

*Receptor* Cell (or group of cells) specialized to react to energy impinging on it (e.g. light, mechanical distortion) and to respond by initiating nerve impulses in sensory nerve fibre to which it is connected. Also, a molecule on a cell membrane that combines selectively with some specific chemical.

"*Reciprocal altruism*" Repayment of an altruistic act (one that puts the organism at a short-term reproductive disadvantage) by a similar act at some later time.

*Reflex* Simple form of behaviour in which a given stimulus rapidly and reliably evokes a given response; mediated by the *central nervous system*.

*Reinforcer* In *operant conditioning* an event which when made contingent on a response increases the probability of that response; in *classical conditioning* another term for the *unconditioned stimulus*.

*Releaser* Term used in *ethology* for the stimulus that triggers a *fixed action pattern*.

*Rhombencephalon* Hindbrain: the hindmost of the three divisions evident in embryonic brain of vertebrates; includes the *cerebellum* and *medulla oblongata*.

*Ritualization* Evolutionary process whereby a behaviour pattern becomes modified so that it functions as a signal for communication.

*Schizophrenia* A form of *psychosis* characterized by a withdrawal from reality and often accompanied by hallucinations and delusions.

*Searching image* Hypothesized mechanism underlying the ability of a predator animal (usually a bird) to capture efficiently a given form of prey (often camouflaged) perhaps at the expense of missing other forms of prey.

*Second-order conditioning* In *classical conditioning*, a procedure in which a previously *conditioned stimulus* is used as the *reinforcer*.

*Sensory cortex* Areas of *cerebral cortex* receiving information (via the *thalamus*) from sensory nerves and in which electrical changes can sometimes be recorded when the appropriate sense organs are stimulated.

*Sensory-motor period* According to Piaget the first stage of cognitive development in which a child's behaviour is controlled by events in his immediate environment; up to age 2 years. In this period the child fails to show *object permanence*.

*Sensory preconditioning* In *classical conditioning*, a procedure in which two neutral stimuli are paired prior to one of them being used as the *conditioned stimulus* in an orthodox conditioning procedure. The other stimulus thereby acquires the capacity to elicit a *conditioned response*.

*Serial reversal learning* Procedure used as a test of *intelligence* in non-human animals. After the subject has learned to choose one of a pair of distinctively different stimuli, the roles of the stimuli are reversed so that the previously negative stimulus becomes the positive. After a period of training a further reversal occurs, and so on.

*Sexual dimorphism* Of a species: having (two) sexes that differ in form (size, structure, etc.).

*Short-term memory* Mechanism involved when behaviour is controlled by information acquired only a short time (i.e. a few seconds) previously; often conceptualized as being a "store" of limited capacity in which information can persist for only a short period of time.

*Skinner box* Term used by almost everyone except Skinner to describe an experimental chamber in which an animal can be isolated from outside events, and containing a device by which the animal can respond (e.g. a lever for rats) and a system for delivering a *reinforcer* (e.g. a food magazine).

*Sociobiology* In general, the study of the biology of social behaviour in animals; more recently, applied specifically to the approach that stresses the evolutionary and genetic background of social behaviour.

*Somatic nervous system* That part of the nervous system that serves the skeletal muscles and sense organs (cf. *autonomic nervous system*).

*Species* The smallest unit of biological classification; those individuals capable of fertile interbreeding under natural conditions.

*Specific nerve energies (law of)* The assertion (generally justified) that a given sensation is generated by nervous activity in specific sensory pathways and cerebral centres, irrespective of the manner in which the receptor is stimulated or where along the pathway the activity is initiated.

*Stimulus control* When, in *operant conditioning*, the response occurs more (or less) readily in the presence of a given stimulus than in its absence.

*Sulcus* A fold or fissure in the surface of the *cerebral hemisphere*.

*Sympathetic division* Part of the *autonomic nervous system* having *efferent* outflow from the spinal cord to internal organs, skin, and limbs. Active in response to stress and to some extent antagonistic to *parasympathetic* activity.

*S–R theory* Stimulus–response theory: in general, the view that behaviour can be interpreted as consisting of a series of responses to specifiable stimuli; more particularly the theory of learning and behaviour developed by Hull from the beginnings provided by Thorndike and Watson.

*Synapse* Point at which distinct nerve cells come into close contact and across which nervous activity can pass upon release of a *transmitter* substance.

*Taxis* Movement of an organism in response to a directional stimulus, the direction of the movement being orientated in some specific way with respect to the stimulus.

*Teleost* A sub-grouping of the fish; includes most of the species of bony fish.

*Temporal lobe* The area of the *cerebral hemisphere* lying below the lateral fissure and anterior to the *occipital lobe*.

*Thalamus* Part of the *diencephalon* of the forebrain, containing nuclei that relay sensory input to the *cerebral cortex*.

*Tectum* the roof of the midbrain in vertebrates, serving a visual function in most of them but especially so in non-mammals where it is sometimes known as the optic tectum.

*Telencephalon* The end-most part of the forebrain consisting of olfactory structures, the *cerebral hemispheres*, and subcortical *ganglia*.

*Territory* An area occupied by an animal or group of animals and defended by fighting or by display.

*Transmitter* A chemical released by one nerve cell that causes activity in another (at a *synapse*) or in muscle (at the *neuromuscular junction*).

*Transposition* In *discrimination learning*, tendency to choose a stimulus not on the basis of its absolute properties but on the basis of the relationship it bears to the alternative. Thus a subject trained to choose a mid-grey rather than a dark grey shows transposition when it chooses a light grey in preference to the original positive stimulus.

*Two-process theory* Theory of learning and of *reinforcement* that accepts the reality of both *instrumental* and *classical conditioning* processes.

*Unconditioned (unconditional) response* The response evoked by a stimulus before the subject has been exposed to any explicit training procedure involving that stimulus (e.g. the *orienting response* to the onset of a noise; salivation to the presentation of food).

*Vacuum activity* Pattern of behaviour (usually a *fixed action pattern*) appearing in the apparent absence of the external stimulus that usually elicits it.

*Variance* A statistical parameter describing the spread of a set of scores computed using the deviation of each score from the mean.

*Ventricle* Fluid-filled cavity in the brain of vertebrates.

*Vertebrate* A member of the animal group (that includes fish, amphibia, mammals, reptiles, and birds) having a skull surrounding a well-developed brain (hence Craniata, as an alternative name for the group).

*Zygote* A cell formed by union of two *germ cells*.

# References

*Note:* where two dates are given for a work the earlier (and that cited in the text) is the date of original publication (this sometimes being of historical interest); the latter refers to the edition consulted.

ADAMS, C. D. and DICKINSON, A. (1981). Instrumental responding following reinforcer devaluation. *Quarterly Journal of Experimental Psychology*, **33B**, 109–121.

ANREP, G. V. (1920). Pitch discrimination in the dog. *Journal of Physiology*, **53**, 367–385.

ARDREY, R. (1967). *The Territorial Imperative*. London: Collins (1969).

ASCHOFF, J. (1965). Circadian rhythms in man. *Science*, **148**, 1427–1432.

BENNETT, T. L. (1982). *Introduction to Physiological Psychology*. Monterey Calif.: Brooks/Cole.

BINDRA, D. and STEWART, J. (Eds.) (1966). *Motivation*. Harmondsworth: Penguin.

BITTERMAN, M. E. (1965). Phyletic differences in learning. *American Psychologist*, **20**, 396–410.

BITTERMAN, M. E., LoLORDO, V. M., OVERMIER, J. B. and RASHOTTE, M. E. (1979). *Animal Learning: Survey and Analysis*. New York and London: Plenum Press.

BLAKEMORE, C. and COOPER, G. F. (1970). Development of the brain depends upon the visual environment. *Nature*, **228**, 477–478.

BLOOM, B. S. (1964). *Stability and Change in Human Characteristics*. New York: Wiley.

BLURTON JONES, N. and SIBLEY, R. M. (1978). Testing adaptiveness of culturally determined behaviour: do Bushman women maximize their reproductive success by spacing births widely and foraging seldom? In REYNOLDS V. and BLURTON JONES N. (Eds.), *Human Behaviour and Adaptation*. London: Taylor and Francis.

BOAKES, R. A. (1983). *From Darwin to Behaviourism*. Cambridge: Cambridge University Press.

BOLLES, R. C. (1967). *Theory of Motivation*. New York: Harper and Row.

BOLLES, R. C. (1979). *Learning Theory*. New York: Holt, Rinehart and Winston.

BORGER, R. and SEABORNE, A. E. M. (1982). *The Psychology of Learning*. Harmondsworth: Penguin. (2nd edition).

BOWER, T. G. R. (1974). *Development in Infancy*. San Franciso: Freeman.

BOWLBY, J. (1965). *Child Care and the Growth of Love*. Harmondsworth: Penguin.

BOWLBY, J. (1971). *Attachment*. Harmondsworth: Penguin.

BRELAND, K. and BRELAND, M. (1961). The misbehavior of organisms. *American*

*Psychologist*, **16**, 681–684.

BROWER, L. P., BROWER, J. Z. and WESTCOTT, P. W. (1960). The reaction of toads (*Bufo terrestris*) to bumblebees (*Bombus americanorum*) and their robberfly mimics (*Mallophora bomboides*) with a discussion of aggressive mimicry. *American Naturalist*, **94**, 342–355.

BROWN, J. L. (1975). *The Evolution of Behavior*. New York: Norton.

BRYANT, P. E. (1974). *Perception and Understanding in Young Children*. London: Methuen.

BUDZYNSKI, T. H., STOYVA, J. M., ADLER, C. S. and MULLANEY, D. J. (1973). EMG feedback and tension headache: a controlled outcome study. *Psychosomatic Medicine*, **35**, 484–496.

BURT, C. (1962). The concept of consciousness. *British Journal of Psychology*, **53**, 229–242.

CARMICHAEL, L. (1926). The development of behavior in vertebrates experimentally removed from the influence of external stimulation. *Psychological Review*, **33**, 51–58.

CARR, H. and WATSON, J. B. (1980). Orientation in the white rat. *Journal of Comparative Neurology and Psychology*, **18**, 27–44.

CHANNELL, S. and HALL, G. (1983). Contextual effects in latent inhibition with an appetitive conditioning procedure. *Animal Learning and Behavior*, **11** 67–74.

CLARKE, A. M. and CLARKE, A. D. B. (Eds.) (1976). *Early Experience: Myth and Evidence*. London: Open Books.

CLUTTON-BROCK, T. H., and HARVEY, P. H. (1978). *Readings in Sociobiology*. Reading and San Francisco: Freeman.

COHEN, D. (1979). *J. B. Watson: The Founder of Behaviourism*. London: Routledge and Kegan Paul.

CRESPI, L. (1942). Quantitative variation of incentive and performance in the white rat. *American Journal of Psychology*, **55**, 467–517.

CULLEN, E. (1957). Adaptations in the kittiwake to cliff-nesting. *Ibis*, **99**, 257–302.

DABROWSKA, J. (1963). An analysis of reversal learning in relation to the pattern of reversal in rats. *Acta Biologiae Experimentalis*, **23**, 11–24.

DARWIN, C. (1859). *The Origin of Species*. Harmondsworth: Penguin (1968).

DARWIN, C. (1871). *The Descent of Man*. London: John Murray (1901).

DARWIN, C. (1872). *The Expression of the Emotions in Man and Animals*. Chicago: University of Chicago Press (1965).

DAVEY, G. C. L. (1981). *Animal Learning and Conditioning*. London: Macmillan.

DAWKINS, R. (1976). *The Selfish Gene*. Oxford: Oxford University Press.

DE CASPER, A. J. and FIFER, W. P. (1980). Of human bonding: newborns prefer their mother's voice. *Science*, **208**, 1174–1176.

DENNIS, W. (1973). *Children of the Crèche*. New York: Appleton-Century-Crofts.

DENNIS, I., HAMPTON, J. A. and LEA, S. E. G. (1973). New problem in concept formation. *Nature*, **243**, 101–102.

DICKINSON, A. (1980). *Contemporary Animal Learning Theory*. Cambridge: Cambridge University Press.

EBBESON, S. O. E. (1972). New insights into the organization of the shark brain. *Comparative Biochemistry and Physiology*, **42A**, 121–129.

EVERETT, N. B. (1965). *Functional Neuroanatomy.* Philadelphia: Lea and Febiger.

EYSENCK, H. J. (1971). *Race, Intelligence and Education.* London: Temple Smith.

FANTZ, R. L. (1961). The origin of form perception. *Scientific American*, **204**, 66–72.

FECHNER, G. (1860). *Elements of psychophysics.* New York: Holt, Rinehart and Winston (1966).

FLAVELL, J. H. (1963). *The Developmental Psychology of Jean Piaget.* New York: Van Nostrand Reinhold.

FODOR, J. A., BEVER, T. G. and GARRETT, M. F. (1974). *The Psychology of Language.* New York: McGraw-Hill.

FOREE, D. D., and LoLORDO, V. M. (1973). Attention in the pigeon: differential effects of food-getting versus shock avoidance procedures. *Journal of Comparative and Physiological Psychology*, **85**, 551–558.

FREEMAN, B. M. and VINCE, M. A. (1974). *Development of the Avian Embryo.* London: Chapman and Hall.

FREEMAN, D. (1980). Sociobiology: the "antidiscipline" of anthropology. In MONTAGU, A. (Ed.), *Sociobiology Examined.* New York: Oxford University Press.

GALTON, F. (1869). *Hereditary Genius: An Enquiry into its Laws and Consequences.* London: Macmillan.

GARCIA, J. and KOELLING, R. A. (1966). Relation of cue to consequence in avoidance learning. *Psychonomic Science*, **4**, 123–124.

GARCIA, J., ERVIN, F. R. and KOELLING, R. A. (1966). Learning with prolonged delay of reinforcement. *Psychonomic Science*, **5**, 121–122.

GARDNER, R. A. and GARDNER, B. T. (1969). Teaching sign language to a chimpanzee. *Science*, **165**, 664–672.

GARDNER, R. A. and GARDNER, B. T. (1975). Early signs of language in child and chimpanzee. *Science*, **187**, 752–753.

GIBSON, E. J. and WALK, R. D. (1956). The effect of prolonged exposure to visually presented patterns on learning to discriminate them. *Journal of Comparative and Physiological Psychology*, **49**, 239–242.

GILLAN, D. J., PREMACK, D. and WOODRUFF, G. (1981). Reasoning in the chimpanzee: I. Analogical reasoning. *Journal of Experimental Psychology: Animal Behavior Processes*, **7**, 1–17.

GRAY, J. A. (1971). *The Psychology of Fear and Stress.* London: Weidenfeld and Nicolson.

GRAY, J. A. (1979). *Pavlov.* Glasgow: Collins (Fontana).

GRAY, S. W. and KLAUS, R. A. (1970). The Early Training Project: a seventh-year report. *Child Development*, **41**, 909–924.

GREGORY, R. L. (1966). *Eye and Brain.* London: Weidenfeld and Nicolson.

GREGORY, R. L. and WALLACE, J. G. (1963). Recovery from early blindness: a case study. *Experimental Psychology Society Monograph*, No. 2.

GRINDLEY, G. C. (1932). The formation of a simple habit in guinea-pigs. *British Journal of Psychology*, **23**, 127–147.

HALL, C. L. M. (1971). *The Role of Genetics in the Study of Behaviour.* Cambridge University: Unpublished PhD thesis.

HALL, G. (1979). Exposure learning in young and adult laboratory rats. *Animal Behaviour*, **27**, 586–591.

HALL, G. (1980). Exposure learning in animals. *Psychological Bulletin*, **88**, 535–550.

HARLOW, H. F. (1949). The formation of learning sets. *Psychological Review*, **56**, 51–65.

HARLOW, H. F. (1958). The nature of love. *American Psychologist*, **13**, 673–685.

HARLOW, H. F. (1962). Development of affection in primates. In BLISS, E. L. (Ed.), *Roots of Behavior*. New York: Harper.

HAYES, L. A. and WATSON, J. S. (1981). Neonatal imitation: fact or artifact? *Developmental Psychology*, **17**, 655–660.

HEARNSHAW, L. S. (1964). *A Short History of British Psychology*. London: Methuen.

HEARNSHAW, L. S. (1979). *Cyril Burt: Psychologist*. London: Hodder and Stoughton.

HEBB, D. O. (1949). *The Organization of Behaviour*. New York: Wiley.

HEBB, D. O. (1953). Heredity and environment in mammalian behaviour. *British Journal of Animal Behaviour*, **1**, 43–47.

HEBB, D. O. and WILLIAMS, K. (1946). A method of rating animal intelligence. *Journal of General Psychology*, **34**, 59–65.

HEIM, A. W. (1954). *The Appraisal of Intelligence*. London: Methuen.

HINDE, R. A. (1966). *Animal Behavior*. New York: McGraw-Hill.

HINDE, R. A. (1974). *Biological Bases of Human Social Behaviour*. New York: MacGraw-Hill.

HINDE, R. A. (1982). *Ethology*. Glasgow: Fontana/Collins.

HIRSCH, J. (1963). Behavior genetics and individuality understood. *Science*, **142**, 1436–1442.

HIRSCH, J. (Ed.) (1967). *Behavior-Genetic Analysis*. New York: McGraw-Hill.

HOFER, M. A. (1981). *The Roots of Human Behavior*. San Francisco: Freeman.

HOGAN, J. A. (1973). How young chicks learn to recognize food. In HINDE, R. A. and HINDE, J. S. (Eds.), *Constraints on Learning*. London and New York: Academic Press.

HOLLAND, P. C. and STRAUB, J. J. (1979). Differential effects of two ways of devaluing the unconditioned stimulus after Pavlovian appetitive training. *Journal of Experimental Psychology: Animal Behavior Processes*, **5**, 65–78.

HOWARTH, E. and EYSENCK, H. J. (1968). Extraversion, arousal, and paired-associate recall. *Journal of Experimental Research in Personality*, **3**, 114–116.

HUBEL, D. H. and WIESEL, T. N. (1979). Brain mechanisms of vision. *Scientific American*, **241**, 130–144.

HUXLEY, L. (Ed.) (1900). *Life and Letters of Thomas Henry Huxley*, Vol. 1. London: Macmillan.

INGLIS, I. R. (1975). Enriched sensory experience in adulthood increases subsequent exploratory behaviour in the rat. *Animal Behaviour*, **23**, 932–940.

JAMES, W. (1890). *Principles of Psychology*. New York: Holt.

JENKINS, H. M. and MOORE, B. R. (1973). The form of the autoshaped response with food or water reinforcers. *Journal of the Experimental Analysis of Behavior*, **20**, 163–181.

JENSEN, A. R. (1969). How much can we boost IQ and scholastic achievement? *Harvard Educational Review*, **39**, 1–123.

JENSEN, A. R. (1971). Do schools cheat minority children? *Educational Research*, **14**, 3–28.

JERISON, H. J. (1969). Brain evolution and dinosaur brains. *American Naturalist*, **103**, 575–588.

JERISON, H. J. (1973). *Evolution of the Brain and Intelligence*. New York and London: Academic Press.

JOHANSON, D. C. and EDEY, M. A. (1981). *Lucy: The Beginnings of Humankind*. London: Granada.

JOHANSON, D. C. and WHITE, T. D. (1979). A systematic assessment of early African hominids. *Science*, **203**, 321–330.

KAMIN, L. J. (1974). *The Science and Politics of IQ*. Harmondsworth: Penguin (1977).

KOESTLER, A. (1967). *The Ghost in the Machine*. London: Hutchinson.

KONORSKI, J. (1967). *Integrative Activity of the Brain*. Chicago: University of Chicago Press.

KUFFLER, S. W. and NICHOLS, J. G. (1976). *From Neuron to Brain*. Sunderland, Mass.: Sinauer.

KUO, Z-Y. (1967). *The Dynamics of Behavior Development*. New York: Random House.

LASHLEY, K. S. (1929). *Brain Mechanisms and Intelligence*. New York: Dover (1963).

LASHLEY, K. S. (1951). The problem of serial order in behavior. In JEFFRESS, L. A. (Ed.), *Cerebral Mechanisms in Behavior*. New York: Wiley.

LASHLEY, K. S. and MCCARTHY, D. A. (1926). The survival of the maze habit after cerebellar injuries. *Journal of Comparative and Physiological Psychology*, **6**, 423–433.

LENNEBERG, E. H. (1967). *Biological Foundations of Language*. New York: Wiley.

LIEBERMAN, P. (1975). *On the Origins of Language*. New York: Macmillan.

LINDEN, E. G. (1976). *Apes, Men, and Language*. Harmondsworth: Penguin.

LINDSAY, P. H. and NORMAN, D. A. (1977). *Human Information Processing*. New York and London: Academic Press. (2nd edition).

LIPSITT, L. P. (1967). Learning in the human infant. In STEVENSON, H. W., HESS, E. H. and RHEINGOLD, H. L. (Eds.), *Early Behavior*. New York: Wiley.

LOLORDO, V. M. (1979). Selective associations. In DICKINSON, A. and BOAKES, R. A. (Eds.), *Mechanisms of Learning and Motivation*. Hillsdale, NJ: Erlbaum.

LORENZ, K. Z. (1937). The companion in the bird's world. *Auk*, **54**, 245–273.

LORENZ, K. Z. (1950). The comparative method in studying innate behaviour patterns. *Symposium of the Society for Experimental Biology*, **4**, 221–268.

LORENZ, K. Z. (1958). The evolution of behavior. *Scientific American*, **199**, 67–78.

LORENZ, K. Z. (1965). *Evolution and Modification of Behaviour*. London: Methuen.

McFARLAND, D. J. (Ed.) (1981). *The Oxford Companion to Animal Behaviour*. Oxford: Oxford University Press.

MACKINTOSH, N. J. (1965). Overtraining, transfer to proprioceptive control and position reversal. *Quarterly Journal of Experimental Psychology*, **17**, 26–36.

MACKINTOSH, N. J. (1969). Comparative studies of reversal and probability learning: rats, birds and fish. In GILBERT, R. M. and SUTHERLAND, N. S. (Eds.), *Animal Discrimination Learning*. London and New York: Academic Press.

MACKINTOSH, N. J. (1973). Stimulus selection: learning to ignore stimuli that predict no change in reinforcement. In HINDE, R. A. and HINDE, J. S. (Eds.), *Constraints on Learning*. London and New York: Academic Press.

MACKINTOSH, N. J. (1974). *The Psychology of Animal Learning*. London and New York:

Academic Press.

MACKINTOSH, N. J. (1975a). Critical notice. *Quarterly Journal of Experimental Psychology*, **27**, 672–686.

MACKINTOSH, N. J. (1975b). A theory of attention: variations in the associability of stimuli with reinforcement. *Psychological Review*, **82**, 276–298.

MACKINTOSH, N. J. and LITTLE, L. (1969). Intradimensional and extradimensional shift learning by pigeons. *Psychonomic Science*, **14**, 5–6.

MACPHAIL, E. M. (1982). *Brain and Intelligence in Vertebrates*. Oxford: Clarendon Press.

MANNING, A. (1972). *An Introduction to Animal Behaviour*. London: Edward Arnold.

MARLER, P. and HAMILTON, W. J. (1966). *Mechanisms of Animal Behavior*. New York: Wiley.

MASTERTON, R. B., CAMPBELL, C. B. G., BITTERMAN, M. E. and HOTTON, N. (Eds.) (1976a). *Evolution of Brain and Behavior in Vertebrates*. Hillsdale, NJ: Erlbaum.

MASTERTON, R. B., HODOS, W. and JERISON, H. (Eds.) (1976b). *Evolution, Brain and Behavior: Persistent Problems*. Hillsdale, NJ: Erlbaum.

MAYR, E. (1958). Behavior and systematics. In ROE, A. and SIMPSON, G. G. (Eds.), *Behavior and Evolution*. New Haven: Yale University Press.

MELTZOFF, A. N. and MOORE, M. K. (1977). Imitation of facial and manual gestures by human neonates. *Science*, **198**, 75–78.

MILES, R. C. (1971). Species differences in "transmitting" spatial location information. In JARRARD, L. E. (Ed.), *Cognitive Processes of Nonhuman Primates*. New York and London: Academic Press.

MILLER, G. A. (1962). *Psychology: The Science of Mental Life*. Harmondsworth: Penguin (1966).

MILLER, G. A. (1981). *Language and Speech*. San Francisco: Freeman.

MILLER, N. E. (1959). Liberalization of basic S–R concepts. In KOCH, S. (Ed.), *Psychology: Study of a Science* Vol. 2. New York: McGraw-Hill.

MISHKIN, M. (1966). Visual mechanisms beyond the striate cortex. In RUSSELL, R. W. (Ed.), *Frontiers in Physiological Psychology*. New York and London: Academic Press.

MONTAGU, A. (1980). *Sociobiology Examined*. New York: Oxford University Press.

MOORE, B. C. J. (1982). *Introduction to the Psychology of Hearing*. London and New York: Academic Press. (2nd edition).

MORGAN, C. L. (1894). *An Introduction to Comparative Psychology*. London: Scott.

MORRIS, R. G. M. (1981). Spatial localization does not require the presence of local cues. *Learning and Motivation*, **12**, 239–260.

MUIR, D. and MITCHELL, D. E. (1973). Visual resolution and experience: acuity deficits in cats following early selective visual deprivation. *Science*, **180**, 420–422.

MURCHISON, C. (Ed.) (1936). *History of Psychology in Autobiography* Vol. 3. New York: Russell and Russell.

MURTON, R. K., ISAACSON, A. J. and WESTWOOD, N. J. (1966). The relationship between wood-pigeons and their clover food supply and the mechanisms of population control. *Journal of Applied Ecology*, **3**, 55–96.

OATLEY, K. (1978). *Perceptions and Representations*. London: Methuen.

O'KEEFE, J. and NADEL, L. (1978). *The Hippocampus as a Cognitive Map*. Oxford: Clarendon Press.

PASSINGHAM, R. E. (1975). Changes in the size and organization of the brain in man and his ancestors. *Brain, Behavior, and Evolution*, **11**, 73–90.

PASSINGHAM, R. E. (1982). *The Human Primate*. Oxford and San Francisco: Freeman.

PASSINGHAM, R. E. and ETTLINGER, G. (1974). A comparison of cortical function in man and other primates. *International Review of Neurobiology*, **16**, 233–299.

PAVLOV, I. P. (1906). The scientific investigation of the psychical faculties or processes in the higher animals. *Lancet*, **ii**, 911–915.

PAVLOV, I. P. (1927). *Conditioned Reflexes*. New York: Dover (1960).

PEARCE, J. M. and HALL, G. (1978). Overshadowing the instrumental conditioning of a lever-press response by a more valid predictor of the reinforcer. *Journal of Experimental Psychology: Animal Behavior Processes*, **4**, 356–367.

PEARCE, J. M. and HALL, G. (1980). A model for Pavlovian learning: variations in the effectiveness of conditioned but not of unconditioned stimuli. *Psychological Review*, **87**, 532–552.

PIAGET, J. and INHELDER, B. (1969). *The Psychology of the Child*. London: Routledge and Kegan Paul.

PLOMIN, R., DEFRIES, J. C. and MCCLEARN, G. E. (1980). *Behavioral Genetics: A Primer*. San Francisco: Freeman.

PREMACK, D. (1976). *Intelligence in Ape and Man*. Hillsdale, NJ: Erlbaum.

PREMACK, A. J. and PREMACK, D. (1972). Teaching language to an ape. *Scientific American*, **227**, 92–99.

PREWITT, E. P. (1967). Number of preconditioning trials in sensory preconditioning using CER training. *Journal of Comparative and Physiological Psychology*, **64**, 360–362.

RESCORLA, R. A. (1968). Probability of shock in the presence and absence of CS in fear conditioning. *Journal of Comparative and Physiological Psychology*, **66**, 1–5.

REYNOLDS, G. S. (1961). Attention in the pigeon. *Journal of the Experimental Analysis of Behavior*, **4**, 203–208.

RIESEN, A. H. (1947). The development of perception in man and chimpanzee. *Science*, **106**, 107–108.

RILEY, D. A. (1968). *Discrimination Learning*. Boston: Allyn and Bacon.

ROE, A. and SIMPSON, G. G. (Eds.), (1958). *Behavior and Evolution*. New Haven: Yale University Press.

ROEDER, K. D. and TREAT, A. E. (1961). The detection and evasion of bats by moths. *American Scientist*, **49** 135–148.

ROMANES, G. J. (1882). *Animal Intelligence*. London: Kegan Paul (1886).

ROMER, A. S., and PARSONS, T. S. (1977). *The Vertebrate Body*. Philadelphia: Holt Saunders.

ROSENZWEIG, M. R., BENNETT, E. L. and DIAMOND, M. C. (1972). Brain changes in response to experience. *Scientific American*, **226**, 22–29.

RUTTER, M. (1972). *Maternal Deprivation Reassessed*. Harmondsworth: Penguin.

SCALIA, F. AND EBBESON, S. O. E. (1971). The central projections of the olfactory bulb in a teleost (*Gymnothorax funebris*). *Brain, Behavior, and Evolution*, **4**, 376–399.

SCIENTIFIC AMERICAN (1979). *The Brain*. San Francisco: Freeman.

SELIGMAN, M. E. P. (1970). On the generality of the laws of learning. *Psychological Review*, **77**, 406–418.

SHETTLEWORTH, S. J. (1975). Reinforcement and the organization of behavior in golden hamsters: hunger, environment, and food reinforcement. *Journal of Experimental Psychology: Animal Behavior Processes*, 1, 56–87.

SHIELDS, J. (1962). *Monozygotic Twins Brought Up Apart and Brought Up Together*. London: Oxford University Press.

SHIRE, J. G. M. (1968). Genes, hormones and behavioural variation. In THODAY, J. M. and PARKES A. S. (Eds.), *Genetic and Environmental Influences on Behaviour*. Edinburgh: Oliver and Boyd.

SINNOTT, E. W., DUNN, L. C. and DOBZHANSKY, T. (1958). *Principles of Genetics*. New York: McGraw-Hill.

SKINNER, B. F. (1953). *Science and Human Behavior*. New York: Macmillan.

SKINNER, B. F. (1967). In BORING E. G. and LINDZEY, G. (Eds.), *A History of Psychology in Autobiography* Vol. 5. New York: Appleton-Century-Crofts.

SLUCKIN, W. (1970). *Early Learning in Man and Animal*. London: George Allen and Unwin.

SMITH, J. M. (1975). *The Theory of Evolution*. Harmondsworth: Penguin.

SMITH, M. C., COLEMAN, S. R. and Gormezano, I. (1969). Classical conditioning of the rabbit's nictitating membrane response at backward, simultaneous, and forward CS-UCS intervals. *Journal of Comparative and Physiological Psychology*, 69, 226–231.

SPENCE, K. W. (1937). The differential response in animals to stimuli varying within a single dimension. *Psychological Review*, 44, 430–444.

SULLIVAN, J. O. (1978). Variability in the wolf, a group hunter. In HALL, R. L. and SHARP, H. S. (Eds.), *Wolf and Man*. New York and London: Academic Press.

TAUB, E. and BERMAN, A. J. (1968). Movement and learning in the absence of sensory feedback. In FREEDMAN, S. J. (Ed.), *The Neuropsychology of Spatially Oriented Behavior*. Homewood Illinois: Dorsey Press.

TERRACE, H. S., PETITTO, L. A., SANDERS, R. J. and BEVER, T. G. (1979). Can an ape create a sentence? *Science*, 206, 891–902.

THODAY, J. M. (1965). Geneticism and environmentalism. In MEADE, J. E. and PARKES, A. S. (Eds.), *Biological Aspects of Social Problems*. Edinburgh: Oliver and Boyd.

THODAY, J. M. and PARKES, A. S. (1968). *Genetic and Environmental Influences on Behaviour*. Edinburgh: Oliver and Boyd.

THORNDIKE, E. L. (1911). *Animal Intelligence*. New York: Macmillan.

THORPE, W. H. (1961). *Bird Song*. Cambridge: Cambridge University Press.

TINBERGEN, N. (1951). *The Study of Instinct*. Oxford: Clarendon Press.

TINBERGEN, N. (1963). The shell menace. *Natural History*, 72, 28–35.

TOLMAN, E. C. (1932). *Purposive Behaviorism in Animals and Men*. New York: Appleton-Century-Crofts.

TRIVERS, R. L. (1972). Parental investment and sexual selection. In CAMPBELL, B. G. (Ed.), *Sexual Selection and the Descent of Man*. Chicago: Aldine.

VAN TETS, G. F. (1965). A comparative study of some social communication patterns in the Pelecaniformes. *Ornithological Monographs*, No. 2. 1–88.

VINCE, M. A. (1969). Embryonic communication, respiration and the synchronization of hatching. In HINDE, R. A. (Ed.), *Bird Vocalizations*. Cambridge: Cambridge

University Press.

WAGNER, A. R. (1976). Priming in STM: an information-processing mechanism for self-generated or retrieval-generated depression in performance. In TIGHE, T. J. and LEATON R. N. (Eds.), *Habituation*. Hillsdale, NJ: Erlbaum.

WATSON, J. B. (1913). Psychology as the behaviorist views it. *Psychological Review*, **20**, 158–177.

WATSON, J. B. (1916). The place of the conditioned reflex in psychology. *Psychological Review*, **23**, 89–116.

WATSON, J. B. (1924). *Behaviorism*. New York: Norton (1970).

WILCOCK, J. (1972). Water-escape in weanling rats: a link between behaviour and biological fitness. *Animal Behaviour*, **20**, 543–547.

WILLIAMS, G. C. (1966). *Adaptation and Natural Selection*. Princeton, NJ: Princeton University Press.

WILSON, E. O. (1975). *Sociobiology: The New Synthesis*. Cambridge: Harvard University Press.

WILSON, E. O. (1978). *On Human Nature*. Cambridge: Harvard University Press.

YOUNG, J. Z. (1971). *An Introduction to the Study of Man*. Oxford: Clarendon Press.

ZANGWILL, O. L. (1950). *An Introduction to Modern Psychology*. London: Methuen.

ZANGWILL, O. L. (1961). Lashley's concept of cerebral mass action. In THORPE, W. H. and ZANGWILL, O. L. (Eds.), *Current Problems in Animal Behaviour*. Cambridge: Cambridge University Press.

ZENTALL, T. R. and HOGAN, D. E. (1975). Key pecking in pigeons produced by pairing the keylight with inaccessible grain. *Journal of the Experimental Analysis of Behavior*, **23**, 199–206.

# Author Index

# Subject Index

*Note:* numbers in italics refer to entries in the glossary.

Acetycholine, 144, *290*

Action potential, 142, *290*

Acquired versus inherited, 63–67

Adaptive behaviour, 50–52, 83, 242–249

Adrenal cortex, 137, 138

Adrenaline, 93, 137, *290*

Adrenal medulla, 93, 137–138

Aggression, 25–27, 29–30

Altruism, 23, 282–283

Antidiuretic hormone, 137

Appetitive behaviour, 209, 212, *296*

Association cortex, 157–158, *291*
  lesions of, 170–171
  and mass action, 167–169
  pathways through, 166
  and subcortical connections, 173–174
  visual processing by, 171–172

Associative learning, 99, 218, 291
  language acquisition, role in, 273, 274–275
  and non-associative learning, 250, 260
  *see also* Classical conditioning, Instrumental learning

Attachment, 121–123

Attention, 195–197, 255–257
  *see also* Stimulus selection

Autonomic nervous system, 137, 144, *291*

Autoshaping, 220, 222, 224, 249, *290*

Avoidance learning, strain differences in, 81–82

Axon, 140, *291*

Behaviour genetics, 76–83
  *see also* Breeding experiments, Pedigrees, Strain differences

Behaviourism, 8–12, 16, *291*

Biofeedback, 180, *291*

Bird song
  alarm-calls, 23
  development of, 112–113
  and isolating mechanisms, 32

Blocking, 223, 228–229, *291*

Brain
  early experience and, 127
  general structure of, 149–152
  human, 156
  and intelligence, 159–160
  lesions of, 155, 167–168, 170–172
  lobes of cerebral hemisphere of, 156–157
  relative size of, 158–159, 265
  theories of functioning of, 161–174
  *see also* individual parts e.g. hypothalamus etc.

Breathing, 184

Breeding experiments
  and single-gene effects, 79–80
  as tools for analysis, 92–94
  in quantitative genetics, 80–81

Bushmen, 285–286

Causality
  and conditioning, 231, 242, 276–277
  and reasoning, 278

Central nervous system, 139, 145, 147–152, *291*